D1519458

Ethnography After Antiquity

EMPIRE AND AFTER

Series Editor: Clifford Ando

A complete list of books in the series
is available from the publisher.

ETHNOGRAPHY AFTER ANTIQUITY

FOREIGN LANDS AND PEOPLES IN BYZANTINE LITERATURE

Anthony Kaldellis

PENN

UNIVERSITY OF PENNSYLVANIA PRESS

PHILADELPHIA

Copyright © 2013 University of Pennsylvania Press

Published by
University of Pennsylvania Press
Philadelphia, Pennsylvania 19104-4112
www.upenn.edu/pennpress

Printed in the United States of America on acid-free paper
10 9 8 7 6 5 4 3 2 1

Library of Congress Cataloging-in-Publication Data
ISBN 978-0-8122-4531-8

CONTENTS

This book is a study of ethnography as a literary practice in Byzantium; that is, it focuses on accounts of foreign peoples the Byzantines themselves wrote. It is not a study of the population of Byzantium according to the methodologies of modern ethnography, something that would be impossible to do given the nature of the evidence. In ancient texts that the Byzantines inherited and studied, ethnography formed a relatively coherent genre (or subgenre), though its emphases and goals varied by author. Its standard topics, to quote a recent book on Roman views of India, included: "mythic or historical origins, populousness, somatic features, warfare, clothing, conditions of living (including eating and accommodation), social structure and political organization, religious practice, gender relations and marriage," and of course geography.[1] Hellenistic and Roman authors wrote ethnographies devoted to specific foreign nations (e.g., Hekataios' *Aigyptiaka*, Megasthenes' *Indika*, and Tacitus' *Germania*), indicating that it was perceived as a potentially separate genre. Even when embedded in other types of literature, it still retained a more or less fixed form.[2] Occasionally I will use the term *ethnology* to denote not a literary passage written in the tradition of ancient ethnography but a general view of a foreign people that shaped the way they were represented textually.

In most extant ancient and Byzantine literature, ethnography is an auxiliary genre, being a "guest" subgenre in epic, imperial panegyric, and especially historiography.[3] In antiquity the *Odyssey* could be regarded as the first account of different peoples and places,[4] but the usual point of reference was the *Histories* of Herodotos.[5] In its supporting roles, one could even call ethnography a symbiotic subgenre, in that it retained its own identity while simultaneously supporting the goals of its host genres, whether those were histories, military manuals, or imperial orations. Its inflection in each case was shaped by the goals and circumstances of its host. There were even parodies of ethnographic discourse, for example, Virgil's account of the bees (in book 4 of his *Georgics*) and Lucian's *True History*. To discuss ethnography as a genre, then, does not require a strict blueprint, nor do we need an ancient (or Aristotelian) definition of the genre in order to speak about it ourselves.[6] A number of ancient genres were not theorized in antiquity. We will find late ancient texts that were devoted primarily to the description of foreign peoples, and the author of the *Notitiae Urbis Constantinopolitanae* (ca. 400) mentions texts on "the customs of foreign peoples" as distinct from geography.[7] But most extant ethnographic texts, as we will see, were auxiliary.

The goal of my discussion will not be to interrogate the facts contained in these texts to ascertain how much of their information the modern historian can use. That has usually been done for most of them, albeit on an individual basis. My approach will rather be a literary and comparative one, that is, it will analyze the politics of each representation in relation to its context, considering the specific goals of the text in question and comparing different representations of the same foreign people across contexts. In scholarship on classical texts, ethnography has long been studied as a system of representation that speaks to the analytical categories and political goals of the author rather than the "realia" of the subject matter. It is my purpose to extend this type of analysis to Byzantine material. This does not mean that the literary study of ethnographic texts does not have serious historical implications, for ethnographic representation cuts to the heart of how the Byzantines viewed themselves in relation to other peoples, and their views on these matters turn out to have been alternately firm and flexible in surprising ways. In fact, a study of ethnography can cause us to revise our notions of just who the Byzantines themselves were, or thought they were, in relation to the wider world they inhabited.

The focus of this study is on literature of the middle and later Byzantine periods. After discussing the historians of late antiquity, who provided powerful models to their successors for the writing of ethnography, I turn to the problem of the relative decline of ethnography in the middle period, between the Arab conquests of the seventh century and the colonization of the Aegean by western powers in the thirteenth. That period witnessed great historical transformations. The rise of the Arabs, Slavs, Bulgars, Hungarians, Scandinavians, Turks, and others changed the political, cultural, and ethnic map of what remained of the ancient world. The Byzantines were at the heart of these transformations, in the middle of that map, fighting for their own survival, steering events as best they could in their own interest, conducting diplomacy and waging war against many new enemies. Byzantine ambassadors and spies traveled widely, from Spain to the steppes and to Baghdad, collecting information for use by Constantinople. There can be no doubt that they had abundant information and sometimes even a global perspective on these geopolitical and ethnic changes. Also, Byzantine writers had direct access to ancient texts that provided models for talking about such historical developments. The Byzantines imitated this tradition with great success when writing the history of their own society, the Orthodox Roman empire governed from Constantinople.

The Byzantines of the middle period thus had the knowledge and means to continue the ancient ethnographic tradition and tell us much about the Arabs, Slavs, Bulgarians, Pechenegs, and others they knew so well. And yet they did not do so. They knew more than they tell us. The question then is, why do middle Byzantine texts avoid following in the footsteps of their ancient models in this regard? Their authors learned to imitate those models in virtually every other respect, so why not in this one? This is an inquiry into a literary problem, and more precisely about a comparative silence in the record, a difficult sort of thing to explain. But their silence does not require us to be silent too. Sherlock Holmes once solved a murder from the fact that a dog did *not* bark. Silences may hold the key to crucial issues in the study of culture; on their basis is it even possible to argue that "in the end, cultural differences are irreducible."[8] Ultimately, the question concerns the Byzantines' underlying mentalities, what we might even call their ideologies, the parts of the world they avoided putting into words in order to sustain their view of that world and their place in it. It is often in the things that we do not tell ourselves, the things that we "know" and take for granted, that our limitations, anxieties, and values can be found.

I do not mean to imply that there is simply no ethnography in Byzantine literature; there is exactly enough to fill a volume of the size you hold. The genre actually was revived in the later Byzantine period, and I devote a long chapter to its various manifestations in the Palaiologan period. The problem I have drawn attention to is the perceptible drop in density in the middle period compared to late antiquity. Byzantine ethnography has never before been made the object of systematic study, and only a few scholars have noted the problem that I have defined, usually in vague terms and without positing explanations.[9] This is the first book to examine this subject.

I note in conclusion the striking paucity of representations of foreigners in Byzantine art, especially that of the middle period. There are almost none. It was difficult to locate an appropriate image for the cover of this book. From late antiquity we have sculpted images of barbarians being defeated in battle (e.g., on the arch of Galerius in Thessalonike) or bearing tribute to the emperor (e.g., on the Theodosian Obelisk Base and the Barberini Ivory), but all we can do for the middle and late Byzantine period is to identify foreign "elements" incorporated into icons or manuscript depictions of saints or Old Testament figures.[10] Some such images did once exist, however. In 1200, Nikolaos Mesarites described a palace in Constantinople that was built in the Persian style and that featured ceiling images of "Persians in their various costumes."[11] This is now sadly lost. All we are left with in this case too is a text.

CHAPTER I

Ethnography in Late Antique Historiography

An Analytical Survey

This chapter will focus on "classicizing" ethnographies that we find embedded mostly in historical texts. I distinguish this secular mode of ethnography, which was an extension of ancient genres and could be written by both Christian and non-Christian authors, from specifically Christian genres of ethnography that appeared in late antiquity and after, which I will discuss in Chapter 3. In the texts in question here, ethnography usually takes the form of digressions from political narratives and is generally subordinate to their objectives, even while it maintains its own distinct conventions.[1] A broad view of the evolution of the genre reveals that the late antique historians continued the traditions of earlier periods, maintaining almost all the modalities of classical ethnography. They wrote in classical Greek about a complex international scene of competing and emerging cultures at whose center stood the Christian Roman empire. This tradition, however, came to a crashing end in the seventh century. This must be emphasized, because scholars sometimes assume that the practices of the late antique historians were typical of Byzantine historiography as whole. When it comes to ethnography, at least, they were not. The texts discussed in this chapter represent the end of the ancient tradition, not the beginning of a new one.

There were two distinct subcategories of late antique ethnography: the classical "objective" description of a land, its people, and their customs, usually written from a distant standpoint (we find this practiced chiefly in Prokopios, Agathias, and Theophylaktos, to cite the main extant authors); and the first-person account of a Roman embassy to a foreign people that presents the ambassador's experience, not a "global" perspective on a foreign culture (this is represented by Priskos' account of the embassy to Attila and other accounts reported at second hand by later authors). The weight of the evidence favors the first category, so I begin there.

The first thing to note is that ethnographic digressions were self-conscious literary artifacts created for a competitive literary scene. In one sense, they were part of the basic check-list for a successful work of history. One needed a high level of Greek style laced with classical references and allusions that required a high level of education to be understood; detailed narratives of wars, battles, sieges, and diplomacy that were preferably based on information obtained from inside sources or eyewitnesses; speeches of exhortation (before battle), persuasion (in diplomatic contexts), and even legal argumentation—this also showcased the author's own professional skills, as most late antique historians were trained advocates;[2] and some geography and ethnography of foreign peoples. A detailed account of a natural disaster such as a plague or earthquake added to the importance of the work. One also needed a moral purpose, whether to exhort readers to embrace virtue and shun vice (heroes and villains exemplified this message in concrete form) or to help future generations cope with like adversities. Meeting these requirements ensured that the historian would be regarded as authoritative and that his work might be valued and thus survive.[3] It also put on display the author's skills and credentials in ways that were socially and professionally advantageous. But within these parameters, there was much room for variation. Reading each of the historians is a unique experience.

Ethnography, then, was a crucial component of a multi-faceted authorial performance that catered to an audience with lofty and varied expectations. But it could take many forms, as we will see, given that the ancient tradition from which it sprang had itself authorized a range of models. In the late historians, the longer ethnographic accounts take the form of digressions and are not always strictly necessary for the exposition of the main military narrative. For example, the wars of the Romans did not really require Prokopios to discuss Thule, Agathias to digress (twice) on ancient Persian lore, or Theophylaktos to describe what he knew of China.[4] In this way ethnography retained a measure of generic autonomy and can be discussed separately from its textual environment. At the same time, we cannot overlook the competitive dimension of this genre: each historian was anxious, if not to surpass, at least to match his predecessors, so that each generation looked farther and farther away for new material or showcased "inside" source-finds for familiar themes. We will review instances of this phenomenon below. This was true not only for ethnography. Prokopios had written a superb account of the plague of 541–542, so his successor Agathias concentrated his literary talents on the two earthquakes of 551 and especially 557, devoting a smaller discussion to a later outbreak of the plague.[5] Besides, it was wars, plagues, and earthquakes that made history momentous and worth writing about in the first place, as Agathias admits in his preface.[6] This conscious literary rivalry resulted in a proliferation of ethnographic writing.

We can consider Prokopios as a "benchmark" writer among this group, as he was admired and imitated by his successors. His narrative of the wars with the Persians, Vandals, Goths, and others contains a large amount of information about foreign peoples and perhaps even more about their geography. Much of this information is indebted to classical models for both its shape and contents but also reflects the world of the sixth century, albeit in politicized ways.[7] However, Prokopios does not offer full-fledged ethnographies of the main opponents (the Persians, Vandals, and Goths). Much information about them can be gleaned from his narrative, so much so that his information on, say, Sasanian Persia can preoccupy an entire book of modern analysis.[8] These occur mostly in the form of "parentheses" or glosses when an office, place, or institution happens to be mentioned, so that the reader can follow the narrative. It was part of Prokopios' ability as a writer that he placed information generally at the point where it would most help the reader, not necessarily grouping it by theme or chronology.[9] These ethnographic asides do have an auxiliary character.

Prokopios assumed that his readers knew who the Persians, Vandals, and Goths were, in the latter two cases perhaps from reading his predecessors, mainly Priskos. It is possible that he did not offer digressions on the Vandals and the Goths because this had already been done, in one fashion or another, by those predecessors. Still, each of the three parts of the *Wars* begins by recounting the recent history of Roman relations with the rival in question. Moreover, he does occasionally reflect on the *mores* of these peoples, as in his famous digression on how the Vandals went soft by indulging in the pleasures available in Roman North Africa, in contrast to the Moors who did not.[10] This juxtaposition proves, contrary to what is sometimes maintained, that classical theories of climate did not strictly govern ethnography in late antiquity, for these two peoples shared the same land. The governing principles of this passage are moral stereotypes that evoke antithetical ancient tropes: one stems from models of ancient luxury, which had their own rhetorical conventions (Sybaris, Baiae, imperial Persia); the other offers an image of extreme primitiveness that correlates with hardiness and endurance (at one point in the passage Prokopios explicitly compares the Moors to animals with regard to their diet).[11] We will return to this passage in the next section when we consider its political subtext.

As for the secondary barbarian players in his narrative, including lesser-known or distant peoples, Prokopios will sometimes provide a brief introduction, presenting aspects of their social order, religion, history, or customs; for example, about the Ephthalitai Huns faced by the Persians; the Christian Iberians caught between Rome and Persia; the Canaanite origin of the Moors who were driven out of Palestine by the Jews under Joshua; and the "democratic" (i.e., anarchic) society and frightening atrocities of the Slavs and Antai.[12] These are summary statements, but serve to orient the reader who may not know much about the peoples in question either because they were "new," such as the Slavs, or lay beyond Rome's proximate neighbors, such as the Ephthalitai. Sometimes he devotes whole chapters to wars between neighboring peoples, such as the Ethiopians and Himyarites in the south and the Lombards and Gepids in the north. These are circumstantial narratives, authenticated by the names of their kings and dealings with Roman diplomats.[13] What Prokopios is most fond of, however, is geography. He loves describing the location of forts and the course of rivers from the mountains to the sea, including the names of the peoples who live alongside them, and pauses to comment on natural oddities and curiosities such as Mt. Vesuvius.[14] There is more geography in the *Wars* than there is in any other Roman historian before or after him, so we must assume a special interest here, perhaps linked to his extensive travels (he stands comparison with Polybios and Poseidonios, both of whom had traveled extensively in the lands they described). Accordingly, Prokopios' narratives of the Vandal and Gothic wars begin with major digressions on the geography of the Mediterranean and Europe, situating the history of those peoples in relation to the overall shape of the Roman world.[15] And, finally, in the first seven books of the *Wars* (finished in 550), he includes two major digressions on people and places, one on the geography and ancient tribes of Italy and the other on the origin of the Heruls, which extends into a long account of Scandinavia ("Thule") and the customs and names of its inhabitants.[16] Prokopios adds that he desired to go and see it for himself, having spoken with people from there, but this never proved possible.[17] This is a strong assertion of the role that sheer intellectual curiosity played in ethnographic literature, the likes of which we do not often encounter in the middle Byzantine period. It was not until the end of Byzantium that we begin to find such intellectual explorers.

Two years after finishing the first seven books of the *Wars*, Prokopios published a supplemental book which carried the narrative down to 553. A huge proportion of this book is taken up with geographic and ethnographic material, including a *periplous* of the peoples and places of the Black Sea and a discussion of the debate over the exact boundary between Europe and Asia. It also includes smaller sections on the Sabeiroi Huns and the silk industry of China, and a long discussion of the Varni and the curious traffic in souls to a place Prokopios calls Brittia (either Denmark or Britain).[18] It is not clear why this final book of the *Wars* contains so much more material of this kind than the first seven. Perhaps Prokopios did not have enough military narrative to fill a book of the same size (book 8, after all, covers only two years).

Before we take leave of Prokopios, let us note a bold statement that book 8 has in store for the reader. At one point during his geographical digressions, the author notes that "I am not talking about intelligible or intellectual matters or other such invisible things (οὐ περὶ νοερῶν ἢ νοητῶν τινος ἢ ἀφανῶν ἄλλως), but about rivers and lands."[19] *Noera* and *noēta* are words chosen carefully: they were technical terms of metaphysical speculation in late antiquity, referring to specific levels of Being in Neoplatonic thought but serving also in Christian theology.[20] This is a striking declaration of a materialist and skeptical orientation in an age that was addicted to metaphysics, an interest in *this* world and its physicality rather than in the next world (in which Prokopios evinces no interest). He would not bother to make this statement if he were not alienated from current standards of discourse. Accordingly, and in stark contrast to the metaphysicians, Prokopios admits ignorance (about major aspects of the world's geography) and does not advocate preset formulas.[21] This is complemented by a statement that he makes earlier in the *Wars*, in connection with Christian theological controversies, where he states that the search for the nature of God, a preoccupation of his emperor and contemporaries, was an "idiotic" waste of time.[22] These too are not attitudes that found many adherents in later Byzantine centuries.

Prokopios had traveled to many of the lands that he wrote about. Also, he was the *assessor*—secretary and chief of staff—of the most important general of the age, Belisarios, so that he had personal contact with soldiers, officers, spies, diplomats, and merchants, situating him ideally at a nexus of information. There were probably few men in the sixth century who knew as much about the world as did Prokopios, from autopsy, reading, and interviews, and probably none who had the same curiosity and freedom from metaphysical bias. He set a high standard for his successors. Let us look briefly at some of their strategies and priorities.

In Agathias, who continued the history of Prokopios, we find a number of the same brief "introductions" of barbarian peoples that smooth the narrative, usually peoples whom Prokopios had overlooked, such as the Alamanni and Dilimnitai (Daylami). Agathias is not consistent in his coverage, discussing primarily the religion of the first group and the military tactics of the second.[23] This is one way in which he manages to contribute something new, writing as he was so self-consciously in the wake of Prokopios. His main new contribution, in which he took pride and to which he repeatedly drew attention, was on Persian culture and history. He claims to have obtained heretofore-unknown information from inside the Persian archives through an interpreter named Sergios, who had visited the Sasanian court during an embassy. We can tell that this information contains authentic Iranian traditions, especially religious ones, as well as the sequence of Sasanian kings, which Agathias supplemented and embellished with events and figures from classical lore and history.[24] What is important here is how Agathias showcases this material as an advance upon what could be found in Prokopios: "I believe that all this information is entirely true and presented in an accurate way, for it has been taken from Persian books. . . . So even if Prokopios has narrated some of the facts regarding Kavades in a different way, my version should be preferred as being much closer to the truth because it is based on the Persian manuscripts."[25] Moreover, this new material revealed that one did not always have to go farther afield geographically for the sake of ethnographic digressions: discoveries could still be made about otherwise familiar neighboring nations, so long as one had the right access or found a new source. But the lure of the distant and unknown always beckoned. Agathias' continuer Menandros looked to Central Asia and the Turks for material, and Theophylaktos cast his gaze from there into China, of which he gave a fairly long account—obviously not at first-hand.[26] Theophylaktos, the last historian to write in this style, exhibits all the modalities of ethnography that we have seen in his predecessors. He also features an earthquake and a long account of the Nile, including philosophical speculation about its flooding. He was, after all, from Egypt, so this is another example of how "insider" knowledge or interest could enable accounts of curiosities closer to home.[27]

The second subcategory of late antique ethnography (mentioned above) was the first-person account of an embassy, but these reports have not fared as well in terms of survival. Of course, much information in the historians derived from such sources, so they might survive at second hand. Libanios mentions in a letter his relative Spektatos who accompanied an embassy to Persia in 357–358:

> Spektatos has returned from the embassy; some people regard him as fortunate in that he has seen vast lands, mountains and rivers, others that he has seen the manner of life of the Persians, their civilization, and the laws under which they live. Others again think the spectacle of the monarch and the jewels that adorned him to be of great moment, while yet others consider it noteworthy that, after presenting gifts, he should come away in receipt of gifts.[28]

It may have been a common practice for Roman ambassadors of the imperial era to submit reports.[29] But it is difficult to reconstruct exactly when such accounts became a literary genre. Perhaps it split off from traditional historiography, as many historians offered first-person narratives of military and diplomatic events (for example, Ammianus Marcellinus and Olympiodoros of Thebes). The first major narrative of this kind that we have, Priskos' account of the embassy to Attila, is embedded in a traditional historical narrative, and Priskos was not the ambassador himself, only his secretary.[30] The first self-standing narrative written in the first person by the ambassador himself was probably that of Nonnosos, ambassador in 530–531 to the Ethiopians and Saracens, small fragments of which are quoted by later authors. Unlike those of Priskos, they focus on the cultural and animal exotica encountered along the journey rather than on the politics itself.[31] Accounts more like those of Priskos in emphasis can be attributed to the diplomats Petros *patrikios*, Justinian's long-serving *magister officiorum* (who wrote a Roman history and manuals for court ceremonies) and Zemarchos, though these survive mostly in the fragments of the late sixth-century historian Menandros, the continuer of Agathias.[32] Therefore, not a single example of this genre survives in its original form. The fragments of Menandros, in turn, are known from the tenth-century Byzantine excerpta *De legationibus* (*On Embassies*), which we will discuss below. Zemarchos' account of the embassy to the Turks in Central Asia (in ca. 569–572) seems to have been known also by the late sixth-century Monophysite writer Yuhannan of Amida (called "John of Ephesos" by modern historians), who used it for his own ecclesiastical history. After recounting the confrontation between the Roman and Persian ambassadors at the Turkish court, he concludes:

> Such, then, were the facts which occurred, according to the relation of the ambassadors, of which we have given a brief abstract. For on their return, after an absence of two years, they detailed much besides that was extraordinary and wonderful of the great populousness of these tribes, and the astonishing character of the regions they inhabit, and of their military institutions, and the uprightness of their morals.[33]

This sounds much like Libanios' description of what Spektatos would have seen on his embassy. What is interesting is that Yuhannan was writing not long after the embassy, meaning that the text came into his hands relatively soon. The same was true of Malalas' use of Nonnosos (the embassy was in 530–531, while the first version of Malalas, containing the quotations from Nonnosos' account, appeared soon afterwards).[34] At the very beginning of the supplementary book 8 of the *Wars*, Prokopios boasted that the first installment of seven books had, in the two years since it was completed, circulated throughout the Roman world. There was, then, a demand for such works, and they circulated quickly.

The loss of the diplomatic ethnographies of Nonnosos and Zemarchos is regrettable, given the richness of the information they seem to have contained. If all that we had of this genre was Priskos' embassy, we might have concluded that these narratives did not offer comprehensive overviews of the geography, peoples, and customs of a foreign kingdom or land, but rather only recounted the experiences of the travelers themselves, often on a day-to-day basis.[35] What they lost in scope they made up for in detail, personal observation, and quotidian information. It is because of this kind of narrative (in Priskos) that we know, for example, about the dining customs at Attila's court and about his concubines and personal habits. Prokopios does not offer such information about foreign rulers. However, our evidence for the narratives of Nonnosos and Zemarchos suggests that this distinction is not absolutely valid. The former especially seems to have offered more ethnography than politics. Moreover, as we will see in the next section, both types of account could be deployed to serve the same political and literary purposes.

This brings us to the most challenging aspect of this genre, namely a close reading of its literary strategies, its meanings, nuances, and implications, usually unstated and possibly subversive. There is too much ground to cover here. In the following section, I will trace a common theme of Roman self-criticism through the ethnographic digressions in three of our authors, but it will be only one type of reading among many other possibilities. Scholarship has traditionally focused on how the "raw" information of ethnography, which was never fully objective to begin with, was formatted according to conceptual categories and literary standards of the classical tradition before being presented to the reading public.[36] In part this meant "formatting" the raw information to preset types, so that Huns became like the nomadic Skythians of Herodotos, while the people of the north were cast as tall, blond, and reckless in battle, like the ancient Celts. In the case of some Goths living north of the Black Sea, Prokopios explicitly states that "they were called Skythai in ancient times, as all nations dwelling in those lands are commonly called Skythians."[37] This literary strategy has traditionally called the accuracy of the information about foreign peoples into question. This is too vast a topic to treat here, as it implicates, by extension, almost every aspect of the representation of reality by these authors. For my part, I doubt that ethnographic accounts can safely be used by modern historians, but not because they uncritically imitate ancient models. It is because they are too political, for they were designed to score points in internal Roman debates and not primarily to present objective information about foreigners.

I would like to stress that our authors were not uncritical imitators of ancient tropes. For example, while we may detect the influence of climate theory from time to time, inherited from ancient sources such as Hippokrates, we should not press it too far when it comes to Prokopios and his contemporaries. They were not determinists in this respect, and too many people were moving around in their own times and changing their customs for that model to work. After all, both the decadent Vandals and the rough Moors lived in North Africa, to say nothing of the native Roman population. Prokopios even claims that the majority of the inhabitants of Thule (Scandinavia) did not differ much from the rest of mankind.[38] Ancient theory, we will find, was more a useful tool than a mental straitjacket.

The one nation in Scandinavia that Prokopios singles out as living more like beasts than men are the Skrithiphinoi, who inhabited the extreme north. We are reminded here of the north-south polarities established by Herodotos,

which made the Skythians the polar opposites of the Egyptians in all ways.[39]
But there is no correlation in the late antique historians between distance
from Constantinople and the barbarians' level of culture. For example, Theophylaktos presents the Chinese as advanced in their civilization, and, as we
will see, Prokopios speaks highly of the Ephthalitai Huns, who lived to the
northeast of the Persians. So while the historians' view of the world was
based on the distinction between Romans and barbarians (the Romans
having long since replaced the Greeks in this polarity), not all barbarians
were necessarily barbaric. But before we draw conclusions about the cultural
politics of late antique ethnography, we should first consider its political
functions. Often it was not primarily about barbarians at all; rather, the barbarians constituted a literary mirror in which Roman society could be reflected
indirectly.

The Politics of Ethnography in Late Antique Historiography

Late antique ethnography was premised on the difference between Romans
and barbarians. If we do not read some of the texts too closely, we might
reasonably conclude that their purpose was to (yet again) expose, emphasize,
nuance, and narrate the moral and cultural superiority of the Romans over
the barbarians, even at the cost of dehumanizing the latter; in other words,
that this was a discourse of chauvinism. Some have even extended this accusation to the whole of the Greek ethnographic tradition, starting with Herodotos.[40] To be sure, passages abound that rhetorically dehumanize the barbarian,
though, in our period, these tend to be found in panegyrics praising emperors who had just been or still were at war with them. It is rarer to find such
passages in the historians. Ammianus Marcellinus' excursus on the Huns is
one such passage,[41] bearing in mind that he was also bitingly critical of his
fellow Romans. Prokopios' representation of the Moors as primitive and poor
is similar: a recent analysis has expertly shown how he distinguishes them
from Romans through "the whole range of traditional markers of ethnic
identity. . . . They did not live like Romans, they did not dress like Romans,
they did not eat like Romans, and they were not even properly human."[42]
Their primitiveness, unfamiliar diet and dress, and darker skin correlated
also with negative moral characteristics, such as treachery and the use of violence against Roman cities. In Chapter 4 we will look closely at a case-study
from the middle Byzantine period: the Pechenegs, as yet another instance of

the "Skythian" type, were routinely dehumanized in order to affirm Roman civilized values by contrast.

But in many cases, the more closely we read the sources and the more familiar we become with literary approaches to classical historiography advanced in the past three decades, the less useful and applicable the charge of chauvinism (however dressed up) becomes. Ethnographers, beginning with Herodotos, have emerged as admirers of many aspects of barbarian culture, as authentic transmitters of barbarian points of view, and, crucially, as subtle (or even outspoken) critics of their own societies and dominant paradigms, moral and conceptual. "It is an irony that the history of barbarism has had to be written in relation to the most literary of texts, which themselves often challenged the common opinions of their day."[43] A classicizing historian, then, operating in the theoretical ground created by Greek philosophy, should not be compared to modern racists, religious zealots, or propagandists of empire.

Ethnography could serve to reinforce (or create) the distinction between Roman and barbarians, but it could also question that distinction or even critique Roman preconceptions about it. I will be focusing here on the latter forms, in part because much of the literary analysis of our texts has been written not by scholars of literature but by social historians who tend to homogenize the outlook of elites. Authors are interpreted against their presumptive social class and seen as expressing conventional imperial views. There are still scholars who, for all intents and purposes, seem to be unaware that Prokopios wrote the *Secret History*, and they discuss his *Wars* as a straightforward expression of Justinianic propaganda.[44] It is time to inject some classical scholarship into these readings by recognizing that elite texts were often critical of elite notions. Even negative portrayals of the barbarians could be complicit in broader arguments that were critical of imperial society as well. Subversion was one of the main functions of ethnography in both classical and late antiquity. Subversion: that is, helping readers think past the dominant beliefs of their society, not necessarily to impose one's own but to help them question what they might previously have regarded as unquestionable. Ethnography presented unique opportunities for this. Discussing the unknown could free the mind from the shackles of the familiar and predictable. Amazement and surprise can be used to convey "novel" ideas. The foreign could become a terrain for mapping out alternative political and social views. Moreover, the farther you go, the safer you are from the rulers of your world, and this works at the level of discourse in ethnography too. As Herodotos had shown, and even Tacitus in the *Germania*, it is possible to criticize aspects of your own world by praising foreign customs, by highlighting things that foreigners do better, even if in other respects their lives are barbaric. Here the "other" becomes a mirror for the "self."[45] We begin with a straightforward example from Priskos and follow the themes that he raises through to Prokopios and Agathias.

At the narrative climax of his account of the embassy to Attila, Priskos describes his chance meeting with a *Graikos* (i.e., a Greek-speaking Roman) who had been taken captive by the Huns but later chose to live among them when his master set him free. He made this choice because he had been thoroughly disillusioned with the corruption of the Roman polity (*politeia*) and found to his surprise (and that of Priskos' readers, no doubt) that life with the Huns was in some respects morally healthier. His tale leads to a debate between him and Priskos over the merits and flaws of the Roman way of life and political system. Some scholars suspect that Priskos invented the entire exchange, and perhaps the anonymous Greek as well, precisely to air his own criticisms of the Roman state. These would be less credible if he presented them in his own voice, and perhaps dangerous.[46] What makes it even more likely that this Greek is mostly if not entirely invented is the fact that he is an inversion of the legendary figure of Anacharsis, a Skythian who adopted Greek customs and thereby enabled Greek authors to ironize their own position and engage in self-critical autoethnography.[47] Priskos' interlocutor is a Greek who has adopted Skythian customs for largely the same reason.

The passage in Priskos is well known, but I will quote it at length to set the stage for the rest of this section.

> He considered his new life among the Skythians better than his old life among the Romans, and the reasons he gave were as follows: "After war the Skythians live in inactivity, enjoying what they have got, and not at all, or very little, harassed. The Romans, on the other hand, are in the first place very liable to perish in war, as they have to rest their hopes of safety on others, and are not allowed, on account of their tyrants, to use arms. And those who use them are injured by the cowardice of their generals, who cannot support the conduct of war. But the condition of the subjects in time of peace is far more grievous than the evils of war, for the exaction of taxes is very severe, and unprincipled men inflict injuries on others because the laws are practically not valid against all classes. A transgressor

who belongs to the wealthy classes is not punished for his injustice, while a poor man who does not understand business suffers the legal penalty, that is if he does not depart this life before the trial, so long is the course of lawsuits protracted and so much money is expended on them. The climax of the misery is to have to pay in order to obtain justice. For no one will give a court to the injured man unless he pays a sum of money to the judge and the judge's clerks."

In reply to this attack on the empire, I asked him to be good enough to listen with patience to the other side of the question. "The creators of the Roman polity [*politeia*]," I said, "who were wise and good men, in order to prevent things from being done haphazardly made one class of men guardians of the laws, and appointed another class to the profession of arms, who were to have no other object than to be always ready for battle and to go forth to war without dread as though to their ordinary exercise, having by practice exhausted all their fear beforehand. Others again were assigned to attend to the cultivation of the ground, to support both themselves and those who fight in their defense, by contributing the military grain-supply. Still others they appointed to take thought for those who had suffered wrongs, some to have charge of the cases of those who, through their own natural incapacity, were unable to plead for themselves, and others to sit in judgment and uphold the intent of the law. . . .

As to the long time spent on lawsuits, that is due to a concern for justice, that judges may not fail in passing correct judgments by having to give verdicts offhand; it is better that they should reflect and conclude the case more tardily than that by judging in a hurry they should both injure man and transgress against the Deity, the institutor of justice. The laws apply to all, and even the emperor obeys them. It is not a fact," as was part of his charge, "that the rich do violence to the poor with impunity, unless one escapes justice through escaping detection; and this is a recourse for the poor as well as for the rich. These offenders would go unpunished because of lack of evidence, something which happens not only among the Romans but among all peoples. For your freedom you should give thanks to fortune [*tyche*] rather than to your master. He led you out to war, where, through inexperience, you might have been killed by the enemy or, fleeing the battle, have been punished by your owner. The

Romans treat their servants better than the king of the Skythians treats his subjects. They deal with them as fathers or teachers, admonishing them to abstain from evil and follow the lines of conduct which they have esteemed honorable; they reprove them for their errors like their own children. They are not allowed, like the Skythians, to inflict death on them. They have numerous ways of conferring freedom; they can manumit not only during life, but also by their wills, and the testamentary wishes of a Roman in regard to his property are law."

My interlocutor shed tears, and admitted that the laws and polity [*politeia*] of the Romans were fair, but deplored that the governors, not possessing the spirit of former generations, were ruining the State. As we were engaged in this discussion a servant came out and opened the door of the enclosure. I hurried up . . . (tr. J. B. Bury, modified)

Let us examine, first, the terms of the debate and its underlying logic, and then the function of this passage in Priskos' *History*.

The debate concerns the Roman *politeia*. Now, the *politeia* happens to be the single most important concept in late Roman and Byzantine political thought, though it has received virtually no attention in the scholarship, which focuses instead on the (theoretically subordinate) concept and practice of the *basileia*.[48] In writers of late antiquity, we should not see *politeia* as a "Greek" term. It was, in fact, the Greek translation of Latin *respublica* and referred to the state and society of the Romans, even under imperial rule. The distinction between "Republic" and "Empire" was seen by late Roman and Byzantine thinkers only as a change in the way that the *politeia* was governed. It was not until the modern period that republics were finally viewed as antithetical to monarchies. In our period, and until the sixteenth century, the Roman empire could be viewed as a "monarchical republic,"[49] the conjunction of *politeia* and *basileia* that we find in Priskos' debate. *Politeia*, then, did not refer to the type of regime by which a state was governed, as it did in Greek political theory, but to a political society whose sovereign was the people, that was relatively homogeneous, and whose political institutions, especially the laws, aimed to encode and enforce shared values. The stability and legitimacy of the Roman *politeia* rested, in theory, on social consensus and the rule of law, not on the imposition of arbitrary power—this is what made it an *ennomos politeia*, a "lawful" polity—even less on the theocratic notions that are popular in modern surveys. The source of political authority always remained popular, not religious. The conception of the *politeia* in the debate in Priskos (as in most other late antique political theorists) is secular and Roman (not Greek or Christian), and subordinates the *basileus* to the social consensus policed by the laws.[50]

The encounter with the Graikos enables Priskos to stage a debate on the ideals and practices of the Roman *politeia*. The Graikos attacks the way in which the *politeia* operates in practice, while Priskos defends the rationale behind many of its arrangements, conceding that they do not always work as intended. At the end of the discussion the Graikos concedes that in theory the *politeia* is good, but it is being ruined by the people in charge of it. So there is a partial and theoretical rapprochement between the two men, though significantly the conversation is interrupted and remains unfinished. This is Priskos' way of signaling that the fundamental question of the governance of the Roman *politeia* remains open.

Specifically, the Graikos bases his preferences on his personal experience of life with the Huns. Beyond that, he questions the monopoly exerted by the Roman state on weapons and war, along with the inequality in the application of the laws and the social injustice that is caused by corruption. In his response, Priskos invokes the advantages of social and economic differentiation and specialization, which he discusses in the terms of Plato's *Republic* (a work whose Greek title is in fact *Politeia*). He defends the principles of Roman justice but concedes that they are not always adhered to, among both Romans and others. His key sentence in defense of the *politeia* is that "the laws apply to all, and even the emperor obeys them." This was not precisely correct, however, as Priskos surely knew, for the emperor had the right to make and unmake laws, which, in a sense, set him above the law, a fact that was recognized by jurists.[51] Still, it was also understood, and conceded by many emperors and theorists, that an *ennomos politeia* required a lawful authority, so all but the most ham-fisted emperors paid careful attention to this matter. The emperors understood that they were allowed to act outside the law only in order to benefit the republic better than the current laws themselves would, under the circumstances. But a tension remained. We see here Priskos' strong stance in favor of one solution to this problem; perhaps he was even suggesting that to redeem the *politeia* from the Graikos' accusations the emperor had to be subordinated even more firmly to the law.

While Priskos does not exactly go on the counter-offensive, he responds to the Graikos' comparison of life among the Huns with that in the Roman *politeia*. "You got lucky," he tells the Graikos: that you are better off here with the Huns than among the Romans is due purely to chance, *tyche*, that you were not killed or that your master was generous. Roman life, we infer, is less subject to chance, given that it is regulated by the laws and norms of the *politeia*, even if they are not perfectly applied. Priskos is saying that one should not generalize from the experience of the Graikos to form the impression of a Hun *politeia*. Life among the Huns is governed either by chance or by the whim of all-powerful individuals (such as Attila); perhaps the two are the same thing. Since there can be no possibility of a *politeia* under such conditions, such a comparison is never attempted. The advantages of the *politeia* emerge strongly even from what Priskos does *not* say. Can there be a barbarian *politeia*? To answer this, we turn to Prokopios and Agathias.

But before we take leave of Priskos, we must emphasize that none of the labor performed by this passage would have been as effective had it been set in any other context. Roman society could be neither analyzed nor criticized as fundamentally as in a debate set well outside its borders, where real alternatives were vividly present and choices could be made (e.g., to forsake Rome and live with the Huns), choices that were simply not available in Constantinople. The presence of a viable "Other" required Priskos to dig deeper in his analysis, precisely what he wanted to do. This was the reason he crafted the entire scene in the first place. Without compromising his loyalty to Rome or the emperor, he managed to level strong criticisms of his own society, to hold up a necessary and subversive mirror, and speak, albeit safely, through the mouth of one who was, like himself, an ambiguous insider-outsider. This strategy had ample precedent in classical literature.[52]

Nor, on the other hand, did Priskos dehumanize the Huns, as Ammianus had done in the previous century. Knowing them first-hand, he "was determined to offer his readership a description of a society that, at least in part, they could understand." Christopher Kelly, while not focusing on the debate with the Graikos, has revealed the humanizing touches and observations in Priskos' account of his own stay with the Huns. They were not beasts; they had table manners of their own, which Priskos, unlike Ammianus, had actually seen. He "set out to challenge earlier versions of the Huns as impenetrably foreign. . . . It doesn't take much to spot the differences, but it takes an open-minded and observant inquirer to isolate those precious moments when two worlds, if only briefly, can be seen to touch."[53] His Huns are ordinary in many respects, and the background of the embassy—a plot by a palace eunuch to assassinate Attila —gives them a moral edge in the narrative.

Attila certainly had more honor than Chrysaphios. There were, in late antique historiography, many techniques by which the masters of Rome could be criticized by using the "Other" as a mirror or mouthpiece, one of which was speeches attributed to the empire's barbarian foes. In Prokopios there are many such speeches that deliver scathing criticisms of Justinian and Roman policy in general, which the historian would not dare to put in his own mouth (except, of course, in a secret work). These speeches air the legitimate grievances of Goths, Armenians, and others, creating sympathy for them among readers. It is also through his speeches that Prokopios enhances the nobility of the Gothic king Totila, Justinian's enemy in the west and the tragic hero of the final books of the *Wars*.[54] These speeches do not make Prokopios any less a Roman patriot. What they indicate is an ability to see events through the eyes of the victims of his own government.

Let us turn, then, directly to Prokopios and the question of the *politeia* in connection with barbarian societies. In the introductory chapters of the *Persian War*, where he recounts episodes from fifth-century Persian history, Prokopios comments on the Persians' relations with the Ephthalitai Huns, a people of Central Asia. This leads to a brief ethnographic digression.

> The Ephthalitai are of the stock of the Huns in fact as well as in name; however, they do not mingle with any of the Huns known to us, for they occupy a land neither adjoining nor even very near to them; their territory lies immediately to the north of Persia. Indeed their city, called Gorgo, is located over against the Persian frontier, and is consequently the center of frequent contests concerning boundary lines between the two peoples. For they are not nomads like the other Hunnic peoples, but for a long period have been established in a goodly land. As a result of this they have never made any incursion into the Roman territory except in company with the Medic army. They are the only ones among the Huns who have white bodies and countenances that are not ugly. It is also true that their manner of living is unlike that of their kinsmen, nor do they live a savage life as they do; but they are ruled by one king, and since they possess an *ennomos politeia*, they observe right and justice in their dealings both with one another and with their neighbors, in no degree less than the Romans and the Persians. Moreover, the wealthy citizens are in the habit of attaching to themselves friends to the number of twenty or more, as the case may be, and these become permanently

their banquet-companions, and have a share in all their property, enjoying some kind of a common right in this matter. Then, when the man who has gathered such a company together comes to die, it is the custom that all these men be taken alive into the tomb with him. (*Wars* 1.3.2-7; tr. H. B. Dewing, modified)

Except at the very end of this passage, Prokopios tries to present these Huns as a people whom Romans might recognize as civilized. They have at least one city, good land, boundaries with their neighbors, and white skin, and are not ugly like the other Huns. More important, they do not live like savages and have an *ennomos politeia*, which means that they recognize the rule of justice, like the Romans and the Persians. Barbarians can have a *politeia* after all. In fact, not only the historians of this period but the Roman authorities themselves believed that the Persians had a legitimate *politeia* that was formally equivalent to the Roman one and equal in rank.[55] Therefore, beyond designating the Roman *respublica* specifically, the term *politeia* operated on a formal level as well. Its cultural "content" may have varied from nation to nation, but so long as a nation was politically organized, socially and economically sophisticated and settled, and lived according to laws, it qualified as a *politeia*. This is why the historical and diplomatic sources will typically qualify it as (for example) "the *politeia* of the Romans" or "of the Persians."

According to Prokopios' information, the Ephthalitai qualified to have a *politeia* too. This Roman historian, then was able to think highly of a group of Huns, even if only the white-skinned ones. This passage would no doubt have come as a bit of a surprise to many of his readers, who would have thought of the Ephthalitai as barbarians who lived even beyond the Persians and who had on occasion raided Roman territory in typical barbarian fashion.[56] What induced Prokopios to present them so positively? The questions surrounding this passage become more complex when we read to the end, where, in a Herodotean move, built-up impressions are suddenly shattered.[57] It turns out that the Ephthalitai practice a form of ritual human sacrifice akin to that of the Skythian kings of Herodotos, those Skythians who are the opposite of settled civilized life. This should make us wonder exactly how just and civilized Prokopios' Ephthalitai really are. Granted, culture and customs differ from *politeia* to *politeia*, but a Roman would probably not recognize a society that practiced this as morally equivalent to his own. Yet is the purpose of Prokopios' sudden revelation to destabilize the positive picture that he has presented of the Ephthalitai? They were hardly that important, and had just been introduced to readers who might not previously have heard of them. Why does he lift them so high (parity with Rome) only to pull them down (parity with Skythians)? The equation, we must remember, cuts both ways. If the Ephthalitai are "no less" civilized than the Persians and Romans, this logically means that the Romans are no more civilized than the Persians and Ephthalitai. Rather than elevating the latter, the purpose of the equation might be to question just how *ennomos* a *politeia* the Romans have. We must not forget that Prokopios was, at the very same time, writing the *Secret History* to denounce Justinian as a bloodthirsty tyrant who drenched the earth with Roman blood, destroyed the *politeia* and the laws of the Romans, and "acted like a barbarian in his manner of speech, dress, and thinking."[58] In fact, the historian contrived to compare Justinian to a number of oriental despots in all three of his works.[59] Therefore, the equation of Romans, Ephthalitai, and Persians at the start of the *Wars* undermines the claim of the Roman *politeia* to be lawful, given that Prokopios also presents the kings of Persia (Chosroes and his father Kavades) as consistently acting beyond the law. Neither they, nor Justinian in the *Secret History* (and in part the *Wars* too), "observed right and justice in their dealings both with one another and with their neighbors," as the passage on the Ephthalitai has it. The question of the justice of the Roman *politeia* is raised here too, then, with disturbing implications.

We may, in this context, revisit Prokopios' famous comparison between the Vandals and the Moors, an exercise in contrasting classical stereotypes, between the decadence of luxury and the hardiness of primitive poverty.

> For of all the nations we know the Vandals happen to be the most luxurious and the Moors the most hardy. Since they gained possession of Libya, the Vandals used to indulge in baths, all of them, every day, and enjoyed a table loaded with all things, the sweetest and best that the earth and sea produce. They wore gold almost all the time and clothed themselves in the Medic garments, which now they call "seric,"[60] and passed their time in theatres, hippodromes, and other pleasurable pursuits, above all in hunting. They had dancers and mimes and all other things to hear and see that are of a musical nature or otherwise happen to be sightworthy among men. Most of them lived in garden parks, which were well supplied with water and trees. They had great numbers of banquets and they diligently studied all the arts of sex. But the Moors live in stuffy huts, in winter, summer,

and every other time, never leaving them because of the snow or the heat of the sun or any other discomfort due to nature. They sleep on the ground, the prosperous among them, if it should so happen, spreading a fleece under themselves. Moreover, it is not customary among them to change their clothing with the seasons, but they wear a thick cloak and a rough shirt at all times. They have neither bread nor wine nor any other good thing, but they take grain, either wheat or barley, and, without boiling it or grinding it to flour or barley-meal, they eat it in a manner not at all different from that of the animals. (*Wars* 4.6.5-13; tr. H. B. Dewing, modified)

The context is significant. The last Vandal king, Gelimer, has taken refuge at a mountain fort in 533–534 with some Moors. The passage purports to explain why the Vandals were not able to endure the hardship of the siege, whereas the Moors were. Realizing this, the imperial officer conducting the siege, Pharas, wrote to Gelimer and persuaded him to accept becoming an honored "slave" of the emperor rather than endure such misery. Charles Pazdernik has expertly unraveled the skein of references that link Prokopios' version of these events to an episode in Xenophon's *Hellenika*, where the Spartan king Agesilaos attempts to persuade Pharnabazos to escape from the slavery of submission to the Persian king and become a free man.[61] Prokopios has Pharas raise the question of slavery at this point so that the reader may be able to apply this concept to the status not so much of Gelimer (after his surrender) but of *Belisarios*—indeed, to the status of all Romans serving under Justinian.[62] This, again, correlates with the themes of the *Secret History*, where Justinian's despotism reduces all Roman free men to a servile status. In connection with his empress Theodora, Prokopios declares that "the *politeia* was reduced to a slave-pen and she was our teacher in servility."[63] It is therefore no accident that Pharas' letter to Gelimer is laced with references to the power of *tyche* over human life, a persistent theme in Prokopios. Submitting to a despotism is presented as accepting the power of chance, which is a way of recasting Priskos' observation to the Graikos, which we examined above, that his happiness among the Huns was a matter of luck. Where the free *politeia* ends, the power of chance starts, and with it the arbitrary will of the despot. On which side of this divide did Romans really live?

What, then, of the ethnographic comparison between the Vandals and the Moors? Prokopios' description of Vandal decadence resonates in many details with ancient Greek views of Persia.[64] This makes the intertextual comparison of Gelimer with Pharnabazos viable, in fact productive, in terms of explaining the course of subsequent events: Gelimer was *prepared* to accept Justinianic "slavery" (identical to Persian). But the description can be read in a complementary way as well. The lifestyle of the Vandals in North Africa is virtually identical to that of the Roman elite in Constantinople as described in the *Secret History*, with all the same details (baths, gold, silk, theaters, hippodromes, dancers, mimes, banquets, and unconventional sexual practices; only the hunting and the parks are absent in the *Secret History*). The ethnography of the Vandals turns out to be a covert ethnography of the Roman elite, and in this instance also is designed to explain why they too acquiesced in the rule of the quasi-Persian despot Justinian. The fall of a great and martial people is described in both cases, one openly and the other covertly.

There was, in other words, room in the late Roman psyche for an "inner barbarian." The philosopher-politician Themistios said as much to Valens and the Senate of Constantinople: "there is in each of us a barbarian tribe, extremely overbearing and intractable—I mean the temper and the insatiate desires, which stand opposed to the rational elements just as the Scythians and Germans do to the Romans."[65] The normative polarity could be reversed in order to stimulate self-criticism: the "good" barbarian might point to the "bad" Roman just as the "bad" barbarian might be a surrogate for the average Roman. Such reversal was as old as Herodotos and Thucydides, who suggested (indirectly, of course) that imperial Athens was behaving almost as badly as the Persian empire when it invaded Greece and so was destined, unless it changed course, to suffer the same fate.[66] Therefore, in terms of its potential, ethnography was an intimate indicator of a society's willingness to engage in self-criticism and the sophistication with which it could do so. The late Roman historians hold up well here. Theirs was anything but an elitist and chauvinistic projection of Roman imperial values—unless we redefine those values to include self-criticism.

The final author we will consider is Agathias, who also wrote a perplexing passage on the *politeia* of a foreign people. But if we read it against the tradition that we have traced from Priskos to Prokopios, we already know that we should not take it as a literal and factual description but as yet another way of talking about Rome in the "mirror" of the barbarian.

> The Franks have a common frontier with Italy. They may be identified with the people who in ancient times were called "Germans," since they inhabit the banks of the Rhine and its territory, and,

though they occupy most of Gaul, it is a later acquisition since they did not previously live there; and the same is true of the city of Massilia, which was originally settled by Ionians. Massilia was colonized long ago by Phokaians who had been driven out of Asia by the Persians in the reign of Dareios the son of Hystaspes. Once Greek, it has now become barbarian in character, having abandoned its ancestral constitution and embraced the ways of its conquerors. But still it does not seem to fall short of the dignity of its ancient inhabitants, for the Franks are not nomads, as some barbarians are, but their *politeia* and laws are modeled on the Roman pattern, apart from which they uphold similar standards with regard to contracts, marriage and religious observance. They are in fact all Christians and adhere to the strictest orthodoxy. They also have magistrates in their cities and priests and celebrate the feasts in the same way as we do; and, for a barbarian people, strike me as extremely well-bred and civilized and as practically the same as ourselves except for their uncouth style of dress and peculiar language. I admire them for their other attributes and especially for the spirit of justice and harmony which prevails amongst them. Although on many occasions in the past and even during my own lifetime their kingdom has been divided between three or more rulers they have never yet waged war against one another or seen fit to stain their country's honor by the slaughter of their kith and kin. Yet whenever great powers are seen to have reached a state of parity, arrogant and uncompromising attitudes are inevitably engendered and the logical outcome is rivalry, the lust for domination and a host of other passions that constitute a fertile breeding-ground for unrest and dissension. Nevertheless, nothing of the kind occurs in their case regardless of the number of kingdoms into which they are divided. In the rare event of some dispute arising between their kings they draw themselves up ostensibly in battle-order and with the apparent object of deciding the issue by arms and then confront one another. But once the main body of the army on either side has come face to face they immediately lay aside all animosity, return to understanding and enjoin their leaders to settle their differences by arbitration, or failing that by placing their own lives at stake in single combat. For it is not right, they say, or in keeping with ancestral precedent for the common good to suffer injury and upheaval on account of some personal feud of theirs. The immediate result is that they break their ranks and lay down their arms. Peace and quiet are restored, normal communications resumed and the horrors of war are forgotten. So law-abiding and public spirited are the subject classes and so docile and amenable to reason, when need be, are their masters. It is for this reason that the basis of their power remains secure and their government stable and that they have not lost any of their territory but have actually increased it greatly. When justice and amity are second nature to a people, then their *politeia* is guaranteed happiness and stability and rendered impregnable to enemy attack. (*Histories* 1.2; tr. J. D. Frendo, modified)

Passages such as these have typically received only fact-checking analyses.[67] But we do not need to dig into western sources to realize that this picture of Frankish harmony is a fiction.

We see here even more clearly that *politeia* is a function of the way that a society is organized with respect to its laws, magistrates, and procedures. Like Prokopios' Ephthalitai, the Franks are not "nomads," which is apparently the anthropological state opposite to that of having a *politeia* (in this digression the term *politeia* both opens and closes the discussion of the character of Frankish society). There can be different *politeiai* that correspond to different people: the Franks have a different language and culture from that of the Romans and, while they have the same religion, being Orthodox is not a requirement for constituting a *politeia*. Agathias, like other Romans of his age, recognized the Persians as having a *politeia* too.[68] It is also clear that he is trying to make the Franks look as much like Romans as possible, in fact violating historicity in order to do so (Prokopios, writing only a generation earlier, had presented the Franks as utterly savage and faithless barbarians, Christians in name only).[69] What explains Agathias' reversal of that negative picture? The answer is probably to be found in the moral agenda that shapes his *Histories*, which he lays out in the preface and in later sections of the text. History, in his view, should try to make people more decent by teaching them through examples of virtue and vice. There are many passages in the work where he tweaks factuality in order to render a satisfying lesson, and I think that this is one of them.[70] The literary strategy behind this is simple and is found in many types of ancient literature: the more similar you make two things seem, the more you highlight their differences (this, for instance, is Homer's strategy with respect to gods and mortals in the *Iliad*). Over half of the digression on the Franks is devoted to their internal harmony. So these are a people with a *politeia* just like that of the Romans—except that they have managed to control internal strife. Pure fiction, of course, but a potent lesson for the Roman reader.[71]

Two final examples from Agathias. Agathias was writing as a Christian, though I believe that he was not one and that this persona was imposed on him by his circumstances. At any rate, in the midst of a conventional and Christian-sounding attack on the pagan animal sacrifices of the Alamanni, he slips in this observation, which sententiously fulfills the Herodotean function of expressing the author's personal opinion: "They would be deserving of pity [ἐλεῖσθαι] rather than censure, and complete forgiveness [πλείστης συγγνώμης], who fail to reach the truth. For they do not willingly slip and fall, but in seeking the good, they form a mistaken judgment and thereafter firmly hold to that opinion, whatever it happens to be."[72]

Using Christian terminology but a thoroughly Socratic argument that failure to attain the good is due to ignorance and should be forgiven, Agathias effectively advocates the "forgiveness" of those who currently practice pagan sacrifice, not something that Christians of the period were wont to do, especially those linked to the repressive policies of Justinian. He rejects the practice of sacrifice itself, but also harsh responses to it that are not infused with an understanding that pagans too seek the good. Might he have had someone in mind other than the Alamanni, someone nearer to (or at) home? We note that he says that the *politeia* of the Alamanni was just like that of Franks except for religion (in the same way as the Franks were just like the Romans except for language and dress).[73] In other words, the Alamanni are like pagan Romans, of which we know the empire still had many. These equivalences assist his readers to make equations with sectors of *Roman* society; the barbarians are again a useful tool for the indirect discussion of domestic issues.

In the following book, discussing strange Persian customs, Agathias goes further:

It is obvious that *each* of the nations of mankind, if they have lived under some law that is generally accepted among them, believes that this law is excellent and sacred, and if something is opposed to it, then that seems to be something worth avoiding, ridiculing, and dismissing. But people have found reasons and arguments from diverse sources to justify their own customs, of which some may happen to be correct, but the rest are specious inventions. So I do not consider it remarkable that the Persians should also attempt to prove that their own traditions are better than those of anyone else.[74]

This picks up from Herodotos' observation that each person would prefer the customs of his own country over all the rest, given a choice;[75] this is the rule of *nomos* over men. We also do not need to point out that when Agathias says "each of the nations," he implicitly includes his own Romans as well. What vistas for critical self-reflection do these comments open up?

In conclusion, we have found that ethnographic digressions often play an indirect instrumental role in the works of the late antique historians: they exist, and take the forms that they do, in order to encourage Roman readers to think more deeply and critically not about barbarian societies but about their own, and often resort to fictions about the barbarians to achieve this goal. They can be seen as a continuation, within the realm of historiography, of the ancient practice of devising *mythoi* "in order to achieve a literary effect."[76] When reading such passages we would do well to supply the "missing Roman," the implied referent that explains why what is being said is being said at all. This is not to say that all ethnography in late antiquity follows this model; it is only the one I have chosen to pursue here. Without discounting the abundant information these texts provide on foreign peoples, we have to consider that the authors also use their foreign subjects as foils by which to discuss their own societies indirectly, just as "Greek sources on Persia were often in fact writing (through Persian fantasies) about their own worlds."[77] But this "instrumental" model of covert self-reflection explains many of the oddities that we encounter in the digressions in question and allows our authors to escape the false dilemma of being regarded either as bad historians or as chauvinist Romans.

CHAPTER 2

Byzantine Information-Gathering Behind the Veil of Silence

Byzantine Sources of Information About Foreign People

The contention of the next section will be that the writing of ethnography declined severely in the middle Byzantine period (in fact, until the fourteenth century), certainly in comparison to the rich collection of sources that we have for late antiquity. This decline was not, however, due to a lack of knowledge, and that is what this section establishes. There were many people in Byzantium who had extensive and detailed information about the empire's neighbors and peoples farther away. This section will document the channels of its transmission. To say, then, that ethnography declined is to say that Byzantine authors *chose not* to put that information into literary form. We have seen that they had the models for doing so, but refused to take up the challenge. For now, we must document the indirect traces of this knowledge.

To start at an obvious place, we know from many texts that the Byzantine state used spies (κατάσκοποι), but our evidence is patchy and indirect (these spies would not have been worth much if our evidence for them was extensive). We do not have any "classified" state information about their activities, which were presumably as secret as the manufacture of Greek Fire. One cannot but cite here the testimony of Prokopios, even though it is earlier than the period under consideration. In the *Secret History*, he says this about the κατάσκοποι: "Many men had always been maintained at public expense who would infiltrate the enemy and enter the palace of the Persians on the pretext of trade or something else, and there they would carefully investigate everything. When they returned to Roman territory, they were in a position to reveal all the enemy's secrets to the magistrates."[1] His accusation that Justinian fully decommissioned this corps may be exaggerated;[2] nevertheless, his account provides us with an explicit statement about their activities as state agents. It was not only foreign lands, then, that spies would investigate, but even the very palace of the Persian kings.

Syrianos' treatise *On Strategy*, now dated to the ninth century, contains a brief but intriguing section on spies.[3] Their function was still primarily military. They are advised to pose as merchants (as Prokopios says too). "They must never be of the same race as the enemy" but "must be acquainted with the customs (τὰ ἔθη) of the enemy to whom they are assigned, fluent in their language, and experienced travelers in their country." In short, the spy network consisted of men with considerable "local" ethnographic expertise. It is for this reason that modern states employ anthropologists and archaeologists as spies. However, by stipulating that they must leave their families behind to guarantee their loyalty, the author of this text indirectly expresses his fear that spies may go over to the other side. Insider knowledge was a double-edged asset.

Emperor Leon VI also discussed military spies briefly in his *Taktika*, saying that they should be able to pass as natives among the enemy.[4] As we will see, these military manuals, and the *Taktika* in particular, are among our best sources for middle Byzantine ethnography. At the end of the *Taktika*, Leon addresses his generals and instructs them that in times of war they need to know the "nature" (φύσις) of the enemy.[5] This is a demand for military ethnography, which he in part provides earlier in his text. Likewise, an anonymous military treatise from the tenth century specifies that generals posted along the borders are to place their spies among Bulgarians, Pechenegs, Turks (i.e., Hungarians), and Rus'.[6] Conversely, we hear of Byzantine scouts being tricked by Persian spies who were dressed as Romans.[7]

Historical sources occasionally reveal Roman spies in action. They were sent by Konstantinos V to abduct enemy leaders among the Bulgarians in 764 and to inform him about Bulgarian movements in 773.[8] In 970, in advance of his massive campaign against the Rus' in Bulgaria, Ioannes Tzimiskes "sent bilingual men, clothed in Skythian garb, to the camps and abodes of the enemy, to learn their plans and communicate them to the emperor."[9] In the tenth century, Ibn Hawqal suspected that Byzantine merchants in Arab lands were actually spies.[10] If they were, they would have been following the prescriptions of the treatises that we read above. Another disguise for spies, well known since antiquity, was the defector. The double agent flees his people, usually because of an alleged crime, and seeks refuge among the enemy, even going so far as to convert to their religion. Consider Nikolaos, a Byzantine tax collector who had fled to Baghdad and converted to Islam, ostensibly in order to practice astrology more freely. Yet in 913, during the revolt of Konstantinos Doukas, he sent a secret message to the *logothetes tou dromou* Thomas, couched as an astrological message in Arabic (the *logothetes*, among other functions, coordinated the empire's diplomacy). Thomas handed this message to his Arabic interpreter Manuel (ἑρμηνεύς) for translation.[11] Unfortunately, too much is obscure in the abbreviated version of this story that has come down to us. We do not know the full story of Nikolaos the astrologer.

The early medieval period witnessed dense and regular contact among the many courts of Europe, Asia, and the Near East, and diplomats were a rich source of information about foreign peoples and events, possibly the most important one.[12] Was this knowledge codified in Byzantium? Starting already in the Republic, Roman generals and governors submitted reports to various state bureaus regarding their activities, mostly on the judicial and financial side.[13] In late antiquity, ambassadors brought back and reported much ethnographic information (we saw how quickly the works of Nonnosos and Zemarchos were put into circulation). For the middle Byzantine period, it is not clear how much of the information that the state gathered in this way was written down rather than reported orally;[14] not all generals, at least, were literate,[15] but most ambassadors were. We even know of many Byzantine writers and intellectuals who went on missions to the east and north. For example, in 829–830 future patriarch Ioannes Grammatikos went to Baghdad, as did, later in that same century, future patriarch Photios (or to Samarra).[16] Courtier and philosopher Leon Choirosphaktes was sent by Leon VI to both Bulgaria (under king Symeon) and Baghdad; many others could be named. But we have no reports of narrative or descriptive texts written by them containing ethnographic material (we will discuss this silence in the next section). By contrast, we do have accounts by foreign ambassadors who visited Constantinople, for example, and most notoriously, Liudprand of Cremona, and Ibn Shahrām's embassy from Baghdad to Constantinople in 981–982.[17]

Diplomats were sometimes expected to function as spies. In 714, emperor Anastasios II, learning that the caliph Walid was about to invade Roman territory, sent an embassy led by Daniel, prefect of Constantinople, ostensibly to make peace but really to observe military preparations.[18] But knowledge obtained through diplomatic channels need not have been secret or covert. One could just ask foreign rulers and ambassadors for information about their people and land, out of curiosity. This was easier when the foreign people in question lived far away and there was no risk of direct conflict, or when it concerned matters that were not militarily sensitive. Through an interpreter (ἑρμηνεύς), for example, Justin II questioned Turkish envoys in 568/9 about their leaders, land, foreign relations, and recent events in Central Asia.[19] Agathias reports that his contact at the Persian court, Sergios, found the palace archivists happy to share with him their knowledge of Persian history and culture, finding it a flattering request that the Romans would want to know that sort of thing.[20] The leading powers of late antiquity seem to have kept each other informed of major events within their respective realms.[21] In the early medieval period too, rulers seem to have regularly recounted important events in their diplomatic correspondence, obviously always presented in a self-serving way. Traces of this on the Byzantine side survive mostly in Latin texts (though their authenticity is sometimes suspect). Michael II (820–829) recounted the rebellion of Thomas the Slav in a letter to Louis the Pious.[22] Manuel I Komnenos sent a detailed account of his defeat at the battle at Myriokephalon (1176) to Henry II Plantagenet, king of England (a source that has been underutilized by modern historians).[23] It is likely that Byzantine emperors received news as well as dispatching it. Manuel's letter, in fact, was part of an exchange. Gerald of Wales claims that Henry responded when Manuel had "asked for information about the geographical conditions, way of life, and things worth seeing in the island of Britain. Manuel sent envoys to deliver his letter." Gerald apparently had access to Henry's response with information about the Welsh.[24] But we do not hear about this exchange and the information that it yielded from Byzantine sources, a lack which is crucial for our purposes.

Hosting foreign ambassadors by itself also provided (and required) a great deal of cultural awareness at the court, especially regarding the foreign elites, who were, after all, the main subjects of ethnographic writing even in antiquity. Foreign customs had to be scrupulously observed, unless it was the intention of the court to give offense (as sometimes it was). Liudprand's account of his embassy to Constantinople in 968 as the representative of Otto I offers many illustrations of this. Amid the negotiations, arguments, and insults traded between Liudprand and the court, much information was exchanged, and many cultural sensitivities were revealed and discussed. For example, Nikephoros II asked Liudprand whether Otto had a park for hunting and showed the ambassador his own. While they were touring it, the Byzantine chief of staff noticed that Liudprand was wearing a hat rather than a hood, which was what imperial protocol required. But Liudprand responded:

> Our women ride wearing tiaras and hoods; we men ride wearing hats. Nor is it proper for you to compel me to change my ancestral custom here, as we allow your ambassadors to keep your ancestral customs when they visit us. For with us they ride, walk, and sit at table long-sleeved, wrapped up, with brooches, long-haired, and wearing a long tunic.[25]

It is safe to assume that the Byzantine court had detailed information about the attire, preferred food, language, and religious customs of all nations who sent ambassadors to it. We hear repeatedly from Arab sources that Arab prisoners were not made by the Byzantines to eat pork (Arab prisoners were included in processions in the capital and even at banquets in the palace, playing a symbolic role).[26] In an oration of 1173/4 for emperor Manuel I, Eustathios noted the sheer variety of languages and clothing from the ends of the earth that one could observe at the court, listing Skythian, Dalmatian, Arab, Armenian, Ethiopian, German, and Italian.[27] Yet he gives us no specific information. Once we set the rhetoric aside, we see that we have concrete information about the observance of national customs at the Byzantine court only from the Latin and Arabic sources, in other words from outsiders who had visited it.

Prisoners, as mentioned, were another source of information, especially high-ranking ones who were taken to the court. We learn from former Arab prisoners that they were engaged in discussions with the emperor and patriarch on religious, political, and cultural topics. Some of them wrote detailed accounts of their stay in Constantinople after being released, but this obviously counts as *Arab* ethnography, not Byzantine.[28] There were presumably as many Byzantine as Arab prisoners who could have recorded their experiences of foreign lands, but we have an account by just one, Ioannes Kaminiates, who was captured in Thessalonike in 904. And yet even this text says almost nothing about the customs of the people who took the author into captivity or the lands and cities that he allegedly visited. Moreover, the text may be a later forgery, revealing nothing of Byzantine perspectives of the tenth century. Even if it is authentic it does not contribute much to the study of ethnography, except to reinforce how determined the Byzantines were to avoid discussing Arab culture.[29] It is from Arab accounts that we learn that some of the interpreters serving in the palace had previously been slaves of Arab masters.[30] These men would also have been valuable sources of information and cultural mediators, but we hear nothing *from* or *about* them on the Byzantine side. It is also an Arab source that recounts, rather romantically, the experiences of a Byzantine patrician captured by Bulgarians, but this too does not count for our purposes.[31]

Most foreign prisoners, of course, were not treated as ethnographic informants but rather interrogated for information of immediate military use, before being either ransomed or enslaved. But they could also be converted into spies. The anonymous tenth-century military manual mentioned above argues that they can in fact be more useful than spies, especially if their families are held hostage. "After they have investigated how everything is going among their own people, they can return and report the facts."[32] Even without resorting to threats, the Byzantines were masters at suborning agents and notables of foreign states. In 773, Konstantinos V was warned in advance about a Bulgarian offensive by what Theophanes calls his "secret friends in Bulgaria" (κρυπτοὶ φίλοι).[33] Niketas Choniates claims that Manuel I had men sworn to him in all the cities of Italy and in regions even farther away, who would covertly investigate and report to him every attack that was secretly being planned against the Romans.[34] These appear to be not Byzantine spies but local notables, i.e., traitors. After all, it is a small step from a Byzantine spy so well trained in foreign customs that his loyalty may be jeopardized (a concern of the military manuals, as we saw) to foreigners who worked for Roman interests. Orthodox bishops in foreign lands could also act as spies. In the late 750s, Theodoros, bishop of Antioch, was deposed by the Arab governor for allegedly sending sensitive information about Arab affairs to emperor Konstantinos V.[35]

In short, the Byzantine state had multiple sources of information about foreign peoples, not only about military movements but also their geography, history, society, political organization, economy, and customs. According to a tenth-century treatise, the emperor (or his representative when the emperor was absent) was to "constantly write and receive reports from the border themes [i.e., the military provinces], and to keep an eye on neighboring hostile peoples, to learn."[36] Much of this material was kept in written form. Yet surprisingly little of it turns up in Byzantine texts; almost none of it, in fact, appears in the Byzantine historians, which is where one might most expect to find it. This information was filed in archives and was presumably available to men with access.[37] Byzantium was, after all, a bureaucratic state. Wherever this material was kept, like most of the paperwork of the now-lost Byzantine archives it has left a small imprint on the surviving literary sources. Of course, using those archives might not have been easy to begin with, given that the material would not have been stored in a user-friendly way, to put it mildly, and not with the convenience of historians in mind.[38] The most sustained look that we gain into this archive is the treatise on foreign policy and barbarian history that was compiled by Konstantinos VII and his writers that we call *De administrando imperio*. It has long been recognized that this work is at least partially based on reports by ambassadors and spies, mostly the former.[39] We will look at this unique text more closely below. Our next-best sources of ethnographic material are military treatises, especially the *Taktika* written or issued by Konstantinos' father Leon VI. Emperors obviously had the highest level of "security clearance," but is it a coincidence that most of our information comes from this father-and-son pair? It is unlikely, however, that only emperors and high-ranking officials had access to these archives, even though it is only in their works that we encounter it. Still, archival traces in the corpus of Byzantine historiography are slight.

The problem is not only that the historians did not use the archives, or did not interview ambassadors and spies when writing their narratives, but, beyond that, the fact that they apparently did not make use of the informants who were available all around them in the cosmopolitan streets of their own capital. The kind of ethnographic information that one could get from, say, prisoners could also be obtained by just heading to a mosque or finding a person with a strange hat and simply asking him about the customs of his fatherland.[40] An all-too-brief glimpse of how that might have been possible is provided by a famous poem by the twelfth-century classics professor Ioannes Tzetzes. Tzetzes boasts that he can act like a Skythian among the Skythians and a Latin among the Latins; in fact, that he can pass as the member of any nation. He then explains how he would banter with Skythians, Persians, Latins, Alans, Arabs, Rus', and Jews in their own language, transcribing the phrases he knew into Greek. For example, he could ask a Latin, κόμοδο, φράτερ, βενέστι ἰνίσταν τζιβιτάτεμ; This is banal. A more curious passage that has been bowdlerized by editors and translators occurs later in the poem. If an Alan woman is having an affair with a priest, Tzetzes knows how to tell her, τὸ φάρνετζ κίντζι μέσφιλι καίτζ φουὰ σαούγγε, which means, he translates into colloquial Greek, "are you not ashamed, my lady, to have a priest fuck your cunt?"[41] I quote the last example not because it provides invaluable evidence for the language of the Alans and the evolution of Greek sexual terms, but because Tzetzes must have specifically asked an Alan to translate the dirty question into Greek for him. It is so odd and specific a question that it could not have formed part of a basic conversational repertoire.

The streets of Constantinople would have been alive with folk customs, whether recently transplanted or already sanitized and adapted to the tastes of the dominant culture, and so subject to potential appropriation by the Roman populace. From the same century as Tzetzes, Ioannes Zonaras attests that mimes made comedic sketches of Arabs and Armenians.[42] There was, then, "popular ethnography." Stereotypes were well known, and the household servants of the wealthy seem to have been a multi-lingual bunch.[43] Ethnography did not require access to the palace archives. It is possible that in Byzantine art specific objects or dress were used to designate foreigners.[44] Byzantine merchants were active throughout the known world that could be reached by sea and, conversely, foreign merchants from almost all places were present in Constantinople and other cities of the empire.[45] It is now being recognized that curiosity to see the world played a greater role in pilgrimages than was thought by scholars previously.[46] Many private Byzantines had traveled extensively and taken note of what they had seen. At the end of the twelfth century, the bishop of Athens, Michael Choniates, commented that "most people who arrive at some city like to inquire out of curiosity about the temper of its climate, its shape and location, and, if it happens to lie on the sea, whether it imports goods from both overland and overseas."[47] Obtaining sources of information was not a problem for the Byzantines. But they left few for us, a challenge to which we now turn.

The Decline of Middle Byzantine Ethnography

We come, then, to the mystery surrounding middle Byzantine ethnography. Given that the Byzantines had so much information about foreign peoples at their disposal, and given also that they possessed and admired the literary models of ancient ethnography,[48] they seem to have produced remarkably little of it themselves. In this section, I will sketch the contours of this problem by focusing on literary sites where it is especially troubling. Moreover, by attending to the silence we may identify some misconceptions about the Byzantines that circulate in the scholarly literature, especially concerning their perceptions of the outside world and their own place in it.

In general, the Byzantine historians who wrote between the late seventh and fourteenth centuries, while commonly praised for setting a high standard and continuing the traditions of ancient historiography, offer us few digressions on the customs of foreign peoples and rarely analyze their social structure or describe their geography. Instead of ethnography we find brief snippets of information relating to barbarians in direct contact with the imperial armies or within the empire's borders. Texts are often utterly uninformative or frustratingly vague about neighboring nations and about major events taking place outside the empire. Chronicles often refer to foreign leaders by their titles and not their personal names; this is true not only for Arabs and pagan Bulgars but even for Orthodox people such as the Serbs.[49] Sometimes they do not even do that much, referring vaguely to "the enemies of Christ" or to classical ethnonyms such as Skythians, making some modern historians complain that this obscures the contemporary identity of the group in question (though this problem is often overstated).[50] This silence or vagueness envelops not only enemies with whom the empire was at war for centuries but also peoples who had recently been conquered, mostly between the ninth and early eleventh centuries. Nor did anyone think to produce an "ethnic geography" of the empire, as Strabo and others had done for the earlier Roman empire.[51] The Byzantines also made few original contributions to geography,[52] and sometimes display a garbled understanding of European geography.[53] So for late antiquity we may know the layout of Attila's tent and his daily habits, but for the middle period we often do not get even the names of enemy leaders who raided deep into Byzantine territory. What ethnography we have comes mostly from the pens of the two emperors mentioned above, Leon VI and Konstantinos VII, who were writing not histories but manuals of state policy or internal propaganda. This, then, is the impression we gain if we read through the Byzantine sources looking for ethnography.

The silence is not absolute, of course. We will later consider snippets and minor versions of ethnography embedded in various literary genres of the middle period. But there are some striking ways of framing the overall problem. I will consider three famous aspects of the culture, namely Byzantine diplomacy, historical memory, and the conversion of the Slavs, that have acquired such weight and canonical status in the scholarship that their odd deficiency in this one regard has not yet been noticed.

We learn almost nothing about the impressions or information gleaned abroad by Byzantine diplomats (including writers such as Ioannes Grammatikos, Photios, Leon Choirosphaktes, and Nikephoros Ouranos) about the customs of the peoples they visited. Foreigners tell us of their experiences in Byzantium, but the Byzantines do not speak about what they saw elsewhere. We have letters that Choirosphaktes wrote during his various missions to Bulgaria and Baghdad, but they reveal nothing about local conditions; they mostly concern his relations with contacts in Constantinople. In one letter to the emperor, Choirosphaktes accuses a eunuch, a political enemy of his, of engaging in debauched sex while on the embassy to Baghdad.[54] Internal Byzantine polemics dominate these texts, as we will see also in the histories. While chronicles tell us something about what these envoys did during their embassies (for example, giving gifts and arranging the release of prisoners), they reveal nothing about what they saw or heard there. The closest that we have is the embassy of Ioannes Grammatikos to the Arabs. The account in Theophanes Continuatus focuses on the expensive gifts that emperor Theophilos gave to "the lord of Syria" through his ambassador in order to impress "Ismael," or "the barbarian," or "the Saracens" (no proper names are given, except Badga, the city). A return of prisoners ensues, and, when Ioannes arrives in Constantinople, he persuades the emperor to emulate the Saracen palaces that he had seen, but no details are given.[55] The same holds true across genres. In the early tenth century, saint Demetrianos, bishop of a small town on Cyprus, traveled to "Babylon" (probably Baghdad) to secure the release of some captives taken in a raid by the "Babylonians." The "leader of the barbarians" was moved by the saint's entreaty, and so his "natural cruelty" abated.[56] Again, we do not learn much. In short, we have no description of a foreign court written by a Byzantine, no accounts like those of Priskos, Nonnosos, and Zemarchos. This silence breaks only in the fourteenth century, with Metochites' *Presbeutikos* to Serbia.[57]

It is not only that Byzantine ambassadors did not record their experiences in a literary medium that stood a chance of surviving; they also did not as a rule document the visits of foreign rulers and ambassadors, including visits by two Scandinavian kings at the time of the Crusades deemed "totally unproblematic events apparently not worth mentioning."[58] Other examples of such omissions were cited in the previous section, but a striking instance, dating from 1204, can be mentioned here. A Nubian prince, possibly Lalibela, who had had a cross branded on his forehead in childhood in accordance with the custom of his people, "appeared at the Byzantine court of emperor Alexios V Mourtzouphlos to fulfill his vow to visit the city whence Christianity had spread to his country. None of the Byzantine sources bother to mention his visit, which has been recorded only by French author Robert de

Clari."[59] Even more troubling is the fact that the Byzantines paid no attention to Christian Nubia in general, although it was still largely an orthodox country. But similar examples can be found in late antiquity.[60]

Perhaps the Byzantines knew little about Nubia. But what about Venice? There was probably no western power that the Byzantines knew better in the late eleventh and twelfth centuries. Many Byzantines had been there or had dealt with its agents and merchants, and many Venetians lived in Constantinople, often on good terms with leading Byzantine writers. For example, the statesman and historian Niketas Choniates sought refuge with Venetian friends during the chaos that followed the sack of the city in 1204.[61] Imperial officials must have had a good working knowledge of Venetian institutions. Yet Byzantine sources tell us virtually nothing about them or about Venetian society. Before 1204, we basically have only three sources. The first is Konstantinos VII's brief account of the city's origins.[62] The second is found in the twelfth-century historian Ioannes Kinnamos, who pauses briefly to attack the Venetian character. After describing the city's peculiar geographical location, he says this about its people: "The nation is corrupt in character, vulgar and servile more than any other, because it is filled with sailors' coarseness."[63] Kinnamos had good reason to write this way. His *History* was a work in praise of Manuel I, and the Venetians had given that emperor much trouble. What he is alluding to here is an episode that had taken place by a small island near Ithaca: to insult the emperor, who was dark-skinned, they had dressed up an Ethiopian, probably a slave, in the imperial vestments and, before Manuel's eyes, they had crowned and paraded him in the imperial barge (which they had captured), making racial slurs. This episode, recounted by Choniates, explains all the terms of Kinnamos' abuse.[64] His "ethnography" is only politics by other means, hardly redeemed by the morsel of geography at its head.

Later in the same chapter, Kinnamos quotes a letter in which Manuel correctly claims that the Venetians "used to be vagabonds and very poor before they poured into the *politeia* of the Romans, toward whom they now behave arrogantly. . . . This nation did not merit a name of its own in the past and has only recently become known, solely on account of the Romans." This might actually explain why the Byzantines did not write much about Venice before the twelfth century. Before then they might well have perceived it as an insignificant place on the fringe of their empire. Even Herodotos did not write about outlying Greek fishing villages.

Eustathios' comments on the Venetian constitution reveal an awareness that something new was emerging there. He slipped them into a most unlikely place, a *Commentary on Ioannes Damaskenos' Pentecostal Hymn*, written in the late 1180s. Eustathios was toying with the idea of the Church as a mixed constitution with God as the king, the Trinity as the aristocracy, and the Christian faithful as the *demos*. He adds, as a side-note, that Venice was such a mixed constitution, listing the three elements: the doge, the *konsouloi* (by which he means some kind of "elected counselors," and the popular element). Rome, both the Republic and the empire, had been seen in antiquity as a mixed constitution. His application of the notion to Venice was innovative, made centuries before western theorists hit upon it, but it does not reveal much about this Italian city; or rather, it reveals that Eustathios knew a lot more than he is telling us, and he expects us to know it too, which is perhaps why he does not disclose it. He seems favorably disposed to the political arrangement he describes: "By this triple-wound cord, plaited in a usable way, they are bound together in their own unbreakable allotment of functions."[65]

Another index of the problem, especially when it comes to embassies, is visible in the series of vast anthologies, covering 53 topics, commissioned in the tenth century by Konstantinos VII Porphyrogennetos. Of these only one survives in its entirety, the one *On Embassies*, including both embassies of the Romans to the barbarians and of the barbarians to the Romans (some other topics survive in fragments, in two cases substantial ones). Its orientation was fundamentally historical, as the preface explicitly states.[66] The volume on Roman embassies consists of 227 pages in the modern edition and includes passages from fifteen authors, about half of them classical and half late antique. Only two wrote after Theophylaktos, Georgios the Monk and Ioannes of Antioch, and they account for only two pages of the collection. But the material taken from Ioannes of Antioch seems to have been entirely from the ancient portion of his narrative. The section on barbarian embassies consists of 370 pages; here there are no authors after Theophylaktos. It is not that Konstantinos' team had a bias against recent history, that is, the 350 years since Herakleios took the throne. Rather, they simply had less material to work with when it came to historical narratives from which to excerpt passages. What we would like to have, in this regard, is the lost volume "On Nations" (Περὶ ἐθνῶν), though here too I suspect the bias would likewise have been classical and late antique.

It was not merely that Byzantine writers after the seventh century did not practice contemporary ethnography, but also that in many cases they seem to have excluded the ethnography that they found in their ancient sources. This is another example of how they bracketed what they knew, in fact making a choice to omit it. In the middle period many chroniclers composed "universal" histories, either from Creation to the present time, or of Roman or world history from antiquity to the present. For the period that we call late antiquity they had the same historians we have, in addition to others who have been lost. Well, in producing summaries of these earlier historians they suppressed more or less all their ethnographic discussions. Theophanes wrote a *Chronicle* covering the years 284–815. He relied heavily on Prokopios and Theophylaktos but omitted almost all their discussions of distant lands and peoples. With a few exceptions, Ioannes Zonaras in the twelfth century did the same.[67] Obviously they had reasons for doing this, but we need to know what those reasons were.

A partial exception to this rule is Photios. In the mid-ninth century, before he became patriarch, he began writing a long series of summaries and reviews of ancient and Byzantine authors, known as the *Bibliotheke*, including many of the later Roman historians. Photios gives a long summary of the first two books of Prokopios' *Wars*, which recount the Persian war, and does not discuss the other books on the Vandals and Goths, even though he had them. Reading Prokopios, Photios is mostly interested in Persian affairs, even internal Persian history, and repeats the brief accounts of the Ephthalitai and the Caspian Gates. But most of Prokopios' ethnographic digressions are not in the two first books, so they do not appear in Photios' summary. Likewise with his long summary of Theophylaktos: he concentrates again on Persian history and the wars with Persia, and is less interested in the Avars and the Slavs (the Balkan wars take up about one half of Theophylaktos' narrative). He omits the passages on China. He is, however, interested in Nonnosos' account of the Ethiopians and Saracens and copies some passages on geography and foreign customs from Olympiodoros (a historian of the early fifth century). As for ancient authors, he provides a long summary of Ktesias' *Persika*, including the oriental exotica. His summary of Herodotos is merely a page long and focuses on the succession of Persian kings, as though Herodotos had written a *Persika*.[68] This reading does actually contain a kernel of truth: the backbone of the *Histories* (including the ethnographic *logoi*) is in fact the sequence of the Persian kings and their conquests.[69] In sum, Photios was not *uninterested* in barbarian ethnography, but paid attention to it only when it was linked to his main historical interests, which included the history of Persia. As it happens, Photios begins the preface of the *Bibliotheke* by alluding to an embassy to the "Assyrians" to which he had been assigned. Perhaps Persia was on his mind for that reason and stayed there after what he saw during the embassy (if he actually went on it). It has been proposed that, as a Christian Roman, he "was interested mainly in the succession of Empires in the East (Persia, Macedonia, and Rome)."[70] But what is important for us is that all this interest is antiquarian to begin with, and possibly connected to Biblical exegesis. Photios evinces no interest in contemporary "Assyria," as he calls it.

I will give two more illustrations of the silence of Byzantine sources when it came to foreign peoples; the second will sound surprising and even counter-intuitive to historians who take their cue from modern surveys rather than the Byzantine sources. First, it is now becoming apparent that the Byzantines adopted many technologies, practices, and forms of knowledge from their neighbors. The spheres that have been researched most with regard to Byzantine-Arab relations, for example, are military technology and the occult sciences.[71] But whatever links are discovered will not change the fact that the Byzantines, in contrast to the ancient Greeks and Romans, did not view their culture as being in dialogue with any other; that they did not have a theory of appropriation and exchange; and that they rarely acknowledged that others might have been doing something better than they were. Only scattered signs of such anxieties can be found (which actually point to fundamental historical transformations that were nevertheless suppressed or subdued in Byzantine awareness).[72] Yet, as with ethnography in general, silence should not interpreted as ignorance. Here too they knew more than they were willing to discuss. The Byzantines cultivated a view of themselves as discrete and isolated, and we must try to understand this even if, as historians, we do not agree with it.

Second, many historians believe that one of the Byzantines' greatest achievements was the conversion to Orthodox Christianity of the Slavs who settled in Greece, the Bulgarians, the Rus', and others, between the ninth and the eleventh centuries. Yet how these conversions took place is poorly understood, because the sources are meager, unreliable, or late. The Byzantine sources in particular are almost completely silent about those events, their leading agents, and the missionaries' experiences and the challenges they faced. They tell us nothing informative about the customs and societies of these peoples before their conversion. For example, we have no idea at all how the Slavs who settled in Greece were converted. All we have is a brief statement by Leon VI in the *Taktika* that his father Basileios I (867–886) persuaded them to abandon their ancient customs and to accept Roman rule and baptism, and also that he "Graecized" them, that is, got them to speak Greek.[73] Beyond this passage and a few others like it, historians have had to simply invent theories for how this process of conversion, Hellenization, and imperial incorporation worked on the ground, for obviously the emperor did not do this all by himself.[74] Thousands of Byzantine agents must have been involved in this process in Greece over the course of decades and even centuries, but all we know about it comes from such brief statements.

Likewise, the famous missions of Cyril and Methodios are known almost entirely from non-Greek sources; even if the Slavonic *vitae* were based on Greek originals, few later Byzantines seem even to have known who those men were. The various conversions of the Rus' and the baptism of Vladimir are mentioned only briefly in Byzantine sources.[75] In fact, "so indifferent were the Byzantines to foreigners that the earliest certain appearance of the Rus' at Constantinople passed entirely unrecorded. . . . This is the embassy of 839."[76] (We mentioned above other foreign envoys whose visits to Constantinople are not recorded in Byzantine sources, including Liudprand, Ibn Shahrām, and Lalibela.)

The longest Greek account that we have of the experiences of a Byzantine missionary of the middle period is contained in the *Life of the Emperor Basileios I*, a mostly fictional narrative in which a bishop is sent by the emperor to convert the Rus'. It is worth quoting this at length because it shows how such accounts could be written on the basis of no concrete information.

> The emperor also conciliated the indomitable and utterly godless nation of the Rhos with the lure of generous gifts of gold, silver, and of silk garments: he concluded a treaty of peace with them, persuaded them to partake of the salutary baptism, and made them accept an (arch?)bishop who had received his ordination from Patriarch Ignatios. Having arrived in the country of the said nation, the archbishop gained their acceptance by the following deed. The ruler of that tribe convened an assembly of his subjects and presided over it, together with the elders of his entourage; the latter clung to their superstitions even more tenaciously than the rest, because they had so long been accustomed to them. In discussing their religion and that of the Christians, they called in the prelate who had recently arrived among them and inquired what his message was and what instruction they were about to receive. The prelate held out the Holy Book of the Divine Gospel and recited to them some of the miracles performed by our Savior and God; he also revealed to them some of the marvels wrought by God in the Old Testament. Forthwith the

Rhos said, "unless we are shown some similar thing, especially something like that which, as you say, <happened to> the three young men in the furnace, we shall not in the least believe you, nor shall we again lend our ears to what you tell us." The prelate put his trust in the truth of Him Who said, "Whatsoever ye shall ask in my name ye shall receive," and, "He that believeth in me, the works that I do he shall do also, and greater works than these shall he do" (provided that whatever is done, is done for the salvation of souls, not for the sake of display), and said to them: "Though one ought not to tempt the Lord God, yet if you have resolved from the bottom of your hearts to join God, then you may ask Him whatsoever you wish, and God surely will accede to it because you have faith, even if I myself be lowly and the least of men." They asked that the very book of the Christian faith, that is, the Divine and Holy Gospel, be thrown into a fire built by them; should it be preserved without damage and remain unconsumed, they would join the God of whom he preached. These words having been uttered, and after he lifted his eyes and his hands to God and said, "Jesus Christ our God, this time as well glorify Thy holy name in the presence of all that nation," the Book of the Holy Gospels was thrown into the fiery furnace. Several hours passed, the furnace was put out, and it was found that the holy volume remained unscathed, unharmed, and having suffered no injury or shrinkage from the fire – even the tassels at the book's clasps suffered no corruption or outward change. When the barbarians beheld this, they were astounded by the greatness of the miracle, and abandoning all doubts, began to be baptized.[77]

This bishop is not named, nor are any of the Rus'. None of their customs are indicated in the text nor their beliefs, history, social orders, or geography. This is a purely rhetorical miracle-and-conversion narrative, no more than two pages long, and set against a generic barbarian background. It could have been used in almost any other context and might well be largely invented, as is so much in the *Life of Basileios*. Again, we note that even the meager evidence that we have about these events comes from emperors or writers working for them, from the same milieu that produced the *Taktika* and the *De administrando imperio*. This hardly means, of course, that this information is reliable, especially when its aim is to praise Basileios, the founder of the dynasty. The rhetoricity of this passage stems from its appearance in what is essentially a panegyrical text (we will later examine what happens to ethnography when it is deployed in imperial orations). Such texts cannot be "used" by modern historians in the traditional way. It is specious to speak of the conversion of the Rus' in the ninth century, just as it is to speak of the conversion of the Slavs settled in Greece at the hands of Basileios I.

In the vast modern bibliography on the conversions, this passage (rightly) receives little attention; conversely, Cyril and Methodios, and all the historically attested missions to the Slavs, receive almost no attention in Byzantine sources. This is a paradox that has not generally been noted. Historians are now realizing that the initiative for most of the medieval conversions came from the barbarians themselves and not the Byzantines. The same is true of the ensuing conversion narratives. The emperors also sent craftsmen to assist in the building of churches in Christian lands and mosques in Muslim lands, but these too receive no notice in Byzantine sources: "the initiative generally sprang from outsiders."[78] In short, the Byzantines paid little attention to these processes in their own writings and never let a people's conversion to Orthodoxy get in the way of looking down on them as "barbarians."[79] We see this tension in the writings of Theophylaktos, bishop of Ochrid in the late eleventh and early twelfth centuries. When he turns to discuss his flock, the Bulgarians, he wants to love them as Christians and find some positive place for them in his view of the world, but he simply cannot get over the fact that ultimately they were filthy, uncultured barbarians. Nothing that he wrote about them quite merits the title of ethnography (or was intended in that spirit). Theophylaktos did, however, write a *Life* of St. Kliment of Ochrid, his predecessor, a disciple of Cyril and Methodios, and a Bulgarian at that. This is one of a tiny set of Greek texts on such subjects (though it seems to have been based on Slavonic sources). Most of it is theological, and the rest is conventional hagiography, though it does mention Bulgarian notables and some place names. Other than that, all we learn is that Bulgarians do not speak Greek and that it can get cold in Central Europe during the winter. One cannot speak about Bulgarian culture on the basis of this text at all.[80]

Dimitri Obolensky attributed this phenomenon to "Greek chauvinism," but this is imprecise. It was *Roman* chauvinism. Converting to Orthodoxy did not make one a Roman in Byzantine eyes, and it was this that ultimately separated the Byzantines from other Orthodox nations.[81] But this is one of many issues that we will have to consider when we attempt to explain the silence of ethnography. Notoriously, conversion to Christianity made little or no difference to how these barbarian peoples were viewed. The famous "missions to the Slavs," described in our scholarship as a glorious achievement of Byzantine civilization, are a dead end in terms of how the Byzantines themselves viewed the world. They paid little attention to this alleged achievement of theirs.

The following chapter will explore the problem of the relative silence of Byzantine ethnography in the middle period, seeking explanations in the new directions of historiography, the Christianization of literary culture, and the ideological problem posed by Islam. The discussion will then turn to a positive examination of surviving specimens of Byzantine ethnography and the rebirth of the genre in the later period.

CHAPTER 3

Explaining the Relative Decline of
Ethnography in the Middle Period

The Genres of Historiography

The decline of Byzantine ethnography draws our attention first to the genre of historiography, for that, given ancient precedents, is where we most expect to find it. If we look closely at the historical sources for the middle period, and also realize that our expectations are preconditioned by the classical and late antique evidence that we wrongly take to be normative, some of the mystery is lifted. This section will offer a partial explanation for the silence of ethnography by examining the main subgenres of Byzantine historiography and the specific goals of each historian. Chapter 4 will then look closely at the few pages of ethnography that made it through these filters.

It is conventional in the study of Byzantine historiography to note that its authors imitated ancient models such as Herodotos, Thucydides, and Prokopios. But most scholars fail to draw a distinction among the early, middle, and late historians, treating, for example, Prokopios and Agathias as representatives of the genre in later periods as well.[1] But this is misleading. It is best to treat the historians of late antiquity as *ancient* rather than *Byzantine* and to postulate a fundamental rupture occurring in the seventh century. The model of history practiced by Prokopios and Agathias was not followed in middle Byzantium, at least not in all respects. Their manner of imitation of the classical sources, in both generic mode and their intellectual attitudes, was not the norm among later Byzantine authors. It is our expectations that are the problem here. What type of history, then, were the later Byzantines writing that can explain why there is so little ethnography in it?

There is, for example, no reason to expect any ethnography along classical lines in the Chronicle of Theophanes, which covers the years 284–813. The goal of Georgios Synkellos, whose work Theophanes was continuing, was chiefly chronological: to align important events and reigns in world history into a linear schema. We noted that Theophanes relied on the classicizing historians for his narrative of late antiquity but that he bypassed their ethnographic digressions. Many of those digressions, however, were static descriptions of the customs of a people or concerned their ancient history or geography, so were not amenable to his annalistic format. Moreover, many concerned people and places with which the Romans did not have direct military contact (e.g., Scandinavia, China, and even the Franks), or who appeared briefly only to then disappear from the stage of history. It did not promote Theophanes' chronographical purposes to include such material; much of it did not consist of "events" in the first place. As for his coverage of the period after 602, when the narrative of Theophylaktos ends, it is likely that Theophanes did not find much ethnography in his sources to begin with. Those sources, from the so-called Dark Ages of Byzantium (640–780), were likely to be annalistic in nature too, and Theophanes was condensing them.[2] Thus, we greet with surprise, not as a confirmation of the norm, the extended digression in Theophanes on the origin of the Bulgars in Central Asia and their establishment in Thrace, lodged under the year 678/9 A.D. (because that was when, according to Theophanes, they settled south of the Danube).[3] We will examine this passage more closely in Chapter 4,[4] which will assemble and reclassify the scraps of ethnography in the historians of the middle period.

The project of synchronization we find in Georgios and Theophanes was the last of its kind in Byzantium. Despite the popularity of their combined chronicle, they were to have no imitators, especially in their recording of events under the Caliphate and even the reigns of the Caliphs alongside those of the emperors and the leading bishops of the Church internationally. Cyril Mango has noted that after Theophanes the horizons of the Byzantine chronicle shrank to Constantinople and the court. For Mango the ninth century was a "pivotal period, which witnessed the transition from a universal to a local perspective." He attributes this to the breaking away of the communities under Arab rule and their Arabization, which made them less interesting to a Byzantine public.[5] One could view the same development in the following terms. Theophanes made the last attempt to write a chronography that was both Christian and Roman in its outlook, that coordinated the fortunes of both Romans and eastern Christians who found themselves outside the empire, whereas later Byzantine historians were more narrowly Roman in outlook. Contrary to what is often assumed, the Byzantines generally did not have an ecumenical outlook or adhere to the notion of an panorthodox common- wealth, which is a modern, not a medieval, concept.[6] From this point of view, it was Georgios and Theophanes who were exceptional, especially in that they regarded events that occurred outside the borders of the Roman state as proper to their historiographical task rather than as "digressions" or exotica. After Theophanes we rarely learn even the names of Arab rulers or much about what happened under them in the formerly Roman and Christian lands.

Theophanes' exceptionally "universal" outlook should caution us against assuming that historical narratives in Byzantium conformed to any one stan- dard, even in the middle period or distinct subgenres.[7] If we assess the goals of individual historians without such preconceptions, it may be possible to explain their lack of interest in ethnography on the grounds that it was not useful to them for promoting their authorial goals. Ideally, this analysis should be carried out on a case-by-case basis, but there are authors who may be grouped together, broadly speaking, into the categories of chronography and imperial biography. And historiography is not the only genre that must be examined in this way. We noted earlier the absence of concrete information about "Babylon" in the *vita* of St. Demetrianos, who went on an embassy there to liberate pris- oners. But the purpose of hagiography was to testify to the saintly credentials of its subject and possibly provide a model of a Christian life for future gen- erations. Ethnographic information was irrelevant to this goal. The fact alone that he went, the moral dynamic of the story, and the virtues revealed—these things sufficed.[8]

Let us consider our main authors and subgenres in roughly chronologi- cal order. Ethnography is the last thing that we would expect to find in the world chronicle of Georgios the Monk, writing in the 870s. Theologically dogmatic, in many ways Georgios was not a historian. "Events for him are simply an excuse for moral and theological lessons expressed through lengthy quotations from the Fathers."[9] He compiled pious but entertaining stories that had little regard even for chronology.[10] His chronicle (or whatever it was) was also a dead end in the overall evolution of historiography. In the tenth century, Genesios and the Continuers of Theophanes wrote imperial biogra- phies, or accounts of individual reigns, focusing on Constantinople and the palace. This was only to be expected, as their goal was to glorify the Macedo- nian dynasty at the expense of its rivals and predecessors. They rarely offered much detail when discussing the emperors' activities outside the City, and even chronology took a back seat to the praise or blame (as the case may be) of the imperial protagonist. Ethnography would not contribute much to this project. After all, there is little ethnography in Plutarch or Suetonius either, who are sometimes taken as their models.[11] This applies not only to imperial biographies but also to laudatory secular biographies written in this period, for example, the eight books written by a certain Manuel on the wars of Ioannes Kourkouas (an early tenth-century general),[12] and the pro-Skleros or pro-Phokas texts of the late tenth and early eleventh centuries which some believe lie behind the histories of Leon the Deacon and Ioannes Skylitzes.[13] As these men were generals, it would not have been inappropriate for historical panegyrics to describe the foreign enemies they defeated, but it was not necessary.

There was a reason for this. Like the imperial biographies in Genesios and Theophanes Continuatus, the main purpose of these works seems to have been to highlight their subjects' preeminence within Byzantine society against the claims of internal rivals and not against the empire's external foes. Their goal was to persuade segments of the elite to back their right to rule. The tenth and eleventh centuries witnessed intense competition among the families that constituted the emerging aristocracy.[14] In such a context, to highlight the martial exploits of a general was primarily to make a bid for the rule or the influence of his family within the court system against his internal rivals, and less to trumpet Roman victory over the barbarians. Faceless generic barbarians served this purpose fine, so long as they were defeated; in fact, some of the wars recounted in these texts were civil wars, against rival families. Ethnography might have been distracting.

Specifically, in the late tenth century Leon the Deacon wrote an account of the reigns of Nikephoros II Phokas and Ioannes I Tzimiskes. We might expect to find ethnography here, because he used Agathias as a model in his preface and in parts of his narrative,[15] and also because he offers a detailed narrative of warfare against foreign peoples. But his information about the latter is meager, consisting of little more than what we can infer from the battles themselves. For instance, all we learn from him about the Saracens beyond how they fought is that they were addicted to magic and wore white robes.[16] The latter is trivial, though not worthless, while the former comes from the sphere of religious polemic (and Muhammad is duly mentioned as one of their teachers in the evil arts). And that is all—with one significant exception on the religion of the Rus' to be discussed below. In general, we can ascribe this gap to Leon's goals as an author too. His aim was to glorify the military campaigns of the leading Byzantine families and to narrate their conflicts from a political point of view. The barbarians were secondary to this project, a mere screen onto which to project Byzantine martial virtues. His main sources have been hypothesized as pro-Phokas and pro-Skleros documents; at any rate, his focus is always on those families and on the emperors themselves. There is no agenda like this in classical historiography, so we should not expect Leon to conform to any ancient models, despite his use of Agathias. Leon's *History* shows that even military narratives written in imitation of ancient authors did not necessarily lead to ethnography if their goal was to highlight the virtues and victories of the Byzantines, especially against other Byzantines. The *History* is thus an elaborated version of imperial biography.

By the eleventh and twelfth centuries chronography and the recounting of imperial reigns had more or less fused in the works of Skylitzes and Zonaras. They moved away from the strict annalist format of Theophanes to a reign-by-reign approach, but still they were basically writing summaries; in their case too ethnography was not helpful. Skylitzes, whose work is entitled *Synopsis of Histories*, is known to have excised the antiquarian and ethnographic bits of information that he came upon in his sources for the period after Leon V.[17] He did, however, include a briefing on the origins of the Seljuk Turks (which we will study separately, along with Theophanes' briefing on the origins of the Bulgars). He entirely omitted the Herodotean account of the religion of the Rus' that he had from the source he shared with Leon on Tzimiskes' campaign of 971. Zonaras, whose work is entitled *Epitome of Histories*, likewise excised most of the ethnography he encountered in his sources, whether relating to ancient or to Byzantine history.[18] Ethnography would also have contributed little to the verse epitome of world history written by Konstantinos Manasses in the twelfth century.

Before we turn to the major historians of the eleventh and twelfth centuries in whose works it is more reasonable to expect to find ethnography, we must first reflect on the type of explanation that we have offered for its absence in the others so far. It is clear that the genres that they worked in (chronography and imperial biography) were not conducive to this, but why were these the genres that were produced? Taking a broader perspective, as we must eventually, the silence of ethnography in the centuries following the Islamic conquests appears at first sight to be a function of the absence of "histories" in the classical and late antique manner, that is, detailed narratives that focus on warfare with speeches as well as geographical and other digressions. The absence of such histories can in part be attributed to the general collapse of

Byzantine literature in that period, but not entirely, for other genres, mainly theological, hagiographic, liturgical, and even annalistic continued to be produced, albeit in smaller quantities.[19] I will propose later that the absence of "histories proper" in this period is, in turn, linked to the requirement that a history *explain* the events it records, whether in terms of the virtues and vices of the protagonists, the military and political institutions of the state, or divine providence. The defeat of the Roman state in the seventh century and the nature of the new antagonist on the world scene made any such history difficult to write. The two main historical genres that emerged from this so-called Dark Age, however, were precisely those that did not have to come to terms with such problems, that is, to interpret the failures of the state and the check that had been dealt to Christian expansionism. They were designed to promote practical interests (to coordinate chronology) or specific dynastic or moral-theological agendas; to these purposes ethnography would not have contributed much. Neither genre displays remarkable analytical capacities.

Our inquiry must now be directed to the great historians of the eleventh and twelfth centuries, who were more ambitious in their discursive modes and analytical aims, and some of whom tried to explain the decline of the empire in their age, especially Psellos, Attaleiates, and Choniates. In comparison to their predecessors, their modes of writing were more indebted to the classical authors and, especially in the twelfth century, their literary context was shaped by the self-conscious revival of ancient genres. It is now, when the Byzantines seemed to be writing proper "histories" again, and not in the chroniclers and panegyrists of previous centuries, that the absence of ethnography is especially perplexing.

Perhaps we can partially explain this absence. We can quickly dispose of the panegyrical historians of the Komnenoi emperors: Anna, who wrote about her father Alexios (1081–1118), and Ioannes Kinnamos, who wrote about Ioannes II (1118–1143) and most of Manuel I's reign (1143–1180, reaching only until 1176). Anna's purpose was to glorify her father as a Homeric hero and ideal emperor, so in this respect she was writing a text much like the *Life of the Emperor Basileios I*, only longer and with more material on foreign wars. She does, of course, offer much information on barbarian history, Latin and Turkish, but no ethnography. Her account of the internal Turkish history of Asia Minor in the 1080s reveals nothing about their customs or beliefs and serves to contextualize diplomacy and wars by introducing a strategic situation; we will discuss it too separately, as it belongs with Theophanes' account of the Bulgars and Skylitzes' account of the Seljuks.[20] Anna also features histories of Robert Guiscard, including the rise of the Normans in southern Italy, and of his son Bohemond. These are character portraits that verge on biography but actually reveal little about their culture beyond stereotypes (the Latins are warlike, whether courageous or reckless, and greedy).[21] Anna basically offers a (hostile) biography of Robert, and to produce it she may have reworked material that was originally more neutral.[22] At any rate, her account of Robert is the longest in Byzantine historiography of the life of a barbarian in lands outside the empire. Anna devotes more pages to his son Bohemond, but only insofar as he warred against Alexios.

Anna's version of imperial biography is slightly more contextualized in the international scene than earlier works in that genre, and her physical-moral portraits of Robert and Bohemond are superior to previous representations in Byzantine literature of barbarian rulers.[23] But those portraits conform to Byzantine rhetorical norms and reflect little of the culture of their subjects: they serve primarily the role of the anti-heroes in the *Alexiad*, and to this degree the panegyrical logic of imperial biography remains intact. One might even hazard a guess that Anna's biographical narrative highlights Robert and Bohemond over, say, the Turks in Asia Minor for the sole reason that Alexios did manage to defeat the former. Thus, they made for more satisfactory villains in the drama of the text. That is why the Normans are "built up" in the *Alexiad* and their manliness highlighted, while the Turks remain more generic and bland as opponents. The defeat of Robert and Bohemond distracts us from the failure to reclaim Asia Minor. There is thus no ethnography in the work, for its focus is on the virtues of Alexios. This absence, and Anna's concomitant inability to understand the overall context of her father's reign, have been noted by scholars who have given different explanations, though none has realized that the absence of ethnography had characterized historiography generally since the mid-seventh century (again, late antique historians are a false standard).[24]

Kinnamos evinces a greater awareness of events in western Europe than most previous historians and often digresses to discuss them briefly in order to set the stage for the military and diplomatic encounters between the Latins and Byzantium. He offers brief statements on the customs of royal succession in Hungary, the fighting styles of the various nations in the West, the politics of the German empire, Italian and Sicilian politics, Kiev, and Venice.[25] But there is no ethnography as such. The purpose of these asides is only to contextualize the narrative, whose primarily focus is imperial action and the greatness of Manuel I.

It is, instead, in the three historians who tried to analyze contemporary history and to offer explanations for imperial decline, rather than to praise specific emperors, that the absence of ethnography becomes especially problematic. I mean Michael Psellos, Michael Attaleiates, and Niketas Choniates. While their narratives are organized on a reign-by-reign basis, following conventions that were, by then, established, their outlook is far more critical than panegyrical.[26]

Psellos, who wrote about the emperors of the eleventh century, many of whom he knew personally, actually does have two lonely pages of ethnography regarding the Pechenegs, a subtle but hostile representation of their beastly and uncivilized nature that we will examine in a separate chapter on the role of the Skythian type in imperial ideology.[27] Otherwise, his lack of interest in foreign peoples is perhaps the easiest to explain, for his work is really a kind of court memoir whose underlying goals are philosophical. Again, there is nothing quite like this in the ancient tradition, so we should not look there to find its basic modes.[28] Psellos rarely discusses events outside the City, and his military narratives are vague. His focus is on the personalities of emperors and courtiers, producing a quasi-farcical drama set on the stage of the court and capital. If he had delineated the character of foreign nations with the same nuance, humor, and attention to detail, that would have been magnificent ethnography. Instead, what he offers is an incisive diagnosis of the political ills and philosophical state of Roman society. He repeatedly draws attention to the mismanagement of the empire's institutions and resources and offers incisive analyses,[29] but when it comes to foreign policy his analysis extends no further than the (internal and political) causes that led to the neglect of the Roman army.

In this respect Psellos set the tone for, or at least conformed to the same pattern as, his fellow analysts of defeat, his contemporary Attaleiates and, later, Choniates, who also looked inward to find the causes of decline and generally neglected the wider international scene. They were more interested in diagnosing the symptoms of Roman faults than in working out international relations. Attaleiates' choices are especially difficult to understand, because he was fixated on exposing the causes of what had happened[30] and narrated foreign wars in detail, in some of which he had participated personally, and yet he still offers almost no ethnography. Likewise, Hans-Georg Beck has noted the absence of detailed information about foreign peoples in Choniates and his concomitant inability to make sense of the waves that struck the empire in the twelfth century. "His information about the Venetians is meager in comparison to that provided by Prokopios about much more distant peoples."[31] Choniates makes no attempt to understand the motions of foreign peoples on their own terms. But Beck does not provide an explanation of this failure; he only observes that Choniates seems to have been "trapped" in the same Constantinopolitan frame of mind as Psellos. Both men were reluctant to look outside the capital. But why?

In part, Constantinopolitan introversion was a legacy of the genre of imperial biography, or the summary sequential accounts of individual reigns out of which these "histories" evolved in the eleventh and twelfth centuries. The works of Psellos and Choniates take individual reigns as their building blocks and focus extensively on the personalities of the emperors, their ministers, and courts, only from a mostly critical (rather than a panegyrical) point of view. We should also not forget that Choniates began to write his *History* before 1204; originally it could not have aimed primarily to explain in international terms (or any kind of terms) the decline that led ultimately to the fall of the City. Its original version included more flattering material, drawing on the author's own orations in praise of the same emperors as well as on the panegyrical mode of imperial biography favored by the Komnenoi (as reflected, for example, in Anna and Kinnamos). It was, then, natural for Choniates to concentrate his revisions on the evaluation of imperial policies and personalities and their effects, and not, in the difficult conditions of the exile at Nikaia, to embark on a Herodotean effort to describe the known world in order to explain the events of 1204.

We could, in fact, turn the problem around and suggest that Psellos and Choniates were performing a kind of "internal ethnography." They bring to bear on their fellow Romans, especially the powerful, a keen eye for character flaws and the gap between reality and official rhetoric, which they represent through a subtle system of allusive language. This language draws on a code that would have made sense only to Romans educated in the Greek classics and the Bible. Psellos and Choniates were master analysts and psychologists, but only of their own culture, of the immediate world in which they personally operated. Writing about foreign cultures may have been too distant and formal a project perhaps, and one for which they lacked a knack for spotting moral contradictions and contextualizing them. The allusive language in which they performed their moral dissections, which is their chief virtue as authors, would not have been relevant when applied to a foreign culture. These men were not, therefore, historians of the world scene but social commentators on the vices of their own society. Unlike Prokopios, who traveled the world and expressed a desire to visit Scandinavia, Psellos and Choniates would have preferred never to have left Constantinople. Both did so only under duress: Psellos to flee the court of Konstantinos IX and become a monk in Bithynia (and for only one year), and Choniates when the city was captured by the Fourth Crusade. Their outlook was not Herodotean. In fact, if we must understand their projects in late antique terms, what they were doing was closer to Prokopios' *Secret History* than to his *Wars*. The stated goal of the *Secret History* was to expose all that went wrong inside the Roman empire rather than along its frontiers, and to expose the crimes and vicious personalities of its rulers, Justinian, Theodora, and their henchmen. Prokopios' nuanced character portraits here, painted in the same allusive classical language, are similar to those of Psellos and Choniates.[32] In fact, the file of negative information that Choniates was keeping (mentally or in writing) and that he added to the *History* after 1204 can be compared to the file of the *Secret History* that Prokopios would have wanted to add to his *Wars*.[33] Again we find that ethnography was not suitable to the specific authorial goals of these historians.

In fact, in Choniates, barbarians, especially the Latins, are made complicit in this project of internal ethnography. Rather than telling us anything informative about their culture, Choniates uses them as mouthpieces to expose the flaws of his own fellow Romans. We saw in Chapter 1 how the historians of late antiquity discussed the Roman *politeia* indirectly, by describing various barbarian societies. Choniates instead presents us with foreign views of Roman society, what we can call "autoethnography by proxy." For example, he has a Norman general artfully mock Isaakios Angelos for having spent his childhood in fear of a schoolmaster and not in deeds of war;[34] German envoys at the court of Alexios III are inflamed with a passion to conquer the effeminate Romans whom they observe all decked out in gold and silk;[35] and when the city falls in 1204, he has the Latin conquerors mock Byzantine customs, dressing their horses in silk and taking up pens to pretend to write in books, "mocking us as secretaries."[36] These are but a few examples of this practice, and my summaries do not do justice to the rich and suggestive language with which Choniates elaborates each episode. At first sight, this seems to allow his Byzantine readers (and he had no others) to see how they were perceived by those who conquered them. It is also a way by which Choniates externalized and objectified his own comparative observations.

The more difficult case to account for is Attaleiates. He too was critical of Roman leadership, but he did not have the same Constantinopolitan bias.

His *History* unfolds largely on the frontiers or wherever barbarians raided within the empire. He paid detailed attention to the geography of war, had participated personally on campaigns, and desired to uncover the "causes" of what had gone so horribly wrong by 1078. His work, unlike that of Choniates, had not originally included panegyrical material; that was tagged on at the end, to make a plausible dedication to Nikephoros III. Other aspects of his outlook raise the expectation of ethnography. He had read Agathias, even modeled his account of the earthquake of 1063 on his,[37] and also revealed strains of cultural and religious relativism in his thinking about foreigners. After the battle of Mantzikert, he stressed the personal virtue of the sultan and claimed that God rewarded him with victory because of his nobility, despite the fact that the Seljuks did not accept his Word.[38] Later, in a long digression, he tried to understand why the ancient pagan Romans were so victorious while contemporary Christian Romans were such losers. To reproach the latter for corruption and possibly deflate their religious pretensions, he ends this digression with a formulation of religious relativism: "It is said that even foreign nations honor justice, preserve their ancestral customs without change, and always ascribe every piece of good fortune to the Creator, given that those things which get us ahead are the same for all people and are required by every religion (θρησκεία)."[39] Such an outlook could not but shape one's view of foreign nations and their motivations. At one point in the *History*, for example, he notes that the Saracens of Hierapolis resisted the armies of Romanos IV, "fighting on behalf of their religion (θρησκεία) and their city, as was their ancestral custom."[40] When suspicion fell on the Pechenegs that they might desert in battle, Attaleiates was there, in the emperor's command staff: "So I made them swear, according to their own ancestral custom, that they would unswervingly keep faith with the emperor and the Romans, and I did not fail in my purpose, for not one of them went over to the enemy in this war."[41] In other words, Attaleiates practiced as an officer what he proclaimed as a theorist of history and cultural difference.

And yet there is hardly any ethnography in the *History*, except for a brief and hostile account of the Pechenegs, which stresses their incorrigible barbarism and faithlessness. We will examine this passage in a later chapter, in a synthetic view of the Pechenegs' image in eleventh-century Byzantine texts.[42] But what are we to make of this discrepancy, or rather the continued failure of ethnography? The study of Attaleiates as an author is just beginning,[43] but an argument can be offered based on what appear to have been his goals. It is likely that the *History* was a contribution to an internal Byzantine discussion about imperial failure, a debate that was all about apportioning blame after the fact and evaluating rival counter-factual theories about what policies and strategies would have averted the catastrophe of the 1070s. For instance, Attaleiates reveals nothing about the culture of the Seljuks who prevailed at Mantzikert. He praises the sultan in generic moral terms so as to ameliorate the defeat of Romanos IV, with whose regime Attaleiates was personally associated, and to push the blame for the loss of Asia Minor onto the administration of the Doukas regime. He has no interest in Turkish culture: the game is all about which *Romans* to blame. Likewise, his account of the Pechenegs at Mantzikert is positive, because this reflects well on his *own* role which may have come under fire in internal discussions, while his earlier account of that people—the passage referred to above—was more hostile because he wanted to criticize the naïve policies of emperor Konstantinos IX. Philosophically, Attaleiates wanted to steer his readers away from an Orthodox interpretation of history. The main comparison that he deployed to do this was not between Romans and barbarians but between ancient and modern Romans, the former being of the Republic (in some respects just as foreign).[44] He hints at the possibility of "barbarian" alternatives when he praises the sultan, but he does not follow through on this promise. So his analysis and comparative thought remain bounded by Roman horizons. In the end, the "causes" that he was seeking were similar to those that Prokopios promised in the preface of the *Secret History*: the faults of Roman leadership.[45]

Therefore, whereas late antique historians regularly used ethnography as a covert medium by which to discuss the flaws of their own society indirectly, Psellos, Attaleiates, and Choniates seem to have eliminated the middleman and taken direct aim at their target. In part, this was because they lived in a more vibrant political culture (but that is a separate discussion).

However, we can invoke the later historians' authorial goals to explain the absence of ethnography only up to a point. We may legitimately wonder why no one else wrote ethnography in the middle period, and cannot avoid the suspicion that it was actively avoided. Under the Komnenoi there was increased contact with people from both east and west, certainly among the ruling class, which became more diversified, and the presence of foreigners at the capital and court seems to have become more pronounced, especially under Manuel I. The context of diplomacy became more complex than it had ever been and also more crucial for the empire's survival. Whatever else they set out to do, historians such as Attaleiates and Choniates did attempt to explain the decline of the empire in the eleventh and twelfth centuries respectively, and it is a flaw in their analysis that they did not try to explain to their read-ers *who* all these foreign peoples were and *why* they were coming toward Byzantium. Men in their position had access to information that would have provided that context. At the same time, the twelfth century witnessed an intense revival and imitation of ancient literary forms and even an experimen-tation with new discursive forms in order to represent new social and moral realities.[46] We have, for example, the revival of the genre of the romance novel. There is, perhaps, more fictional ethnography to be found in the Byz-antine novels about the barbarians who kidnap the pretty girl than in the historians of the period who wrote about the very real barbarians who sealed Byzantium's fate.[47]

What we are left with is a literary scene that seemed reluctant to engage in ethnography, despite the fact that its political culture had detailed informa-tion about other cultures and states. Alexios I, for instance, would certainly have been monitoring the broader international situation closely, though it is possible that his daughter and biographer Anna lacked that knowledge and wrongly depicted him as reacting with surprise to developments that he could neither predict nor shape in advance.[48] Attaleiates and Choniates, on the other hand, certainly knew more than they wrote about, but they were engaged in different kinds of literary projects from those of their late antique predeces-sors. The latter strove to emulate a model that had gradually evolved since classical antiquity and focused on wars with the barbarians; with a few ex-ceptions, they tell us comparatively little about the culture and factions of the court, about the private lives and personalities of its leading members. Psellos, Attaleiates, and Choniates were not emulating that model. They were all about the court and are but three voices in what must have been extensive internal debates about political scandals and the success or failure of imperial policy, whether at home (in terms of succession) or in the wars. They wrote exactly what they set out to write. Ethnography might have enabled them to explain the broader world better, but in the end they were but commentators on the ruling class of their own society, and brilliant at that.

Ethnography and Christianity

All people, and perhaps especially those living in the eastern Mediterannean, have to face the raw human fact of cultural, ethnic, and religious differences. The question is how they respond to it. An interesting coincidence is that the sources for two outlooks that rubbed shoulders in late antiquity, namely Herodotos and the prescriptions of the Old Testament, originated in the same context, namely the multicultural Achaemenid empire, though they represented opposite reactions to it.[49] Herodotos and his heirs deployed a range of mechanisms by which to cope with and understand the fact of human diversity, even with regard to "enemy" cultures such as the Persians. They postulated equivalences between Greek and foreign gods and practices, suggesting that differences were only nominal (e.g., Zeus = Baal); they looked beyond cultural differences to uncover the ultimate nature of reality, humanity in its pure form perhaps (the *nomos-physis* debate); or they investigated foreign cultures for the sheer intellectual pleasure of it, in order to derive knowledge, evaluate respective strengths and failings, and possibly to understand or critique Greek society by contrast. This was Greek ethnography as a quasi-philosophical literary genre. I am not discussing here general perceptions of foreigners in Greek society, which could be as chauvinistic as those of any other. Ethnography was often a conscious *challenge* to such views.[50]

The Old Testament consistently takes the opposite approach. In the face of difference, it insists uncompromisingly on the absolute truth of one set of beliefs and rejects all others as both false and pernicious, as a pollution that must not be allowed to enter. Its basic narrative is one of repeated contamination followed by punishment. To be sure, the same qualification must be made here as in the case of the Greeks: most of the people who figure in Old Testament narratives were open to foreign ways; this is precisely why the strictures had to be applied so vigorously.[51] But it was the text that survived to stamp future generations, not the practices it condemned. To its schema, Christianity added the imperative of conversion, which aimed to absorb and finally eliminate difference. While this presupposed the uniformity of humanity's spiritual being, it posed challenges regarding where to draw the line between religion and the secular world in each culture. At best, secular culture was a matter of indifference, so long as it did not impinge on the religious issues of the day. This made it unlikely to generate interest among Christian thinkers, as there were always more pressing religious controversies to resolve within the Church. It is no surprise that early Christian writers add little to classical knowledge about foreign peoples.[52]

This is not to say, however, that early Christian writers were indifferent to classical ethnographic typologies. There were two polemical contexts where the sheer diversity of human culture revealed by the Herodotean tradition proved to be a valuable asset: refutations of astrology, or "astrocide" as it was dramatically called. The Hesiodic-Herodotean idea that "custom is king," which Agathias also endorsed, was trotted out to refute the idea that it was really the configuration of the stars that determines human character. Here lists of weird and contradictory customs, taken from classical literature, proved useful. The second was to refuse Julian's defense of Helllenism by playing up the virtues of the barbarians.[53] But this was for a specific tactical purpose: in all other contexts it was understood that God's Word was to supersede such customs.

Early Christianity did not imagine itself as a "pure" religion that transcended ethnicity and culture. Early Christian writers, enmeshed in the modes of Graeco-Roman knowledge, defined religion precisely in terms of ethnography: Christians were themselves a new *ethnos* (or *genos*) superior to all others, especially the Jews and Greeks but also Phoenicians, Egyptians, and Skythians.[54] To be sure, they were a new *ethnos* that emerged from other *ethnē*, but differentiation was premised on polemical ethnography. Other peoples represented false ways of viewing and worshipping the divine, their "secular" cultures also complicit in that error. Thus, the apologists accepted Herodotos' categories and even his data wholesale, but only to put them in the firing range. To become proper Christians, barbarians had to reject their distinctive national cultures and values and accept the mores of the Christian nation. Their separate cultures had no autonomy or legitimacy. There was little "celebration" of difference. Ethnic labels were stigmatized by association with their pagan traits: "Egyptian" signified the worship of animals, "Phoenician" human sacrifice, and "Greek" a term for a pagan generally.[55] As for nomads, Eusebios basically equated the beastly life of early fallen man to the state of nomadism: no cities, laws, philosophy, or morality.[56] "Nomadism" was apparently not a neutral anthropological category, and we will see that later the Byzantines did not think nomads could make proper Christians. Conversion entailed a civilizing process premised on acceptance of Roman norms.

When Eusebios boasted that bishops attended the Council of Nikaia from all over the world, including barbarian lands, he was basically extending to the Church and spiritualizing the Roman rhetoric of triumph, conquest, and taming of the barbarian.[57] He was not "celebrating diversity." This brings us closer to what was going on here: compared to barbarian alternatives, Christian identity was inflected in a *Roman* way and projected Roman imperial values.

While the Christianization of the Roman world is a standard analytical category in our scholarship, its converse—in fact, its corollary—has received far less attention: the pervasive Roman character of late antique Christianity.

The imbalance in coverage can be explained in part because historians traditionally regarded Christianity as a more profound, spiritual, and historically momentous force than the mere "state" that was Rome. Christianity, many assumed, was surely the dominant partner in terms of identity and ideology. But this is now changing as scholars begin to recognize that the *orbis Romanus* generated normative orders that in many respects were more fundamental than the moral and doctrinal systems of its late religion. In effect, this meant that when "the Romans became Christians, the Christians had become Romans."[58] In many social contexts, late antique imperial Christianity became merely another way of inflecting *Romanitas*, in fact a rather conservative version of it. So "the parameters for orthodoxy were increasingly equated to those for being Roman."[59] This contributed to the process by which the distinction between Christians and pagans morphed back into a version of the familiar distinction between Romans and barbarians. Becoming Christian increasingly meant taking on the distinctive cultural traits of a Roman.[60] When Christianity was packaged and exported to barbarian kings after the fall of the western empire, it was as a distinctly Roman product that could bring its bearers into closer association and alignment with Rome.[61]

Historians who have explored the overlooked interstices of this process have realized that "Christian Romans in general showed no more sympathy for barbarians than their pagan predecessors."[62] They display the very same types of Roman chauvinism. "Christian cosmopolitanism never became the official policy of the Roman state. . . . What happened, rather, was the absorption of Christianity into *Romanitas*; [while] the moral barrier separating civilization and barbarism stood its ground . . . the ideals of Christianity were narrowed sharply to coincide with Roman ethnocentrism."[63] The new religion not only "perpetuated traditional Greek biases against barbarian otherness,"[64] it infused them with religious exclusivity and polemic. Therefore, we should not overestimate the degree to which Christianity, despite its occasional rhetoric, creates universal communities of faith. Historically, it has underwritten exclusivist national ideas and movements just as often as it has created bridges between peoples and cultures.[65] It did not weaken the cultural chauvinism of the Romans, but rather gave it a new religious valence.

In most early Christian ethnology, foreign customs are identified with the false religions that underwrite them. Proper Christians were expected to comport themselves according to models of culture that were based on Greek and Roman social norms. No thought was given to the elaboration of alternative and foreign cultural models compatible with the faith. Ethnography proper largely remained a secular genre. Even though the faith traveled far beyond the empire already in late antiquity, a fact that was noted with pride by many of its apologists within, these extramural conversions produced little ethnography. Hagiography and ecclesiastical history are almost completely silent regarding the local conditions of these distant Christians, and about who they had been before they converted. Three martyr texts stand out, from three points of the compass. The martyrdom of St. Sabas the Goth (372 A.D.) reveals a bit about the background and conditions of the Christian community in the Gothic kingdom north of the Danube, but it dismisses pagan Goths as a "twisted race" of "barbarians,"[66] saying little more about them. The martyrdom of Arethas recounts the death of the hero and his companions at the hands of the Jewish king Dounaas of the Himyarites, in sixth-century Yemen. The text offers information on the cities, geography, and recent political history of the Red Sea region, but, while it was translated from a Syriac original, the drama of the text is framed by conventional coordinates: Orthodoxy, heresy, and Judaism as understood in the Roman empire.[67] That is not the case in the martyrdom of Sire (Persian Shirin), the daughter of a Sasanian notable who was executed (in 559) for embarrassing her family and insulting the Zoroastrian religion and dignity of the Persian elite. The text is full of incidental details that pertain to the hierarchy, rituals, and vocabulary of Sasanian Zoroastrianism, but this is certainly because the text was translated from a Syriac original written in that context. Put differently, the degree to which this text is ethnographically interesting to us is the degree to which it is not Byzantine to begin with.[68] And looking farther, to "India" (in late antique and Byzantine texts this meant both Ethiopia and the subcontinent),[69] we face a variety of genres. The apocryphal *Acts of Thomas*, also written originally in Syriac and translated into Greek, is set partly in India and even mentions by name a historical king of the first century (Goundaphoros). Other than that, however, its setting is a purely imaginary oriental fantasy, and its plot is a Christian romance. The text may have promoted a specific theology, but it has no ethnography.[70]

A much later Byzantine chronographer would claim that Constantine the Great sent out bishops to the foreign nations "both so that they could investigate their lands (ἐπὶ ἱστορίᾳ τῶν τόπων) and preach the faith."[71] But these "histories" have not survived, nor is the claim factual. Amazing stories of cross-cultural travel and encounters can be glimpsed only through bare summaries. The early fifth-century Arian ecclesiastical historian Philostorgios recounts the story of Theophilos the Indian, a native of an island in the

Indian Ocean (possibly one of the Maldives), who was alternately employed as a missionary-ambassador and exiled by Constantius II (337–361). Theophilos established churches among the Himyarites (in Yemen) and the Persian Gulf and visited Axum (Ethiopia).[72] His story enables Philostorgios to give an ethnography of Himyar; how long it was we cannot be sure exactly, for we know it only through the summary made by Photios in the ninth century.

> He [sc. Philostorgios] says that Constantius sent an embassy to the people called of old Sabaeans and now known as Himyarites. The people is descended from Abraham through Keturah. Their country is called Great Arabia and Arabia Felix by the Greeks. It borders on the outer ocean. Its capital is Saba, from where the queen set out to journey to Solomon. The people practice the custom of circumcision on the eighth day [after birth]. They also sacrifice to the sun, the moon, and the local demons. There are quite a few Jews living among them.[73]

It was probably Theophilos' mission in the Persian Gulf that stimulated Philostorgios to embark on a major digression that fuses geography with Biblical exegesis. He summarizes the courses of the Tigris and Euphrates and argues that they actually originate in Paradise, only they travel long underground before bursting to the surface at the places traditionally believed to be their sources (so too the Nile, for which he offers a complicated argument).[74] Philostorgios also digresses on the exotic fauna of the east, including both real and (what are to us) imaginary creatures. This is unconnected to biblical exegesis, but it also omits the actual *people* who lived in the places he describes. In all this, he belongs squarely to the literary world of late antiquity. The digression hinges on the activities of Theophilos but is not required to understand them. It begins with a narrative of his missions, mixes geography and Scripture, and finally indulges in Herodotean exotica. Philostorgios was trying to inject some of the tropes of classicizing literature into a Christian genre, a literary trend that would generally accelerate during the fifth and sixth centuries.[75]

A contemporary of Philostorgios was Palladios (d. ca. 431), the author of the famous *Lausiac History*, an account of Egyptian monasticism. A brief text *On the Peoples of India and the Brahmans* has also survived under his name. It consists of two parts, of which only the shorter first part will concern us here, as only this *may* be by Palladios. The second, an account of the encounter between Alexander the Great and a Brahman sage with parallels in the *Alexander Romance* tradition, is attributed to Arrian, and sections are attested on a papyrus as early as the second century A.D. The question of Arrian's authorship is open, as is whether its teachings are of Cynic origin or authentically Indian.[76] The narrator of the first part, "Palladios," admits he was unable to converse with the Brahmans as he reached only the edges of the "Indian" ocean. Like Philostorgios, he correlates exotic geography with that found in the Bible, though only once: the Ganges is one of the four rivers of Paradise.[77] He attributes the remainder of his account to a disenchanted lawyer from (Egyptian) Thebes, who traveled to Adule and Axum but failed to reach the island of "Taprobane" (usually identified with Sri Lanka), though he heard reports about it; in the end, he reached India (while he places it by the Ganges, he situates it in the southern hemisphere by noting that the seasons were reversed). He could not communicate with the people but did infer their intentions from their hostile facial expressions, which he describes in detail, just as they inferred his fear from the fact that he went pale.[78] For six years he was made to work in a flour mill, and managed to learn the language. He was finally set free because the king feared Roman reprisals.[79] His account focuses on geography, fauna, and flora, and the diet of the people. He includes wonders, some taken directly from pseudo-Kallisthenes: the Makrobioi in Sri Lanka who live up to 150 years; magnetic islands that attract ships with metal nails; the pygmy Bisades in India who have large heads; and the Fanged Tyrant, a beast that could swallow elephants whole.[80] The Theban concludes with an account of the ascetic lifestyle of the Brahmans, who have no clothes, four-legged animals, agriculture, iron, buildings, fire, wine, or bread. They worship God in their own way and live like nomads in the forest, resting on the leaves.[81] They mate with their women only once a year and have only two children each.[82]

There is no account here of Christian communities in these far-off places, and no descriptions (or condemnations) of paganism. The only comment about Brahman religion is that "they worship God and have knowledge but it is not sophisticated, nor are they able to penetrate the workings of providence; still, they pray unceasingly."[83] This is a unique text coming from a Christian author and therefore difficult to interpret. It may have been offered up as a curiosity and a foreign parallel to connoisseurs of Christian asceticism,[84] though this explains only the section on the Brahmans. Palladios' detached view is enabled by the sheer distance and exotic nature of his subject: any group closer to home who practiced the same customs would probably have been condemned harshly by the monastic and ecclesiastical establishment. Distance and "ethnography" again enable the toleration of otherness. Some seem to have accepted that the Brahmans did worship "our God."[85] One must always wonder, of course, how much of the personal story was true and whether the monsters and wonders were added to give an air of unreality to the whole tale. The Brahmans may have functioned as a kind of literary "utopia" for monastic communities, not to be taken literally but only "good to think with." In fact, the narrative framework of this story and its geography may be based on Iamboulos' tale of the Island of the Sun.[86]

It is interesting that early Christian explorations of literary ethnography occur in generically unique forms, occupy the margins of literary production, are possibly pseudonymous, and have no imitators in later centuries. I have in mind also the *Narrations* of pseudo-Neilos of Ankyra (fifth–sixth century) and *Christian Topography* of Kosmas Indikopleustes (sixth century). The first is a hagiographical romance, indebted to the ancient novel, except that the protagonists, who are separated by barbarians and reunited at the end, are not a pair of young lovers but a father-and-son pair of ascetics on Mt. Sinai. The crucial sections for our purposes are the parallel ethnographies of the savage Saracens and the monks of the peninsula; in many respects, the writing of an ethnography of monks is the more innovative aspect, but the two parallel passages call out for a juxtaposed literary reading.[87] They are embedded in a quasi-historical romance whose purpose is pious. The Saracens are desert nomads who live beastly lives, side by side with their animals. They offer human sacrifice, or else a camel they hack to pieces and eat. Christian perceptions of nomads here follow Graeco-Roman norms. Yet the ethnography of the monks that follows interestingly does not affirm the ideals of urban life, the traditional antithesis of nomadism, but celebrates a life devoid of luxury, economics (the monks have no money), and pride. These monks are "philosophers of the desert." Ironically, they too, like the Saracens, are cast as the opposites of city dwellers.[88] Ethnography in late antiquity again emerges as a vehicle for indirect social commentary.

By contrast, the *Christian Topography* attributed to Kosmas is a rambling attempt to prove, through biblical exegesis, that the world is flat and shaped like the Ark of the Covenant. Into this argument the author throws information about people and places along the trade route to the east, such as the Red Sea, Ethiopia, India, Sri Lanka, and China, which he seems to have visited himself.[89] Not all his digressions are strictly relevant, and we can attribute them to his tendency to show off. (If only later Byzantine travelers had done the same.) He discusses Red Sea trade, the Ptolemaic inscriptions there, and the Christian communities of the Far East.[90] An entire book is dedicated to Ethiopian fauna and the ethnography of Sri Lanka (Taprobane); some scholars believe these passages were appended to the *Christian Topography* later, from a separate book the same author had written on geography.[91] This material is jumbled together with discussions of the angels, the Flood, Moses, and the like. All in all, it is a fascinating attempt to marshal the modes of ancient ethnography and autoptic travel-writing to argue a Scriptural point, but it remained a non-starter, at least in Byzantium. Its conspicuous display of knowledge about exotic places positions it within the agonistic context of the otherwise secular ethnographic scene of the sixth and seventh centuries.

Before moving from the early to the middle Byzantine period, mention must be made of an "alternative" ethnologic schema some early Christian writers spun out of Scripture, though they only occasionally deployed it as a system of classification. This was their attempt to identify all the peoples of the world with their putative Old Testament ancestors, usually tracing them back to the sons of Noah. We can see this as a Christian alternative to the classical habit of finding common ancestors in Greek myth. It was this schema that has saddled us with concepts such as "Semitic" and the like.[92] There was no ethnography here. Its sole concern was to satisfy and validate Scriptural typologies, basically effacing cultural distinctions in order to promote Biblical exegesis over empirical inquiry. This exegetical scheme had no room for the representation of cultures and so could generate no ethnography. But it persisted among those who would use the Old Testament to make sense of the medieval world.

If we turn to the middle Byzantine period in search of Christian ethnography, we encounter a bleaker picture. As we saw, the Byzantines did not write much about their missionaries to foreign lands, in contrast to modern historians, who have fixated on them (for nationalist reasons).[93] Also, the function of hagiography was to extol the virtues of the saint, which were often otherworldly and opposed to the secular values even of his own society. Herodotean digressions were here irrelevant. If the foreign society visited by the saint was Christian, it sufficed to simply say that, because it was the only thing that mattered from the standpoint of the story, as cultural difference could unnecessarily complicate the narrative. If that society was not Christian, its otherness could be conveyed briefly and in polemical terms, which sufficed; the story would not be advanced by discussing the details of foreign customs. Certainly, there was no sympathy for them, or interest. We saw how little the *vita* of Demetrianos, a tenth-century Cypriot bishop, reveals about his experiences among the Arabs when he went to petition for the liberation of captives.[94] Likewise, saint Elias the Younger (tenth century) lived among the Ismaelites for a while and even converted some of them, but nothing is revealed about their way of life and religion; he then traveled to the Holy Land, Egypt, and even "Persia," but his *vita* reveals almost nothing of his experiences there.[95] The same is generally true of the *vitae* of itinerant saints of this period.[96] In part, this was because these texts were usually written after the saints' deaths, when few people (if any) knew much about their early travels. The authors had not accompanied the hero on them and did not know and did not care to invent the details. The texts, besides, had a religious purpose, though the absence of even an aside is striking.

If hagiographers were unskilled or uninterested in discussing the foreign places visited by their heroes, they were even less forthcoming when it came to barbarians who attacked the empire. The following passage on the Rus', from the ninth-century *vita* of Georgios of Amastris, is typical of many lives, sermons, and chronicles of the period: "The Rus', a tribe that as everyone knows is very savage and cruel and endowed with no shred of humanity—beastly in manners, inhuman in deeds, showing its bloodthirstiness in its very aspect, delighting in nothing else to which men are inclined so much as in murder."[97] This is a generic image of the bloodthirsty barbarian; the passage continues on in this vein. Moreover, we will see that raids by *Christian* barbarians were not depicted differently in later centuries.[98] The key factor behind the representation of barbarians was whether they were friendly or hostile to the Roman state, and this was true of hagiography as well as secular genres.

The picture does not change much when we turn to hagiographic fictions, that is, stories about nonexistent saints who lived in or traveled to distant locations, sometimes beyond the edges of the known world. Though we may regard these texts as fictions, they were not necessarily read that way by contemporaries, who even instituted cults in honor of their heroes.[99] Still, these texts were meant to provide literary entertainment by describing exotic locations. Yet there is still no ethnography. According to his long *Life*, Gregentios was a saint and bishop of Zaphar (Yemen) in the early sixth century, although he was invented probably in tenth-century Constantinople. He traveled from his birthplace somewhere in the Avar empire to Italy and Rome, Carthage, Alexandria, and finally Himyar. But the text's grasp of western geography is garbled and bears only a distant relation to reality. While there is some knowledge of the topography of Rome, "all persons from the 'country of the Avars,' Italy and northern Africa down to Egypt and Yemen speak the same language."[100] The hagiographer does know a bit about the geography, cities, and kings of Ethiopia and Himyar in the early sixth century, through a complicated chain of textual transmission.[101] But there is really no ethnography here either: the background is generic.

The same is true of *Barlaam and Ioasaph*, a long hagiographic romance whose ultimate ancestor was the story of the Buddha and which circulated in various versions and languages before it was translated from the Georgian into Greek in the late tenth century.[102] The story is set in India, but only the location of that land is briefly described at the beginning. The narrative is thereafter set in a generic distant land with a king, a royal family, ministers, and so on; there is nothing culturally distinctive. When Nachor delivers the refutation of paganism, it is a refutation of the cults of the ancient eastern Mediterranean, especially of the Greeks. He says nothing about the cults of the people he is ostensibly trying to convert. The Byzantine reader may have read this text through the prism of the *Acts of Thomas* and the *Narrations* of pseudo-Neilos, texts that were probably drawn on for the composition of *Barlaam and Ioasaph*.

If we waive the requirement of historicity, the distant places beyond India appear in the *Life* of Makarios of Rome, composed between the fifth and the tenth centuries. It tells the story of three monks from Mesopotamia who journey toward the saint, who lives in a cave close to the gates of Paradise. After visiting the Holy Land and Persia (specifically the royal city of Ktesiphon), they begin to encounter a range of fabulous races and animals, including basilisks, unicorns, and the Dog-Headed people (*kynokephaloi*). The latter "only gazed upon us and did us no injustice, sitting around with their women and children, naked; each of them had a lair under a rock and they were wild like animals."[103] Before they reach the saint's cave, they pass through the realm of the damned. This type of narrative, of course, is not exactly ethnography, but rather belongs to a parallel or rather complementary sibling genre which describes the fabulous things to be seen at the edges of the earth when one goes beyond the borders of the known world. Ethnographies of the *kynokephaloi* and accounts of the beasts that lived in the far reaches of India could be found in Ktesias' *Indika* (summarized at length by Photios) and especially in the so-called *Alexander Romance*, which inspired the *vita* of Makarios.[104] This "ethnography of the fringes" has distinctive goals and methods, being implicated in the construction of specific types of sanctity, and it would take us far from our purpose to investigate them.[105]

"Travel literature" was not a genre as such in antiquity or in Byzantium. Unlike the Greeks and Romans, the Byzantines did not send out missions of geographical exploration,[106] and their literature "is notoriously deficient in travel accounts."[107] Most extant specimens are religious in nature.[108] While late antique accounts of pilgrimage could feature detailed ethnographic information, as in the sixth-century "Piacenza Pilgrim," we have nothing like this for the later period. In the ninth century, a monk by the name of Epiphanios wrote a *Life* of the Apostle Andreas, recounting, among his many travels, his journey around the Black Sea. Epiphanios claims that in order to flee from the Iconoclasts he and his companions followed in the footsteps of the Apostle, with earlier accounts of his travels in hand, looking for signs of his passage and for relics.[109] The text then includes a first-hand account of the north Black Sea peoples, though the actual nondevotional information that it purveys is limited. We learn that at Sousania the men were apparently ruled by the women in the Apostle's time; the Zichians were barbarous but the Sougdaians gentle.[110] The late twelfth-century *Ekphrasis* of the Holy Land by Ioannes Doukas (misnamed "Phokas" in modern scholarship) consists mostly of static descriptions of places with few references to people; his only ethnographic digression, which we will examine below, is on the Assassins (and it is more heresiological than ethnographic). Of course, *ekphraseis* of places were not meant to be ethnographic in the first place.[111] The *Hodoiporikon* (or *Travel Account*) of Konstantinos Manasses (1161/2 A.D.)—the title is modern—recounts a mission to the Crusader states to secure a bride for Manuel I, but it gives only brief descriptions of places, leaving most of the people out of the picture (and the purpose of his journey was secular, not religious).[112] His text, which is generically unique, largely removes the sights of the Holy Land from their current historical context.

Ethnography, then, played a limited role in Byzantine religious literature. The classical ethnographic "types" of the Skythians, Egyptians, Phoenicians, and others, which were identified with diverse forms of paganism by the Apologists, disappeared into the catch-all category of the pagan "Hellenes." Thereafter, the goal of Christian writing was largely to project Christian values and beliefs and to police their boundaries against rival religious types: Jews, heretics, pagans, and, later, Muslims. The one genre that did highlight difference was polemical and aimed to repress it. This was the list of theological errors that were attributed to heretical groups which, in some cases, were defined as ethnic groups. There was ample precedent for such composite lists in late antiquity, especially the *Panarion* of the "heretic-hunter" Epiphanios of

Salamis (on Cyprus). Some heresies could be defined and disposed of in a paragraph, but some discussions could expand to near-ethnographic amplitude. A striking example from the ninth century is the *History of the Paulicians* written by Petros of Sicily, which recounts not only the (false) doctrines of that sect but also the (execrable) history of their leaders and community in Asia Minor over the course of centuries, as well as some of their customs. This treatise is in many ways *like* an ethnography except its purpose is entirely polemical, based on Scripture and theology. Moreover, the Paulicians were a group in the process of distinguishing themselves from the Romans: they recruited mostly within the empire, so it is not clear that they were an altogether foreign group.[113] Heresiology here verges on becoming polemical ethnography.

In the eleventh century, the Byzantines began to compile lists of the theological and other errors of foreign peoples, especially the Latins. Most of these were of a theological, liturgical, or ecclesiastical nature, but the lists gradually were expanded to include "errors" relating to customs that had only slight religious valence (e.g., regarding food, clothing, and names). Tia Kolbaba has argued that these lists were not only weapons in doctrinal or ecclesiastical controversy but boundary-markers that were constructed around their authors' Orthodox and Roman culture, to define and defend it at a time when it was being threatened and aggressively invaded by the Latins.[114] These are, of course, not ethnographies in a classical sense, and they attribute "errors" to the Latins generally without saying too much about who, where, how, and why. Nor can they be relied on to present a reliable composite picture of Latin culture, for they served a polemical purpose by rhetorically highlighting perceived differences. It is not always easy to know whether the latter actually corresponded to real ethnic differences (and Kolbaba argues that some did not). Still, the lists probably do reflect what many believed about Latin culture, especially in the twelfth and thirteenth centuries.

The Latins (and Armenians) were not the only targets of such attention. Ioannes II, the Byzantine metropolitan of Kiev in the late eleventh century, condemned any customs of his flock that deviated from "the current piety and decent way of life of the Romans."[115] This brings us back to the point we made earlier about the specifically Roman inflection of Byzantine Christianity. As we will see repeatedly below,[116] the Byzantines, even their clergy, had a specifically *Roman* Orthodox outlook and, when they were exporting religion, did not readily distinguish its norms from those of their national culture. Byzantine Christianity was *not* understood to be a "universal" faith that ignored cultural differences. It could accommodate itself to them, but grudgingly. Conversion was understood as a civilizing process for the barbarians,[117] and the standard for civilization was always Romanía. Leon VI was as explicit about this as had been the historians of Justinian's time: "the Bulgarians have embraced the faith of the Christians and have gradually taken on Roman customs."[118]

Unfortunately, we know little about how the Church "civilized" the customs of the barbarians and brought them into alignment with Roman norms. We have only snippets, such as the case of Ioannes II of Kiev mentioned above. The most detailed document relating to this issue that we have from the early Middle Ages is the letter sent in 866 by pope Nicolaus I to Boris-Michael, the king of the Bulgars, who had posed to him a series of questions regarding the changes that conversion would entail to Bulgar culture. The topics addressed by the pope range beyond what we would consider to be strictly religious.[119] But this is not a Byzantine document. What we have instead is a slightly earlier and far more rhetorical letter by Photios to Boris.[120] Unfortunately, these are too often juxtaposed: the pragmatic, down-to-earth Catholic pope and the aloof, rhetorical Orthodox patriarch, a contrast that is supposed to reflect something deep about the two religious cultures. In reality, we are dealing with texts that had different objectives and should not be compared. There is every reason to believe that the Byzantine missionaries in Bulgaria, and possibly the patriarch himself, dealt with the same practical issues on the ground in the usual ad hoc way.

A fascinating but little-known patriarchal text, sent probably to a bishop in Bulgaria in the twelfth century, demands the reform of the nocturnal "satanic games that the Bulgarians call *nedalai* in their barbaric tongue," which seem to have involved sex among men and criminal acts.[121] Were it not for this bureaucratic disciplinary text, we would not know about this custom, whatever it was. But this does not apply only to foreign customs. The same is true about Byzantine popular culture, which scholars reconstruct in part from the canons of the Councils that sought to regulate or stamp it out. Popular beliefs, plays, festivals, and cross-dressing are documented by the canons and their commentators, such as Theodoros Balsamon in the twelfth century.[122] We should note that the Church was mostly ineffective at eliminating many of these customs, partly because it had limited means of enforcement when the state was unwilling to intervene, as it usually was. This "negative autoethnography" deserves more study, even though it reflected the views of a minority. Still, the spirit of systematization was absent from these texts as well. No Byzantine writer attempted to document all the customs of a people like a new

Herodotos, even if only to "discipline" them. As with the historians, we are dealing with scattered ad hoc notices, in the typical Byzantine manner.

We can now relate the findings of this survey to the question of the decline of ethnography in the middle Byzantine period. The first conclusion is that Christian genres had little need for, or interest, in ethnographic discourse. In late antiquity it appears in marginal and idiosyncratic authors whose quasi-fictional experiments were dead ends, such as Palladios, pseudo-Neilos, Kosmas, and the Arian historian Philostorgios. Their digressions are generically recognizable and reveal the influence of secular geographic and ethnographic writing. One could say that these digressions belong to the general late antique literary milieu: they are attempts to adapt secular modalities to Christian needs. In the middle period, by contrast, there is almost no Christian ethnography.

The second is that Christianity did little or nothing to counter the Roman bias against barbarians. Instead, religious differences were now regarded with pious abhorrence, and what we regard as merely cultural differences were often interpreted as sins stemming from theological errors. When a *pope* in the ninth century could, in his official correspondence with a Roman emperor, take it for granted that "all barbarians live like ignorant animals, do not know the true God, and worship trees and stones," we see that Christianity had done nothing to counter ancient anti-barbarian rhetoric. In fact, it had assimilated it and combined it with scriptural exclusivities.[123] No one advocated a theoretical distinction between culture and faith that would enable Romans to regard other Orthodox peoples who were not Romans as true peers. We will see later that in Byzantium the recognition of religious affinity with Christian barbarians was situationally contingent and could not hide the depth of cultural difference and condescension that it was meant to disguise.[124] In fact, there was a tendency after the eleventh century to view cultural differences as religious ones, thereby reinforcing the difference between Byzantines and other Christians with religious polemic.

Religious exclusivity certainly contributed to a proliferation of polemical views of other cultures. In late antiquity, the survival of secular historiography and its ancient philosophical roots allowed some authors to project a pluralist attitude which recognized Graeco-Roman culture as One Among Many. Yet they lived side by side with advocates of a *pensée unique* (There Can Be Only One),[125] an approach that steadily gained in strength and hardened. Practices and beliefs that the Greek tradition represented ethnographically would come rather under the purview of theology in Byzantium and, accordingly, be treated polemically. This was a major reorientation from Man to God, as a previous generation of scholarship would say—or from rivers and mountains to "invisible things" as Prokopios had complained.[126] Some historians date the onset of introspection to the seventh century.[127] It is a potent correlation that around 600 another shift seems to have occurred in the empire from an elite culture shaped by classical forms and images to one dominated by Christian ones, for example icons and Biblical themes.[128] Byzantium's Christian identity became more strident when the empire was suddenly surrounded on all sides by non-Christian enemies. This had consequences for intellectual life that have not been fully investigated. It makes a difference whether you take your bearings from the Old Testament or Herodotos. Consider, for example, Agathias' ability (in the late sixth century) to recognize that all cultures believe in their own superiority even when they are wrong, and yet that all people strive for the good, even if they sometimes fail, and that they should be forgiven for failing. Agathias was transposing the terms of Herodotean philosophy into a Christian idiom.[129] In the sixth century, then, ethnography was a viable option.

Now consider the late seventh-century text called the *Questions to doux Antiochos* (questions on thorny religious problems posed to and answered by a sage). Question 42 is: "How is it certain that the Christians' faith is better than any other under heaven; for every faith believes that it is holier than the rest?" To this reasonable "Agathian" challenge the sage offers an answer that lowers the bar intellectually. He replies, first, that no other nation has ever been fought by so many enemies and yet still survived, which is false, as it forgets the Jews. Second, no Christian emperor has been killed by the barbarians—which is relevant only because Christianity is here linked to one state, Byzantium (plenty of non-Roman Christian rulers were killed by barbarians).[130] This is no longer a position above history, and it nails Christianity to the mast of the Roman state, making it hard to separate the sage's faith from his Roman outlook. And even here, in the realm of historical apologetics, he has omitted the Arab conquest; he will not admit that most of his precious emperors were heretics; and he does not for a second consider that the question requires him actually to investigate the truth-claims of the other religions or the cultures that lie behind them. So no ethnography can be based on his position or be generated by it. The argument is so weak that we can assume only that the answer was predetermined. At least the sage admits the existence of conflicting claims to religious truth and the fact that this could be perplexing; this is itself rare in Orthodoxy. But he does this only because too many thinking men and women were having doubts, doubts that, in the aftermath of the Bush adminstration we may ironically call "reality-based."[131] He would rather ignore the whole thorny issue, because, not being Augustine, he had no means to address it. He could not think outside the Roman box. This was perhaps part of the seventh-century "drawing-in of east Roman horizons."[132]

To come full circle, like Herodotos and the writers of the Old Testament, both Agathias and the author of the *Questions* realized that the world was full of nations and religions with incompatible truth-claims. Their responses diverged because they were drawing upon such different traditions. The one that became dominant for centuries reduced the appeal of Agathias' "ethnographic tolerance" and, with it, the possibility of ethnography generally.[133] It is not a coincidence, then, that the revival of Herodotean ethnography at the very end of Byzantium, by Laonikos Chalkokondyles, was inspired by the Platonist ethnophilosophy of the anti-Christian thinker Georgios Gemistos Plethon.[134]

Ideological Blockage: The Islamic Challenge to Roman and Christian Narratives

We have so far avoided the elephant in the room: Islam. The Arab conquests entirely changed the dynamics of state power and the configuration of peoples. This posed unprecedented challenges to the literary representation of the non-Roman world, reinforcing some of the negative factors we have examined already and also imposing significant silences of its own. The Byzantines were willing to discuss Islam on the theological, exegetical, and doctrinal level but not as a culture or a historical reality. In accordance with the early Christian equation of "foreign" cultures with theological error, they considered what we would call Islamic culture as the product of theological choices, not really a culture at all but a series of exegetical errors that only led to abhorrent practices. This was, of course, an interpretive choice. Behind it lay the most traumatic fact in all of Byzantine history. In the seventh century the Christian Roman world contracted dramatically because of the rise of Islam and the concomitant loss of the East, but also because of the prior establishment of the Lombards in Italy and the Slavs, Avars, and Bulgars in the Balkans. The entire context of imperial history changed, and along with it the implications of ethnography for imperial ideology. Let us look back again to late antiquity.

Despite the loss of the western empire in the fifth century, the writers of the sixth century, such as Prokopios and Agathias, were secure in the dominant position of the Roman empire. It was culturally superior, militarily powerful, and ideologically supreme. The barbarian states in the west were perceived as being somehow under Roman authority and, it seems likely, saw themselves as quasi-Roman and looked to Constantinople for recognition. This was especially true of the kingdom of the Goths in Italy under Theodoric, who said as much in a letter to emperor Anastasios: "our royalty is an imitation of yours, modeled on your good purpose, a copy of the only empire."[135] The sentiment was shared by the Romans, for their part. As we saw, Agathias had presented the Frankish states as equivalent polities modeled directly on that of the Romans. Regardless of whether the Franks saw themselves in those terms, it is crucial that a historian writing in late sixth-century Constantinople was willing to do so. A Roman could imagine that *Romanía* was the normative standard against which the civilization of its neighbors could be measured. Moreover, the reconquest of western lands was not beyond imagining. Justinian actually did reconquer North Africa, Italy, and a part of Spain. Besides, the loss of the West in the fifth century seems not to have shaken the Romans of the East too much in the first place.[136] New Rome could function as a self-contained unit and had suffered no losses. The only other superpower that was able to generate a cultural system around itself was Persia, but the two states had long coexisted, if at times in uneasy recognition of each other. They fancied themselves "the two eyes of the world."[137] The kingdoms between them were liquidated,[138] and the continued spread of Christianity in all directions reinforced Roman pride and enhanced imperial prestige.[139] "New peoples," such as those described by the late Roman historians, sought validation and legitimacy from the empire, along with an alliance and possibly conversion. Their description in literary ethnographies likewise incorporated them into a world-system that was dominated by Rome.

This was not at all the situation facing the writers of the middle Byzantine period, especially those of the first centuries after the rise of Islam. The Caliphate did not merely change the relations of power in the Mediterranean and Near East by its sheer size, it offered a different religious and ideological model and cast the reduced Roman empire into the margins. Peter Heather has contrasted the "profoundly alternative ideology" of Islam that "generated a cultural as well as political revolution" to the Romano-barbarian client states in the west, where the disruption was, "in the first instance at least, limited to politics."[140] Romanía was now a smaller place in the global geography of power, and its leading opponent much larger than anything the Romans had known. This was a defeat that the Byzantine writers could not explain, or did not care to explain beyond ascribing it to God as a punishment for their sins. Certainly, the discussions that must have been held about it in the corridors of power may well have been of a different nature, far more pragmatic, informed, and worldly. Behind the feverish denunciations of the false religion and a horror of coming into contact with its polluted practices and fatal beliefs, there lay a pragmatic approach on the part of the state and its diplomats, who treated the powers of Islam as yet another part of the world to be dealt with like any other. It was only textually that Islam could not be represented "normally"[141] because the norms of representation could not accommodate it. We can discuss only what was written by those who were willing to write. Our subject is literary representation, not what the Byzantines knew. We have seen that these were not the same.[142]

Our sources ascribe the rise of Islam to the anger of God. But the emphasis on theodicy is a function of the types of sources we have. We will examine its impact on ethnography below, especially the way it represents the agency of the "other." First, we must complete the picture. The pagan Bulgars concurrently established themselves south of the Danube and warred against the empire, reaching the walls of Constantinople. They would not convert for another two centuries, and even that did not end their aggression. For centuries the empire was on the defensive against non-Christian states in a way that a contemporary of Prokopios could scarcely imagine. Meanwhile, the kingdoms in the west, now more post- than sub-Roman, created their own systems of power and ideological claims that conflicted with those of Byzantium, especially regarding the crucial ownership of the legacy of Rome itself. This was a different world-system in which to write ethnography. What were the implications of this system-shock for the ethnographer?

In one sense, the lack of ethnography from the two centuries after the rise of Islam is not surprising, as this was a period when the Byzantines wrote little in general.[143] It would be long before they reconstituted the literary and intellectual skills that are required for the nuanced representation of human character, even of Byzantine character, to say nothing of representing the oddities of a different culture.[144] But the ideological implications of the new world-system would have compounded the problem. To explain Arab culture the Byzantines would have had to come to terms with Islam as a historical phenomenon, and ethnography would have had to turn into a religious anthropology. This might have been possible for non-Christian authors such as I think Prokopios and Agathias were, following in the tradition of Herodotos, but thinkers capable of this emerged only later in Byzantium. A religious anthropology of victorious new peoples would have required a thorough revision of the schema of Christian triumph and imperial victory, ideological pillars of the late Roman state and Church.[145] Ethnography would have to be therapeutic, for its subject was in itself a trauma. But "a God-protected empire simply could not admit to defeat: the image of control had to be maintained, come what may . . . especially at the hands of non-Christians."[146] Since the third century, at least, Christian writers had adhered to a narrative of inexorable expansion and had no language with which to explain Christian *contraction*, because it was not something that they had yet faced, not even when the west fell to the barbarians. Likewise, on the imperial side, the emperors and their spokesmen had no language with which to explain a reversal such as this. These new peoples were established on formerly imperial territory and most emphatically did *not*, as had happened in the fifth-century west, recognize the primacy of Rome in the overall world-system. An ethnography of the Arabs—or, for that matter, of the pagan Bulgars—would have to overcome formidable ideological blockages. This presumably is one of the main reasons why the Byzantines never wrote those histories.[147] Into what ideological framework could ethnography be fitted? Prokopios had faced no dilemma like this. He could make his subversive comparisons only because he could take the hegemonic standing of Romanía for granted.

It is astonishing how little Byzantine authors tell us about the Arab world. Muslims lack a real portrait, character, or personality in Byzantine sources.[148] To give a striking illustration, there are few enemy speeches in middle Byzantine historiography, and most of these are generic.[149] The Byzantines not only were unwilling to step outside their own culture and view it philosophically (which is what an ethnography would require), they could not even bring themselves to do so *rhetorically*. It was evidently impossible for them to compose speeches for Arab leaders that referred to the Christians as infidels. Prokopios had not only composed speeches for Justinian's foreign enemies, but had made those speeches especially powerful and biting. They generate considerable sympathy for the emperor's most heroic enemy, the Gothic king Totila.[150] But in the middle period, Byzantine historians saw everything flatly from the Roman and Christian point of view and were not interested, not even for the sake of plausibility, to entertain an enemy's point of view. They were uninterested in or incapable of performing rhetorical and intellectual exercises that their late antique predecessors, based on classical models, were able to do, and do well; put differently, they were unable or unwilling to experiment with their own subjectivity, to bracket it even if only provisionally.

Some Byzantines did write about Islam, but they tended to attack it as a theological and exegetical error, that is, as a theoretical problem,[151] not as a living religion sustaining a thriving culture. This was perhaps because they felt that they could defeat it in theory, whereas the reality that was the Muslim world was beyond reach. Those polemical treatises could be written without ever speaking to a Muslim. (The reverse was, of course, not true, as the Arabs did write a lot about Byzantine culture.[152]) We witness the reduction of ethnography to religious polemic—or rather, that religious polemic *blocked* ethnography—every time a chronicle refers to the Saracens simply as "the enemies of Christ." We see it in some of the military treatises. Consider Syrianos in the ninth century. "The barbarians who fight against us," he writes, "fight against us because of our faith; if we had the same faith, they would not fight against us."[153] (This was a spectacularly wrong prediction, as the conversion of the Bulgarians proved.)

As we will see, the Byzantines were far more comfortable writing about enemies who were less threatening, especially if they had already been defeated. The most original ethnographic excursus in Byzantine literature is that of Leon the Deacon on the religion of the Rus', who had just been defeated by Ioannes I Tzimiskes and sent back north (and they were defeated again on the way by the Pechenegs). Leon's source was a panegyrical history of Tzimiskes' campaign. By contrast, Leon says nothing about the culture of the Arabs, though he narrates victorious campaigns against them too. Mauropous and Psellos wrote similar ethnographies of the Pechenegs that were framed within panegyrics extolling imperial victory.[154] The tenth-century encyclopedia *Souda* has a long entry on the Bulgarians that discusses their preference for Avar clothing and narrates brief but colorful episodes from their history. By contrast, its entry for the Arabs is: "name of a people," and, for the Saracens: "a people." It would be difficult to reconstruct a history of Islam or the Arabs based on middle Byzantine sources alone. Howard-Johnston has also argued, on the basis of the *De administrando imperio*, that Konstantinos VII Porphyrogennetos was starting to write a history of Islam.[155] But most of Konstantinos' material was taken from the *Chronicle* of Theophanes, who, in turn, is now recognized to have received it, via a translation, from the eighth-century Syrian history of Theophilos of Edessa, who was writing in the Caliphate.[156] So this is "Byzantine" material only by appropriation and some tampering, not origin and manufacture.

Defeat in religious war made it difficult for the Byzantines even to discuss their enemies and impossible to understand their motivation. This problem was further compounded by the most typical Byzantine interpretation of such events, namely that military defeat was a punishment imposed by God on the empire for its sins (or the sins of its rulers). This schema constitutes the most basic theory of history in the Old Testament and would be applied by the Byzantines repeatedly to their own reverses.[157] A striking example is offered by Euodios' account of the Forty-Two Martyrs of Amorion, who were captured when the city fell in 838 and executed seven years later after refusing to accept Islam. He applies the scheme mechanically in his summary of Roman-Arab relations: whenever the rulers of the Romans lapse into some heresy, the Arabs win territory (but divine mercy prevents them from making the conquest total), and when the emperors return to Orthodoxy the Romans win back some territory.[158]

Let us consider the implications of this schema for ethnography. While there are two parties involved in this relationship, this theodicy applies its logic to only one of them, the victims. They have a linear and "logical" relation to God: he punishes them for their transgressions as he later rewards them for their piety. But what about the other party, the Persians, Avars, Arabs, or, later, Turks? Their victory is not understood according to this schema as a reward by God. It cannot be, because they are not even Christians. They are worse than bad Christians, yet still they win. So the same logic cannot apply to them. Their victory is exclusively a function of Byzantine sin and has nothing to do with the barbarians' virtues. In fact, to be useful in this schema, they must be stripped of their identity and be recast as passive tools of God's anger against the Romans. Paradoxically, then, Saracens were both God's instrument (when they were winning) and an offense against all that was holy (when they were losing).[159]

This schema effectively denied them agency. It is as though the Christian Romans were the only real people in the world, and history was defined as the vagaries of their relationship with God; otherwise they were surrounded by a veil of darkness out of which came periodic punishments, whether earthquakes or Turks. The latter were thus "passive instruments" that "possessed no self-will."[160] That is why the enemy had to be depicted as a raging wild beast, a blind force of nature (though when defeated "arrogant lions" quickly became "humble rabbits").[161] One might go so far as to claim that the whole goal of this view was to safeguard the integrity of the Christian subject, even or especially of the sinful, chastised subject, and to deny the very existence of the Muslim as a human being. A human being, after all, might choose to become a Muslim. Ducellier has noted that Byzantine literature was far more likely to stress episodes of martyrdom at the hands of Muslim persecutors than conversion to Islam by Christians under Muslim power.[162] The humanity of the Muslim is only indirectly affirmed when he is imagined as sent to Hell for his sins to suffer a punishment far worse than that which God was using him to inflict upon the Romans.[163] The fundamental logic governing the world, then, did not apply to him. Ethnography and mutual understanding were impossible under these ideological conditions. Islam proved to be the great impediment to ethnography because of the Christian logic that governed Byzantine responses to it in literature. This mode of interpretation had ancient roots, that is, Biblical ones, but it was only after the seventh century that it became the standard response in many Christian genres.

Consider the beginning of Photios' second *Homily on the Rus' Attack* of 860 that expounds precisely such a type of theological ethnography.[164] For Photios the attack, which was repelled, constituted a manifestation of divine punishment and was a part of *Roman* history; it was not part of Rus' history, for which he had no concept (just as in the U.S. the "Vietnam" war is seen as a chapter in *American* history, not Vietnamese history). The Rus', according to this schema, were but incidental instruments in a relationship that had only two partners, the Romans and God. Photios describes them as utter savages, hardly as human beings at all. After all, blind, raging, "wild beasts" are like earthquakes when they happen to you. The only motivation he allows is that they were envious of the fame of the Roman nation and sought to bring it down (much like the explanation set forth by the Bush administration after 9–11: "they hate us for our freedoms"). Again, we should not confuse what Photios may or may not have known about the Rus' with what he was saying here. He was, after all, preaching a homily, and his message was subject to the goals of the genre. Certainly he knew more about the Rus' than he was saying—just as the Byzantines generally knew much but wrote little about all barbarians. The question is not what they knew but what, in each situation, promoted the contingent goals of the text (whether a sermon, imperial panegyric, etc.) The type of knowledge that we find, say, in the *De administrando imperio* would have been useless or would have undermined his message that day. It was the logic of punitive theology that bounded the horizons of inquiry and representation in his sermons. It instrumentalized the "other."

In the Christian genres of theodicy the barbarian has a negative but purely instrumental role: he mediates the relationship between the Romans and God. But the same was also the case when the barbarian was given a positive image, especially in sermons. When preachers wanted to shame their congregations into behaving better, one approach they could take was to contrast the Christians' bad habits with the piety, morality, and good order allegedly kept by pagans, heretics, Jews, or barbarians.[165] An example from Photios shows how the same speaker could offer this opposite picture to make a different point. Here he is trying to persuade his audience to follow the Golden Rule. Note the different role that infidel barbarians now play.

> Use the same standard for yourself as for your neighbor. . . . The precept is simple, the law is common to Greeks, barbarians and, if you will, to both the faithful and the unfaithful. Many infidel nations live by this inborn law; many barbarians, while being barbarians in other respects, observe steadfastly this natural law, having made sure, by not wronging others, that they are not themselves wronged by them. What then? Is justice sought after by infidels and barbarians, even without a written law . . . while for us faithful, who call on Christ . . . is it not a shame to be called faithful unless we observe justice toward one another?[166]

There can be no reconciling such an image of the Rus' or Arabs with that in the sermons on the attack of 860. They are simply operating in different discursive universes. This double-pronged approach to the "bipolar" image of the barbarian goes to the heart of the ideological framework of the Christian representation of radical alterity. There was no paradox here, only genre-specific instrumentality. Moreover, exhortations that made use of a positive image of the barbarian were never accompanied by an analysis of foreign ways or even relevant information. They tended to be purely rhetorical. In other contexts, the preachers viciously attacked those same groups and would never countenance the suggestion that one had to examine their customs and see whether they deserved imitation. In neither case do we find ethnography.

The Byzantine reaction to early Islam was dominated by theological and literary modalities that precluded ethnography. Byzantine literature continued to ignore Arab and Islamic culture, along with the fate of Christian and other populations under Arab rule, even after Byzantium had gone on the offensive and the power of the Arabs had begun to wane. But the intellectual sophistication of a number of Byzantine thinkers outgrew many of those assumptions and was not confined to outdated paradigms during the next round of Islamic invasions, in this case by the Turks in the eleventh century. While many churchmen were perfectly happy to repeat the same refrains, Michael Attaleiates was not. As a brief epilogue to this section, we may consider how he either rejected or recast the modalities we have seen so far.[167]

For one thing, Attaleiates was not afraid to face the fact of imperial decline square-on and to view it, moreover, in mostly pragmatic and worldly terms. For him, something had gone horribly wrong with Byzantine political leadership.[168] He was not bound by the paradigm of eternal victory and wanted to understand the actual causes of defeat. He set out to recount and explain the sudden decline of empire in the third quarter of the eleventh century. For starters, he rejected the widespread view that defeat is God's way of punishing religious deviance.

> For it seemed that such a large uprising of the foreign nations and the cutting down of those who live under Roman authority could be attributed only to His anger against the heretics, that is the Armenians dwelling in Iberia, Mesopotamia, and as far as Lykandos, in Melitene, and in the vicinity, and those whose religion was the heretical, Jewish one of Nestorios and the Akephaloi. Those lands abounded in such bad beliefs. But when disaster also struck the Orthodox, all who followed the religion of the Romans were unsure what to make of it.[169]

Moreover, he does not view the victorious barbarians as passive instruments of God's will and does not depict them as raging wild beasts. He highlights the virtues of the Seljuk sultan and makes it clear that he deserved to win in spite of the fact that he was not a Christian.[170] Also, in a major digression, he explains why the ancient Romans had won in their wars and explicitly draws attention to the fact that they were not Christian.[171] It is not that he wants the Byzantines to give up their religion. To the contrary, he wants them to be more sincere and genuine Christians, because he believes that all religions promote values that are good for social justice and military victory. "It is said that even the foreign nations honor justice, preserve their ancestral customs without change, and always ascribe every piece of good fortune to the Creator, given that those things which get us ahead are the same for all people and required by every religion (θρησκεία)."[172] This effectively leaves the field open to a rational analysis, one that goes beyond religion and stresses secular, especially intellectual, virtues such as planning and foresight. In the end, Attaleiates has likewise used the model of the virtuous barbarian, in this case the sultan, to shame his fellow Romans, but his argument operates on an altogether different intellectual and analytical level from the sermons of Photios.

CHAPTER 4

The Genres and Politics of Middle Byzantine Ethnography

The *Taktika* and *De administrando imperio*: Military and Diplomatic Ethnography

The genre of Byzantine ethnography that has received the most attention is the military manuals, especially Maurikios' *Strategikon* (ca. 600) and Leon VI's *Taktika* (ca. 900), but largely from a positivist point of view, that is, from historians who are searching for facts about military history and are evaluating the reliability of the manuals from that standpoint. In the process, it was discovered that Leon basically copied Maurikios in his description of many nations, thereby rendering his information suspect. At the same time, it was found that in many instances he modified his template in order to reflect contemporary reality better, so the picture presented by the *Taktika* is mixed. On the one hand, the text must always be checked against its model, but it is not an anthology.[1] Yet additional clarity can be brought to our understanding of Leon's literary strategy when it comes to ethnography.

As we saw above, in the epilogue to the *Taktika* Leon instructs his generals to know the *physis* (or "nature") of the empire's enemies.[2] They are presumably to acquire such knowledge in the field and at their posts, but Leon provides his own survey in *diataxis* 18 of the text (out of 19), just as Maurikios discusses each of the *ethnē* in book 11 of the *Strategikon* (out of 12). Maurikios begins with the Persians, but in following him and copying much of his information Leon has actually done something interesting that has largely passed unnoticed: he turns Maurikios' *descriptions* of Persian military customs into a series of *prescriptions* for the Roman generals of his own day.[3] For

example, the Persians endure toils and wars on behalf of their *patris*, and this
is exactly what Leon tells his generals that the Romans should do, though
without saying that he is borrowing this from a description of the Persians.[4]
The notion that generals should win by strategy rather than by rashness is
also lifted from the *Strategikon* on the Persians, in fact the very next lines.[5]
The following lines on Persian endurance Leon interprets as a Christian virtue that will be rewarded by God.[6] He reveals his source in the next section,
where he says that there *were* some nations, such as the Persians, who would
not initiate negotiations even when they were hard pressed but waited for the
other side to do so. By speaking about them in the past tense, he implies that
the Persians are not a current threat. Note that Leon does not necessarily
want to advise his generals to do the same thing, so he switches here to a descriptive mode, leaving it unclear whether he recommends this policy or not.[7]
Moving along, he turns the Persians' encampment policies into positive rec-
ommendations for his generals, though without admitting what he is doing,
and likewise with their battle formations and exploitation of the summer
heat.[8] Only at the end he does attribute some of these recommended maneu-
vers to the Persians.

In the case of the Sasanian Persians, then, it is as though Leon, intending
to write his own *ethnika* based on Maurikios, realized that the first *ethnos*
that is discussed in the *Strategikon* was no longer a threat and thus omitted it
from his discussion; but, liking much of what was said about their practices,
he adapted it to contemporary Roman use, even adding a patina of Christian
virtue to it. But this improvised method introduces structural problems into
the text, as these prescriptions should have been placed in earlier, more thematically relevant *diataxeis* (e.g., on making camps). This indicates that Leon
had not planned how to handle book II of the *Strategikon* in advance, but was
reacting to it as he wrote, almost as if he had not read it before.[9] In this case,
he effectively erased the Persian name in order to redirect the ethnographic
"content" associated with them to a different purpose, albeit one that is out of
place in an ostensibly ethnological *diataxis*. As a result, military ethnography
is slightly postponed.

The next section in the *Strategikon* is on "the Skythians, namely the
Avars, Turks, and other Hunnic nations with the same lifestyle." Leon was
not concerned about the Avars or the Turks of ca. 600, who were not a problem for the empire of ca. 900. But the generic category "Skythian" enabled
him to transfer this material to their typological heirs in terms of geography
and lifestyle, namely the Bulgarians and Hungarians.[10] Here Leon does

something subtle, which also has implications for the cynicism with which the Byzantines treated the religious ideology of their empire, a topic we will explore at the end of this chapter. The *Taktika* were written soon after king Symeon of Bulgaria had won in a major offensive against the empire. Leon carefully states that he is not going to discuss how to fight the Bulgarians, because they are Christians and Romans should not be fighting other Christians. But he does discuss the Hungarians instead, and repeatedly states that the Bulgarians are just like them in all ways except religion, thereby providing the requisite coverage of Bulgarian warfare, albeit covertly (and covert action is a strategy that Leon generally recommends to his generals).[11] Moreover, Leon reveals that the Romans did have a military *parataxis* (a special formation) for fighting Bulgarians and that Bulgarians had their own *parataxis* for fighting the Romans, so religious sensibilities merely prevented him from *speaking* about this matter at that time; it did not prevent actual warfare between the two Christian states. Symeon, after all, was a dangerous neighbor who had been trained in Greek rhetoric during his childhood stay as a royal "guest" in Constantinople (at the very same time as Leon himself was being schooled at the court),[12] and he still had contacts in the capital and palace. It could be imagined that a text such as this might fall into his hands, and Leon probably wished not to antagonize him at that delicate diplomatic juncture. Leon makes the curious claim that during the recent war Providence sent the Turks, whom the imperial fleet ferried across the Danube, to attack the Bulgarians "who were unjustly attacking the Christians," in order that "Christian Romans not spill the blood of Christian Bulgarians."[13] There was, of course, something other than *divine* providence active behind the scenes here. Leon's son Konstantinos VII revealed that his father had invited the Turks to attack Symeon from the rear and facilitated their crossing.[14] We are entitled to a cynical view of Leon's Christian scruples.

Leon's decision to use the Turks as a foil for the Bulgarians is reminiscent of the late antique historians' use of other foreign peoples as foils for discussing Roman society, but there is a difference between using a set of foreigners as a foil by which to discuss your own group (the Romans) indirectly, and using them to discuss another foreign group (here, the Bulgarians). Leon's is not self-critical ethnography. His move from Turks to Bulgarians was facilitated by the generic nature of the Skythian model. Also, Leon's ethnographic focus is limited mostly to military matters, and posits military customs as independent of culture. For example, he observes that the difference between Hungarians and Bulgarians is that the latter are Christians and so have partially accepted Roman customs and shed their savage nomadic past along with their lack of faith (καὶ τοῖς Ῥωμαϊκοῖς ἀπ᾿ ὀλίγον μετεβάλοντο ἤθεσι, τό τε τό ἄγριον καὶ νομαδικὸν τῷ ἀπίστῳ συναποβαλόντες).[15] This statement points to fundamental cultural changes about which, however, we are told almost nothing specific in Byzantine sources, Leon's own works included. Turks and Bulgarians have for him an identical military persona regardless of their cultural differences.

Following the order of the *Strategikon*, Leon gives us a brief section on the Franks and the Lombards, whom Maurikios called "the blond nations."[16] Most of this section is also copied from the *Strategikon*, but Leon includes two curious contemporary references. Where the *Strategikon* begins by emphasizing that both peoples value freedom greatly, Leon goes on to add that the Lombards have lost this virtue for the most part.[17] Later, following the *Strategikon* word for word in noting their uncontrollable greed, Leon adds that "we know this from our own experience, as many of them come over from Italy for some business or other."[18] He adds that these nations have become Christian and are generally friendly to the empire.[19] He does not say whether this has improved their level of culture.

Next are the Slavs.[20] They are introduced identically as in the *Strategikon*, but Leon quickly notes that their love of freedom was especially pronounced when they used to dwell in their proper country, north of the Danube. When they crossed over to the south and entered Roman territory they were initially reluctant to accept any leaders other than their own, but in time they converted and were made, by the author's father Basileios I, to accept Roman culture and military orders.[21] Leon then returns to the exposition in the *Strategikon*, but here something interesting happens. The *Strategikon* at this point gives what we might call a proper ethnography of the Slavs, discussing their customs of hospitality, their food, their women's devotion to their husbands (to the point of death), and their habitat. Only then does it disclose their fighting style and dispense advice on how to defeat them and march through their country. Leon repeats most of the ethnographical information, but changes all the *Strategikon*'s verbs to the past tense. It is only the custom of hospitality which he explicitly says that they still preserve (ἔχουσιν ὁμοίως), but here he indicates his own incredulity (οὐκ οἶδ᾿ ὅπως εἰπεῖν).[22] When he reaches the military section, he begins to copy that too, again changing the verbs into the past tense, but then cuts it short after only a paragraph. "As for the raids that the Romans used to make against them," the reader is now referred to the previous *diataxis* of the *Taktika* (17), where Leon had placed the *Strategikon*'s material on how to fight the Slavs and other barbarians who fight in that way, although there he recasts it as generic (not specifically Slavic). Apparently, he realized that a section on how to fight the Slavs would have been useless, as they were now basically Romans. But then why include them as a separate category in the first place? Why rehearse outdated information about their previous culture? Did Leon grasp the futility of this section as he was writing it and so cut it short midway through? This would reinforce our earlier conclusion about the similarly improvisational way in which he handled the Persian section of the *Strategikon*.

Finally, Leon turns to the "Saracens."[23] To them is devoted the single longest section, obviously because it was the most urgent for the empire of his time. It is not primarily based on the *Strategikon*, though parts of it are. Leon cites as sources his generals, the histories of previous emperors, and Basileios I ("our father"), who fought against them many times.[24] The section begins with a brief history of the Saracens, focusing on their conquest of the eastern provinces when Muhammad became the leader of their false religion.[25] They think that they are pious but they are not, because they do not worship Christ. He then declares that "we will fight back against their impiety on behalf of piety and our orthodox faith."[26] He does not discuss Islam or Saracen culture, but sticks to military matters. In fact, he applies some of the *Strategikon*'s Persian material to the Saracens: they are hampered by cold, and their bows are useless in the rain.[27] He has transposed information again, though remaining in the same geographical environment. He notes that the Saracens harass the Romans today just as they had harassed the Persian kings in ancient times, and adds that it is primarily because of them that he has undertaken this *polemikē diataxis*.[28]

Earlier in *diataxis* 18, Leon had briefly and confusingly mentioned the Saracens' motivations in war: "They do not march out because they are subject to anyone else or owe military service, but rather because of their love of gain and freedom, or one might say for plunder and their own faith, or better stated their lack of faith due to false religion, as if on account of these things they suffer at our hands, thinking that God is their enemy and that they are unable to endure the harm of it all."[29] It is hard to know what this rambling sentence even means, assuming that it has been transmitted correctly. Does he mean to imply that the Saracens think that God is not on their side? Leon discusses Saracen recruitment again in the proper section on them: they are not drafted but join up voluntarily, the rich in order to die on behalf of their people and the poor to gain plunder. In the subsequent chapters Leon seems to propose recruitment policies by which the Romans can offset the advantages this system gives to the Saracens, and emphasizes the Romans' duty to defend the true faith against Saracen attacks. It is less clear, however, whether he is actually trying to borrow and adopt Arab institutions at this point.[30]

Military manuals naturally treated foreign cultures in a confrontational way. Gilbert Dagron has in fact suggested that they can be seen as a form of heresiology, a catalogue of different types of deviance from the (Roman) norm, potentially infinite in number but reducible here to a common denominator (in this case barbarism rather than atheism).[31] Also, they focus overwhelmingly on tactics, terrain, and strategy. One does not learn much about culture from them, other than clichés, for example, that the Franks "love freedom." Only the Slavic and Arab sections contain information beyond the strictly military, but the Slavic is outdated (by Leon's own admission), while the Arab is confusing and polemical (and hardly represents Arab culture as we might know it from its own sources).

To conclude, along with historiography, it is the military manuals that contain the most information that can be labeled ethnographic. In the case of Leon's *Taktika*, however, we are dealing with information that has mostly been recycled from Maurikios' *Strategikon*. However, it has been carefully adapted to fit the conditions of Leon's reign. The Persians were no longer a threat, so their material is cast into a series of positive prescriptions for Leon's generals. The Skythian material, on the other hand, has been transferred to contemporary peoples who bore that name in the classicizing Byzantine outlook (Bulgarians and Hungarians), given that the Avars and Huns were no longer relevant. The Slavic material has been put into the past tense, as the people in question had, by that point, mostly been absorbed into the empire. Leon thus omits most of the military discussion that pertained to them, for it was irrelevant, but it was too late: he had already begun to write the section and had to cut it short. Finally, the material on the Saracens is mostly new, though it becomes confusing when it goes beyond the strictly military aspect. In sum, the *Taktika* is hardly a strict anthology; it is, rather, a modulated adaptation, though not consistent or always well planned, and it remains unclear how useful it could actually have been in the field.[32]

That same question can be asked of the so-called *De administrando imperio* written (or compiled) by Leon's son Konstantinos VII (or his team of scholars) about half a century later. Its original address (not exactly a title) was *Konstantinos, Eternal Emperor of the Romans in Christ, to his son Romanos, Crowned by God and Born in the Purple* (i.e., Romanos II, reigned 959–963).[33]

In the preface and first chapter, the author explains that his intention is to "instruct" the imperial heir and make him wiser about the nations that surround the empire and about the best ways to handle them, adding that he has chosen to write not in Attic but in spoken Greek. While many historians want to take this declaration at face value, it is difficult to see this text as usefully didactic. It does stress the centrality of the Pechenegs to the geopolitics of the north Black Sea region (ch. 1–9); recommend specious lies by which to fend off impertinent barbarian requests for Greek fire, vestments, and brides (13); contain some geographical digressions (esp. 9, 30, 40, 42); and rehearse recent relations with the Caucasian principalities (43–46), all of which might have been of use to Romanos, unlike the majority of the text, which has little contemporary relevance or practical advice. It is hard to see, however, how Romanos' policy-makers could have relied on these passages to run the empire and its foreign policy, which had never depended on manuals before, or that Romanos could have kept up with events on the basis of this book.[34]

The *De administrando imperio* contains more information on the empire's neighbors than does almost any other Byzantine text, which by itself makes this a unique, even perplexingly aberrant text, though I will argue below that this impression should be tempered. Its core, ch. 14–46, begins with the Arabs and moves clockwise around the Mediterranean, focusing especially on the Balkans and then on the Caucasian regions, though it strangely omits the kingdoms of the Franks and Bulgarians; also, except for the Caucasus, its narratives end short of the present. The text is nevertheless considered the showcase of Byzantine ethnography, even though the theory that its core was based on the volume *On Nations* (περὶ ἐθνῶν) of the Constantinian *excerpta* has been questioned.[35] Given that the problem of Byzantine ethnography as a literary genre has not attracted attention, most of the debate about the text has focused on its date (or phases of revision), authorship (or editorship), sources, coherence, and relation to foreign policy on the one hand, and on the factual reliability of its chapters on the origin of the Serbs, Croats, and Hungarians on the other, as modern historians of those nations find themselves in the unhappy position of having to rely on this text to reconstruct key aspects of their national history. These debates have not always been pleasant or conclusive, and we do not need to involve ourselves in them here. Most have focused narrowly on specific passages or even single words and have not considered the overall structure, purpose, and meaning of the work.

But to talk about the structure or meaning of the *DAI* (as it is often called) is just as challenging as sifting through the details, if not more so. It is obviously a compilation, some would say a patchwork, put together from a diverse range of sources. Some of the latter are known; for example, the historian Theophanes, who is quoted verbatim. Others can be plausibly inferred; for instance, the reports of Byzantine envoys,[36] but after that all we have is speculation, usually based on what "interests" each report seems to be supporting. References are thus thrown about to "at least one Magyar source," a revised seventh-century account of the Serbs and Croats, a ninth-century papal account of the conversion of the Serbs and Croats,[37] and "a chronicle otherwise unknown from the town of Cherson in the Crimea."[38] Sometimes different sources are proposed on the basis of slight variations in presentation between one passage and the next.[39] One solution is simply to accept that the text was formed through the operation of heterogeneous literary and ideological influences, including classical geographical determinism, encyclopedism, etymology, and *origines gentium* that were meant to bolster Byzantine imperial hegemony over client states, especially in the Balkans and Caucasus; and also that a paucity of easily digestible written information about current cultures was responsible for its frequent lack of contemporary relevance, as imperial information-gathering was limited to military operations and was not always in writing.[40] James Howard-Johnston has recently set forth two ingenious proposals about the omissions in the text.[41] Current enemies, he argues, such as Arabs, Franks, Bulgars, and Khazars, were excluded "*deliberately*, because . . . they were not actual or potential allies or clients (the subject of *DAI*) but major rivals." They "were the proper subject-matter of a different category of text, a military manual," specifically Leon VI's *Taktika*, which discusses precisely Arabs, Franks, Bulgars, and "Skythians" generally. Second, he argues that it was in fact Leon VI who began to compile the *DAI* and that his heir Konstantinos began to update it later (but never finished the job). That is why, he explains, so many chapters of the "core" section finish around 910 and bear indications that they were written around that time. If true, this would not only justify but require the arrangement of the present section, which treats the *Taktika* and *DAI* in succession, though the thesis certainly requires further discussion. At least it salvages the coherence of the authors or editors' *intention*, if not the text itself, which remains "a ramshackle collection of disparate materials."

But just because we do not instantly grasp how a text coheres does not mean that it does not do so. For example, the authors of the modern commentary were certain that ch. 9, on the river routes of the Rus', was a later addition that did not sit well in the first part of the text, which seems to be devoted otherwise to relations of power among the peoples north of the Black Sea, and especially to the Pechenegs. Since then, however, scholars have noted the passages where the author of this chapter highlights those places where the Pechenegs can most easily attack the Rus' convoys.[42] Is there a way to salvage the unity of the text as we now have it? As far as I know, no scholar has engaged with the unitarian interpretation proposed by Telemachos Lounghis in 1990, in part because of its enigmatic (Greek) style and elusive thesis. Lounghis seems to think that the work reflects the ideology of the Macedonian dynasty, which he takes to be a form of "limited ecumenism" that was opposed to unlimited Roman imperialism. The Macedonian emperors were apparently willing to concede the west to the Franks—or to the popes; the point is confusing as the *Donation of Constantine* weaves in and out of Lounghis' roller-coaster argument. This explains the omission of the Franks from the *DAI* (in the opposite way from Howard-Johnston's, it should be noted, which requires them to be potential enemies).[43] Lounghis has a strong card to play in Konstantinos' open advocacy in ch. 13 of historical fictions to fend off barbarian requests for brides, silk, and Greek fire.[44] Could he not have used fictions of his own in the *DAI* to advance a political agenda? The careful excision of the Justinianic *reconquista* could fall into this category, and the dating in c. 27 of Narses and the coming of the Lombards to the eighth century (rather than the sixth) would then be not a mistake but a lie. Not all aspects of Lounghis' argument are easy to follow, and I find problematic the notion that medieval states operated on the basis of "doctrines" (like the U.S. Monroe Doctrine) that are never spelled out in any source. But in a looser form the argument has plausibility, and Lounghis' astute observations require further exploration.

The state of research on this important text poses two major problems for the student of Byzantine ethnography: first, we do not know the source and date of much of the information in it and so cannot control for the interests that each morsel was meant to serve (nor it is certain, if the source was foreign, that it was transmitted correctly or understood on the Byzantine side);[45] and second, we are faced with contradictory theories regarding the overall meaning and purpose of the text within Byzantine court circles, which makes it hard to interpret specific passages. These are obviously not problems we can solve here. What we can do, however, is make the *DAI* less intimidating and less unique in the corpus of Byzantine literature. The text does offer much information about the geography, history, and rulers of many foreign peoples, but it does not for all that contain much *ethnography*. As Howard-Johnston has noted, there is more history in it "than the Herodotean-style geography and anthropology promised in the proem."[46] He is referring to the programmatic statement according to which the third part of the *DAI* (what I have called its "core") will be devoted to "the differences among other nations, their origins and customs and manner of life, the position and climate of the land they dwell in, and its geographical description and measurement." This is then repeated verbatim at the end of ch. 13 in order to introduce the "core."[47] This sounds like the classical genre of ethnography and is therefore promising.

Yet none of the chapters that follow do actually reflect this blueprint, and the aspect in which they are most deficient is the "customs and manner of life" category. There is, for example, the reference to Rus' rites in ch. 9. At the island of St. Gregorios, along their route to the south,

> they perform their sacrifices because a gigantic oak-tree stands there; and they sacrifice live cocks. Arrows, too, they peg in round about, and others bread and meat, or something of whatever each may have, as is their custom. They also throw lots regarding the cocks, whether to slaughter them, or to eat them as well, or to leave them alive.[48]

This report is the only one of its kind in the text. The commentary at this point is trapped in the modern Scandinavian versus Slav debate,[49] but from the standpoint of ethnography it is more interesting to point out a curious coincidence, namely that the most extended digression in middle Byzantine literature on another people's "customs" is the (independent) account of the pagan religion of the Rus' in Leon the Deacon later in that century (derived, I believe, from a source written in or soon after 971, scarcely more than a decade removed from the *DAI* itself).[50] The patterns of discussing foreign customs and religions in the *DAI* are broadly similar to those in Byzantine historiography as a whole with respect to their general silence, treatment of Islam, and rare moments of rich description, as in the passage quoted above.[51]

To give another example, Byzantine historians, as we will see, sometimes rely on the format of the military manuals to convey relevant information about foreign peoples (who, after all, often appear in the context of a military narrative). The *DAI* occasionally features this ethnographic mode too. Consider its account of the otherwise unknown Fatemites, with whom Muhammad supposedly won many victories. In accordance with the proem's programmatic statement, the text tells us about their origin (they stem from Fatem, Muhammad's daughter, which of course directly contradicts the claim that he used them in his own wars) and their geographical location (north of Mecca). The rest of the entry would not have been out of place in a *Strategikon* or a classicizing history:

> They are brave men and warriors, so that if they be found to the number of a thousand in an army, that army cannot be defeated or worsted. They ride not horses but camels, and in time of war they do not put on corselets or coats of mail but pink-colored cloaks, and have long spears and shields as tall as a man and enormous wooden bows which few can bend, and that with difficulty.[52]

Yet the most important respect in which the ethnographic modes of the *DAI* conform to broader Byzantine patterns observable in historical texts is the Byzantine version of *origines gentium*, a narrative form that is distinctive to texts written in Byzantium between the seventh and the twelfth centuries (and is different from classical narratives to which scholars give the same name).[53] We will encounter and study this type again in the next section, when we turn to the historians, but it is prevalent, in fact fundamental, in the *DAI*, a fact that diminishes that text's isolation from the broader literary scene. The typical Byzantine *origo* has the following features. It tracks the geographical movements of each people from its "original" homeland to its current location, and often notes changes in its relations to surrounding powers and geopolitical configurations. Peoples are normally grouped under leaders, whose children typically split off, taking segments of the group with them. There is no discussion of their customs, social structure, only rarely of their political organization (mostly in the section on the Pechenegs in the DAI), and almost nothing of their religion before baptism (if we are dealing with a currently Christian nation), and even their conversion is mentioned only in passing.[54]

These are, then, not ethnographies as such but sober, factually oriented geostrategic narratives that do not pass judgment on foreign cultures because they are not about "culture" to begin with. It is likely that as a group, from the seventh century to the twelfth, they originated in official reports or briefings on the many "new peoples" that entered the empire's orbit in this turbulent period. We might be glimpsing here the analytical categories in which imperial officials (and not only emperors) wanted their information prepackaged. Ethnography was not something they cared about. Again, the *DAI* is found to conform to the general patterns of Byzantine representation of foreign peoples.

Ethnographic Moments in the Byzantine Historians, and a New Subgenre

Despite the predominantly negative argument made so far, ethnography can be found in a number of Byzantine historians. Few are full ethnographies in the classical sense, being either too brief or partial in their coverage. They fall into three categories. The largest, I propose, is a type of official "briefing" on the origins and geopolitical situation of a new foe that enters the empire's military horizons. This is a subgenre of historiography that I propose we recognize, and has close links to the sources that lay behind the *De administrando imperio*, a text that no longer has to stand in isolation. The second consists of discussions of the Pechenegs in the eleventh century that we will examine in a later section, because they offer a coherent case study of how a group's image was modulated to serve different literary goals, mostly in historiography and imperial rhetoric. The third, smallest, and least coherent category consists of those moments when a historian decided to say a few words about a neighbor of the empire. By far the longest and most innovative text in this category is on the religion of the Rus'. It is found in Leon the Deacon, but originated in a source that he used for Tzimiskes' Balkan campaign of 971.

Briefings on the Origin of New Peoples in Historiography

Methodologically, we could use the material in the *De administrando imperio* as a benchmark and search for its like in other texts, to see where else this kind of material appears. We do not have to look far. The controversial information in the *De administrando imperio* on the Serbs, the Croats, and the Dalmatian cities, telling how they gained autonomy and then allegedly returned to the imperial fold under Basileios I, recurs in the *Life* of that emperor. Granted, this material is not ethnographic, being more about Byzantine foreign policy, but it does recount the relations of foreign states to each other, taking us outside the boundaries of Romanía (though it mixes history, anecdotes, and legendary motifs).[55] But the *Life of Basileios* does not go far enough from a methodological point of view, as it and the *De administrando imperio* are attributed to the same initiative and are not independent of each other.[56] Ideally, we would prefer passages in sources much earlier or later than the age of Konstantinos VII, as this would establish a continuous and distinctively Byzantine mode of discussing foreign peoples that might then be linked to state sources. Such texts do in fact exist: I propose Theophanes' digression on the origin of the Bulgars;[57] Skylitzes on the origin of the Seljuks and on the Pecheneg crossing of the Danube under Konstantinos IX;[58] and Anna Komnene on the internal history of the Turks who had entered Asia Minor.[59] These texts have comparable points of emphasis and omission and play parallel roles in the narratives in which they appear, and other passages may yet be identified as belonging to this category.[60] I will focus first on Theophanes, whose digression traces the origin of the Bulgars north of the Black Sea and their establishment in Thrace, placed under the year 678/9 AD.

> In this year, too, the tribe of the Bulgars assailed Thrace. It is now necessary to relate the ancient history of the Ounnogoundour Bulgars and Kotragoi. On the northern, that is the far side of the Euxine Sea [Black Sea], is the so-called Maeotid Lake [Sea of Azov] into which flows a huge river called Atel [Volga?], which comes down from the Ocean through the land of the Sarmatians. The Atel is joined by the river Tanais, which also rises from the Iberian Gates that are in the mountains of the Caucasus. From the confluence of the Tanais and the Atel (it is above the aforementioned Maeotid Lake that the Atel splits off) flows the river called Kouphis [Kuban?] which discharges into the far end of the Pontic Sea near Nekropela, by the promontory called Ram's Head. From the aforesaid lake is a stretch of sea like a river which joins the Euxine through the land of the Kimmerian Bosphoros, in which river are caught the so-called *mourzoulin* and similar fish. Now on the eastern side of the lake that lies above, in the direction of Phanagouria and of the Jews that live there, march a great many tribes; whereas, starting from the same lake in the direction of the river called Kouphis (where the Bulgarian fish called *xyston* is caught) is the old Great Bulgaria and the so-called Kotragoi, who are of the same stock as the Bulgars. In the

days of Konstantinos [Konstas II], who dwelt in the West, Kroba-
tos, the chieftain of the aforesaid Bulgaria and of the Kotragoi, died
leaving five sons, on whom he enjoined not to depart under any circumstances from their common life that they might prevail in every
way and not be enslaved by another tribe. A short time after his de-
mise, however, his five sons fell out and parted company, each with
the host that was subject to him. The eldest son, called Batbaian observed his father's command and has remained until this day in his
ancestral land. His younger brother, called Kotragos, crossed the
river Tanais and dwelt opposite his eldest brother. The fourth and
fifth went over the river Istros, that is the Danube: the former became subject of the Chagan of the Avars in Avar Pannonia and remained there with his army, whereas the latter reached the Pentapolis,
which is near Ravenna, and accepted allegiance to the Christian
Empire. Coming after them, the third brother, called Asparouch,
crossed the Danapris and Danastris (rivers that are farther north
than the Danube) and, on reaching the Oglos [Danube delta?], settled between the former and the latter, since he judged that place
to be secure and impregnable on both sides: on the near side it is
marshy, while on the far side it is encircled by the rivers. It thus provided ample security from enemies to this tribe that had been weakened by its division. When they had thus divided into five parts and
been reduced to a paltry estate, the great nation of the Khazars issued forth from the inner depths of Berzilia, that is from the First
Sarmatia, and conquered all the country beyond the sea as far as the
Sea of Pontos; and they subjugated the eldest brother Batbaian,
chieftain of the First Bulgaria, from whom they exact tribute to this
day. Now, when the emperor Konstantinos [IV] had been informed
that a foul and unclean tribe had settled beyond the Danube at the
Oglos and was overrunning and laying waste the environs of the
Danube, that is the country that is now in their possession, but was
then in Christian hands, he was greatly distressed and ordered all
the *themata* to cross over to Thrace. He fitted out a fleet and moved
against them by land and sea in an attempt to drive them away by
force of arms; and he drew up his infantry on the land that faces the
so-called Oglos and the Danube. . . . (tr. C. Mango and R. Scott,
modified)

This is not the place to provide a historical commentary on this important passage.[61] What we are interested in are its contours as a literary artifact. The first sentence enables the digression to be slotted into Theophanes' annalistic entries. The digression then explains the movement of a new people into their "current" geostrategic location and concludes by returning to the temporarily suspended narrative of imperial history. The digressions in Skylitzes and Anna work in the same way. There is a heavy emphasis on geography, much of it erroneous in this case, and the reference to the fish suggests that this may be an abridgment of an original version that contained more extensive information on fauna and natural curiosities. The building blocks of the narrative are barbarian names, as tribal groups are naturally subsumed under the names of their leaders, whose movements are tracked in relation to the established imperial powers in their proximity. While we can discern the operation of classical themes here (in aetiology, the conflation of tribes with their leaders, geography, and ecology), the purpose of this text is to brief us on the origin of a people that only now enter the picture. Theophanes' digression, like those in Skylitzes and Anna, does not offer information or value-judgments on their culture, religion, or society. It is, in this way, "neutral," like much of the *De administrando imperio,* with the exception that Theophanes calls the Bulgars "foul and unclean," that is, non-Christians (no such judgments appear in the other authors). But this is said only when their arrival is announced to the emperor so it may belong to the imperial narrative that resumes at this point rather than to the original ethnographic report that has been inserted into it. The only report that we have on the culture of the Bulgars during this period is found in the *Souda* entry on them, which states that "they so liked the attire of the Avars that they adopted it for themselves and still wear it to this day." It is possible that this brief statement comes from the same original source that contained the account of their origins.[62]

Let us compare the latter to Skylitzes' account of how the Seljuk Turks, in the early eleventh century, moved south from Central Asia to replace the Arabs as overlords of the Near East.[63] It is a dry, self-standing narrative of warfare and diplomacy, dense with names and events, whose purpose is to explain the origin of a new geostrategic situation so as to enable the main narrative to continue. The digression likewise ends at the "point of first contact" with the Romans. Events are dependent on the actions and decisions of tribal leaders, and Skylitzes is also concerned to situate the new power in relation to its neighbors and predecessors, for he begins with a geographical overview of the Caliphate and its dissolution. Unlike Theophanes (or, rather, Theophanes' source), he does not have an interest in geography for geography's sake. His digression too is not exactly ethnography but narrow military and geostrategic history; it is silent about culture, religion, and society, and says nothing about Islam, not even in relation to the previous dominion of the Saracens (who merely replace the ancient Persians and expand their empire). Anna's narrative of internal Turkish history is similar, in that its purpose is only to explain a new geopolitical situation by recounting the internal history of the Turks whom it groups under their leaders, with no commentary on their culture. Her digression also ends by slotting into her narrative of the reign of Alexios, again at the point of contact. She has less need for geography or Great-Power analysis, however, as her narrative unfolds in central Asia Minor, in territory taken from the Romans.

We are fortunate, in the case of Skylitzes on the Turks, to be able to track the speed with which such information could sometimes be generated and used by historians (just as we saw how quickly the travel memoirs of Nonnosos and Zemarchos were taken up by Malalas and Yuhannan of Amida, respectively, in late antiquity). Despite much interest in the problem of Skylitzes' sources,[64] his account of the Seljuks has not yet received attention. Skylitzes, a high official under Alexios Komnenos writing perhaps in the 1090s, probably obtained his information from the intelligence services, and it appears to have been fresh. We can infer this from the fact that Attaleiates, another high official who finished writing his *History* around 1079 (so in the previous decade), gives only a brief and vague account of the Turks' movements. It is only a sentence long and differs on many points with Skylitzes' longer account. For instance, on two key points it is wrong where Skylitzes is right: the river separating the Turks from Persia was the Oxus, not the Ganges, and the Turkish leader was not of servile origin.[65] The information recounted by Skylitzes was, therefore, probably generated between 1080 and 1100, for Attaleiates, a high-ranking state official, would surely have had access to it if it had existed earlier.[66] It was precisely that generation, under the leadership of Alexios Komnenos, which was coping with the aftermath of the Turkish settlement of Asia Minor, and knowledge of their background would have been accumulating. Here, perhaps, we glimpse how quickly such information could be incorporated into a work of history. On the other hand, it is shocking how little Attaleiates seems to have known about the origin of the Seljuks, who had been a major problem for at least three decades before he finished his *History*. It was, in any case, Skylitzes' information, not his, that was copied by the historians of the following century.

One of those historians was Nikephoros Bryennios, writing the history of the civil wars of the 1070s. Bryennios copied Skylitzes' account of the origin of the Seljuks, but made some minor changes to it in order to highlight the role of civil war and the reliance on foreign, notably Turkish, mercenaries, in the decline of the Abbasid Caliphate. Like the ancient historians we saw, he too thereby converted ethnography into an indirect vehicle for commentary on the Byzantine empire of his own time, which was likewise riven by civil war and was debating the utility of Turkish mercenaries.[67]

What has emerged here is a quasi-ethnographic subgenre of Byzantine historiography, which we might define as a succinct, factual, and secular briefing on the origins of a barbarian people that had recently established itself within or beside the Roman borders. These briefings typically reveal nothing about these peoples' culture or religion, but trace the geography of their origins, relate their rise and movements to surrounding powers in that region, and explain how the actions of their leaders led to the current geostrategic configuration that the Romans now had to face. These are not *origines gentium* in the classical sense;[68] rather, they track group movements to a new strategic context. These reports have not yet been identified as a distinct genre, but the *De administrando imperio* contains many of them, suggesting that the others also originated in the state services before finding their way into the hands of the historians, between the seventh and the twelfth centuries. This diminishes the uniqueness of the *De administrando imperio*, suggesting that at any point in middle Byzantine history one could have drawn up a similar compendium, and it may provide a glimpse into the generic format in which imperial officials obtained their basic narrative information about foreign peoples. One still wonders, however, why this type of material was not used more often by the Byzantine historians, as they probably had the access.

Ethnography in Bits and Pieces

If by a "standard" ethnography we mean a historiographical digression that includes "mythic or historical origins, populousness, somatic features, warfare, clothing, conditions of living (including eating and accommodation), social structure and political organization, religious practice, gender relations and marriage,"[69] and geography, then there is probably no ethnography in Byzantine literature before the fifteenth century. But some historians do occasionally convey information that fills in a part of that overall picture (just as the military manuals discussed the dimension of warfare), ranging from small asides to more extended (if thematically limited) digressions. No point would be served by compiling all the small asides, and I doubt that anything coherent would emerge from such an exercise. Some examples will suffice. A Pecheneg leader named Kegenes who had taken up Roman service advised the Romans to slaughter all the Pechenegs they had captured recently under Konstantinos IX, "citing a barbarian proverb (παροιμία βάρβαρος), which was actually intelligent, that one should kill the snake while it is still winter and he can't move his tail" (the Romans chose to disperse them instead and settle them in empty lands).[70] Narrating the civil wars before the accession of Alexios Komnenos, Bryennios notes how some Frankish mercenaries switched their allegiance from Botaneiates to Bryennios (the author's ancestor): "dismounting, they placed their hands into his, following their ancestral custom, and swore allegiance to him."[71] Attaleiates offers extended *ekphraseis* of an elephant and a giraffe from Egypt that Konstantinos IX paraded in Constantinople to delight his subjects. Descriptions of exotic animals were a staple of ancient ethnography, but in this case the animals are severed from the world of their origin, which remains opaque in Attaleiates; but this passage may yet be shown to tie in somehow with the political themes of his *History*.[72]

It is unclear that any kind of coherent "ethnography" would be reflected in the sum total of such references even if they were assembled; and each would first have to be investigated individually in its "local" literary context before being synthesized with others. Some such ethnographic asides or glosses are ambiguous or may simply be rhetorical. In the *Capture of Thessalonike*, Ioannes Kaminiates refers to facial expressions that "barbarians are accustomed to make" (involving jaw and eye motions) and to "the way in which barbarians are accustomed to cross their legs."[73] Presumably, both expressions are meant to signify that we are witnessing "uncivilized" behavior, though it is not clear what exactly. Moreover, all the ethnographic fragments that I have quoted so far refer to barbarian peoples (or animals) present on Byzantine soil, not in their "native" environment. This is typical of Byzantine introspection and stands in contrast to late antiquity, when authors cast their gaze far from the center to find exotic new material and project Roman values. It also reflects the recurring invasions that Byzantium endured in the middle period. The foreign was never sufficiently distant. Ideally, for a genuine ethnography, we would like to have information on foreign peoples that does not stem from their direct military interaction with the Byzantines. But this we rarely get. It is military victory or defeat at the hands of barbarians that loosens, ever so slightly, the Byzantines' ethnographic tongue.

A notch above the ethnographic "asides" are mini-digressions. There are few of these in Byzantine historiography. Two are found in Niketas Choniates, though they are different in approach, one on the Cumans and the other on the cult of the Assassins. In his imperial orations, Choniates provides limited information on the fighting style of the Cumans, a couple of lines at most.[74] But in his *History* he offers a mini-military ethnography that recycles the same brief descriptions of their equipment as do his orations but then moves in a new direction. Here is the whole of it:

> Crossing the Danube was easy for them, even more so their raids for plunder, nor was there any toil or labor in their departure. Their equipment consists of a quiver slung crosswise across the waist, curved bows, and arrows. They also have spears, which they wield and twirl around in battle. The same horse bears the Skythian, carries him through furious melee, and provides him with nourishment when its vein is cut open; they even say that, being mounted, it satisfies the barbarian's irrational lust.[75]

This digression reports mostly on military equipment and, as such, would be appropriate for an updated *Taktika*. But it becomes more interesting toward the end. The Cuman is bestialized, for he is said to drink his horse's blood and have sex with it when his own animal urges become too strong. Man and rider are fused. Not only that, the final clauses are reported *from the horse's point of view*, for it is the "bearer" of Cuman culture.[76] This has the effect of lowering the people to an animal level: they are best understood through their horses, which they treat in an inhuman way, and they do not rise above that level. It has been suggested that this dehumanizing passage is indebted to Ammianus' account of the Huns, which includes similar descriptions.[77] But Ammianus wrote in Latin, and it is not clear how his account could have entered the Byzantine historical tradition. An argument about the indirect lines of that influence is, however, now gradually taking shape (independently of Choniates).[78] Be that as it may, it is interesting that such colorful (and preposterous) ethnographic motifs were being recycled at least eight centuries after their first appearance and that they were being applied to a different people, as if the world contained a limited number of types and it was only a matter of matching up "new" peoples with ancient types (and even names). We will confront this issue in a later section on the Pechenegs, who were seen as interchangeable with the Cumans and were also bestialized in Byzantine writing, both historiographical and rhetorical. The persistence of such images since late antiquity stemmed from the conventions of imperial rhetoric, on the need to construct oppositions between civilized Romans and barbarians who were little better than wild beasts in order to highlight the emperor's role in taming them. We will return to this issue.

Not all mini-ethnographies were so indebted to ancient rhetorical models, as we realize when we read Choniates' account of the Assassins, certainly a new phenomenon on the world stage.

> The Assassins (Χασίσιοι) are a group of people (*genos*) who are said to be so bound to their leader and eager to obey his commands that they would throw themselves from a cliff if he but nodded in that direction, or dance with swords, leap into water, or hurl themselves into the fire. The leaders of the Assassins send them out to kill people they want dead. They approach these men as if they were friendly to their cause, or claiming to have some business with them, or pretending that they are envoys from some other nation, and then strike them many times with their daggers and kill them as enemies of their lords, never letting the difficulty of the deed even enter their mind, nor the possibility that they themselves might be killed and not bring about the other man's death.[79]

In analyzing this passage, it would be useful to compare it to another, roughly contemporary one. The sect drew the attention of a Byzantine traveler to the Holy Land who wrote after the death of Manuel I, one Ioannes "Phokas" (though this surname is an error: his name was Doukas). His account is a set of *ekphraseis* of cities and religiously significant monuments from which the *people* have more or less been omitted, so there is no question of ethnography. The major exception to this pattern are the Assassins (Χασύσιοι) near Tripolis.

> They are a Saracen nation (*ethnos*) but neither Christianize nor follow the teachings of Muhammad; instead, they have their own heresy, but do believe in God. Their leader they call God's ambassador, and at his bidding they go out to the rulers of great countries and

cut them down with knives, jumping upon them in a sudden attack and themselves dying in the attack, for they are few and are killed by the many when the deed is done. They believe this is martyrdom and a guarantee of immortality.[80]

Phokas' approach (to use his conventional name) is heresiological, that is, this passage may well have been lifted from a Byzantine manual listing heresies and their doctrines (a genre that was flourishing in the twelfth century). There is an initial concern for classification, and then references to the title of the group's leaders, their practices, and their beliefs about obtaining immortality. Choniates' discussion, by contrast, avoids the religious dimension altogether and is more ethnographic in tone, insofar as it focuses on the astonishing mental state of the group's members and the strange behaviors in which they engage. In modern terms, we could say that where Phokas is defining a *cult* Choniates is discussing a *culture*, though both emphasize its strangeness. It is Phokas, in this instance, who is concerned to define it in terms of preexisting groups, whereas Choniates does not make comparisons or rely on ancient (or stock) motifs to make the new group intelligible.

Beyond these brief accounts, there is possibly only one of medium length in Byzantine historiography that conveys what may be authentic foreign beliefs and traditions.[81] This is a digression on the religious beliefs and practices of the pagan Rus', and is embedded in Leon the Deacon's account of Ioannes Tzimiskes' campaign against them in 971, when he expelled them from the Balkans after hard-fought battles. I argue elsewhere that Leon's account of this campaign is based on a heavily classicizing source whose goal was to glorify the emperor's victories.[82] Part of this text's strategy was to model specific episodes on ancient Greek and Roman history, something that Leon was also inclined to do, mostly by using Homer and Agathias, on whom he even modeled his preface. Thus from a methodological point of view we must be doubly cautious: while the digressions on the Rus' do go back to the original panegyrical source, we cannot with certainty ascribe all their classical notes and associations to that source: they may represent Leon's additions to it. Moreover, any authentic raw data here have already passed through a classicizing filter, but this does not mean that they do not exist. Specifically, after one of the fierce battles before Dorostolon, the Rus', who are here called Skythians or Tauroskythians, come out to collect their dead.

And they collected them in front of the city wall and kindled numerous fires and burned them, after slaughtering on top of them many captives, both men and women, in accordance with their ancestral custom. And they made sacrificial offerings by drowning suckling infants and chickens in the Istros [Danube], plunging them into the rushing waters of the river. For they are said to be addicted to the Hellenic mysteries, and to make sacrifices and libations to the dead in the Hellenic fashion, having been initiated in these things either by their own philosophers, Anacharsis or Zamolxis, or by the comrades of Achilles.[83]

Anacharsis and Zamolxis are linked to the Rus' via the classicizing term that Leon and his source used for them, that is, Skythians. Leon goes on to cite theories that Achilles was also a Skythian banished to Thessaly on account of his cruelty. He (or his source) adduces ethnographic proof of this connection: "the style of his clothing with a brooch, his fighting on foot, his red hair and grey eyes, and his reckless and passionate and cruel temperament" (for the latter, Leon quotes Agamemnon from *Iliad* 1.177): "For the Tauroskythians are still accustomed to settle their disputes with killing and bloodshed. That this people is reckless and warlike and mighty, and attacks all the neighboring people, is attested by many people." He cites Ezekiel among the witnesses, mixing classical with Biblical authorities.

There is much in this account that refers the reader back to classical and Biblical texts. Occasional poetic language (πυρὰς θαμινὰς; τῷ ῥοθίῳ τοῦ ποταμοῦ); links between the Rus' and Achilles based on common ethnographic *indicia* (at the end of the narrative, Leon provides an *ekphrasis* of Svjetoslav's appearance as well); the adducing of ancient and Biblical texts; and the Herodotean borrowings all make this a complex, multi-layered literary-antiquarian digression. The Rus' are partly calqued on Herodotos' Skythians: this emerges from their addiction to Hellenic religion, sacrifice of captives, and instruction by Zamolxis.[84] But does this invalidate the specific information about their practices? This fear was raised already in the nineteenth century in connection with late antique historians such as Prokopios who modeled their narratives on classical authors, often word for word, but it was observed subsequently in closer readings that both subtle and blatant deviations guaranteed the distinctive identity of the contemporary events that they related, and non-classicizing sources confirmed their testimony on key points.[85] The same can be said about this account of Rus' religion. Despite all the classical associations, what is actually reported does not exactly match anything in Herodotos or other classical sources. The closest I know is a passage in Prokopios, though its vocabulary is completely different and was not the likely model here: When the Franks invaded Italy in 538–539, they seized a bridge over the Po and began to sacrifice Gothic women and children and throw their bodies into the river.[86]

A historical study of the information reported by Leon about the Rus' military equipment and human sacrifices has attempted to explain his testimony by using external sources.[87] The conclusion is that his reports are likely to be authentic. Thus we face the same problem that is posed by any ethnographic source, whether ancient or Byzantine: the data have been processed through literary and analytical categories and embellished with associations that make them relevant to the target audience, making extraction difficult. Leon (or his source) has tried to render the Rus' intelligible to his learned readers by modeling them on Herodotos' "Hellenizing" Skythians and the "wrathful" Achilles of the *Iliad*, but at the same time he reports scenes that may have been perfectly authentic and distinctive to Rus' culture. The passage stresses novelty and authenticity and yet still remains anchored in familiar typologies and allusions. In this it was following the ancient ethnographic tradition, which did the same.

The same is true of Leon's description of the beliefs of the Rus' regarding the afterworld, which follow a few pages later. At a war council, they decide to die fighting rather than surrender, but this puts them in a bind. Leon explains:

> This is also said about the Tauroskythians, that never up until now had they surrendered to the enemy when defeated; but when they lose hope of safety, they drive their swords into their vital parts, and thus kill themselves. And they do this because of the following belief: they say that if they are killed in battle by the enemy, then after their death and the separation of their souls from their bodies they will serve their slayers in Hades. And the Tauroskythians dread such servitude, and, hating to wait upon those who have killed them, inflict death upon themselves with their own hands. Such is the belief that prevails among them.[88]

Whatever we make of this, it is not borrowed from any surviving classical source, nor on the other hand has any independent evidence yet been found to confirm it.[89]

This sudden burst of ethnography can be explained only in the context of the classicizing ambitions (both Roman and Herodotean) of its original author. The goal of that lost text was to glorify the wars of Tzimiskes, and its culmination was the triumph that the emperor celebrated in Constantinople upon his return. The Rus' in this text, like Robert and Bohemond in Anna's *Alexiad*, are set up in such detail only to enhance the victor's glory. That is why this Hellenic material can be related in so dispassionate a way: it magnifies the victory over the forces of pagan savagery. But it also seems that this text did not reflect a trend or set a new one in this regard. For example, Theodosios the Deacon's highly classicizing and panegyrical poem on the *Capture of Crete* (of the early 960s) reveals almost nothing regarding the culture and beliefs of the Arabs defeated by Nikephoros Phokas. It is possible that the original source Leon was using for the campaign of 971 was written as a Tzimiskean "response" to Theodosios' poem. Be that as it may, we may suspect that it was easier to discuss the pagan rites of the Rus' than to touch the many thorny issues raised by Islam. As we saw,[90] Leon says almost nothing about Islam in his lengthy accounts of Byzantine wars against Arabs.

Finally, it is in this brief burst of classical ethnography that we obtain the most detailed description of a foreign ruler in Byzantine literature since the sixth century, one that would not be rivaled until Anna's character portraits of Robert and Bohemond.[91] Svjetoslav, the ruler of the Rus', almost emerges as a character, albeit in the shadow of his victor, Tzimiskes. His actions during the war reveal a bellicose and savage but not dishonorable character, and a detailed *ekphrasis* of his barbarian appearance is given at the end, when he agrees to terms.[92] This is balanced by the heroic *ekphrasis* of Tzimiskes himself at the beginning of the account of his reign.[93] I suspect that this juxtaposition and the appearance of the conquered Svjetoslav at the end derives from the symbolism of the Roman triumph, or at least of ancient descriptions of the triumph that survived in Byzantium, which prominently featured the defeated king in their representation of victory.[94] Leon's source reflects this triumphal outlook, which culminates in Tzimiskes' entry into Constantinople, modeled word for word on the triumph of Camillus in Plutarch.[95] In this context, the detailed description of Svjetoslav's regalia is basically a literary surrogate for the parade of such items in the Roman triumph (Svjetoslav was not captured, and so not paraded).[96] Captives were still paraded in Byzantine triumphs (in that of Tzimiskes, it was the Bulgarian royal family).[97] The text is here making up for the absence of the vanquished enemy ruler. So it is not only the ethnographic material that has been processed through literary filters.

At any rate, it was the political need to cast the emperor in the guise of a glorious Roman hero and to honor him with a military narrative in the classical tradition that produced the best ethnographic digressions in Byzantine literature.

The Classicism of Byzantine Ethnography:
A Partial Rehabilitation

No discussion of Byzantine ethnography can avoid the topic of the classicizing tendency of its writers to give ancient ethnonyms to contemporary barbarian peoples (for example, "Skythian," "Celt," and "Persian"), a habit that we have observed often and that has caused concern among modern historians, eliciting generally negative commentary. In fact, more than the Byzantine practice itself it is this negative modern reaction, which consists often of condescending comments rather than analysis, that calls for discussion. Byzantine classicism is conventionally filed under "imitation," if not "affectation," and is believed to have had detrimental effects on the Byzantines' ability to perceive and discuss reality. Ancient ethnonyms and their semantic baggage displaced contemporary names that might have given narratives more historical "authenticity," so classicism has been accused of functioning as a "literary atavism" or "distorting mirror" of reality. Moreover, the use of ancient names creates confusion: in the twelfth century, does "Skythian" mean "Pecheneg" or "Cuman"? "Turk" was used for people in Central Asia, the Near East, and eastern Europe (i.e., Hungarians). The use of these labels is noted disapprovingly by many scholars, though usually in passing, without going beyond what have by now become the stereotypical references to "imitation."[98]

I will argue that the Byzantines' use of ancient ethnonyms, even of ethnographic "types," was far less problematic than many scholars assume. It is the modern accusations that are drenched in ideology, rely on double standards, miss Byzantine cues that signal onomastic "translations," and fail to make crucial distinctions between generic and specific ethnonyms and between classical and late antique prototypes.

"Distortion," for starters, is an explosive word to throw around. It implies that an objective, nondistorted system of representation is available, or might have been available in late antiquity and Byzantium, yet no scholar has provided such a system, whether relating to ethnographic or any other kind of knowledge. We certainly need to expose and overcome the (usually unspoken) assumption that groups have a "true" name and that classicism either distorts it or obscures it behind an alien substitute.[99] There probably does not exist today, even among the universally recognized nations of the world, a single group that is called the same thing by all others, and there are many whose official names abroad are utterly different from what they call themselves. In some cases, for example, Greece, the national name (Hellenes) is used only by the nation itself and no one else. The many names by which the German nation is known today had separate historical trajectories and ideological connotations before entering "official" use. None of them were ever "objective" or "undistorted" prior to that point. Our task is to understand those histories and the politics they reflect, not to defend a magical ("true-name") theory of language.

Modern historical scholarship, far from being undistorted, is just as guilty of using generalized ethnic categories (e.g., "Turkic," "Slavic," "Germanic") that are often not based on any primary sources at all and do not correspond to how the historical people in question viewed themselves, assuming that they had coherent group identities in the first place, as was not always the case. So whereas the Byzantines' "distorting" labels came from classical and late antique texts, modern distorting labels are derived from racial and national ideologies, or "innocently" confuse historical linguistics with cultural identity.[100] Some of these modern labels have recently been questioned and even undermined (especially the "Germanic" one), but more remains to be done. Moreover, Byzantinists are vulnerable to the charge of hypocrisy on this front, as they have systematically occluded and even flatly denied the Roman identity of the Byzantines, which is loudly proclaimed in the primary evidence and which we all now recognize the "Byzantines" positively claimed for themselves. These so-called Byzantines knew exactly who they were (Romans) and what they wanted to be called, yet they are the one medieval people whose own name modern historians refuse to use. In fact, the modern term "Byzantine" is itself a species of classicism, in that it links the entire culture to the *Greek* city on the Bosporos rather than to its primary *Roman* dimension (Constantinople being "New Rome").[101] The existence of a Greek-speaking, Orthodox living Roman empire has not sat well with western ideologies (at least since the ninth century), and the basis of Byzantine civilization has been systematically denied and distorted so as not to offend these sensibilities. Far from resisting this ideological distortion, many modern Byzantinists have in fact led the charge. Tu quoque, then.

Byzantine classicism had its political overtones, which we will consider below, but it was fundamentally a literary phenomenon. Cyril Mango's famous paper on "Byzantine Literature as a Distorting Mirror" suggests that courses in Greek composition may have unintentionally had a harmful influence in shaping modern perceptions of Byzantine classicism. He found that newspaper articles sound strange when turned into Attic prose and concluded that the Byzantines must have distorted the reality—the "flavor," as he called it—of their world by writing in that register and adopting its conventions, including ethnonyms.[102] Setting aside the question of whether it is possible to understand anything about the workings of the world today through newspapers, given the high level of both internalized and cynical distortion they purvey, it is important to recognize that any society that has newspapers has also undergone transformations affecting the totality of its life and language such as were not imaginable from either an ancient or a Byzantine standpoint. The changes that even Christianity introduced to the ancient world were slight by comparison. The difference between warfare in the first century and warfare in the tenth is almost zero when both are compared to that of the twentieth. It has yet to be proved that Attic Greek, enhanced by the Christian vocabulary that middle Byzantine writers could also draw upon, ever produced *that* level of distortion when used to describe the events of, say, the tenth century. As Peter Brown wrote about emperor Julian,

> no discontinuity even remotely like that to which a modern, post-industrial society can be exposed had come between the men of the fourth century and their models. It is only with the nineteenth century that the teaching of the classics finally reached that degree of preciosity and inapplicability to the present that we judge so harshly in fourth-century men. . . . [We have become] less certain that it is not we who have distorted those parts of reality that the old mirror continued to reflect none too badly.[103]

For that matter, it has yet to be proved that an elevated Attic register was not at least as adequate for representing Byzantine realities as modern English is, about which scholars do not seem to have doubts.

Also, the case for distortion must offer a modicum of *proof.* Too often it is just assumed that classicism entails distortion and that classicizing Byzantine historians were out of touch with the world in which they lived. A confluence of distinctively modern ideologies has created a field receptive to such assertions and has set an astonishingly low threshold of proof for what is a serious charge. These ideologies include the modern bias in favor of vernacular over learned, "elite" languages; the view that the "flavor" of a period is to be found in its *Volk* and in what Mango calls "low-brow" elements; the aesthetics of "authenticity," which is the product of modern alienation; and skepticism about the relevance of transhistorical, "classical" concepts, reinforced by a heightened awareness of periodization. These factors shape modern instincts, but it is time to ask for real proof: not only must independent evidence be provided, but so must methodologically grounded arguments for why modern constructs of "authenticity" are to be preferred over "artificial" classical terms. It should go without saying that rhetorically to invoke "flavor" is insufficient.[104]

We should contextualize and try to understand the literary phenomenon in question, not disparage it. It is crucial to emphasize that this classicism was a *literary* phenomenon: it was not a feature of how all Byzantines perceived their world at all times, or the conceptual world in which the state planned its foreign policy, but a function of how *some* authors *sometimes* chose to represent their world in writing. Literary representation does not always reflect the sum total of one's understanding of the world, just as the scarcity of literary ethnography did not accurately reflect the limits of the Byzantines' knowledge of foreign peoples. Classicism had to do with the choices that some authors made when they wrote narrative texts that, they hoped, would pass the test of time. Emulating classical texts was a sensible strategy, for the language of those texts was rightly seen as one of the keys to their transhistorical success.

The literary issue at stake, whether we call it classicism, Atticism, or imitation, is too broad in its implications to be discussed fully here. It cuts to the heart of literary production in Byzantium, an activity that deliberately operated along a spectrum of linguistic registers that were more or less removed from spoken Greek. It was not only foreign ethnonyms that were recast in this way but, ideally, almost every aspect of a writer's vocabulary, syntax, and style. So let us not be naïve, or unfair. In most modern languages, formal prose deviates from the vernacular, though the cultural nuances, historical roots, and linguistic aspects of this practice vary. Modern scholars also distance themselves from the vocabulary of popular culture by placing quotation marks around words with which they are otherwise perfectly familiar and which they use without trouble in their everyday speech. But for the purpose of maintaining a formal authorial stance, they must alienate themselves from these words in print.[105] The jargon of popular culture is thereby marked off. We can imagine Byzantine writers doing the same, with a notional cut-off point somewhere in the Hellenistic or Roman imperial era.

The ability of Greek to operate on multiple registers should not put off users of modern English. English is a composite language, and formal prose often tends to run toward the vocabulary derived from Latin and French rather than from Old English, just as Byzantine writers shunned foreign or "new" words. They said "Persian" and "Skythian" for roughly the same reasons that a chief of police today, speaking before the cameras, will say "the adolescents who had effectuated forcible entry into the domicile were apprehended" rather than "we caught the kids who broke into the house"[106]—two sentences that mean exactly the same thing. Like Greek in Byzantium, but for different historical reasons, English is a language that can be translated into (other versions of) itself. Robert Browning drew attention to how the *De administrando imperio*, a text that self-consciously eschews Attic Greek, translates the Khazar city name Sarkel as ἄσπρον ὁσπίτιον, whereas the classicizing Theophanes Continuatus translates it as λευκὸν οἴκημα, which mean the same thing ("White House") but in different stylistic registers.[107] Ethnonyms were thus subject to the same diglossia that characterized the Greek language as a whole (and had, in fact, long characterized it already in various forms).[108] Byzantine scholars even compiled lists of places that had changed their names to enable equivalence (or translation) between contemporary and classical times.[109] The question before us is precisely how foreign names were translated into Greek, taking "translation" in the broad sense of "rendered intelligible." The problem of classicism, I will argue, has been greatly overblown. I will offer four qualifications to the "distortion" thesis and then a more general discussion.

First, onomastic classicism as a form of translation never fully displaced the use of contemporary names, even in authors who preferred classical versions. This is confirmed by the lists in Gyula Moravcsik's *Byzantinoturcica: Sprachreste der Türkvölker in den byzantinischen Quellen*. The contemporary form was typically used as a gloss on the first mention of the classical one. Traianos *patrikios* (ca. 700 A.D.) explained that his Skythians were called Goths "in the local language."[110] In one place, Attaleiates refers to "Skythians, popularly called Pechenegs."[111] But he does not offer translations consistently. His "Sauromatai of the West" are the Hungarians, but he does not say so.[112] And it is not clear who his "Myrmidons" in the north are (we will return to them below). Overall, this is a mixed picture. The more "generic" the ancient name (e.g., Skythian), the more likely it was to be glossed. Choniates, to take another author, uses both "Paiones" and "Oungroi" for the Hungarians in his *History*; in his orations, which classicize more consistently, he calls the Cumans "Skythians," but on one occasion he uses their contemporary name.[113] So even composition in the highest register did not exclude barbarian names. Therefore, we should not take Anna's prissy classicism as the norm, as is often done. She famously refused to give all the names of the leaders of the First Crusade because the list was too long (a legitimate problem) and because their barbaric sound offended against her taste.[114] But this was not "merely" a literary choice. It was political: she probably meant to insult them. Elsewhere she cites a barbarian place-name but apologizes for it, invoking the precedent set by Homer in her defense.[115] Otherwise, the *Alexiad* is full of barbarian names and histories, so even her occasional fussing over purity was atypical, and probably meant to be dismissive in an ad hoc way. At the opposite end of the spectrum lies the *De administrando imperio*, which disavows high-style Atticism and opts for what it calls a vernacular idiom (διὰ κοινῆς καὶ καθωμιλημένης).[116] It is no coincidence that this text has the greatest density of barbarian names and avoids classicizing ethnonyms for the purpose of clarity. Other Byzantine texts lie between these two poles; there was not a single standard and no one was completely allergic to contemporary forms.

Second, advocates of "distortion" fail to distinguish between different periods of literary classicism and have treated it as a straitjacket, when in fact it hardly restricted specific, even idiosyncratic authorial goals. Having translated many authors who all wrote in the most elevated register, I can say that each has a distinctive style and voice, even those who were writing in the same period (though it is difficult to render those differences in English). We cannot take Prokopios as representative of the genre of historiography from late antiquity to the Fall of Constantinople in 1453, as is often done; his style is markedly different even from that of his first successor Agathias. Lumping all authors and periods together under one label distorts their significant deviations and points of emphasis. Psellos, Attaleiates, and Choniates can be seen, when read closely, to have been pursuing different projects. Their prose is dissimilar.

Third, many "classicizing" ethnonyms were not "classical" at all, but late antique. The term "Hun," for example, was a common ethnographic label in late antiquity and Byzantium, but it was not classical: it appeared in the late fourth century, in Greek really after 400 A.D. The Goths, Franks, Lombards, and Gepids that populate the pages of Prokopios (and are called by those names) were also not known in classical antiquity. Herodotos would not have recognized most of the peoples of this world, and their names continued in use in the middle period. "Turk" was another "generic" ethnonym used widely in the middle period for a variety of groups, but it is first attested only after the middle of the sixth century. The Byzantines also had collective terms for the people of western Europe that were either not classical or were not used in their classical senses (Frank, Latin, and Italian). Their use was governed by the particular configuration of cultural and political power in the medieval West, at least as that was perceived by the Byzantines, and owed nothing to classical precedents.[117] It was when they were called "Celts" that classical paradigms came into play (see below), but this was rare. In other words, the Byzantines' ethnonymy was not governed exclusively by classical paradigms but also by those that emerged in late antiquity, when the ethnic map of the ancient world began to change into that of the Middle Ages.

Fourth, the use of classical ethnonyms rarely makes it impossible to figure out who is being meant, though some historians profess to be more confused by this practice than others.[118] At this point we must draw a distinction between "generic" ethnonyms such as Skythian, Hun, and even Persian that were used simultaneously for different groups, and one-to-one correspondences between ancient and new peoples, for example, Hungarians as "Paionians" (also as "Oungroi" and "Ounnoi"), Serbs as "Triballoi" (also as "Serboi"), and Bulgarians as "Mysioi." In the case of ancient names "reserved" for one modern people, there is no confusion except in the case of correspondences that did not catch on and so are attested in only a few sources (e.g., "Myrmidons" in Attaleiates for the Rus', or some specific subgroup of the Rus').[119] It can be argued that one-to-one correspondences do not really fall under the category of distortion at all. There were no medieval treaties or conventions regulating what each people or state was to be called, and modern languages use many terms for the same countries. For example, "Germany" can be translated into *Deutschland* or *Allemagne*. We will make a great stride when we simply accept that in the neoclassical language of Byzantine prose Hungary was "Paionia." This is "translation" rather than "distortion."

A more interesting question concerns the politics behind these names, especially the nongeneric ones. Paul Stephenson has proposed that some of these names offered specific advantages for imperial propaganda. By calling Balkan peoples "Dalmatians," "Mysians," and the like, especially in the context of imperial victory, Byzantine writers reinscribed contemporary relationships onto the ethnic map of the early Roman empire—or rather, more significantly, onto the map of the empire's *provinces*—thus legitimizing their (re)incorporation after conquest.[120] Cast as former imperial provinces, they were then "naturally" seen as belonging to the empire. This legitimized their conquest and endowed the empire with an aura of continuity, even immutability, effacing the turbulent centuries in between. This also explains why imperial panegyrics use classical ethnonyms more often and consistently than historiography does. Some Byzantines could be explicit about the matter and directly state that the Bulgarians and others were basically interlopers on Roman land.[121]

A similar purpose was served by the digressions in the *History* of Leon the Deacon on the ancient histories of Adrianople and Dorostolon, both Balkan cities on the route of emperor Tzimiskes in 971. These histories, which were partly fictitious, tied them to the imperial Roman past and so, especially in the case of Dorostolon, legitimized the conquest of Bulgarian territory by the emperor.[122] The Byzantines exploited a range of usable imperial pasts to promote a variety of literary and imperial goals.

As for the generic classical ethnonyms, they encoded broad ethnographic categories in addition to having a geographic component. This was especially true in the case of the "Skythians," a label that was attached to a series of peoples in succession and sometimes to more than one simultaneously. The ultimate point of reference was the people described in the fourth book of Herodotos, but their name was associated with specific cultural traits already by late antiquity. These traits included nomadism, lightly armored and flexible cavalry warfare, and an origin north of the Black Sea or the Danube. Goths, Huns, Avars, Turks, Bulgars, Hungarians, Pechenegs, Cumans, and others were all called Skythians at one time or another.[123] The image did not apply well to the Goths at the end of the fourth century, though some authors tried it out on them, but it did work spectacularly well for their great enemy, the Huns. At any given time it is usually clear who the "Skythians" *du jour* were. The period of greatest confusion was ca. 1100, with the Pechenegs and Cumans, who did not appear all that different from each other. Anna knew they spoke the same language,[124] and, besides, the two groups were internally complex and fluid in membership.[125] A switch from one confederacy to the other may well have been regarded from a Byzantine point of view as an internal "Skythian" matter.

As the Byzantines never sought to clarify or investigate the economy and society associated with nomadism of the Skythian type,[126] and as the military customs of the people in question varied (beyond the fact that they appeared to be "on the move"), the most important criterion in practice was probably, in the end, geographic. "Newer" people inherited the traits and also the generic name of the people who had previously lived in or ruled over those lands, going back to Herodotos' Skythians. In this sense geography could govern ethnography.[127] The principle is nicely stated by Prokopios in his digression on the Black Sea: "all nations which have lived in those regions have been called Skythian in general, some of them with the added name Sauromatai, Melanchlainoi, or something else."[128] If we jump ahead half a millennium, we find that the Rus', who lived in that general area, were called Skythians but simultaneously also Kimmerians, Tauroskythians, and other names, even though the "nomadic" model did not fit them well.[129] In this sense geography trumped ethnography. Another example of geographic determinism in the assignment of names occurs in Attaleiates, who calls the Seljuk Turks "Nephthalitai Huns,"[130] probably because they came from roughly the same place as the Ephthalitai Huns of late antiquity, described by Prokopios. But because they conquered Persia, he also then calls them Persians, and subsequently glosses both terms (Huns and Persians) as those "who are now called Turks."[131]

For reasons we will examine in the next section, "Skythian" was the most important generic ethnonym in the Byzantine repertoire, as it encoded the opposite of the cultural values of the Roman elite and their imperial ideology. It was not, then, simply a matter of geography: there was definitely a perception that the inhabitants of what we call Central Asia were nomadic, regardless whether that notoriously complex term fit them well or not. If we jump ahead another half-millennium, we read in Laonikos Chalkokondyles, the Byzantine Herodotos, that "the name Skythian itself designates anyone who adheres to the nomadic lifestyle."[132] By then, of course, the Mongols had reaffirmed the validity and utility of the model.

"Skythian" was not the only ancient ethnonym with cultural or moral baggage. Consider the "Celts," which is what Anna (among others) called the western Europeans (also "Latins" and "Franks"). There was in antiquity a well-developed tradition of Celtic ethnography, focusing on their large stature, blond features, fearlessness in battle, and the warrior-chieftain relationship.[133] Many of these Celtic qualities reemerge in Anna's Latins, but I will focus here on only one aspect of the comparison. On a few occasions, Anna found herself in the awkward position of having to defend her father's cautious and cunning military strategy, which often involved running away from the field of battle, against the values of the impetuous and even reckless Latin knights, who charged head-on with no fear of the enemy. Anna adapted Aristotle's ethical theory of the mean in order to defend her father. True courage, she argued, lies between recklessness on the one hand and coward-ice on the other.[134] This gave substance to her boast in the preface of the *Alexiad* that she knew the works of Plato and Aristotle. She patronized a cir-cle of philosophers from whom she commissioned commentaries on treatises of Aristotle that had not been much discussed in antiquity, including the *Ethics*.[135] And there we find the connection: in the *Ethics* Aristotle had cited the Celts as a people who fear nothing.[136] Anna's image of Robert's martial wife Gaïta, who accompanied him on campaign, wore armor, and, "like an-other Pallas," rallied the men when they had been routed, also resonates with classical images of manly Celtic women.[137] This is yet another illustration of how classical ethnography provided a series of usable types that could be projected onto the present in order to advance specific political arguments, while still maintaining a modicum of geographical consistency and plausi-bility.

In sum, a variety of literary nuances and political-ideological motives lay behind the names that the Byzantines used for foreign peoples. It is tempting to treat their use of classical ethnonyms as a more or less coherent system of signs which valorized contemporary groups on the basis of ancient tropes and biases. Thus "Skythians," "Celts," "Persians," and others represented fixed moral and political types—here nomads, blond brawny fighters, and Orien-tal despots respectively. These types were deployed to "classify," organize, and so interpret the contemporary world-system as it was perceived by educated Byzantines. To a degree this was true, but not for the majority of cases. The Byzantines were hardly averse to using vernacular contemporary ethnonyms. The terms that they used for Balkan groups, especially in the twelfth cen-tury, projected an ideology not so much of moral and political classification as of geographical ownership, that is, in relation to the former provinces and conquests of the Roman empire. Also, some of the terms used most often—Franks, Huns, and Turks—were not classical at all but late antique, referring to groups with whose descendants the Byzantines were still coping. When used in the middle Byzantine period, "Hun" seems to have been more or less interchangeable with "Skythian." The two other terms, Frank and Turk, were not generic types that could be applied to other peoples: they were used for

Franks and Turks! Moreover, those two ethnonyms were also "vernacular," in the sense that this is what most Byzantines and many others actually called these groups outside the classicizing conventions of their literature. (It is still unclear why they called the Hungarians "Turks.")[138] The use of these names was therefore not a form of classicism, regardless of the fact that the names, like the peoples they designated, may have been old by ca. 950. So was the name of the Romans, which the Byzantines claimed.

Therefore, truly classicizing vocabulary was limited to the terms Skythian, Persian, and Celt, though the last two were used rarely. It also included other ethnonyms such as Triballoi and Illyrians, geographically restricted to the empire's former Balkan provinces. One could argue that all of these terms served to highlight the cultural superiority and even political supremacy of the Romans over whatever foreigners were designated by them. In the following section, we will examine how "Skythian" in particular, by far the most common of the three, was used to highlight Roman imperial superiority. Over the centuries, the Byzantines put more effort into defining themselves vis-à-vis the nomad than the Celt or the oriental despot. Perhaps the former was geographically too distant while the latter was too close, politically speaking. The concept of the Persian, in fact, illustrates the complexity of middle-Byzantine classicism, along the lines of the discussion so far. It is an appropriate case study with which to close.

Contrary to what is often stated, the Byzantines after the seventh century did not normally call the Arabs "Persians" or "Medes." They called them mostly Saracens or Arabs.[139] The people they called Persians in the ninth century were in fact Persians, survivors of the failed Khurramite revolt against the Caliphate who sought refuge in the empire.[140] There was little classicism in this usage, though the romantic tales that the Byzantines told about them were based on classical stereotypes about Persian culture, in this case their penchant for astrology.[141] Before the arrival of the Seljuks, then, the term was reserved for the ancient Persians or for contemporary peoples and states whose rulers were Iranian. The Seljuks, when they arrived on the scene, were called Turks and also Persians, both of which were historically appropriate, but also Huns.[142] Those of them who raided Asia Minor they called Turks rather than Persians, but that changed in the twelfth century when they established permanent states there. It is really only among the writers of the twelfth and early thirteenth centuries that the term "Persian" was used to refer to enemies of the empire in a way that evoked ancient stereotypes about

Persia. It was also at this same time that those writers were gradually coming to identify as much with ancient Greece as ancient Rome, making it convenient to have a Persian enemy. Theodoros Prodromos could thereby refer to the attacks of the new Xerxes against "our Greece."[143] Even so, there was no discussion of the culture and politics of these new "Persians." They were merely a barbaric threat, a foil for the more civilized Graeco-Roman culture they had displaced. It was only in the case of "Skythians" that Byzantine authors discussed the internal constitution of foreign cultures, and then only to promote the propaganda of their own court. To their image we can now turn.

The Pechenegs in the Eleventh Century: The Politics of the Skythian Image

Scholars of ancient ethnography recognize that the way in which a culture talks about others is intimately related to the way in which it perceives itself or, rather, the ideal categories under which it wants to perceive itself. Polar oppositions, such as *Greek and barbarian*, *Roman and barbarian*, and *Christian and pagan*, were driven by ideal images and were as much about defining the first term indirectly and policing its borders as they were about defining the second by exclusion. Some authors, for example Herodotos and Prokopios, talked about foreign cultures in ways that were deeply enmeshed in contemporary debates about the nature of their own societies and aimed less to impart actual information about outsiders. The "other" was here (partly) a rhetorical foil, a strategy for talking about the "self."[144]

In a previous chapter I argued that some late antique historians (Priskos, Prokopios, and Agathias) used digressions on foreign peoples to reflect critically on Roman society, but critical reflection was only one mode of the instrumental use of the "other" in historical literature. The barbarian could, alternately, be demonized or dehumanized in order to highlight Roman values by contrast, a trope typically found in imperial panegyrics. Whether the emperor destroyed the beasts or defeated, "civilized," and converted them, the rhetorical point was the same, to highlight the superiority of Rome. In the present section, I examine this type of "ethnography" by focusing on the image of the Pechenegs in the eleventh century, when they came into military conflict with the empire. My goal will not be to provide yet another typology of images in Byzantine rhetoric. I will, rather, propose a revised understanding of Byzantine identity and ideology, specifically that the Byzantines did not have an ecumenical Christian outlook; they treated the rhetoric of Christianization with cynicism and even opportunism; and, more importantly, conversion was never sufficient to penetrate the ideological barrier between *Romans and barbarians* that I argue was fundamental to the Byzantine outlook. This thesis obviously cannot be argued in full here, but a comparison of how Byzantine writers discussed *pagan* barbarians and *Christian* barbarians, and the moment of transition between the two, is highly illuminating and paves the way for a new understanding of Byzantine ideology. In fact, the modern fiction of "Christian ecumenism" is generally collapsing— the medieval evidence was never there to support it—and with it will fall associated modern constructs such as that of the "Byzantine Commonwealth."

I begin with Psellos' digression on the Pechenegs, the only ethnography written by this multitalented writer,[145] because, while still subtle in its language, it is uncomplicated from the standpoint of the problems identified above. In fact, we can analyze this digression precisely in terms of ethnographic subgenres we have already identified. It begins with a "briefing" on their geographical movements and relations with neighboring peoples (the "Getai") to the point of contact with the Roman border. He then discusses their tactics and weapons, as if he were writing an entry for an updated *Taktika* (in fact, Psellos boasts elsewhere of his familiarity with military manuals, and even compiled one of his own).[146] He presents them as so primitive that one wonders why they posed such a threat to the imperial armies. It is worth quoting his description of their behavior once their ranks are broken in battle, since this assimilates their way of life to that of wild animals.

> they flee in disorder and scatter, each in a different direction. One throws himself into a river and either swims away or sinks, swirling in the whirlpools. Another eludes the attention of his pursuers by running into a deep forest, and the others likewise in other ways. And while all of them disperse in this way, they later meet up again, one coming down from a mountain, another up from a gully, still another from a river, and others randomly assemble from other places. When they are thirsty, if they come across a spring or river, they immediately throw themselves down and lap it up [λάπτουσιν], but if not, they dismount from their horses and begin to drink their blood, opening up their veins with a knife. In this way they overcome their thirst, using blood in the place of water. Then they carve

up the fattest of their horses and start a fire with whatever twigs they happen to find nearby. They barely heat up the dismembered limbs of the horse and devour them (λαφύσσουσι) while they are still dripping with blood and gore. Restoring their strength in this way, they return to their original lairs (καλιάς), and they burrow like snakes in deep gullies and steep cliffs, which they use as protective walls.

Psellos concludes by stressing that they do not honor agreements, regardless of the oaths that they have given, recognize no god, and "believe that death is the end of all existence." They were, in other words, as far from being Christians as possible. The contemporary significance of this pointed statement will emerge in the discussion below.

The purpose of this digression in the *Chronographia* is to showcase the martial qualities of emperor Isaakios Komnenos (1057–1059), whom Psellos, as part of the political argument of his work, portrays positively, at least on the military side.[147] Psellos was not primarily interested in exploring the culture of a foreign people but only in creating an image of utter savagery for the emperor to overcome. There was, of course, more than one way this could be done. We saw how Leon the Deacon (or his source) deployed the modes of Herodotean ethnography to present the heathen religion of the Rus' defeated by Tzimiskes. But Psellos does not report distinctive beliefs and practices. In what can only be called a pure rhetorical artifice, he dehumanizes the enemy by reducing them to the level of beasts, much as we see in the digressions on the Huns and Cumans in Ammianus and Choniates.[148] The imagery of natural habitats and settings, and the suggestive language used to describe their eating and drinking, insinuate that the Pechenegs not only live like animals, but are integrated into the natural world. Psellos need not have conducted any research or ever seen a Pecheneg to create this image. Moreover, by focusing his attention on what the Pechenegs do when they disperse to their lairs, Psellos manages to divert attention away from the fact that Isaakios did not conclusively defeat them, and provides an implicit apologia for his inability to do so. This prevents the reader from witnessing the transformation of savage barbarism by the civilizing power of the Christian Roman empire. But the rhetoric of precisely such a transformation lurks directly beneath the surface of Psellos' account; in fact, his ethnography of the Pechenegs was written against the background of precisely such an account, produced by one of Psellos' closest associates, Ioannes Mauropous.

The reign of Isaakios was not the first time that the Pechenegs had crossed the Danube and raided Roman territory. That had happened in the late 1040s, under Konstantinos IX Monomachos, though Psellos says nothing about those events, as after the revolt of Leon Tornikes (1047) his narrative focuses on the personalities of the court. In 1047, however, Mauropous had written an oration prematurely celebrating the conversion to Christianity of some Pecheneg leaders defeated in the initial phases of the conflict. This oration presents two "ideal" types, the first of pagan barbarian nature in its beastly form, followed by its redemption through the acceptance of Christ and the transformative agency of imperial benevolence (in fact, God and emperor are blurred in this passage from a grammatical point of view).[149]

> Who are these foreign people with the alien language, and where are they from? And who managed, against all expectation, to so tame their strange visages, beastly souls, and weird appearance, granting them more humanity and transforming them utterly? [presumably Konstantinos IX] Who brought this nation (*laos*) to the Lord, which formerly did not know Him? Who brought the enemies of God and the emperor into the Church and into the City? I must say some brief words about them. They were a faithless people, as you all know, an irreverent and lawless people, Skythians by race, nomads in their lifestyle, beastly in manner, abominable and foul in life and habits. One might say that they were not worthy of anything different, for they knew not reason, nor law or religion; they were organized into no kind of civil polity (*politeia*), were joined together by no bounds of solidarity. They inflicted evils upon the land by their sudden raids.

This archetypal picture, basically the same as that presented by Psellos fifteen years later, gives way to another, the transition mediated by a narrated encounter with "the armies of the Romans."

> They threw their weapons far from their hands, which they then stretched out pleading for mercy, and, in their barbarian and unintelligible voices, invoked compassion from the victor. And the latter responded so quickly to their plea and dealt with them so much better than could ever have been hoped that they now stand beside us [the oration was written in the expectation that their leaders would be

present at the court for its delivery, literally standing by the orator],
a miracle to those who behold it, having been transformed into tame
human beings where they were once like wild beasts, converted
from their previous ugliness and wickedness to their present cheer-
fulness and grace. But the brightest and greatest part of this striking
change is that they have become pious and faithful where they were
once impious and faithless, as soon as they partook of the font of
incorruptibility through our god-loving power and God's own love
of humanity. They were marked by him [the emperor or God?] with
the light of grace and received this new appearance and transformation from the Spirit of renewal. . . . And behold this lawless people
has become a holy people (*ethnos hagion*), the impious ones have become a new nation of God (*laos theou neos*). The calling of the nations is active again, the faith has again gained a wondrous increase,
and the Gospel has prevailed to the ends of the earth. Thus does the
emperor leads the atheists to his God, thus does God subject enemies to the emperor.

Passages such as these have been taken to demonstrate that Christianity
enabled the Byzantines to see beyond ethnic differences, with the prerequi-
site, of course, of imperial victory and the enemy's conversion. The faith
could act as a bridge between two alien peoples, though we observe that religious conversion has been fused here with the baggage of ancient Rome's
"civilizing mission." It is not only faith that the Pechenegs received, at least
according to this speech, but also some kind of lawful order too, for Mauropous
refers to their previous lack of a *politeia*, the true mark of culture according to
ancient Greek and Roman writers. After all, "civil polity" is not anything
discussed in Scripture. And if we look at Psellos' ethnography of the Pechenegs, which corresponds to the "before" image in Mauropous' scheme, we
find that "everything happens in a random fashion for them (αὐτόματα
τούτοις πάντα συνέστηκε)," as they believe in nothing and respect no stabi-
lizing conventions.[150] We saw, in our discussion of the Greek late antique
historians, that in the absence of a lawful *politeia*, chance (*tychē*) reigns.[151] So
in Mauropous we still have a *Roman* view of Christian conversion.

Mauropous' celebration is, in the end, only panegyrical boilerplate, a
purely rhetorical transition between two abstract states of being that reveals
little information of use to the historian. The same language had been used
since late antiquity to celebrate the conversion of peoples living along the

periphery.[152] Mauropous was dealing in types here, not history, sociology, or ethnography. Beyond this limitation, historians may wonder whether or to what degree we can rely on the one fact Mauropous does state, that a whole *ethnos* had been converted and had become "a people of God." Just like that?[153] Fortunately, we have other accounts of this event that are more "reality-based," specifically that of Attaleiates. He agrees with Mauropous on the barbarism of the Pechenegs. All they know how to do is raid, he says. "They are loathsome in their food and the other aspects of their life, and they do not abstain from eating foul things." During this raid, however, they were weakened by disease and hardly resisted the imperial armies, surrendering up their leaders. The Romans then deceived themselves into thinking that they had subdued the enemy, but it was not in the latter's nature to be subdued. We note again the deployment of animal imagery in the following exposition.

> When the disease passed, like snakes warmed up by the heat they began to move again with vigor and gave the appearance of possessing a strength that could not easily be subdued. The emperor's plan was to send their leaders back in the hope that they might bring their people (*to homophylon*) to its senses. He had honored them with the rebirth of divine immersion and with the greatest dignities. . . . But then he realized that it is pointless to try "to whiten an Ethiopian,"[154] and that "to benefit a bad man is like feeding a snake": good will is unlikely to elicit gratitude from either one. For when they reached their own *ethnos*, they behaved again in accordance with its customs . . . drenching the Roman land with the blood of the Ausones.[155]

What is going on here? How are we to understand the event in question, or rather these two contrasting texts? Is it true that Mauropous "really believed that barbarians could transcend their nature," whereas Attaleiates and other historians (Psellos and Skylitzes) did not?[156] Is this a difference between a man close to the Church and a secular historian of questionable orthodoxy? Did the latter believe in immutable racial traits whereas the former, perhaps because of his more Christian outlook, saw past them? I believe this is the wrong approach. We are dealing with two genres that have different goals. Mauropous' speech in particular is not a declaration of belief: it is a programmatic statement intended to justify imperial policy. It is unlikely that the orator literally believed his own claims about the total transformation of the Pechenegs. He said only what was demanded by the occasion, specifically a ceremony in the imperial presence that celebrated the baptism of foreign leaders and expressed a hope about its effects. The oration reiterated a set of ideal types, both positive and negative; it did not express anyone's convictions as to the facts. Mauropous, the emperor, and all in attendance *hoped* that things would work out for the better, and the purpose of the speech was to express that hope, but I doubt they realistically expected much. The orator was like a spokesman of a company whose stock is in doubt: he puts on his best face when speaking about it on the news, but what he and everyone else in the real world believe is a different matter. We cannot, as is often done, turn such imperial orations into "ideology" without incurring the risk that the Byzantines were fundamentally deluded (a view that numerous Byzantinists have been willing to embrace). But we have too many cases of writers (among them Psellos, Mauropous' friend) who said one thing in their imperial orations and another in the histories that they subsequently wrote of the same events, contradicting themselves and even admitting that they had lied earlier because that is what one did in imperial orations. Interestingly, in a poem Mauropous tells how he refused to write a history at the instigation of some powerful people because he did not want to lie in order to flatter them: "these things are best kept for panegyrics," he said.[157] It is not that panegyrists did not *want* the emperors whom they praised to embody the virtues that they ascribed to them. There was truth of a general kind behind the praise. Panegyric is a tricky genre that way.[158] The Pecheneg "integration" never occurred in fact; we merely gain a glimpse of it as a theoretical possibility in a speech that was, as we will see, never delivered.

The speech evoked ideals that all agreed on, because its function was to rally support behind imperial policy. But genuine consensus around that policy was not a given. Opponents could invoke a different set of commonly held ideals that justified different policies. Calling the Pechenegs a "new people of God" after a nominal baptism justified emperor Konstantinos IX's decision to settle them on Roman territory by the Danube. As it happens, we know that this speech was not actually delivered due to controversy regarding this policy (a fact that is not always noted by historians who wish to use the speech to reconstruct Byzantine attitudes).[159] Mauropous had to scrap it and quickly write another; he cut all the Pecheneg material but reused other

parts of it word for word. This last-minute change was forced on him by the
emperor, who was facing criticism over his policy from powerful sectors of
the army. *The speech was never delivered because this section of it was regarded
as too controversial.* We do not know what positions its critics invoked to
defend their position. Later that year, the rebel Leon Tornikes tried to depose
Konstantinos and promised the people that "he would increase the territory
of the Roman state by wars and victories against the barbarians,"[160] thus
deploying a different rhetoric that stressed the gap between Romans and
barbarians, even Christian barbarians. Psellos also favored a strong defense
of natural frontiers and wished to keep Romans and barbarians separate.[161]
We are, then, not authorized to treat the Christian *ethnology* of Mauropous'
speech (for it is even less an *ethnography* than Psellos' digression) as embody-
ing any kind of consensus, far less an alleged "Byzantine ideology." We
must be skeptical of its claims, even cynical,[162] for the emperor himself
doubted it would convince the people whose opinions mattered, and feared
that they might even be offended by it. The emperor didn't buy his own
rhetoric.

The savage aspect of the "nomadic Skythian" was, then, a versatile literary construct. It signified the *absence* of cities, agricultural life, lawful society,
a stratified command structure, and civilized customs.[163] In this way, it functioned as the opposite of "Roman," opening up the necessary theoretical space
for imperial intervention, including both the fulfillment of the Romans' civilizing mission and the Church's call to convert the nations (whose success,
Mauropous implied, had waned of late). But its deployment was conditioned
by the specific policies that an author supported at that moment, the "hidden
face" of the texts in question.[164] Mauropous trotted the image out, but with-
drew it when the emperor decided that opponents of his policy would not
buy into the image of a fully converted, civilized Pecheneg. Psellos, who
probably sided with those opponents and who generally wanted emperors to
be more aggressive against barbarians, hammered the failure home by in-
sisting that the Pechenegs were untrustworthy, for they believed in nothing.
He used the same image as Mauropous, but to support an opposite imperial
policy, which he situated, for greater rhetorical effect, under the reign of a
later emperor (in fact, close to the very end of the first version of his *Chronographia*). Like Ammianus, he thereby concluded his history with a call to
action against the "other." Attaleiates seems to have agreed with Psellos that
the Pechenegs were beyond hope (he notes that changing them was like try-

ing to whiten an Ethiopian), but with an interesting, equally opportunistic (in fact ad hominem) deviation we saw above. He presents the Pechenegs as steadfast in their loyalty to the Roman cause at the battle of Mantzikert, against those who accused them of being untrustworthy, but he does so chiefly because he himself was the officer responsible for guaranteeing their loyalty at that moment.[165]

In conclusion, there is little ethnography behind the beastly image of the nomadic Skythian in these eleventh-century texts but much "imperial politics by another means." The image was deployed, modulated, and withdrawn in service to specific agendas. It was a rhetorical mechanism by which Byzantines debated their relationship with a part of the outside world, but always in conjunction with their internal politics. I offer one final observation on the balance of Roman and Christian elements in these debates, to set the stage for the following section. For all his stirring rhetoric of conversion, Mauropous never states or implies that the Pechenegs in his vision had become Romans.[166] They had converted to Orthodox Christianity and accepted the emperor's authority, but he does not regard them as one of "us," not even close. They do not move from being pagan barbarians to being Christian Romans. His speech subtly postulates another category for them: they are "a new people of God." The omission and corresponding invention are significant. They reveal that in a panegyrical speech intended to give full backing to the emperor's acceptance of his newly converted allies, a speech that stresses Christian identity, Mauropous could still not find it within himself to postulate a full affiliation with the Pechenegs. It probably never occurred to him; the notion would have been preposterous. Conversion could move you up one scale (that of *Christians and pagans*) but definitely not the other (that of *Romans and barbarians*). Despite it all, then, the Pechenegs remained barbarians, "friends and allies of the Romans" in the official and archaic terminology of the court.[167] That gap could not easily be crossed. We will see the same devices at work in other discussions of Orthodox barbarians, "people of God" who were also not quite Roman. It was, in fact, not just the fleetingly converted Pechenegs who could be cast as Skythian nomads when the occasion demanded, but some very Christian peoples as well. The image of the savage nomad was flexible enough that it could cross religious boundaries, but it could do so because the Byzantines' primary identity in such contexts was Roman. That is what set them apart from the rest of the world. The fundamental Roman-barbarian polarity continued to operate in Byzantium even when the rhetoric of Christian ecumenism sought to cover it up for the purposes of a propaganda speech.

The Representation of Orthodox Barbarians: The Limits of "Christian Ecumenism" and the "Byzantine Commonwealth"

The Byzantines used multiple, incommensurate polarities for distinguishing between self and other on the contemporary international scene, chiefly *pagan and Christian, Roman and barbarian*, and, in a qualified sense after the twelfth century, *Greek and barbarian*. The signification and moral valence of each polarity varied by occasion, genre, and author, but in general they did not overlap. For example, many barbarians were Christians and even Orthodox, while the Romans of the past, from whom the Byzantines traced the origin of their empire and society, were pagans. So two unsynthesized systems of value were in play. In a striking letter, the scholar-general Nikephoros Ouranos (late tenth century) tried to synthesize them into a single hierarchy, albeit just for the purpose of making a single rhetorical point. He wrote that Christians are supposed to be as morally superior to Greeks as Greeks were to barbarians.[168] But barbarians could be Christian, suggesting that the top and bottom of this hierarchy could meet. And had Christ not dissolved the distinction between Greek and barbarian (or Greek and Jew)? Conflicting schemas were simultaneously operative.

We can imagine how differently a Byzantine might view a foreign people based on which polarity (and hence identity) he was using for the purpose. The Rus', after a certain point, could be regarded favorably as fellow Christians, but from the standpoint of culture they were dismissed as hopelessly barbaric. The Arabs, on the other hand, were "the enemies of Christ" and also of the Roman empire, but grudging respect for their achievements in Greek science could be expressed.[169] Ideally, we should plot each representation of a foreign culture along multiple, changing axes defined by genre and circumstance, but this is not possible for reasons of space, and also because a broader theoretical issue must be dealt with first, relating to how scholars have defined Byzantium's identity and, by extension, its view of foreigners. Byzantium has almost universally been viewed through the prism of its Christian identity rather than its Roman one, and, moreover, its Christian identity has been viewed as inclusive. One reads again and again that anyone could become a "Byzantine" so long as he was Orthodox and "loyal" to the emperor, Byzantium allegedly being, after all, a "multi-ethnic empire." Accordingly, and with a few (albeit notable) exceptions, Byzantinists have denied that the Byzantines "really" had a Roman identity (another way of saying that "it does not matter that the Byzantines almost always called themselves Romans"),[170] and some have argued that Roman just *meant* Christian for them.[171]

I argue that this approach distorts both the Byzantines' view of themselves and their views of others. They had an exclusive sense of identity predicated on their being Romans, not only Christians, and, while it was possible for foreigners to become Byzantines, this process required them to conform to national Roman standards that went beyond the acceptance of Christianity. It was ultimately the Roman dimension that shaped the Byzantines' view of foreign cultures, even of Christian ones. Without that, it is hard to explain why other Orthodox peoples were perceived as foreign by the Byzantines in the first place, and it is impossible to explain why they are commonly represented as beasts no better than heathens. Granted, there is room for nuance, as argued above, especially in rhetorical and institutional sites linked to the Church, which was marginally involved in transnational operations, but by and large there is a large gap between modern theories and Byzantine perceptions, and this section aims to expose it. Moreover, in order to bridge that gap the field has invented a whole repertoire of concepts that have become canonical through sheer repetition, though they have not been subjected to analytical scrutiny. Their weak evidentiary foundation is beginning to tell against them in recent discussions. One of the concepts entangled in this discussion is abstract and religious, while the other is cultural and historical. I am referring, first, to Christian ecumenism or universalism, and second to the notion of the "Byzantine Commonwealth" put forward by Dimitri Obolensky in 1971.[172] In part, the second is a historical manifestation of the first. There is much at stake here, and the ethnography of the Christian "other" is at the heart of the problem. I will first discuss the ethnographic issues and return at the end to the question of ecumenism and the Commonwealth.

Texts can certainly be cited in support of the "ecumenical" outlook, but when they are examined more critically they begin to emit different, less warm signals. For example, the speech on the peace of 927 with the Bulgarians, written probably by Theodoros Daphnopates, invokes Christian universality: "No longer are we called Skythians and barbarians or this and that, but now we are all Christians and the children of God."[173] The Bulgarians

offer an ideal case study, because they began as pagan and barbarian enemies
of the empire; converted to Christianity in the ninth century; remained rivals;
were incorporated into the empire in 1018; and later regained independence
in the 1180s. Yet, as we will see, at no point were they considered Romans or
even cultural equals. As one scholar has noted in a study of Byzantine views
of the Bulgarians, "there is no Byzantine writer who to one degree or another
is not convinced that the barbarians and the peoples speaking other languages stand at a lower level in their cultural development than the Rhomaioi,"
including Christian barbarians.[174] Despite Daphnopates' pious protestations,
the "Skythian" image remained at the forefront of Byzantine perceptions.
What, then, are we to make of his speech? It is useful at this point to recall
our analysis in the previous section of the speech by Mauropous on the peace
with the Pechenegs, specifically how contingent its Christian rhetoric was
upon volatile political circumstances. In fact, it was withdrawn at the last
moment, and our historical sources suggest that it would have been regarded
as hopelessly naïve. Similar considerations limit the value of Daphnopates'
peace speech for reconstructing Byzantine "ideologies."

The Byzantine representation of the Bulgarians consistently stresses their
otherness, throughout the centuries and overriding religious changes. There
was, however, one moment when they tried hard to highlight their common
faith as grounds for peace and reconciliation. That moment was when Symeon,
the king of Bulgaria, seemed to have the advantage in the war. The rhetorical
guns of Christian brotherhood were then brought out. In letters to Symeon
and the archbishop of Bulgaria, the patriarch Nikolaos emphasized that "Romans and Bulgarians" were both "the one people (*laos*) of Christ,"[175] i.e.,
presumably only insofar as they were both Christian, not that they had become one people in all respects, especially those respects that were designated
by what were apparently irreducibly distinct ethnonyms. Baptism has "united
you to the Roman race as sons to fathers."[176] There can be no doubt but that
this was a concerted Byzantine propaganda campaign, and even this insisted
on a hierarchical relationship and not an equal one. At a meeting of the two
rulers, emperor Romanos I appealed to Symeon's faith, in a speech reported
in many chronicles. The speech is but a page long, but it uses the name
"Christians" nine times, an unparalleled and conspicuous density.[177] This
was the context of the speech on the peace by Daphnopates that gestures toward Christian ecumenism. The speech was about reconciliation, so the appropriate rhetoric was trotted out. But the gap between "Romans and
Bulgarians" had not been bridged. In fact, traces of its irreducible difference

are imprinted here as well. Roman exceptionalism lurks behind even the most Christian rhetoric of religious brotherhood. At one point Daphnopates refers to "the nomadic and wagon-dwelling" past of the Bulgarians and reports that Symeon had been told during the war "that it would be abominable for the Romans to accept as emperor anyone who was not a Roman."[178] In an official diplomatic letter to the king, Daphnopates himself had mocked the hollowness of his assumption of the Roman title: "Of which Romans exactly do you claim to be the emperor?"[179] Contrary to what many historians believe, a Roman was not made simply by the fact that he was ruled by someone who claimed to be the emperor of the Romans, but the reverse. It was the national community of the Romans that authorized a leader to call himself the *basileus* of the Romans.[180]

The concept of the barbarous nomadic Skythian was not, then, applicable only to pagan peoples such as the Pechenegs. It could also be brought out to put Christian Bulgarians in their place, as rhetorical need required. The image even hovers above Daphnopates' speech, though his goal was to make concessions in the interest of peace. Nikephoros II Phokas was in a less conciliatory mood when, in 965 or 966, he had the Bulgarian ambassadors slapped in the face and yelled at them, calling them a "wretched and abominable Skythian people" and their king a "leather-gnawing ruler clad in a leather jerkin," among other colorful insults.[181] Some Byzantines even seem to have thought that the Bulgarians had not been converted, at least not properly, until they were conquered by Basileios II in 1018. A bishop was then sent out, says Psellos, to "those formerly nomadic Skythians, later called Bulgarians . . . and he turned that entire *ethnos* toward God,"[182] as if they were still pagans in 1018. Konstantinos VII, or his court writers, called them "opinionated and boastful."[183] Some sources equate entrusting the Christian faith to barbarians with casting pearls before swine.[184] The source of this condescension was not religious. As one scholar put it, "the Bulgarians failed the Roman ethnic identity test."[185] Nor was this a function solely of imperial rhetoric. Byzantine saints' lives—texts written by Romans about other Romans—regularly portray the Bulgarians as a separate and hostile people, "the nomadic *ethnos* of the Skythians," with whom the Romans were perennially at war.[186] One would never realize that they were Christians from these texts. Ultimately, "Orthodox Christian Bulgaria constituted a rival in the Balkans to Byzantium."[187]

Categorical ethnic distinctions persisted after the conquest and then again after Bulgarian independence. Under Basileios II the *genos* of the Bulgarians, says Psellos, became a part of the territory (*epikrateia*) ruled by the Romans, only they were chafing for independence: their *ethnos* wanted rebellion.[188] In the crisis of the 1070s, we are told by Attaleiates that the rebel Basilakes gathered an army of Franks, Romans, Bulgarians, and Arvanites,[189] implying that Bulgarians were not Romans even though they were then a part of the Roman empire. Narrating the rebellion of Petros and Asan in the 1180s, Choniates uses the ethnonyms Vlach, Bulgarian, and Mysian more or less interchangeably but consistently calls them a different *genos* (or *ethnos*) from the Romans; in any case, they were *barbarians* and had their own *patris*.[190] An interminable debate has raged over the exact ethnicity of the rebels and the kingdom that they founded. Almost none of that debate is relevant to the question of the Byzantine view, which is that they were not the same as the Romans: they were a different, always inferior, national group that only happened to share the same faith. From the vantage point of the thirteenth century, Georgios Akropolites presented the Bulgarians as a race conquered by Basileios who later rose up against their Roman rulers and sought independence. For Akropolites they were a different people who spoke a different language.[191]

National differences, or at least their perception by the Byzantines, were resilient. In the debates of 1206, after the fall of the City to the Latin Crusaders, the Byzantine clergy reminded cardinal Benedictus that it would have been easy for them to flee to the "the lands of barbarians who share our faith" but instead "we remain here enduring a myriad of woes at the hands of your *ethnos*."[192] In the last decades of the empire's existence, Ioannes Kanaboutzes spelled it out to his Latin masters: "One is not a barbarian on account of religion, but race, language, the ordering of one's politics, and education. For we are Christians and share the same faith and confession with many other nations, but we call them barbarians, I mean the Bulgarians, Vlachs, Albanians, Russians, and many others."[193]

The Byzantines used terms of abuse for the Bulgarians similar to those they used for the Arabs,[194] calling them "wild beasts" and "the wolves of the west," that is, compared to the "wolves of the east" (the Arabs).[195] All this causes surprise only if one accepts the framework of alleged Christian ecumenism. In reality, it seems that religious community did not influence military policy either, which was also based on the irreducible distinction between Romans and barbarians. To be sure, these Romans occasionally demanded that Christians not shed Christian blood in war, but we must be skeptical about these pronouncements, for they were made almost exclusively when the Romans were in a position of weakness or facing uncertain odds, specifically against Symeon of Bulgaria and the Crusaders. We saw, in an earlier section, the cynical way in which Leon VI pretended not to give information on how to fight the Bulgarians while doing so covertly under the guise of talking about the Hungarians, and how he used those Hungarians (pagans at the time) to attack Bulgaria from behind.[196] Leon the Deacon reports that emperor Nikephoros II Phokas faced a dilemma when the Taurians (i.e., the Rus') marched against the Mysians (Bulgarians) at the instigation of a Roman rebel. The emperor wanted to make an alliance with one of these two people in order to conquer the other, but he was not sure with which one. The way Leon reports it, Nikephoros ultimately rejected the Taurian option because he would probably not be able to persuade their ruler, Svjetoslav, and turned instead to the Mysians, only now instrumentally enlisting their common faith as an argument and proposing a marriage alliance "between the Romans and the Mysians."[197] On a strategic level, this story resists an "ecumenical" or "commonwealth" reading. The emperor is presented as neutral between two options, one pagan and the other Christian, if not actually leaning initially toward the Taurians (and it is likely that he himself had called them in to attack the Bulgarians from behind, disregarding the bonds of religion). The labels also suggest that the "Mysians" were perceived as being ethnically as foreign to the Romans as were the "Taurians."[198]

These were only two moments against a persistent background of cynical and pragmatic calculations, i.e., politics. The Christianization of Bulgaria did not change how Byzantine sources discussed the relations between the two states: the two continued to be friends or enemies depending on the political, military, or economic exigencies of the moment.[199] Of all Christian peoples the Byzantines were the least interested in (and the most skeptical of) pan-Christian movements such as the Crusades, as western critics pointed out. "In fact, if one were to look simply at the way the Byzantines acted, one would be tempted to conclude that the Byzantines were most reluctant to fight non-Christians, less reluctant to fight Christian foreigners, and least reluctant to fight their fellow Byzantine Christians."[200]

There is, in sum, little evidence that religion influenced Byzantine foreign policy, other than as a tool of diplomacy with other Christians when the odds were against the empire; as such, it was quickly dropped, qualified, or just not invoked when the balance of power shifted. "Christian" and "Roman" were extensionally identical when the empire faced non-Christian enemies,[201] but in facing Christian enemies the Byzantines showed their true Roman colors. All others were barbarians. Two examples (treated in brief) demonstrate how the rhetoric shifted to accommodate the interests and strategies of Romanía.

One comes from sixth-century Spain, still partly under Byzantine rule. "Reccaredus' conversion in 589 [from Arianism to Catholicism] put an end to the use of the otherness of faith as an element of Byzantine diplomacy. Instead, the Byzantines apparently switched to emphasizing . . . that the Visigothic rulers (although now converted to Catholicism), remained essentially *barbari* and thus strangers to the Hispano-Roman tradition of government, which was only to be carried on by a Roman(-Byzantine) administration."[202] Another is from the conflict with Symeon, which forced the Byzantines to discuss matters that they might have preferred not to mention. Professing a concern for the common salvation of "the two races (*genē*), the Romans and the Bulgarians," the patriarch Nikolaos informed Symeon that the emperor was mustering a coalition of Rus', Pechenegs, Alans, and western Turks— what he calls "godless nations"—"against your state and race (*genos*)."[203] If only Symeon would "make peace" for the sake of all Christians, the patriarch might be able to persuade the emperor to hold off.

Despite the perception of irreducible ethnic differences, there is still almost no ethnography in the texts we have discussed. We learn almost nothing about the Bulgarians' customs, the organization of their society and state, or even whether they really were a coherent "people," as the language used to describe them implies. Collectivizing them served the Byzantine goal of setting them off as different. At best, and only when the Byzantines were under duress, Bulgaria was a dignified Christian kingdom, while at worst the Bulgarians were virtually nomadic Skythians whose image differed little from that of the Pechenegs in the eleventh century, their religion notwithstanding. It all depended on the needs of the rhetorical moment, but one thing never varied, and this takes us to the heart of Byzantine ideology: never were the Bulgarians acknowledged to be Romans or the true equals of the Romans, even when they all belonged to the Roman empire. Entirely contrary to scholarly consensus, not everyone in this "empire of the Romans" was a Roman. It wouldn't have been an empire if they were.

Two key texts for the study of Byzantine attitudes toward the Bulgarians during the period of the occupation (1018–1185) are the works of Theophylaktos, bishop of Ochrid, and Gregorios Antiochos, which have been studied extensively from this point of view. Both enjoyed the benefit of a superb Constantinopolitan education and resented being in the provinces, especially among barbarians such as the Bulgarians. Antiochos only visited, but Theophylaktos was posted there for life and tried to ameliorate his alienation by coming to terms with his wretched environment. Past scholars have depicted him as chauvinistic and xenophobic, but recent studies have shown that he tried to imagine the Bulgarians as occupying a higher level than plain barbarism, though, of course, without ever equating them to proper civilized people.[204] On the one hand, he does complain about the barbarism of his surroundings. His letters from Bulgaria are full of references and comparisons to animals, frogs, asses, swine, and sheep; his new home was a swamp, a desert full of scorpions. In one letter, he notes self-deprecatingly but also ironically that he now smells authentically Bulgarian, "like a sheepskin."[205] To be sure, he was trying to ingratiate himself with his correspondents, but this, if it partially exculpates him, only shifts the burden onto a much larger segment of Roman society: this is what they wanted to hear about the Bulgarians. On the other hand, Theophylaktos, almost alone among Byzantine authors, wrote a *Life* of St. Kliment of Ochrid, his predecessor and a disciple of Cyril and Methodios. In a work on the fifteen martyrs of Tiberioupolis he also included an account of the Bulgarian baptism under Boris, where he states that the Bulgarians, who used to be an *ethnos barbaron*, had now become a *laos theou*, "a people of God."[206] This is the exact same "tertium quid" move that we saw Mauropous make in connection with the recently converted Pechenegs. It did not quite make them Romans, and, as we see in Theophylaktos' letters, it did not make them culturally acceptable either. This, then, was the furthest in the direction of Christian ecumenism that an autocephalous bishop of Ochrid and leading exegete of Scripture was willing to go. National and cultural differences never left his sight.

Our second source is the letters of Gregorios Antiochos. In writing about his visit to Bulgaria (in ca. 1173), Antiochos, unlike Theophylaktos, had no religious reason to think more highly of the locals than did any other Roman. He mocked the wretched weather, the sheepskin clothes, poor hovels, and stinking food of the Bulgarians. He mentions the frogs and leeches in their lakes. The only good thing about the land was its flocks, but he complains about "the bleating of sheep, the croaking of goats, the mooing of cows, and the grunting of pigs."[207] Animal imagery dominates his account; it is as though there were no people in the land he visited, or else animals have taken the place of people in his bitterly satirical zoo-ethnography. But there is a crucial difference from the way Byzantine writers normally depicted "beastly" barbarians (such as the Pechenegs): this was that Bulgarians were *tame* animals. Antiochos is conscious of being in a foreign land. It has been proposed that "physical illness becomes yet another metaphor for [his] intensely felt cultural alienation."[208] Perhaps we should not psychologize these letters.

They are, in their own way, a rhetorical exercise addressed to his former teacher of rhetoric, none other than Eustathios of Thessalonike, a kind of invective against a place. Perhaps they were meant to amuse. Even so, they are another nail in the coffin of Byzantine ecumenism.

This rhetoric of contempt, however, was not directed solely toward non-Romans. It has been noted that twelfth-century Constantinopolitan snobs who, for one reason or another, had to travel or live in the provinces could refer to provincial Romans as uncouth barbarians and bemoan their lack of culture. Even Athens and Thessalonike were not spared, and stereotypes for specific provinces were revived from ancient texts (e.g., for Paphlagonians and Kappadokians).[209] Thus, scorn for foreign barbarians by Romans generally and scorn for provincial Romans by more elite Constantinopolitans were rhetorical motifs that converged during this century. We might say that snobbery against provincials was the rhetorical stream into which anti-Bulgarian prejudice was channeled, at least in the few texts that survive from the era of the occupation, given that now the Bulgarians were all under Roman rule and could no longer be cast as nomadic Skythians. Yet there is a potency and inflection to the otherness that our two witnesses ascribe to the Bulgarians that exceeds the complaints that were normally made about the low levels of culture among provincial Romans. The animal imagery is striking, and there was no talk elsewhere of a "new people of God." Provincial Romans were uncouth but they were still Romans. There was no talk of them being *ethnographically* different.

This perception of difference is nicely illustrated by some ethnographic verses of Ioannes Tzetzes, a contemporary of Antiochos. We met Tzetzes earlier as the translator of some vulgar conversation in the language of the Alans.[210] He will not disappoint here either. His so-called *Histories (Chiliades)* is a vast verse commentary on the corpus of his own letters, made up of hundreds of brief poems explaining the references contained therein. One letter is addressed to a certain monk, "Heliopolos," who had left the comforts of Constantinople to go to Thessalonike and the land of the Paionians in order, as Tzetzes would have it, to check out the beautiful asses of Paionian women.[211] In the corresponding section of the *Histories*, which has been overlooked by historians of Bulgaria, he explains that the Paionians are the Bulgarians who had been crushed and enslaved by emperor Basileios II,[212] and follows up with a story from Herodotos illustrating how hard-working Paionian women are.[213] He then continues:

On Paionian daughters, who adorn their buttocks
Hesiod said to his brother Perses:
"Don't let an ass-fancy (*pygostolos*) woman deceive your mind."[214]
There are two ways in which she may be called *pygostolos*.
Either because she adorns her arms and forearms (*pygōn*),
and so is called *pygostolos* for putting on bracelets.
Or because she adorns her buttocks (*pygē*), by her hind-quarters,
with broad girdles done up with tassels and fringes.
Such are the daughters of the Paionians,
And even so they remain today in the total conquest
which the most powerful Basileios the Great
imposed upon the entire race of the Paionians.
For still those women around their own buttocks
wear broad girdles, tattered, many-tasseled.
They adorn their arms likewise,
with bracelets of iron, bronze, and glass.
Sometimes even with small knuckle-bones,
and other such things in the form of bracelets;
they wear scarves that they tie around their arms.[215]

The effect is perhaps not unlike that of the "gypsy woman" of Hollywood films, and this is broadly the historical and cultural milieu on which that stereotype is based. What Tzetzes attests is the sexual attraction that such "otherness" could engender in addition to xenophobia. The two have always gone hand in hand, though the Byzantines were otherwise reluctant to discuss this. We can often count on Tzetzes to tell us these things.

At any rate, neither imperial occupation nor Christian brotherhood in the end managed to assimilate the Bulgarians to Romanía. If we look outside the context of direct imperial rule, we find no exception to the pattern of Byzantine contempt for other Orthodox peoples. In the rhetoric of the twelfth century, the Serbs are "no more than a band of pillagers who devastated some territories of the empire."[216] The persistent themes, across a range of texts and authors, are comparisons of the Serbs to wild animals and the triumph of the Byzantine emperor over them. A whole bestiary is deployed, along with an ecology of mountains and forests. Military encounters with them are cast in the form of wild-beast hunts, with the emperor, of course, as the lead hunter. In defeat, they are partially domesticated. Granted, we are in a panegyrical imperial context where every effort was made to cast the emperor as victorious and his enemies as savage, but it is still striking that there seems to be no reference to the Serbs as Orthodox in any of these texts. Eustathios too, archbishop of Thessalonike, casts them as nomads, refers to "the laws of the wolves in which they are raised," and uses the same verbs of animal behavior Psellos had used in his account of the pagan Pechenegs.[217] The *History* of Choniates, otherwise critical of most of the emperors, uses the same rhetoric for the Serbs, calling them "herds of cattle grazing the green, waiting to be slaughtered."[218] There are no "Christians" here, just "Romans and barbarians," the dominant polarity in the Byzantine view of the world. Choniates has lifted this imagery from his panegyrical orations,[219] but in the critical context of the *History* it expresses Roman pride on his part. He had no more need to glorify those emperors.

Nothing changes if we look at the Rus'.[220] For the Byzantines, *all* peoples, regardless of their religion, were potential enemies of Romanía. In one poem, Manganeios Prodromos (twelfth century) lists the Serbs along with Skythians, Latins, and Persians as defeated by the emperor.[221] "The nations are moving against us," wrote the emperor Theodoros II Laskaris in the following century, listing Persians, Italians, Bulgarians, and Serbs,[222] throwing Catholic, Muslim, and Orthodox peoples together into one category, i.e., enemies of the Romans. Religion did not defuse national differences. This has led one historian recently to refer to the Byzantines' "relentless accent on *Romanitas* and on the superiority of Byzantium and its culture over those around it."[223] It was this perception of irreducible difference that allowed the Byzantines to typecast foreigners into a limited range of images of otherness, images that were ultimately indifferent to the barbarians' social and religious life. The same was true of those moments when circumstances called for the rhetoric of Christian brotherhood: if we look closely, there too we find the traces of the same unbridgeable gap, whether in the context, in what has been sublimated, or simply in what is said elsewhere in the same work.

Certainly, there were at all times individuals who embraced Christian universalism, detached themselves from Romanía, traveled along transnational religious networks, settled in distant countries, and were celebrated in monastic circles.[224] But they were, as always, a small minority, and some were regarded with suspicion by the Byzantines.[225] Christian ecumenism had broad horizons but a small demographic base. Such choices are still possible even in the most nationalist modern states.[226] Conversely, many Byzantine monasteries, both in the capital and on Mt. Athos, were segregated by ethnicity. Suffice it to cite the famous case of the general Gregorios Pakourianos (of Caucasian origin), who founded a monastery for Georgians from which Romans were excluded because they were too "violent and greedy."[227] This document is a case of the provincials striking back with their own ethnic rhetoric.

I would like, in conclusion, to offer a more direct and theoretical response to the notions of Christian ecumenism and the "Byzantine Commonwealth" that have shaped so much recent scholarship about Byzantium. These concepts are flawed by an exaggeration on the part of modern historians, a single-minded insistence on the Christian identity of the Byzantines, and an extreme reluctance, almost a horror, of viewing them as Romans. The Byzantines did recognize, of course, that they shared the same faith with other peoples, and sometimes granted that this had *some* claim on their relations with them. But it did not amount to much in practice, for those peoples never ceased being barbarians in the eyes of the Romans, irreducibly different and inferior. But if we forbid the Byzantines from appearing in our scholarship as Romans, they can then only be viewed as an inchoate, multi-ethnic mix held together only by the Church and monarchy. Obolensky's notion of the Byzantine Commonwealth is but one manifestation of this misunderstanding. But it is crucial to explain in what sense I consider it a misunderstanding. Its original intent was not quite as problematic.

Obolensky's *Byzantine Commonwealth* traces the export and adaptation of Orthodoxy, its associated narratives, and art forms from Byzantium to the Slavic world. It is an eloquent and magisterial study of that process, and my critique has no bearing on the vast majority of its contents, which are mostly descriptive. The problem is that it projects the cultural continuum that ultimately emerged from this process back onto the Byzantines themselves, whereas there was nothing in their vocabulary, mentality, or general perception of the world to correspond to it. There is nothing, for instance, in the evidence that authorizes Obolenksy's near-exclusive focus on the Slavic nations: this was a function of his own interests and biases. It is has often been noted that many more cultures merit inclusion in the alleged Commonwealth on the basis of Obolensky's own criteria, among them Nubia, Armenia, and Georgia, to say nothing of the early medieval West and the early Caliphate.[228] That his concept is modern is demonstrated by its wholesale reproduction in strategic analyses of the alleged "Clash of Civilizations."[229] Jonathan Shepard has recently recast the Commonwealth thesis to save it from its many critics by examining how Slavic cultures treated Byzantium as a repository of cultural capital, both political and religious, from which they continued to draw even after the fall of the empire.[230] I have no quarrel with such an analysis. Shepard, however, carefully avoids the trap that Obolensky set for himself.

The fundamental problem was that Obolensky and the fields that he brought together in his study were not, at that time, sophisticated enough to distinguish between *emic* and *etic* forms of analysis. A modern category was projected onto the past and treated, despite vague disclaimers to the contrary,[231] as if it were a Byzantine mentality. The Byzantines had no concept encompassing the peoples that Obolensky included. No primary source upholds an ideology that incorporated all Orthodox peoples into such a Commonwealth, certainly to nothing beyond the loose, emerging federation of Churches for which we already have a term, namely the Orthodox Church.[232] Given that Obolenksy and some of his followers mistook their own analytical concepts for medieval mentalities, they became frustrated when they realized that the Byzantines did not think (and far less act) in accordance with them. To bridge the gap they engaged in backwards reasoning, faulting the Byzantines rather than the theory. Believing that "Romaios" *meant* Christian Orthodox and that there was no "meaningful" way to distinguish Romans and Christian barbarians, Obolensky attributed the Byzantines' refusal to embrace his Commonwealth to . . . their *Greek* chauvinism (that is, barbarians must be the opposite of Greeks, not Romans, because Roman meant Christian and Christians were by definition inclusive).[233] This tortured logic is entirely the product of the imperative in Byzantine Studies to deny that the Byzantines actually were who they always said they were.

When we take our guidance from the sources, however, we find that what the Byzantines said about foreign peoples was a function of who they thought they themselves were, and served to reinforce it. It is crucial that we have found little significant difference in their depiction of pagan and Christian barbarians, which means that this is the wrong polarity to use in this context. What we have seen of Byzantine ethnography (or ethnology) tallies well with their foreign policy: the distinction between Romans and barbarians was paramount there as well. The Byzantines failed to show much interest or initiative in the events and processes of cultural diffusion that created the alleged Commonwealth; they considered Christian barbarians as little better than animals (at best tame rather than wild); and it seems that they did not allow the bonds of religion to influence the most serious decisions that a people must make, i.e., concerning war. Nor does it seem that religious considerations determined how Byzantium was, in turn, treated by its own

Orthodox neighbors, its cultural god-children.[234] In the end, reconstructions of a people's "ideology" must rest on a bedrock of critically evaluated primary evidence, or else we are building conceptual castles in the air. On the anthropological side, Geertz warned against "impeccable depictions of formal order in whose actual existence nobody can quite believe."[235] This sounds very much like the notion of ecumenism that Byzantinists have constructed, only subsequently to disparage the Byzantines themselves for not adhering to it.

The Byzantines' Roman identity was not without its own internal tensions and possibly even contradictions and moments of revealing silence. But we will never know what those were unless we first try to understand it, an effort that has not yet been made. By contrast, a concerted effort attempts to link them to other Christian cultures on the basis of their religious identity. The most that we can say, however, is that there were moments when the Byzantines were willing to see their Christian neighbors as something better than barbarians though less than Romans, an undefined "new people of God."[236] That status, however, unlike the Byzantines' own Roman identity, was deployed and retracted according to the circumstances of the rhetorical moment.

CHAPTER 5

Ethnography in Palaiologan Literature

An Introduction to the Palaiologan Period and Its Sources

In 1204 the armies of the Fourth Crusade captured Constantinople and set about the conquest and dismemberment of the Byzantine empire. They were to have only partial and temporary success. The Byzantines-in-exile managed to hold on to many regions, chiefly western Greece, Trebizond and its hinterland, and most of western and northwestern Asia Minor, from where they retook the capital in 1261. The Palaiologan dynasty reigned over the reconstituted empire for the next two centuries, but the geopolitical context had changed irrevocably. Asia Minor was gradually lost to a number of post-Seljukid emirates, of which the Ottomans would prove the most ambitious and successful. This process was complete, more or less, by 1337. Mainland Greece and the islands were a patchwork of mercantile, feudal, and mercenary Latin colonies mixed up with regional Byzantine, Slavic, and Albanian principalities. The Palaiologan empire actually made considerable progress against them, especially in the Peloponnese, most of which it managed to recapture by the fifteenth century, but the Byzantine cause was hampered by a series of civil wars that broke out in earnest in 1321 and continued, on and off, until the fall of Constantinople in 1453 and even beyond (the despots of the Peloponnese continued to squabble until 1460). These wars, and the distractions of the Hesychast religious controversy, which tore the Byzantine leadership apart after the mid-fourteenth century, enabled other powers to dominate the Balkans, first the Serbs and then, after 1371, the Ottomans, who had been brought over as mercenaries in the civil wars but decided to conquer the whole for themselves. After the 1370s, Byzantium was on and off a vassal and tributary state of the Ottomans. A grace period of fifty years was granted to its existence by the defeat of sultan Bayezid by Timur at the battle of Ankara in 1402. But the blow to Byzantine prestige and imperial self-confidence had already been struck.

One of the great paradoxes of the Palaiologan period is that it was marked by a thriving and innovative literary culture, for all that it was a period of rapid and demoralizing imperial decline. A great deal of this literature is fault-finding, of course. Who was to blame for the decline? Fingers were pointed and the case made at length against both the Palaiologoi and their critics, as well as against the Latins, infidels, Hesychasts, anti-Hesychasts, Unionists, anti-Unionists, Serbs and Bulgarians, the partisans of innumerable factions, and the sins of the Byzantines generally. At any rate, this vigorous and confusing debate generated a rich body of literary and documentary evidence. The culture's image of self-subsisting and aloof autonomy partly gave way, as foreign influences, especially from the Latin world, made their presence felt both physically and intellectually. There was much more interpenetration now: the borders of the state did not coincide with those of the culture, and the foreigner was now everywhere, at the court, in the army, Church, and aristocracy, as an in-law, or ruling an adjacent territory.

From the standpoint of ethnography, the Palaiologan period presents an extremely uneven picture. There are two main bursts of activity, corresponding mostly to the production of historiography. The first burst occurs in the first half of the fourteenth century. Georgios Pachymeres was born in 1242 in the Nikaian exile and moved to Constantinople after the restoration. He wrote the *History* of the reigns of Michael VIII and Andronikos II, covering the period 1260–1308. His was the generation that experienced the promise of renewal and then the initial disappointments under the first Palaiologoi, including the violent enforcement of Union by the otherwise competent Michael VIII and the disastrous foreign policy of his devout but incompetent son Andronikos II. The leading writer among the next generation, Theodoros Metochites (born 1270), had also moved from Asia Minor to Constantinople to became Andronikos II's prime minister, falling with him in 1328. Metochites was a literary innovator whose large corpus includes the types of works that we found to be missing from previous Byzantine production, such as a first-hand account of an embassy to a foreign court and various essays on comparative politics and ethnography. We will look at some of them in more detail below. The last main figure in this burst is Nikephoros Gregoras, born in the early 1290s, who was a student of Metochites. His *Roman History* covers the years 1204–1358 and reflects disillusionment with the failure of the

Palaiologan restoration, the civil wars, and Hesychasm (whose exponents condemned and imprisoned him).

Some minor texts aside, the next century is a gap for us. It is important to stress, however, that this was not a gap in literary production as such. During this century, between the 1360s and the 1460s, the Byzantines wrote much on the issues of the Hesychast controversy, for and against Union with Rome, and in many traditional rhetorical genres. They did not, by contrast, write works that systematized the world's polities and nations or situated the state and culture of Byzantium in relation to the other peoples of the world, that is, historiography and its related genres. It is perhaps easy to see why. Other, more pressing intellectual debates consumed their interests. Many of the intellectuals of this era were personally involved in its controversies, on whose vagaries their standing and careers often depended, though not their lives (Byzantium was not a society that murdered dissident thinkers). The most interesting intellectual of the second half of the fourteenth century was Demetrios Kydones, who rejected Hesychasm and converted to Catholicism. His works make the case for Union with Rome and describe the west positively.

Moreover, the standing of the empire in the world and its relations with its neighbors and enemies were in rapid decline during this period, leading to the loss of imperial territory and to vassal status. Palaiologan literature reveals a society in a state of shock and bewilderment. Nothing was working as it used to. It was as if the normal rules of the world had been suspended and the old distinctions and hierarchies were overturned. Ideologically, that is exactly what had happened. We can scarcely imagine the humiliation felt by emperors who had no money to pay for passage home, or who had to pawn jewels to western money-lenders, or leave their sons as collateral for loans. By the end of the fourteenth century, the Byzantine emperor had to follow the Ottoman sultan on his campaigns, help him to subject formerly Roman cities, and pay him tribute for the privilege.[1] In many ways, this was even worse than the Arab conquests of the seventh century, which had at least left part of the empire to imagine itself as autonomous and still supreme in its own sphere, reduced though that was. In sum, as in almost all periods of Byzantine history, there still were men with a superb literary training and the knowledge to write ethnography. They chose not to do so. They probably had no idea what it should look like any more.

Ethnography reappeared vigorously, in fact more so than at any other time in Byzantine history, in Laonikos Chalkokondyles, who wrote his *Histo-*

ries after the Fall, and, to a lesser degree, in the other historians of the Fall, Doukas and Kritoboulos. The history of this period could be written only in retrospect, when the City had fallen and it was clear that the Byzantine order would not be reconstituted soon, or again. This called for approaches that dispensed with the fixtures and certainties of the ancient imperial and Christian world view. I will say a few words about these historians here, as the following sections will not focus on them. This book will reach only until the later fourteenth century, when Byzantium was absorbed into the Ottoman empire and relations with the west took on a new aspect. Beyond that was a different world that followed different rules: the three historians of the Fall were basically historians of the Turks, a perspective that sets them apart from the Byzantine tradition as ethnographers (sources before the Fall have little to say about the Ottoman Turks, so they cannot be included here). I have decided to write a separate book on the period of the Fall, focusing on the *Histories* of Laonikos.[2] A word should be said about him here, however.

The most interesting of the historians of the Fall from our standpoint was Laonikos Chalkokondyles (born Nikolaos), an Athenian who wrote a *Histories* in imitation of Herodotos, structuring it after the sequence of Ottoman conquests just as Herodotos had followed the course of Persian expansion. His coverage of people and places ranges from Arabia and Mongolia to Britain, with emphasis on Italy and Spain (the two places from which the rulers of his native city had come in the previous century). Laonikos was not pro- or anti-anyone in particular, and he seems to have cast off both the Roman and the Christian filters of Byzantine discourse. He offers the first ethnographic treatment in Greek of Islam as a living culture. He does not dwell on theology or really ever mention religious debates. In an un-Byzantine way, he treats all peoples and their religions with respect. In part, this was because he was a student of the philosopher Plethon, who revived the pluralist paradigms of pagan late antiquity. Laonikos was, however, critical of the Palaiologan leadership of the empire (for failing "the Greeks") and the cruelty and perfidy of Mehmet II, and he seems to have taken some jabs at the papacy. In many ways he continues the themes that are explored in this volume, though he sometimes takes them in weird directions.

A word on how the following sections are organized. Instead of breaking the material down by author or period, I have decided to approach it by theme, beginning with travel literature and devoting the following two sections to the representations of Mongols and Latins. This division will facilitate comparisons among genres on similar topics and also comparisons with previous

Byzantine categories. An east-west division is loosely based on how the Byzantines themselves saw their new position, "squeezed," as Pachymeres put it
in the preface of his *History*, between "the Persians [Turks] to the east and the
Italians to the west . . . making alliances with the Italians against the Persians and using the Skythians to push back the Italians."[3] An east-west division seemed appropriate for literary reasons too, as the Byzantines used
different categories for each. But within each section, the material will be
examined chronologically. Minor texts, not among those mentioned above,
will also be introduced. As some authors used inherited categories to express
new ideas, parts of the exposition will take the form of close readings.

It must be acknowledged that in comparison to the literature of late antiquity, and even of the middle Byzantine period, the Palaiologan period is
understudied. Sometimes the editions are not good or there is little or no
relevant scholarship. The intellectual history of this period is obscure, though
not for lack of texts. Many facts remain to be established and connections to
be made. It is unclear, for example, whether Laonikos can be placed in a tradition that reached from Metochites to Plethon via Gregoras and Kydones, a
tradition that favored the study and appropriation of ancient philosophy and
became increasingly anti-Hesychast.[4] Can it be a coincidence that our main
ethnographers all belonged to that tradition? Laonikos' revival of Herodotos,
at the end, was performed outside the bounds of the Christian tradition.

The Politics of Palaiologan Travel Literature
and the Case of "Agathangelos"

"Travel literature" was not a fixed genre in Byzantium.[5] It is best approached
as a modality that narratives in a variety of genres could take on to promote
the agenda of the text or, which may have been the same thing, the standing
and authority of its author. Many such texts were produced in the later Byzantine period, either as self-standing briefings or embedded in histories, devotional texts, theological polemics, or political texts. Most of them relate to
diplomacy in one way or another, whether secular or ecclesiastical. These
texts relate to the Balkans, Egypt, and Asia Minor, not to the Latin west.
Despite the frequency of Byzantine travel to Italy and the west,[6] we have no
narrative accounts. All we have are a handful of *ekphraseis*. In a letter from
the 1370s, Kydones wrote a mini-*ekphrasis* of Venice, which I will discuss at
the end of this chapter, for Kydones was instrumental in changing the discus-

sion when it came to the Latin west. Manuel II, a prolific writer who traveled as far as England in 1400, tells us little about the lands he visited, though he did pen a brief description of a tapestry at the Louvre.[7] Manuel Chrysoloras wrote a famous comparison of Old and New Rome in 1411, addressed to his patron Manuel II.[8] For more, and longer, texts, we have to wait for the Council of Ferrara-Florence (1438–1439), but this takes us almost to the generation of Laonikos.

For the Balkans and Egypt, however, we suddenly have a number of texts, though it is difficult to explain why. Byzantium had always been diplomatically active.[9] It is possible that the Palaiologan empire saw an uptick in the frequency and density of diplomatic exchanges in all directions, as the empire was less able to fend for itself in the more dangerous world of the later Middle Ages and was surrounded by powers that it had to play against each other. The emperors now accomplished more through diplomats than through soldiers, which might have led to their skills being valued more, and hence advertised more. One study found a total of fifteen missions to Mamluk Egypt just for the years 1282–1328.[10] At any given time, there must have been hundreds if not thousands of Byzantines who had been on such missions, each of which might have consisted of dozens or over a hundred men. Eventually, even the emperors traveled to the west to seek aid, and in the late fourteenth century they also had to attend upon the Ottoman sultans. Moreover, in the reduced circumstances of the period, one did not have to travel far to reach foreign lands. After the early fourteenth century, going over to Asia Minor would suffice, or to wherever the sultan had pitched his tent.

Many of these dynamics are present in the chronologically first text that falls under this category, Metochites' *Presbeutikos*, an account of his efforts to hammer out a marriage alliance in 1298–1299 between Andronikos II and Stefan Uroš II Milutin of Serbia. This thirty-page text is the first Byzantine embassy-narrative since the days of Priskos, Nonnosos, and Zemarchos in late antiquity. Presumably many others had been written in the meantime, but this is the first to survive. In fact, we have written confirmation of one written just previously. In 1294, Metochites and Ioannes Glykys (later patriarch, 1315–1319) went on a bride-hunting mission to Lusignan Cyprus and Cilician Armenia. Gregoras tells us that Glykys (who was later his teacher) wrote an account of this embassy,[11] but it has not survived. In contrast to his late antique predecessors, however, Metochites' journey in 1299 did not take him to Eastern Europe, Central Asia, or Yemen but only to Skopje, by the Byzantine-Serbian border, a few days from Thessalonike. During the negotiations, moreover, he was able to send messengers back to his masters and receive updated instructions on short notice. The *Presbeutikos*, which is written in Metochites' convoluted and difficult Greek, is basically a report to his superiors. Most of it recounts negotiations over terms that included border arrangements and a prisoner exchange, but without divulging any specifics: it is an abstract drama of persuasion, doubt, pleading, and arguing, that highlights Metochites' central role in the mission's success.

The narrative of the journey to Milutin is interesting, but offers little scope for ethnography. After all, they did not travel far into Serbian territory, and the conditions of the peasantry throughout the Balkans would have been fairly homogeneous. By this time there was hardly much that was new or interesting about the Serbs to an educated Byzantine readership. Metochites does dwell on a Serb envoy who accompanied his party: he was boorish and had to be restrained from abusing the hospitality that the law provided for embassies on the move.[12] He describes the harsh winter. The Serb was so rough that he braved the cold by leaving his head uncovered, but fell ill.[13] In Thessalonike, Metochites received a report by the governor on the unsettled state of the lands through which he would travel, full of cattle- and goat-thieves, barbarians allied to the kral (the Serbian ruler) whose hideouts were in the mountains, and imperial subjects virtually in a state of revolt.[14] He wants us to think that he is heading into the barbarian wilds, and imagines his return as from a world of rustic illiteracy and barbarism back to reasoned speech and Hellenic grace.[15] There is no doubt that he considered the Serbs to be barbarians, but he does not elaborate. After all, any embassy was a journey into the opposite of Constantinopolitan culture, refinement, and order. Metochites carefully notes where and under what conditions they had to spend each night on the road—but much of this was still inside Byzantine territory. Just leaving the capital was an unpleasant adventure. The most we get in terms of ethnography is a brief description of the bejeweled kral and the silk-appointed furniture of his chamber; apparently, the Serbs were going for a "noble Roman" effect.[16] The envoys were looked after during their stay and given food from the kral's table in precious dishes. Metochites itemizes the types of animals and fish that they were fed, making it appear as if he were in a zoo (we recall Gregorios Antiochos' insinuation that Bulgaria was basically a vast animal park).[17] Then the negotiations began.

It is interesting that two ambassadors who knew each other—Glykys and Metochites—wrote self-standing accounts of their journeys in such proximity. It suggests the likelihood of literary emulation or competition.

This was certainly the case with Gregoras, who studied under both men. He also went as an envoy to the Serbs in 1326 and recounts the journey in a way that emulates and even forms a literary sequel to that of Metochites. He first wrote this account in a letter and later incorporated it into his history.[18] The main goal of his embassy was to bring back Eirene, Metochites' daughter, whose husband had defected to the Serbs and had taken her with him before he died. Gregoras' party included one hundred and forty men. He describes how they crossed the Strymon but then could not find shelter, as raids had wasted and emptied the land. As they were wandering during the night, a band of men dressed in black leather appeared, "like demon ghosts" out of the night. They were lightly armed and spoke in a Bulgarian dialect, but began to joke with the Romans and led them to a village where they could camp down. One day's journey from there they celebrated Easter at Strumica, but Gregoras grumbles about the "barbarian" speech and melodies of the locals. Their voices reminded him of mountain shepherds, but they enjoyed the local festival customs nonetheless. At Skopje they managed to persuade Eirene to return to Byzantium. The kral, her son-in-law, saw them off, but Gregoras criticizes him for inadequately performing the formalities: "then again, as they say, monkeys behave like monkeys and ants like ants." Gregoras closes his account by recalling an ancient saying: "consider yourself fortunate that you were born a Greek and not a barbarian."[19] We see, then, that animal images persist for the Christian peoples of the Balkans, as does the distinction between civilized gentlemen and barbarians. The latter are good for some ethnographic flavor in the narrative.

Our next texts take us to Egypt and the eastern Mediterranean. In the 1320s, a twelve-year-old boy named Andreas Libadenos accompanied an embassy to the sultan of Egypt as undersecretary; the group then also made a detour to Jerusalem. Much later (ca. 1355), Libadenos wrote an idiosyncratic account of his life and travels, including the trip to Egypt and a later journey to the empire of Trebizond. The title of the text combines the words for "history," "travel account," and "anabasis," the latter alluding to Xenophon, whose *Anabasis* also took him to Trebizond and then Byzantion. While in some respects this work is a travel account and even an autobiography, it is actually a kind of prose thanksgiving hymn to Christ, the Virgin, and various saints that praises and thanks them profusely for the aid they have given to the author, especially during his many illnesses, which are also described in detail. Travels, storms at sea, and illness, then, function as extraordinary events for which Libadenos can thank his divine patrons. "Autobiography" in this context is only a mode that inflects a work with a different purpose,[20] and many of the descriptions tend to be rhetorical.

The journey to Alexandria and Cairo reveals nothing about the locals. We are given a charming description of the trees along the banks of the Nile, and Libadenos says that they saw the granaries and treasuries of Joseph (i.e., the pyramids). His group then traveled to Jerusalem, with the sultan's permission. As with most Byzantine accounts of the Holy Land, there is little or no reference to the people who lived there, excepting the occasional Orthodox prelate. Libadenos' attitude toward the locals is captured by the phrase "infidel beastly barbarians," which is all he says about them.[21] His main purpose is rhetorically to praise his divine patrons for keeping him safe. We saw earlier how the *ekphrasis* of the Holy Land by the twelfth-century writer Ioannes Doukas mostly omitted the people, as if he were describing an empty film set.[22] In Byzantine texts, these places are inhabited only by the ghosts of events past.

There is little doubt that Libadenos actually went on the journey that he described. The same is not true of a slightly later traveler to the Mamluk realm and the Levant, who, while he may be a fictional person, has left us with a quite fascinating account. We turn back to Gregoras and to one of the best-kept secrets in Byzantine literature, a gem that, if it were found in a classical author, would have inspired many monographs. Gregoras' *Roman History* seems to have been a work always-in-progress and was written in phases. The section that includes his trip to Skopje was in the first part, finished before the onset of the theological debates surrounding Hesychasm and the teachings of Gregorios Palamas that would cloud the end of his life. Gregoras was kept under confinement in 1351–1354 for opposing the theories of Palamas, and his *History* began to reflect those concerns. The work turns into an anti-Palamite argument in which the narrative of events plays an auxiliary role, to prove, that is, that the onset of Palamism was disastrous for the empire.

At a point, however, after the *History* has become a theological treatise, Gregoras suddenly interrupts his exposition with what appears to be completely different material. He tells the story of how he was secretly visited in prison by a former student named "Agathangelos," whom he had not seen in many years. This "Good Messenger" would visit him five times during his captivity, bringing him news of the outside world and materials to continue his theological polemic. Gregoras provides an emotive account of Agathangelos' first appearance to him and their "recognition" scene after his "almost twenty years" of travel, obviously an Odyssean allusion.[23] Agathangelos says that he had spent that time traveling the world to research cities, harbors, and the shape of the earth, mostly for astronomical reasons; he was also moved by disgust at the Palamite turn that Church and State had taken in Byzantium, which, for him, had caused the rapid decline of both.[24] In chapters 24–25 of the *Roman History*, he recounts his long journey to Gregoras, and the work here takes the form of a dialogue between the two men (the genre of dialogue was popular in this period, especially in theological controversies). Agathangelos' tour around the eastern Mediterranean took him to Rhodes, Egypt, Palestine and Syria, Kilikia, Cyprus, Crete, Euboia, and then back to Constantinople.

This narrative frame-device presents obvious problems of interpretation. There was no one actually named Agathangelos. The question has been posed whether he was a fictional character invented by Gregoras, though the few discussions of this possibility shun its literary implications and prefer the task of matching him up to actual contemporaries who may have provided Gregoras with his model. The results, tentative and uncertain, do not help us understand the text.[25] It is best to treat Agathangelos as a literary creation, even if Gregoras modeled him on an acquaintance or derived his information about those places from real sources. The information itself is not fantastic, even if the narrator bears the hallmarks of Odyssean invention. It should also be noted that Gregoras' main expertise as a scholar was in astronomy (he proposed a reform of the Julian calendar, which was not adopted). Agathangelos' narrative utilizes the same calendrical markers as Gregoras uses throughout the *Roman History*. His politics also perfectly match those of Gregoras himself. As we will see, the function of Agathangelos' narrative in the context of the *Roman History* is to prove that the outside world remains hostile to Palamism, and that almost all foreign states and societies were faring better than Byzantium was in the grip of Palamas and his supporters, specifically emperor Ioannes VI Kantakouzenos: political decline had been *caused* by the Palamist shipwreck.[26] Agathangelos frames his narration with that declaration. Let us see, then, how Gregoras uses an account of foreign places to pursue domestic polemics.

At every place, Agathangelos visits the local sights ("things worth seeing" or *theamata*), which for him means mostly ancient ruins and places with classical associations. He is far less interested in Christian antiquities or "holy" sites. While he might spend a page discussing the battle of Issos between Alexander and Dareios and even notes, in connection with Tarsos,

that Alexander bathed in the Kydnos,[27] his only references to Christian antiquities are the mere fact that Palestine was "trod by the salvific feet" and an
allusion to Antioch in the New Testament.[28] He does not mention that St.
Paul was from Tarsos, and he dwells at length on the foundation of Antioch
by Antiochos I (a mistake for his father Seleukos). This fascination with the
physical ruins of classical antiquity was nothing new for the Byzantines, as I
have argued elsewhere in connection with Athens.[29] However, while "Agathangelos" prefers pagan *antiquities*, he is interested in the Christian *present*
and in ascertaining the state of Orthodox communities under Latin and
Muslim rule. At one point he states that his (scotched) plan to travel east
from Damascus was in order to determine how many Christians still survived there, under the impious nations, and whether he could find traces of
ancient Chaldaean and Persian wisdom (i.e., astronomy).[30] This concern for
the contemporary state of "captive" Christianity leads him to make some
interesting observations about the Latin and Muslim polities in question,
to promote his overall polemical purpose. Those, then, are the poles of Agathangelos' narrative: faint traces of classical antiquity on the one hand and
a strong showing by anti-Palamite Orthodoxy under foreign rule on the
other.

At Rhodes Agathangelos looks for the Colossus but finds no trace of it,
not a scrap of bronze or the base on which it stood. Locals showed him the
remains of the ancient cities, whose names he quotes from Homer.[31] The inhabitants, he says, are of our own race, religion, and language. Some were
descendants of an army that had attacked the Latins and had been defeated,
losing their liberty but otherwise now living there prosperously. The Latins,
who "live in arms" (i.e., the Hospitallers), make sure no foreign threat
touched the island. They have created conditions of lawful rule in the mar-
kets and courts, where avarice has been curtailed. "Life is free from trouble"
there. Those Byzantines, at least, were prospering under Latin rule. Agathangelos then sails to Alexandria, offering him the chance to digress on the
Nile.[32] He sees the *theamata* in Alexandria and then wants to see the pyramids and hundred-gated Thebes, and to meet the sacred scribes of Egypt
mentioned in the old books. In all this he was now following in the footsteps
of Herodotos, but, he discovered, it was all just a dream, for only their names
survived (it is unclear whether he is referring to the scribes alone in this
clause or to all the attractions, for the pyramids existed and were well known).
It is interesting that so far he had failed to find the main ancient attractions at
each place.

Agathangelos passes quickly by the "sights" of Palestine, saying nothing specific about them, and moves on to Damascus, which was also under Mamluk rule.[33] He praises its populousness, the equality that governs the market, the good order of the political authorities, and the good sense of the inhabitants. This must refer to the Muslim majority too, not only the Christian minority. Again, Agathangelos has only praise for this foreign society. He compares Damascus to Alexandria, finding the latter superior in military preparation, the lawful regulation of the market, and the administration of justice, but true piety (i.e., Christianity) was freer and more sincere in Damascus.[34] As in Rhodes, there was no fear of foreign attack. We note that while Agathangelos sets out to define the prevailing conditions in these foreign societies, and thus by extension to offer a concise ethnographical itinerary, his definitions are generic. Their purpose is to provide formulaic praise of Hospitaller Rhodes and the Mamluk realm, not to tell us something distinctive about them. This praise is meant to highlight precisely the virtues that Byzantine society lacked. That is why his accounts lack specificity and elaboration (for example, anecdotes). It becomes easier to believe that this is a rhetorical construction by Gregoras, not an actual travel account.

We have already touched on Agathangelos' discussion of Antioch.[35] The one thing that he admired most there was that he could still see signs of ancient Christianity, even though "the foreign Arab religion" was dominant throughout that region. At Issos he describes (though vaguely) the site of the battle won by Alexander and the different tactics employed by him and Dareios.[36] At the start of book 25, Agathangelos says that his original plan was to explore the lands of the east to see how many Christian communities had survived under foreign rule, amid all that impiety, and whether he could find any trace of ancient Chaldaean and Persian learning. He was dissuaded from this, however, by the most respected citizens of Hierapolis (Bambyke, by the Euphrates), who said that it would not be convenient to advance further because of differences in language; also, there was nothing left of ancient wisdom in Persia and Chaldaea because the Mongols had poured over those lands—here he gives a summary of Mongol expansion[37]—most local customs were extinguished, and all the distinctions and boundaries in those lands were thrown into confusion. Moreover, the Mongols were fighting civil wars after the death of their ruler. When Agathangelos saw that Egypt and Arabia were also in dynastic turmoil, he turned to the the sights around Tarsos instead.[38] Again, his search for ancient wisdom was foiled. But his continued references to Alexander take us back to a time when Greek power was expanding rather than contracting; in fact, they take us back to the moment when Greeks first conquered these lands. It is as if Agathangelos, a Byzantine, is bidding them farewell by looking back to their first point of contact. His account is a long farewell to the Hellenistic East.

At this point Gregoras breaks in and asks Agathangelos to tell him also about the current state of ecclesiastical politics in all these lands. *That* is what he really needs to know: the state of the Church is more important than the gold of Kroisos! Specifically, Gregoras wants to discuss the catastrophe that Palamism has caused, and this purpose now explains why we have been entertained by Agathangelos' seemingly irrelevant peregrinations in the first place. The latter have positioned him as a credible source to answer the question posed now by Gregoras: What do the Christians outside the empire think of what we are doing here? Agathangelos says that he was going to keep the two types of "histories" separate, and was going to come to ecclesiastical matters when he had finished discussing secular history, but now he will mix them together, for that is what Gregoras wants.[39] He goes back and presents the ecclesiastical situation in the lands he had visited, leading into a polemic against Palamas. We can now grasp the point of it all: the Orthodox Christians who live among impious races and are enslaved by foreign arms still remain faithful to ancestral piety and the true doctrines.[40] Now we know where this whole journey has been headed.

The most integrated part of the narrative is the next stop, Cyprus. He refers vaguely to the attractions of the island and presents its geography. Most of this long section is actually a panegyric of Georgios Lapithos, a correspondent and ally of Gregoras himself. He is praised for his Christian virtues and good deeds, and for defending Orthodox thought before the Lusignan king in order to confound the Catholic theologians of his court. Agathangelos discusses this at length, probably because he meant to counter the Palamite talking point that opponents of Hesychasm were closet Catholics.[41] It also turned out that Arab thinkers would visit Cyprus to discuss Ptolemaic astronomy based on "the traces of Chaldaean and Persian wisdom," so Agathangelos obtained his wish after all. Other than to meet Lapithos, he went to Cyprus because of its many attractions and hospitable regime. He elaborates on this when Lapithos gives him a tour to show him "all that was sightworthy," such as theaters, marketplaces, and court-houses. Agathangelos presents us with yet another (generic) image of a lawful and orderly society that complements his picture of Rhodes and the Mamluk realm.[42] He then receives a lecture from Lapithos on how good political orders are maintained and how bad ones come about, which turns into an attack on the state of Byzantium and on Palamism specifically.[43] This harangue is followed by the news that Kantakouzenos had taken the capital and sided with Palamas (in 1347), a report which makes Lapithos cry.

His next stop is Crete.[44] He discusses its shape and size, and says that he had always wanted to see the labyrinth at Knossos. We then have something extraordinary. Agathangelos provides a substantial description of the labyrinth, an expansive artificial cave with columns, residences, courtyards, and fountains that he explored with some locals bearing torches. He draws conclusions about how its *technites* (presumably Daidalos) would have carved it out of the living rock. What are we to make of this? As far as I know, Minoan archaeologists are unaware of this passage. Nanno Marinatos, an expert on Minoan Crete, tells me that no part of the complex excavated by Evans could have been in this state in the fourteenth century. If this is the case, Gregoras' narrative is proven to be fictitious, along with "Agathangelos." It is an invention premised on ancient tales of Daidalos' construction of the labyrinth for Minos, whose reign and monster Gregoras goes on to discuss. Still, I know of no other text that describes the labyrinth in this way or that presents it as so accessible.[45] Another possibility is that the description was based on the so-called Labyrinth of Gortyn, a cave-turned-quarry, which early modern travelers mistook for that of Minos (Gregoras' would be the earliest mention of its exploration).[46] It is, however, on the other side of the island, so that Agathangelos' testimony remains questionable. This passage might repay further study.

We have now almost reached the end of Agathangelos' travels. Crete was under Venetian control. He toured the island, whose inhabitants were Romans and held to the true faith. He was going to stay, but was prevented by the war preparations of the Venetians (there was to be a war against the Genoese in the Aegean). Instead of praising the Venetian polity in Crete, Agathangelos gives a fairly, full albeit still rhetorical, description of the assembly of their armada.[47] This, I suspect, is also meant to make Byzantium look bad by contrast, for surrendering control of the seas to these naval powers and scrapping its own fleet. The flurry of activity and ship construction that we witness in Crete could not have taken place in Byzantine territory. From this point on Agathangelos recounts the war between Venice and Genoa that frames his own return to Constantinople. The only stop of interest is at Troy, where he tours the site of the war in the *Iliad* and affects to correct the poet's description of the Skamander.[48] After that, he returns to attacking Palamas and Kantakouzenos as he makes his way to meet Gregoras in his cell.

There is little in this travel narrative overall that required input from an actual traveler. "Agathangelos" is at least a disguise, and may well be a fiction. His descriptions of foreign polities are general. His geography could have been learned from books and is not always correct for places that he allegedly visited, which is suspicious. His account of the labyrinth, while precise, smacks of fiction. Moreover, in my exposition I have drawn out the polemical purpose served by the narrative: to highlight the decline of Byzantium at the hands of Palamas and Kantakouzenos by praising the polities of Latins and Muslims and to enlist the Orthodox communities abroad in a struggle against heresy. Foreign descriptions again hold a mirror up to the vices and failings of Byzantium and are offered in the spirit of self-criticism and diagnosis. Less easy to explain is the emphasis on classical antiquities. I have drawn attention to them, not because they constitute ethnography, but because they are woven into an account of travel in foreign places. But why are they there at all, especially if they were made up by Gregoras and there was no Agathangelos? This is difficult to answer. I suspect that this too may be a projection of Gregoras' intellectual persona onto the shape of the world. Gregoras' opposition to Palamism was caught up in his professed use of ancient thought to understand the world and resolve theological problems. This too was used against him by his enemies.[49] Agathangelos' narrative thereby combines the two aspects of Gregoras' own intellectual profile: a search for ancient wisdom and an opposition to Palamas. This perhaps might also explain why that search is so often frustrated, as at Rhodes and in Egypt, or satisfied in unexpected ways (such as finding Arab experts in "Chaldaean and Persian wisdom" on Cyprus). The journey of Agathangelos around the Levant ultimately encodes the political and intellectual journey of Gregoras himself.

Both Libedenos' and Agathangelos' accounts of their journeys to Egypt aim to promote religious agendas, devotional in the first case and polemical in the second. The same is true of another, exactly contemporary, account written by none other than Gregorios Palamas himself. In 1354, Palamas, the archbishop of Thessalonike, was captured by Turks and taken to Asia Minor, where he had discussions with both Christians and Muslims at the urban centers of the Ottoman emirate. The texts that he wrote about this experience, which recount the itinerary of his captivity, are important for a number of reasons. They offer us a glimpse of life in the emerging Ottoman emirate before the Byzantine sources fall silent about the Turks, a silence that would not be lifted until after 1453 in authors such as Doukas, Laonikos, and Kritoboulos. In the Byzantine sources at least, we jump from the emirate of the 1350s (seen in Palamas and in the *History* of his imperial patron Kantakouzenos) directly to the empire of Mehmet II, with only snippets in between. Of course, Palamas does not provide anything like an ethnography of Ottoman Bithynia, and the information that he does give, especially regarding Muslim-Christian relations in the lost territories, has been picked over,[50] but he makes only general references to Turkish customs.

The bulk of the text actually recounts religious debates that took place between Palamas and various spokesmen for Islam at the Ottoman court. The captivity narrative is only a framework for these debates, so that this text has a religious agenda as well. Of course Palamas "wins," and he depicts the Muslims as admiring his wisdom and learning. He himself yields on no point and deems Islam an impious pollution. In general, later Byzantine polemics against Islam, some of which were written by emperors such as Kantakouzenos and Manuel II, tend to repeat the points made by their predecessors of the middle period, to the point where scholars speak of a "sklerosis" in the genre.[51] No allowances were made for the new circumstances and changed relations of power between the two faiths; the polemics covered the same ground. In his long refutation of Islam, Kantakouzenos never comes to terms with or even acknowledges that he had a Muslim son-in-law.[52] Manuel II saw Islam as something Evil that should one day vanish; he wrote against it only so that no one could say, on Judgment Day, that he did not know the truth.[53]

Palamas' own goal, however, is not so much to attack Islam as to present himself as a defender of the true faith and a man whom the Turks themselves came to respect. By presenting himself in this light, Palamas is putting himself forward, to his Byzantine audience, as a spokesman for Orthodoxy who can effect an accommodation with the Turks in which the Orthodox (Palamite) position would be honored. Gregoras had done something similar with Lapithos in Agathangelos' narrative, except that he had Lapithos win the respect of the Lusignan king of Cyprus on behalf of non-Palamite Orthodoxy. Palamas and Gregoras were effectively bidding for foreign validation, with the Turks and Latins respectively—but all, of course, before the eyes of their Byzantine readers. These Turks and Latins were rhetorical constructions that served the purpose of internal debate. Still, the respective choice is significant. Anti-Palamite thinkers sought validation in the eyes of the Latins, an affiliation that would be taken to the next level in the coming years by Demetrios Kydones, while the Palamite establishment presented itself as able to make deals with the Turks, a popular position as the Turks increasingly acquired Christian subjects.[54] The Palamites held little truck with the Latins. This distinction is nicely illustrated in the *Life of Sabas the Fool*, a Hesychast saint, written by the Palamite patriarch Philotheos Kokkinos. On Cyprus, the saint was almost martyred by the Catholic clergy, but in Egypt he excites the admiration of the sultan, who almost converts because of him.[55]

To Palamas' claim to have the ear of the Muslims Gregoras had a jaw-dropping response, pointing to a different bodily organ. In a later book of the *Roman History*, Gregoras provided a counter-narrative of the future saint's captivity. He says that the barbarians mocked Palamas for "the gold and silver that they found secreted in the orifices of his body." Was this not in violation of the ascetic life that he preached? When they found his books, they would ask him what each one was and then toss it into the sea, inspired to do this, Gregoras claims, by divine providence. Finally, they sodomized him,[56] an episode on which Gregoras dwells for about half a page. The significance of this passage is not clear, for we do not have a study of the sexual dimension of late Byzantine polemics, especially in connection with the Turks. Charis Messis, who is preparing one, tells me that this was a subtle and humiliating way of indicating that Palamas bore the "seed" of Islam within him and that his thought was tainted by this rape. The literatures of sex and travel were both, again, politics by other means.

The Mongols in Pachymeres, Metochites, and Gregoras

By 1300, the Byzantines had, over the course of the previous millennium, applied the Skythian label to a range of different peoples. As we saw,[57] there was a tension between its geographic and ethnographic aspects. The label could be applied to anyone who lived or came from beyond the Danube, but not all of those were nomads of the Herodotean type. The term fit the Huns, Avars, Magyars, and Pechenegs far better than it did the Goths, Bulgarians, or Rus'. The Byzantines were not too discriminating here, because the function of the label was not the advancement of anthropological science but the projection of imperial ideology. In panegyric and historiography, the nomadic Skythian was the antithesis of the urban, cultured Roman, standing for the forces of blind destruction that periodically assailed the empire. In this guise, the Skythian subject existed to be defeated and "tamed" by the emperor, civilized and converted if possible. He was a barbarian slate on which the values of

New Rome were inscribed by the emperor and his men. This process often resulted in caricature, or rather schematic juxtapositions. We saw how this worked in the orations of Mauropous on the Pecheneg settlement, for instance.[58]

Genghis Khan changed all that. The Mongol expansion asserted the power of the Skythian model over all other types of states that lay in its path, and did so, moreover, at a time when the Byzantines were struggling to recover from the most calamitous defeat they had ever experienced, the loss of Constantinople. In the changed circumstances of the thirteenth century, it was not at all obvious that the dominant political model on the earth was represented by the surviving sliver of the Roman empire at Nikaia, not when its antitype stretched from Korea to Poland. The "normal" hierarchy seemed to have inverted. The best an emperor could hope for under these circumstances was to stay out of the Mongols' way, and it must be said that the Byzantines were very lucky in this regard. Certainly, they had many close calls and experienced prolonged anxiety, but overall they fared well. The Mongols inflicted defeats on most of their neighbors to the north (in the Balkans) and east (in Asia Minor), but never came into direct conflict with the Byzantines themselves.[59] One could even say (in hindsight) that it turned out rather well for them.

During these tense years, Ioannes III Doukas Batatzes was well informed about Mongol movements and plans, because he had to coordinate campaigns in the Balkans and Asia Minor. Byzantine envoys were even sent to Karakorum, in Mongolia. Michael VIII Palaiologos played a crucial role in fomenting dissent between the Golden Horde and the Ilkhans of Persia, and two Byzantine brides were married to Mongol warlords, one of whom, Maria "of the Mongols," played an important role in imperial diplomacy after her return in 1282.[60] Therefore, the court had detailed, first-hand, and contemporary information about a major foreign player. The three authors I will examine here, Pachymeres, Metochites, and Gregoras, whose works appeared in the first half of the fourteenth century, no doubt had similar sources of information. My analysis, however, will not so much assess their reporting as expose the agenda behind the images that they constructed. These images drew heavily on the classical tradition and were not overtly or covertly religious in nature, as was so much writing about the Mongols in the west.[61] They were, however, always political, usually covertly.

The historian of the Nikaian period, Georgios Akropolites, mentions the "Tacharians"[62] periodically in his condensed narrative, but does not say much about them that we can use (his Skythians were the Cumans). His readers were apparently expected to know who these people were. We get more background information from his student and continuer Georgios Pachymeres, who covered the period 1260–1308, focusing heavily on ecclesiastical affairs. The "Tocharians" enter his narrative when he mentions their conquest of Seljuk "Persia" (i.e., Iraq), inducing the Seljuk leadership to seek refuge with Michael VIII (ca. 1258–1260).[63] He then goes back to relate that Ioannes III had only heard rumors about them "so obscure had that nation been until then; many said that they were the dog-headed people and ate forbidden foods, including people."[64] This might be a dramatic literary way of depicting "first contact," but it was not true of Ioannes' actual diplomacy. The emperor had acquired excellent knowledge of the Mongols. Pachymeres apparently did not have access to this information; perhaps it was never written down or published. He later mentions the marriage-relation Michael VIII established with Abaqa Khan (of the Ilkhans) via his daughter Maria and a treaty with the Mamluk sultan of Egypt ("Ethiopia"), Baybars (1260–1277). This leads him to one of the few digressions in the *History*, on the natural differences between the people of the north and of the south (the link being Baybars, a Cuman ("Skythian") by origin who became a sultan in the south). Pachymeres asserts a strong version of climatic determinism: northerners are white but have no learning or arts, only martial prowess, while southerners are dark, clever, and advanced in learning, but torpid and soft when it comes to battle. The difference is attributable to how much the sun heats their respective brains. This is why Baybars wanted Cuman soldiers, and after exerting diplomatic pressure on Michael he secured access to the Black Sea route through the Bosporos.[65]

This extraordinary passage is followed by a detailed description of the giraffe, its appearance and behavior, for Baybars sent one as a gift to Michael.[66] Through this agreement, Baybars was able to constitute a powerful army of Cuman youths and proceeded to make war against the (Latin) Christians in Syria, destroying many of their cities, which, Pachymeres is careful to note in his lament, once belonged to the Romans.[67] In his detailed and astute reading of this passage, Petrides shows how Pachymeres has drawn on ancient ethnographic physiology, especially the polar antithesis of the Skythians and Ethiopians, though the way he configures and perfectly balances their qualities without a *tertium comparationis* or doctrine of the mean is unprecedented, as is his too-positive evaluation of the Ethiopians. There may be a subtext of imperial criticism here.[68] Michael's famous diplomatic skills failed to secure peace but were rather outmaneuvered by the sultan, who combined the positive qualities of both Cumans and Egyptians, i.e., strength *and* cunning. "We," the Romans, have failed on both counts. Ethnography, for the first time really since late antiquity, becomes again a vehicle for covert critique of Roman failures. And the giraffe? Its hybrid nature (in Greek it is called a "camel-leopard"), and light and dark colors may signify the mixed nature of the Mamluk regime that prevailed in the Near East. The fascination that it held for the people of the City may also symbolize how Baybars distracted the silly Byzantines in the game of diplomacy and accomplished his anti-Christian purpose.

It is not until book 5 that Pachymeres properly introduces the Tocharians (adding that "Mongol" is one of their names).[69] I paraphrase his account, which is prompted by an attempt by Michael VIII to win over Nogai Khan of the Golden Horde. They are a simple people who enjoy each other's company but are vicious in war. They are self-sufficient and do not unnecessarily complicate their lives. Genghis Khan (Τζιγκίσκαν) was their "lawgiver": he was not a wise man like Solon or Lykourgos but an unknown and wicked blacksmith who taught them how to prevail in war by following these laws: abstain from delicacies, content yourself with whatever lies at hand, support each other, stick together, eat any type of food, live with many women, avoid fixed abodes, and change locations in pursuit of advantage. For food they were either to hunt with arrows or drink the blood of their horses (that old Hun cliché found in Ammianus and Choniates). If they want more substantial sustenance, they were to place blood in a sheep's gut and set it under their saddle, thus heating up a quick dinner (another trope from the same tradition). They were not to busy themselves with refined goods (such as clothes), so as to devote themselves to war. They were to speak the truth and practice justice so that they could trust and rely on each other implicitly.[70]

Familiar images of the Skythian haunt this picture, especially the symbiotic relationship with the horse and the lack of culture and refinement (Pachymeres does leave one wondering whether the Mongol will satisfy his sexual needs with the same immediate pragmatism that he does his hunger). But it is not quite the same picture. These nomads have a *nomothetes*, a law-giver, meaning that they do have laws and customs, at least among themselves, and therefore they have a *purposeful* way of life: like all other systems of laws, theirs has a definite goal, to facilitate conquest. They are not, then, the lawless beasts of the Byzantine rhetorical tradition, but a finely-tuned fighting society. Moreover, their values are not, from the standpoint of the Greek and

Christian traditions, bad. These men are extremely disciplined, self-sufficient, rely on each other, despise the pursuit of refined material goods, practice justice, and tell the truth, at least to each other. The picture verges on being utopian, a sublimation of Spartan military or monastic values—except for the beastly aspects. We note the fictitious emphasis on their internal harmony, which Agathias had projected onto the Franks to draw his readers' attention to perceived Roman deficiencies.[71] The culture of the Mongols—who are winning on the world stage—highlights what the Christians lack, especially the Byzantines, who are losing. Ethnography again becomes a vehicle by which to highlight Roman flaws.

This is brought home in the sequel. Michael kept dispatching embassies to Nogai to win him over, sending him fancy clothes, foods, and aromatic wines. Nogai had learned to enjoy the food and wine—remember that nothing prevents Mongols from eating whatever lies at hand—but would inquire after the practical value of the clothes and other accessories (did those pearls, for instance, protect one from lightning, by any chance?). If not, he would reject them, or put them on briefly just for the sake of politeness, and would then go back to his dog- or sheep-skin. "He kept his eye on what was useful."[72] This is a mirror for the Byzantine to see himself in and shudder. The nomad was no longer a screen on which to project victory but a place to look for the causes of defeat, a mirror in which to see Roman vices clearly. Laiou has likewise argued that Pachymeres' panegyrical obituary of Ghazan, the first Mongol Ilkhan (d. 1304), which almost makes him out to be a Christian and an ideal leader, is meant specifically to offer a pointed contrast to the failings of Andronikos II.[73]

In later books, Pachymeres outlines the internal history of the Golden Horde after Nogai, focusing on changes of leadership and diplomatic relations with the Bulgarians and Byzantines.[74] The material in these passages was probably derived from Byzantine diplomats, and so, as we have come to expect, contains dry, factual accounts with no ethnographic elaboration. I have concentrated instead on the places where Pachymeres constructs a portrait of the type of culture the Mongols represent. Despite its traditional elements, in its precise contours it was something new in the annals of Byzantine ethnography, and was about to receive considerable elaboration. From an antitype used to project victory, the Skythians had suddenly become the wave of the future.

Pachymeres did not explicitly slot the Mongols into the Skythian category, though they certainly fit the type. In his *Moral Essays*, Theodoros Metochites, the leading thinker of the next generation, made the identification explicit; in fact, he assumed that the Skythians were one people and had a continuous history from Herodotos down to the Mongols of his own day. A word, first, on the text of the *Moral Essays*.

Published in the 1320s, it consists of 120 essays with personal reflections on a wide range of topics, including ancient authors, human psychology, moral maxims, political science, and history.[75] There are some thematic clusters, but no overall system of organization. The chapters that will concern us here have not been edited since 1821 and are due for a new edition. Moreover, the prose of Metochites is notoriously obscure, allusive, abstract, and repetitive. There is a strain of pessimism in the work, which is sometimes baffling. The first essay, for instance, argues that it is no longer possible for someone today, "living in the dregs of all time and human history," to say anything, because everything has already been said—yet that does not stop him from going on for another 826 pages of the modern edition.[76] This discrepancy might be ironized, but another cannot, Metochites' laments on the decline of the empire to its curent wretched state, especially the loss of Asia Minor.[77] A later cluster deals with politics and history, covering different regimes, and then the constitutions of the Greeks, Carthaginians, and Romans, culminating in four essays on how the Romans became so great that they aspired to world domination. The last of those essays ends with the early Christian theory that it was no accident that the conclusion of the civil wars and rise of Augustus coincided with the birth of Christ: this was because God decided to bring peace and salvation together to all of mankind.[78] This is an optimistic note on which to end: Roman and Christian values spread to the far corners of the earth. Pompeius had subdued piracy, and the Apostles had subjected the "barbarian, wild, and beastly peoples" to the Word of God.[79] But readers of the *Essays* know that the Roman empire has declined to insignificance. We immediately wonder what has caused this, and what has taken its place.

Well, the next essay, in fact the very last in the political-historical cluster, is "On the Skythians." The Skythians come after and terminate the sequence of Roman essays.[80] This might have been meant as more than a metaphor or image by Metochites. It gives the impression that the Roman world has yielded to that of the Skythians. Let us look closely at Metochites' ethnography.

He begins by saying that for as long as human history can recall they have been the most populous nation, have never been subjected by a foreign

power or ruled by a single one of their own men, and claim the largest portion of the earth in the north for themselves. They are extremely warlike,
even against each other. What follows illustrates how Metochites has fused
the history of all groups ever called Skythian by the Byzantines into one. At
one time, he says, they crossed the Danube and plundered Thrace, then they
went around the Adriatic to raid Italy and all the northern lands, including
Gaul and Spain; then a portion of them went to North Africa and established
themselves there. Metochites is here referring to the Goths and Vandals in
the late fourth and early fifth centuries. This allows him to suggest indirectly
that "the fall of Rome" was due to the Skythians, who are still around causing
trouble. Sure enough, he then refers to "our times" when the Skythians have
enslaved most of Asia "even as far as India." They may have played this role in
the story of Roman decline for a millennium. Metochites then surveys the
sequence of world empires from the Persians to the Romans, leaving us to
wonder whether he is implying that the Skythian empire will follow that of
his own people. For, he goes on, empires come and go according to chance
and the times; they grow old and die, just like people and animals, and are
replaced by others. The providential scheme of history touted at the end of
the previous essay has here been overcome by its exact opposite: Christ and
Augustus have been replaced by chance and natural, animal decay.

The Skythians, however, seem to form an exception to this universal
rule. They have fought against each other at times, but down to this day they
have not been subjected by a foreign conqueror (Metochites recounts at length
the failures of Dareios and Alexander against them). Then begins the ethnography proper.[81] Their way of life is utterly unlike that of any other people and
utterly impossible for anyone else to follow. It is a simple life with no artifice,
similar to that of the animals in that it entails no deliberation, contrivance,
or normal human customs and conventions. Still, they are sociable by nature
because they are human, but this can be seen in many animals too, so it is
not saying much. Few animals are completely solitary. They do not live in
cities, as almost all other people do, or protect themselves with walls, and
have no crafts, trades, or arts that improve life. They live almost in a random
way, with no real administration (we note that this is all in the present tense).
They wander throughout the year and live in the outdoors, content with air
and earth. They do need protection from the cold, but they manage this with
no difficulty. Metochites describes their tent-huts, which they carry around
with them on wagons. They do not use fire much for cooking as other peoples do, nor do they put much effort into meal preparation. A bit of meat

suffices, of both domesticated and wild animals which they hunt with bows. They cook it a little and then eat it, just as it is.

Turning to their society, their lives are simple, and they have none of the complications of a legal system. For Metochites this means no scheming, plotting, trials, verbal contests, slanders, arguments, or the like; they also have no judges, appeals, advocates, commentators, professional teachers and twisters of the law, channels of verbal pain, and punches delivered by the tongue, the sort of things that one finds among the Greeks and other barbarians. Without much by way of material goods, they lead simpler and more just lives than most people. This is all quite fascinating. Like Pachymeres, Metochites has constructed a fantasy of primitive life that verges on being an idyllic pastoral Arcadia.[82] He has honed in on the most disagreeable aspects of the legal culture of more civilized races and made the Mongols seem better for being primitive. They are noble savages and live more justly than other peoples, but apparently have no religion other than Nature.[83] This again highlights the stress that the Byzantine world view was enduring. These are not a people who need to be conquered, tamed, and civilized. They are an antitype that seems to have endured from time immemorial and, for all that it has not produced "civilization," they have managed to remain free and stick to their simple values. (This was probably also a response to ancient authors such as Strabo, who argued that the Skythians may have once been the simplest of men, the least malicious, and most self-sufficient, but have been corrupted by the luxuries, pleasures, and arts introduced by the south.)[84]

This idyllic picture is enabled in part by the suppression of the Mongols' ferocity. We should remember that the Byzantines had largely been spared it. Those who had not, tended toward darker images. Metochites does address the military aspect at the end of his essay, but this too from a positive point of view: no nation can prevail over them in war, given their overwhelming multitude and constant habituation in war such as no other people can show.[85]

One can hardly imagine a greater contrast than that between *Essays* 109 and 110 of the collection, and it is hard to believe that Metochites did not intend to undermine both Roman and Christian ideologies by juxtaposing them with this extraordinary essay on the Mongols. It is as though it points toward a new world order in which their way of life would henceforth rule over Roman-style cultures. This anxiety might be reflected in his ambiguous regard for the value of the classical Greek tradition in which he was immersed.[86] His view of the current crisis was global. In their digressions on the

Mongols, then, both Pachymeres and Metochites express disillusionment with venerable "truths" and profound lack of confidence in the ability of Rome to survive. Their primitive, idealized Mongols reflect that ideological predicament, though it seems Metochites was willing to raise the stakes from critiquing an emperor to the viability of the very ideology of empire itself.

What a fitting irony it was, then, that after his fall from power, in 1328, the floor mosaics of Metochites' own house—he was a great patron of the arts—were lifted up and sent as a gift to "the ruler of the western Skythians, who had asked for this to decorate the floors of his own house."[87] This strikingly symbolizes the transference of power from civilized Rome to primitive Skythia that he himself feared: the very ground on which he stood was literally torn out from under his feet.

But what did an allegedly primitive and unaffected Skythian ruler want with Byzantine mosaics? Pachymeres' Nogai would not have given them more than a glance. The episode of Metochites' floors indicates an avid desire for the finer things of civilized life. To answer this we turn directly to the historian who relates the story, Metochites' student Nikephoros Gregoras. His account of the Skythians, while drawing on those of Pachymeres and Metochites, will provide the necessary corrective and restore a sense of balance and historical proportion to their fantastic quasi-idealization.

Gregoras began writing his *Roman History* in the early 1330s and worked on it until the late 1350s. The later books focus on the Hesychast controversy and contain long theological discussions, but the digression on the Skythians, in the second book, was among the passages written first. For those sections Gregoras used Pachymeres' *History*, but he also had Metochites' *Moral Essays*; in fact, he is our main source for that work's original publication.[88] His account of the Skythians responds to both prior texts. Its rationale is that readers should be told who these Skythians are because they will recur throughout the narrative.[89] This is in fact the longest sustained foreign digression in the *Roman History*, and Gregoras' programmatic statement contains an implicit criticism of Pachymeres, who had not properly introduced this people. In fact, however, the digression is made up of material that is lifted from Metochites (including the same Homeric quotations) and secondarily from Pachymeres, with minor elaboration. The same picture emerges of a primitive and just society. One element that Gregoras adds is the theological comparison of these barbarians to natural catastrophes sent by God, such as storms, floods, earthquakes, hurricanes, and the like. Extending the riverine image, like water that flows into the sea and gradually becomes salty, the

Skythians change their way of life and take on the customs of the places where they settle.[90] But the implications of this will become apparent only at the end.

Gregoras tries to put Skythian history into some order, constructing the Byzantine equivalent of an *origo gentis* for them and tracing the movements of their various branches.[91] There was an original group of Skythians who stayed in the homeland and retained their proper name. Various subgroups broke off and settled in different lands, taking on the names of the peoples they conquered along with their customs, such as the Sauromatai, Massagetai, and Amazons. He adds to this list the Sarmatians, Germans, Celts, Gauls, Cimbri, Teutons, and of course the Vandals and Goths (though not by name). In the next section he turns to the history of Mongols, offering the first proper *origo* of this new phase of the Skythian people. It conforms in all respects to the previous specimens we have seen, especially the emphasis on leaders and geostrategic changes,[92] though it is a century removed from its subject (and contains some genealogical errors). He describes the formation of the Golden Horde and Ilkhanate. Gregoras notes that in this phase of expansion the Skythians encountered the remnants of prior phases of Skythian migration, though these peoples fled before the onset of the Mongols and some had turned to agriculture in the meantime. This, again, goes to the tendency of Skythians to be assimilated.

Specifically, the Mongols who took Mesopotamia "were pleased with the graceful nature of the land and stopped their long peregrinations . . . their leader thus chose for himself the part of Asia that is best suited for every type of human delight."[93] Gregoras has thus injected a hedonistic theme into his narrative that is absent from those of Pachymeres and Metochites. He goes on to explain that at first they knew nothing of gold, silver, and wealth— thus starting his argument from the same idealized point as his predecessors. But nature, he explains—the same Nature that Metochites claimed they worshipped?—will steer one toward the enjoyment of delights, if they are present, just as it can make one content in their absence. The Mongols adapted to their environment, and started to tax and enslave their subjects. The end of his digression effectively neutralizes the Skythian image that both Pachymeres and Metochites had deployed to critical effect:

> In time, as they came into contact with the customs of the Assyrians, Persians, and Chaldaeans, they adopted their religion and left behind their ancestral atheism; they also assimilated to their laws

and customs, which call for luxurious clothes and meals and generally prescribes a hedonistic way of life. They went far down the path
of this life-style change: previously they would cover their head with
a thick and unkempt hat and were happy, when it came to clothes,
to don the skin of wild animals and unworked hides. Likewise, for
weapons they had used makeshift clubs slings, spears, bows and
arrows. . . . But later they began to wear clothes made exclusively of
silk and gold thread. They reached an excessive extreme of decadent
luxury, positioning themselves at the diametrical opposite of their
former lifestyle.[94]

This demythologizes the Skythian type by folding it into the other types
that the Mongols encounter and conquer. It responds to Pachymeres specifically through the reference to the hats, exactly the sort of luxury in which, he
had claimed, Nogai allegedly had no interest. And it responds to Metochites
by arguing that his primitive savages posed no threat to the civilized order.
The Mongols might take it over, even appropriate the domestic mosaics of a
defeated Byzantine statesman, but life would go on as usual, for better or for
worse. In the face of the Skythian model, Gregoras invokes the model of
primitive roughness conquered by the decadent arts of empire—the story,
essentially, of Xenophon's *Education of Cyrus*, especially its last chapter. The
times did not call for paradigm shifts. There, with Gregoras' response, ended
the brief Byzantine flirtation with the new Skythians.[95]

The Latin World: A Hall of Mirrors

The Byzantines collectively labeled western medieval Europeans "Latins" or
"Franks." They knew well that the western world was internally complex,
with many ethnicities and languages, different types of states that were often
in conflict with each other, and a wide variety of military, religious, and commercial orders, but the collective designation made sense, for the whole was a
broad cultural unit of sorts. Modern historians also see its core as the Frankish-
Latin world: it was the modes and orders of the Franks that spread to the
periphery of the north and east, creating what we know as "Europe."[96]

Before the eleventh century, the Franks posed only a peripheral challenge to the Byzantine view of the world. They were descendants of the people
who had conquered (or been given) the Roman provinces of the west, and

after 800 they claimed the title and rights of the Roman emperors, effectively denying these to the Byzantines. But this challenge was intermittent and weak, especially in the ninth and early tenth centuries, so that the real Roman emperors could still collaborate with their western colleagues and even organize joint ventures and regard each other as peers. In the *De administrando imperio*, Konstantinos VII famously exempted the Franks from his strictures against treating any foreign people as an equal.[97] But this balanced dynamic began to change dramatically in the eleventh century, when the Latin world began to expand and make military, economic, and religious advances on the Byzantine sphere. Norman expansion, Venetian commercial interests, and the claims of papal supremacy led to open conflict, not just "tension." Theological differences hardened, battle lines were drawn, and wars were fought— and decisively lost, in 1204, by Byzantium. The Byzantine world was colonized and occupied by the Latins, though attempts to assimilate it failed. "Difference" was maintained, though in too close a contact.[98]

East-west conflict generated new images on both sides to serve the needs of polemic, exchange, and respective self-positioning. The overbearing Catholic prelate, the avarice and grasping of the Venetian merchant, and the impetuous fearlessness of the "Celtic" knight reflected the more defensive psychology of the Byzantines in the face of an "arrogant," aggressive opponent, while the images of fickle, treacherous, and effeminate "Greeks" that were devised by spokesmen for western powers reflect their contempt for a people who, they thought, ought to be subjugated. In terms of classical ethnography, the two sides of this polarity corresponded to ancient Roman stereotypes of northern barbarians (on the one hand) and of decadent *Graeculi* (on the other). This was no coincidence, as these types were brought out of retirement and given new life after the eleventh century. In terms of gender theory, Charis Messis has astutely shown that the Byzantines tended to define the Latins in terms of masculine vices, whereas the Latins defined the Byzantines in terms of feminine vices.[99] In a sense, this battle was lost before it was even fought, for the men dominate, that is their nature, even if they are rough about it. Another way to put it is to say that Byzantium was raped by the West, and had to live with its rapist while struggling to preserve its dignity, values, and faith.

The Byzantine material relating to the Latins is vast and cannot be covered here. Even if we exclude the strictly theological (a large part of the whole), there is still too much left, and that too is fragmentary. There was no one view of the Latins. The contexts that called for literary representation varied, and the French, Italians, and Germans, as well as the knights, bankers, and bishops, all called for different approaches, depending on the goals at hand (to repel their advances? to recruit them against the Turks?). Nor were there any extended ethnographies of the Latins that attempted to "make sense" of them, at least not until Laonikos.[100] We are dealing with hundreds of little bits of literary evidence that do not add up to a coherent picture, so we must necessarily be selective. I have chosen to focus on specific topics such as the military culture of the western knights and the constitutions of the Italian republics because they tended to generate slightly more extensive discussions.

My analysis is also based on the following premises. On the one hand, the majority of Byzantines preferred Turkish (Muslim) over Latin (Catholic) rule. This is a big claim, though hardly original, and I will not make the case here.[101] Turkish rule was exploitative and horrible and the result of violence. But the Turks were also willing to allow the Byzantines to continue to be who they were, Orthodox Romans: their identity was preserved. Catholic rule was exploitative, racist, and the result of violence. But most of the Latins, and especially their Church, were unwilling to recognize the Byzantines for who they were, treating them instead as "Greeks" and heretics who had to be brought into line with western beliefs, practices, and hierarchies, or made to feel that they were inferior to them. The Byzantines understood this perfectly well and made their "choice" accordingly. (Incidentally, the reaction to the current "crisis" in Greece is shaped by perceptions that go this far back, as do the reasons why the Orthodox world is in some ways more hostile to Catholicism than to Islam.) Byzantines under Turkish rule converted to Islam in greater numbers than they did to Catholicism in areas under Latin rule.

On the other hand, the debate was not really framed as a choice between Latins and Turks in a discussion of their relative merits. The choice was always between being pro- or anti-Latin, with the latter option entailing Turkish rule by default. There were articulate spokesmen for choosing the Latins and accepting their rule, and these arguments were made not only by converts such as Kydones but also by the emperors who would thereby lose their territories.[102] There were no equivalent, pro-Turkish advocates, at least none whose works survive. The debate was framed entirely in terms of the Latins. In other words, the Latin west was the Byzantines' primary sparring partner when it came to renegotiating their identities and defining their respective positions. It was onto the Latins that they projected and sought to ameliorate their anxieties; it was the Latins' view of them that mattered most. No one *wanted* to be ruled by the Turks: the question was whether they could stand being ruled by the Latins.

This tendency to "project" onto the Latins is evident already in Anna Komnene's obsessive fixation on Robert Guiscard and Bohemond and her nervous anxiety to use the image of her father Alexios in order to counteract the ideological (not just military) threat they represented.[103] The masculinity they exuded and performed made her insecure about traditional Byzantine values. Niketas Choniates also, in the part of his *History* dealing with the Third and Fourth Crusades, repeatedly forces his (Byzantine) reader to view himself from a western perspective, often with self-critical results.[104] This should not be mistaken for an identification with the cause of, say, Friedrich Barbarossa, as it sometimes is, nor do Choniates' long tirades against Latin greed and brutality make him a confused author. In this context, "Friedrich" is a literary construct that enables an internal dialogue and expresses self-doubts. Niketas rather comes across as almost pathologically concerned about "how they see us." During and after the Crusades, one gains an impression from many Byzantine authors that they feel watched and assessed by the Latin gaze, enabling them to project and externalize their own fears. In fact, many of the policies of Manuel I can be interpreted this way—and were, by his critics.[105]

The Germanic savages of the age of Prokopios, who performed human sacrifices over bridges, had evolved into a peer culture, different enough to be set off but similar also in enough ways to make comparison inevitable. In the later Byzantine period, the balance of power shifted decisively in favor of the Franks. Let us consider some of the ways Byzantine authors coped.

Origins

In studying the fall of the western Roman empire, historians have moved from an older model that stressed the barbarian conquest of the Roman provinces and the establishment of "barbarian Europe" to a model which sees the barbarians as artifacts of the Roman world and thus posits the continuation of a Roman order in the West after the alleged "Fall" (though many are now returning to the older model). Byzantine views of the same event experienced a similar paradigm shift in the later period.

Consider Konstantinos Stilbes, a scholar and bishop who drew up a "list of Latin errors"—104 of them to be exact—after the sack of Constantinople

by the Crusaders. We touched on these lists above under the rubric of polemical anti-ethnography.[106] Indeed, they tell us much about how the Byzantines perceived the customs of the Catholic Church, and, as Kolbaba pointed
out, many of the said customs highlight more cultural differences than religious ones. Stilbes accuses Latin priests of having sex and calling it a wet dream
(no. 37) and of fighting in battle (no. 38), and he rails against the diet of the
Latins, which apparently includes bear, jackal, turtle, and dolphin (no. 66).
He also accuses them of ethnic bias, in that they worship only saints of their
own race (no. 49), but not Constantine the Great, who was one of their own
kind, because he founded New Rome, which they resent. So who are these
Latins? What is their "race"? For Stilbes, they were not Roman. Drawing on
previous Byzantine lists of such "errors," he argues that the nations beyond
the Adriatic Sea, including the Italians, Lombards, Franks, Germans, Amal-
fitans, Venetians, and the like, were once all outside the Church and held to
forbidden barbarian customs, that is, they were pagan barbarians. Then the
Vandals destroyed ancient Rome, wiped out the Romans, and implanted
their Arian and Nestorian heresies in Rome, whence the Franks and Germans picked them up. Only the Calabrians are true orthodox Christians (no.
104). Barbarians and heretics are thus folded into the same category.[107]

For Stilbes, writing in the aftermath of 1204, the Latins were of barbarian origin and out-and-out heretics who had basically destroyed the Roman
order in the west. But compare the very different narrative told by Georgios
Akropolites half a century later. He too was writing a treatise *Against the Latins*, but the Latins are now for him peers who have deviated from a common
Roman matrix. He opens by addressing them as "Romans, you who come
from elder Rome; I wish to call you brothers because we think and believe
the same way."[108] Of course, the bulk of his treatise explains precisely how
they do *not* believe in the same way, but the conclusion makes a remarkable
appeal to a lost unity, treating the Latins and Byzantines as only two halves
of the former Roman empire that have developed in different directions. The
passage deserves to be quoted.

> It seems, O Italians, that you no longer remember our ancient
> harmony. . . . But no other nations were ever as harmonious as the
> Greeks and the Italians. And this was only to be expected, for science
> and learning came to the Italians from the Greeks. And after that
> point, so that they need no longer use their ethnic names, a New
> Rome was built to complement the Elder one, so that all could be

called Romans after the common name of such great cities, and have the same faith and the same name for it. And just as they received that most noble name from Christ, so too did they take upon themselves the national name [i.e., of Rome]. And everything else was common to them: magistracies, laws, literature, city councils, law courts, piety itself; so that there was nothing that was not common to those of Elder and New Rome. But O how things have changed![109]

The Latins are here seen not as the barbarian conquerors who destroyed Rome but as the Latin-speaking half of the Roman empire itself. They are lifted as a whole out of one ethnographic category and placed into another, the very one from which the Byzantines also traced their descent. The history of the Fall of Rome is elided. According to this version, the ancient Greeks and Italians jointly entered into a Roman venture, creating a common culture (Akropolites stresses the Greek contribution). Later, for unknown reasons, their paths diverged. This fraternal picture, we must remember, occurs in a treatise that is theologically *anti*-Catholic. That is, even in opposing the "Italians" Akropolites has already internalized them as a Byzantine alter ego. It is through this process that they became the Byzantines' main interlocutors in the final centuries, the foil against which all issues were framed and discussed, even if it meant constructing new and purposeful narratives such as this one in order to frame the debate and give it emotive purpose.

Postulating a common origin, of course, gave a rhetorical advantage to the Byzantines, who believed that they had remained faithful to the original position and that it was the Latins who had deviated from it. Whether this argument had any effect on the Latins or remained trapped within the Byzantine hall of mirrors constructed by these anti-Catholic polemics remains unclear. But, still, it bound the two sides more closely and allowed them to be compared, to the advantage of the "Greeks." After all, ancient philosophy, the New Testament, and the Church Fathers—the important ones, at any rate—were in Greek. What did the Latins have to show? Here too, however, Byzantine opinion had to accommodate the maturation of medieval Latin thought, especially during the thirteenth century. This posed an additional challenge. It was one thing to redescribe the Latins and place them into the "Roman" ethnographic category. But what if they began to outperform the Byzantines according to the very indexes of Roman culture?

The first trace of such an anxiety that I have been able to discover is in a letter by Theodoros II Laskaris, the pupil and then emperor of Akropolites. An otherwise proud defender of the "Greeks," their language, and their philosophy, he admits there that the latter has slipped away from them and dwells now among the barbarians (i.e., the Latins).[110] By the mid-fourteenth century, it was becoming increasingly apparent to many Byzantines that the balance of intellectual power, and not just military and economic strength, was shifting in favor of the west. For the first time since late antiquity, works began to be translated from Latin into Greek. It was no coincidence that this was also when some Byzantine thinkers began to go over to the Latin side and convert to Catholicism. There would be more after the late fourteenth century, including Manuel Chrysoloras, Ioannes Argyropoulos, and Bessarion. But the man who led the way in the mid-fourteenth century was Demetrios Kydones.

Kydones defended his position in a long *Apologia*, using both arguments and autobiography. This is a fascinating document that deserves more study, but I will focus here on his view of the common origins of Latins and Byzantines and his reconfiguration of ethnographic categories. Kydones did not merely have an "inner Latin" as an interlocutor: he had internalized the entire Latin position and was but expressing it in Greek. He justified his conversion by openly proclaiming not only that the Catholics were right on the issues but that contemporary Latins intellectually surpassed the Byzantines. When he began to translate Aquinas, he says, the Byzantines began to realize that not all Latins were like the ones whom they saw in the east, sailors and merchants. "They were not inferior to the Greeks when it came to wisdom . . . though they may not previously have appeared that way to the locals here."[111] Kydones then goes on to rebut the opposition that this paradigm shift had caused among elements of the Byzantine intelligentsia.

> For too long my countrymen had been content to hold on to the staid old notion that mankind was divided into two groups: Greeks and barbarians. They held fast to their stupid myopic view that the latter were nothing more than oxen and asses; the Latins could not be credited as being capable of anything worthy of human beings. They themselves, of course, claimed the credit for Plato, all his disciples, and all Greek wisdom. To the Latins they attributed the skills of armorers and a dubious skill in trade and in running taverns. In former years, no one among us took any pains to show our country-

men that the Latins also had contributed something of cultural value. . . . The long historic rift between the Byzantine and Latin worlds had caused a deep alienation between us. . . . An alleged devotion to the productions of our own Greek scholars served as a pretext for concealing their envy.[112]

In Kydones, the Byzantines' Latin alter ego is competing to replace his previous identity as an Orthodox Roman. His language swerves in and out of that position, switching from the first to the third person. He cannot decide whether a specifically anti-Catholic Orthodoxy is essential to the identity of his countrymen, and he disingenuously advocates "openness" to western positions and the unanimity of the Fathers in order to insinuate that the Orthodox were wrong (and thereby damned). Nor is he sure who the "Romans" were. The western view was that the Byzantines were ethnic Greeks and religiously either schismatics or heretics (depending on whom you asked), but Kydones refers to the Byzantines alternately as Romans or Greeks, the latter mostly in connection with their language and literature. The westerners he calls Romans, Latins, or just westerners. As a result, in advocating a western alliance for Byzantium, he can ask, "Who but the Romans would make the best allies for the Romans?"[113] Like Akropolites, he seems to have thought that Latin and Byzantine "Romans" had the same origin, "but later, I don't know how, we separated from each other."[114] At any rate, New Rome (Constantinople) owes allegiance to Elder Rome, as a colony to its mother city.[115] Yet while he touted his patriotism—"my fatherland above all else, after God. . . . [I would rather be] there in misfortune than enjoy all advantages among the foreigners"[116]—he also accepted Venetian citizenship and resided in the west for long periods.

Despite Kydones' efforts, some, perhaps even most, Byzantines still regarded the Latins not only as heretics (or schismatics) but as barbarians too,[117] two categories that overlapped, as we saw with Stilbes. Still, that view was clearly on the wane among the literate classes, in addressing whom Kydones was perhaps pushing against an open door. Those classes tended to have extensive dealings with the Latins, mostly financial and mercantile.[118] Moreover, the very existence of Kydones himself illustrated the Byzantine internalization of the Latin world. The debate with the Latins could simply become a debate with the likes of Kydones and, whatever he was, he was no barbarian. He represented the fact that in this debate Byzantium was coming to grips with aspects of itself. By the fourteenth century it was fairly clear that the Latins could not be reduced to a single barbarian ethnotype; their world was too diverse and too similar to that of the Romans. Specific stereotypes could be deployed for limited purposes such as warfare (which we will discuss below), but not for the whole. Kydones was right that the Greek-barbarian distinction was no longer applicable. The two worlds, Byzantine and Latin, were more like estranged siblings than anti-types. Rather than defining the Latins as inverse "others," as they had always done with the Skythians, for example, later Byzantine writers sought rather to see how they measured up against the Latins, who were now expanding dynamically. As we will see, the stance of these writers was mostly defensive.

Looking ahead to the early fifteenth century, converts to Catholicism such as Argyropoulos and Bessarion would fully accept the western view and regard the Byzantines as Greeks, not "really" Romans at all, going further in this respect than Kydones ever did. By that point the appropriation of the Roman legacy by the West was complete, and there was hardly anyone left on the Byzantine side to reclaim it. This had dramatic consequences for the ability to write ethnography, for the Byzantines' own subject-position was in question. One radical solution, proposed by Plethon and his student Laonikos, was to sever their ties to both the Roman and Orthodox legacies and construct a new Hellenic identity. This was an extension and amelioration of the Greek position into which western aggression, both ideological and military, had forced the Byzantines, for all that it rejected Catholicism itself. Plethon and Laonikos enabled a new phase of Greek ethnography, in fact a revival of Herodotos, by resituating themselves amid the categories inherited from the classical tradition and drawing all new boundaries. But that is a story for a different discussion.[119]

Warfare

The "Latin" had taken up residence in the house of the Byzantine self, becoming part of the internal conversation and even a family member—sometimes literally. How could firm lines be drawn, especially as more territory came under direct Latin rule and the emperors themselves ostensibly backed Union and began to travel to Rome? Gregoras explains, for example, that the opponents of the late thirteenth-century patriarch Georgios (or Gregorios) of Cyprus accused him of bringing "Latin habits" with him when, at age twenty, he left Cyprus to take on "Roman customs" (also that he had been ordained by a Catholic). This controversy is attested in contemporary texts as well, including the patriarch's autobiography.[120] "He was born and raised among the Italians, and only affects our speech and dress," said his predecessor Ioannes Bekkos.[121] Gregoras dismisses the charge, but only because he wants to defend Georgios personally. Bekkos and his allies presumably felt that they could tell the difference between Italian and Roman (Byzantine) customs, and Gregoras himself elsewhere complains about the adoption of foreign fashions at the court, not only Latin but Turkish, "so that one could no longer tell who the Roman was."[122] He also relates that Theodoros Palaiologos, a son of Andronikos II by his western wife Yolanda-Eirene, who had been raised as a Catholic and became the marquis of Montferrat, was excluded from the succession by his father because "in his mentality, faith, appearance, the shaving of his beard, and all his other habits he was a complete Latin."[123] So one could still wear a Latin hat and be a Roman, but too much acculturation could make even the son of the Byzantine emperor into a Latin. Cultural boundaries were being monitored and policed intensely. (We will meet Theodoros again below.)

I would like to interrogate another similar distinction made by Gregoras, this time regarding martial culture, because it implicates ethnographic categories too (though not clothing). The *Gasmouloi* were the offspring of mixed marriages, usually between a Latin (Venetian) man and a Byzantine woman, that took place in the context of the Latin empire of Constantinople (1204–1261). Michael VIII recruited many of them into his navy when he retook the city. Gregoras notes that "they had been raised in both Roman and Latin customs, so that they had circumspection in battle (ἐσκεμμένως) from the Romans and daring (εὔτολμον) from Latins."[124] Presumably this means that they could be either circumspect or daring as occasion demanded, not that they somehow combined both qualities. But what boundary is Gregoras policing here? What military ethnography lies behind this distinction?

Gregoras explains the essential differences between Byzantine and Latin military tactics in a later passage describing how Michael VIII's generals went against an army sent by Charles of Anjou.

> They decided that it would not be a good idea or altogether safe to wage open war against the enemy, as the latter had a numerical advantage and were very well armed and armored. Instead, they set ambushes and guerilla attacks and shot at them from the steep hills in the region in order to spur them into a wild rage, an uncoordinated

rush and charge. For the race of the Italians is raised in the following customs. If they advance to battle in an orderly way, they form a
solid and immovable wall. But if they deviate from their accustomed
order even a little bit, there is nothing to prevent their enemies from
taking them prisoner. Sometimes their innate stupidity and arrogance[125] has greatly harmed them as they cannot be marshalled easily when their anger gets the best of them. The Roman army had
long known about this and so engaged them with tricks and strata-
gems.[126]

It is not clear from this account what the "natural" state of the Italian warrior
is. The battle formation to which he is "accustomed" is strict and orderly, so
that he risks defeat by deviating from it even a little bit. But this formation
seems barely able to contain the seething rage and wild impetuosity that
churn beneath the surface. A few guerilla attacks can set them off? This suggests that the orderly formation is actually superimposed on a more primal,
uncontrollable nature to which it is rather unsuited. The task of the Byzantine general is to unravel this combination scientifically and just let the Italian be himself.

That the true nature of the Latin is the impetuous one is suggested by
the reference to the "daring" of the Gasmouloi, which they inherited from
their Latin side. "Essential" differences are at play here. In fact, Gregoras is
replaying an old discussion. Among the many faces that the Latins presented
to Byzantium, none was more striking than the armored knight who charged
the enemy head-on and decided the matter by breaking, chopping, and
grinding his enemy into pieces. The Normans in the eleventh century were
the first to bring this type to Byzantine attention, and its power elicited swift
defensive reactions, on the page as well as the battlefield. This became another arena in which to construct and maintain essential differences in response to the Latin challenge, both the "inner" and the outer.

Byzantine strategy is famous for its calculated avoidance of pitched battles and heroic last stands (with one, final, exception, though that was led by
a Genoese). Victory was to be obtained preferably by diplomacy, bribery,
subversion, tactics of delay, and harassment of the enemy. These preferences
were made explicit in the manuals and implemented in practice.[127] The *Strategikon* of Maurikios (ca. 600) stipulates that "officers should be stationed in
safe places, so they do not dash forward and fall in battle," because this
"would discourage the soldiers."[128] The herald is commanded to shout (in

camp Latin) to the soldiers: "Do not fall back. Do not go ahead of the standard. . . . This is how a brave soldier should act. If you leave the standard, you will not be victorious. . . . Whether fighting, pursuing the enemy, or in the front ranks, do not charge out impetuously and cause your ranks to be broken up."[129] "Bravery" meant staying in close formation. The army was supposed to advance in a disciplined fashion.[130] A tenth-century manual associated with Nikephoros II Phokas advised generals to "avoid not only an enemy force of superior strength but also one of equal strength," *unless* it has already been defeated three times.[131]

The goal was victory through strategy, not heroism, which was not much prized. Byzantium's greatest conqueror had been Basileios II, a master strategist, not a hero. That was how Psellos had described him.[132] He would not return to the City unless he had accomplished his strategic objectives, no matter the weather. He had an exact knowledge of military matters and had studied all the manuals. He micromanaged the battlefield but never took part in battle, knowing how quickly the tide could turn. During battles he maintained close contact with all parts of his army and forbade anyone from rushing ahead of the formation. He did not reward anyone who did so even if it led to a rout of the enemy. There were no prizes for ἀριστεία, a Homeric term, only dishonorable discharge. Basileios had his eye solely on τὸ νικᾶν (winning) and knew that it was best attained by compact formations.

That was before the Latin knight, whose appearance caused discomfort and defensiveness among Byzantine spokesmen. It was at this point that what had previously been taken for granted as good sense now had to be defended. Kinnamos, a secretary who discussed the works of Aristotle with emperor Manuel Komnenos, offered a precise formulation:

> Strategy is an art (τέχνη), and one who practices it must be adaptable and cunning and know how to make a timely alteration at every turn. For there is a time when it is not shameful to flee, if the occasion allows, and again to pursue relentlessly, each according to one's advantage; where success would seem more by cunning than by force, risking everything is to be deprecated. Since many and various matters lead toward one end, it is irrelevant (ἀδιάφορον) which one you use to reach it.[133]

However true this might have been, "win by any means necessary" is not quite as heroic as "stand and fight." Everything was about what Kinnamos labels the "one end," i.e., victory; there was no room for a personal ethic of heroism, which was only a distraction. This could, and did, lead to accusations of cowardice by the Latins,[134] which were painful at a time when the Byzantine aristocracy was itself becoming increasingly militaristic and even heroic in its outlook.[135] But what they perceived as the "reckless impetuosity" and "savage fury" of the knights went beyond what even they aspired to display.[136]

The behavior of the Norman and French knights reminded the Byzantines of the Celts. According to well-known ancient stereotypes, they would rush into battle without any fear, to die or win. As it happened, the classicizing ethnonym which Byzantine authors used for the Normans and French was "Celt." We saw above how Anna Komnene exploited this to magnify her father's wars against them, while simultaneously defending his more "cautious" Byzantine approach to battle by invoking Aristotle's doctrine of the mean (in this case, between cowardice and impetuosity).[137] But we have to remember that all these discussions were internal. The use of classical names and Aristotelian arguments to ameliorate a perceived flaw would make sense only to another Byzantine, not to a Norman knight. We see again the Byzantines seeing themselves in the Latin mirror and trying to fix (for their own sake) the picture they saw there. Deploying Celtic stereotypes was one way to do it. As late as the mid fifteenth century, Laonikos was still calling the French "Celts" and claiming, like Gregoras, that they were impetuous and stupid. It was to these qualities that he ascribed their defeat at Nikopolis, in 1396.[138]

The image of the ferocious Celt, then, was one way by which Byzantine authors continued to cast at least some Latins as barbarians, even in an age when they had to concede intellectual parity to western philosophers. But at the same time this approach revealed a fascination with an otherness whose power and allure they could not quite resist. This emerges from a later passage in none other than Gregoras, with whom we began. He describes the jousts and tournaments (ντζούστρα . . . τορνεμέν) organized in 1332 by Andronikos III, who participated in them himself. He defines these as western customs that the Byzantine court had only adopted.[139] But were they not also Byzantine customs then? At what point does this ethnographic digression cease to be foreign? The emperors had been staging jousts and even fighting in them since the days of Manuel I Komnenos, two centuries earlier, and they had been depicted in both art and literature.[140] To be sure, it was probably an intermittent spectacle, but at some point you can stop pretending that it is not yourself you are really talking about, unless you are insecure about your "inner Latin."

Constitutional Theory

In an earlier chapter we raised the problem of the silence that Byzantine sources of the middle period maintain regarding the political regimes of the Italian cities, especially Venice.[141] The silence is not especially problematic until the twelfth century. Before that there would have been little reason for the Byzantines to recognize those cities as significant enough to merit ethnographies or political commentary. Conversely, when they burst dynamically on the Byzantine scene, there might have been considerable embarrassment or uncertainty about how to explain the dominance that commercial cities of former subjects had attained over the empire of the Romans. Byzantine theorists were certain that monarchy was the best and most powerful type of regime, so the rise of the commercial republics at the empire's expense was best seen as a purely internal failure of imperial leadership. This is precisely how most Byzantine historians approached the theme of decline.[142] Moreover, both classical and Christian genres of literature avoided tackling economic issues, which alone would have explained the rise of the Italian cities in the Aegean. Byzantine statesmen may have understood what was going on perfectly well, but putting it into formal prose was another matter.

We have good surveys of what the Byzantines eventually did write about the constitutions of the Italian cities, especially Genoa and Venice.[143] The topic is of general interest, in no small part because of the centrality of political theory to the rise of Renaissance "civic" humanism and so of modern political philosophy. What I will do here instead is offer a more literary reading of early Palaiologan accounts of Genoa in particular, focusing on how images of the city were crafted to make internal arguments. Aspects of this theme have been explored already, but it should be integrated into the overall argument that this section has made about how the representation of the Latin world functioned as a Byzantine hall of mirrors. When they looked closely at the West, the Byzantines often saw aspects of themselves looking back.

The first Byzantine account of Genoa's constitution occurs in a panegyrical oration of Manuel Holobolos in honor of Michael VIII Palaiologos, dated to 1265. Interestingly, Holobolos was also the first Byzantine to engage in a serious study of Latin literature, for all that he was anti-Union (and suffered for it).[144] He calls Genoa a proud metropolis that has established many colonies. He explains the name as *Ianua*, the Gates (to France), an etymology that would be repeated by later Greek writers such as Laonikos, or as derived from the god Janus. It was settled by Italians who govern themselves in a manner similar to that of the ancient Athenians. They are adept at naval matters, including battles; their city is supplied through trade over the seas. The most noble, wealthy, and senior of its citizens crossed the wide ocean in search of Michael, and when they had found him and tasted his sweet eloquence, they recognized him as their caring father. Holobolos then gives them a page-long speech praising Michael, crammed full of classical references, followed by a description of some embroidered silks that he gave them.[145]

That the Genoese were a naval power was not a striking thing to say in 1265. But why the stretched comparison to Athenian democracy? The speech, made soon after the Byzantine reconquest of Constantinople, praises Michael in classical and Biblical terms for possessing all the virtues and restoring Roman imperial authority. The comparison of Genoa to Athens is actually only the first part of the claim being made in this section of the speech. Its conclusion is stated by the Genoese themselves, in their oration. They come before Michael and submit their city to him, an act presented in constitutional language: "Until now we have regarded democracy as the best type of regime and deemed monarchy to be like tyranny . . . but from now on we wish to be ruled by a true king."[146] In other words, Manuel calls Genoa a democracy only in order to subordinate democracy to monarchy—an argument his audience would have been willing to accept—and thereby explain why Genoa surrendered itself to Michael VIII. The comparison serves this rhetorical purpose only; a realistic account of the Genoese constitution would mess up the argument by disrupting the structural analogies. Genoa is but a foil for the renewed supremacy of Roman monarchy.

Holobolos made "democracy" vanish beneath a wave of panegyrical rhetoric. In his *Moral Essays*, which we examined earlier in connection with the Mongols, Metochites attacked it directly. In fact, democracy is the subject of the long essay (96) that opens the cluster of political meditations that closes with the essay on the Mongols. Metochites depicts democracy as an inherently unstable type of regime. He focuses on Athens, but at the end extends his conclusions to Genoa, which, he says, was careening toward disaster precisely because it had recently introduced a radical form of democracy, a claim that was not entirely devoid of truth.[147] What lies behind this passage? Shawcross has demonstrated that Metochites was actually responding to a treatise on government written by Theodoros Palaiologos, the son of Andronikos II and Yolanda-Eirene, who, as we saw, had been sent to the west to be raised a Catholic and became the marquis of Montferrat.[148] In his treatise, written in Greek but surviving only in a later French translation, Theodoros had advocated a more deliberative and conciliar form of government along western lines that would limit the power of the ruler. Without such institutions a monarchy is only a tyranny, governed by the whim of a chief minister; here Theodoros was pointing to his personal enemy Metochites. Shawcross traces how Metochites' essay seeks to discredit Theodoros' proposals and his credentials for making them.

What needs to be emphasized for our purposes is that this exchange was not so much a conflict between "western" and "Byzantine" ideas, though in part it was that. It could just as well be regarded as a conflict between two factions at the Byzantine court, between the son of the emperor and his minister. Theodoros, after all, was not devoid of support. Theodoros was the "inner Latin," which is why authors hostile to him, such as Gregoras, stressed his Latin way of life and appearance. They were trying to depict him as an outsider who should have no voice in the debate over the Byzantine crisis. His voice is assimilated to that of his subversive mother, Yolanda of Montferrat. Gregoras explains that she had nagged Andronikos II to impose what we might call a feudal order on what remained of the Roman empire, so that its territories should be divided up among all the heirs. When she failed to get her way she moved to Thessalonike and soon agreed to send her son to Italy. Gregoras takes care to note that the latter was married to a daughter of the Genoese Spinola family.[149] So, in the end, Metochites' attack on Genoese "democracy" points home, to yet another Palaiologos and an internal debate.

Metochites had actually discussed the Italian "democracies," comparing them to the ancient Greek ones, in a work written two decades before the 1320s debate with Theodoros. This was a long essay *On Character or on High Culture*.[150] His aim was to reflect on the attitudes of learned Byzantines, not to comment purposefully on Italian constitutions; the latter are brought into the discussion only in order to reveal Byzantine biases. Specifically, Metochites is evaluating the relative importance of the deeds and literature of the Greeks, and he is about to weigh them against those of the Romans. His argument is that Greek literature is more important than Greek history, and the only reason that we care and know so much about the history is that the Greeks were good at writing about it. Many nations throughout history have performed similar deeds, it's just that we don't know about them or don't care. Specifically, many cities in Italy have exactly the same type of constitutions as the ancient cities, lacking almost none of the same institutions. And yet no one cares about them the way we care about the Greek cities, simply because the latter were described by Thucydides and Xenophon. He then goes on to argue that the Romans performed incomparable deeds that are definitely worthy of attention.

It is hard to know what prescriptive conclusion we are supposed to draw from this. Certainly not that we should study modern Italian history more if we want to be consistent, and more likely the exact opposite: we should focus less on the history of the *Greeks*, recognizing that we pay attention to them only because of their literature. In itself, Greek history is as uninteresting as Italian history. The history that we should be paying attention to is that of the Romans, from whom the Byzantine state was descended.[151] Perhaps the point here is merely to offer a comparative reflection on Byzantine reading habits and values.

In all the texts we have examined, Italian constitutions have been defined and discussed negatively in order to affirm Byzantine values, whether political or cultural—or the interests of the author or his patron. Syros has demonstrated that the long account of Italian civic instability in the *History* of Kantakouzenos, especially the 1339 revolution in Genoa, is really an indirect commentary on the same conditions in the Byzantine empire and is meant to justify the aristocratic policies that the emperor had implemented when he had been in power. Italy is again a screen onto which Byzantine debates are projected.[152]

In time positive images were disseminated too, especially, as we would expect, by converts to Catholicism, but not only by them. We have already seen Gregoras praise the governance of Hospitaller Rhodes, Mamluk Egypt and Syria, and Lusignan Cyprus in order to critique the bad state of affairs that, he claimed, the rise of Palamas had caused in Byzantium (ecclesiastically and politically). In the generations after Gregoras, the praise of western regimes was increasingly associated with conversion to Catholicism. Kydones again led the way here, with a brief description of Venice, whose citizenship he would receive at the end of his life. It is remarkable that we have to wait so long for a discussion of Venice in particular. It is a topic that was not discussed for over a century and a half after 1204. Of course, Kydones was hardly an outsider when it came to Venice. In a letter from the early 1370s to Manuel Palaiologos, he launched a new tradition: the praise of Venice (yet without mentioning the city by name).[153] He praised in general terms its location, the beauty of its homes, churches, arts, the market, the ships, and the Arsenal. "Above all," however, he praised

> the prudence of its Senate, the enforcement of the laws, the punishment of criminals, the rewarding of the virtuous, the sharing of goods among the citizenry, their unanimity about what is expedient and what harmful, the fact that no one is a lazy drone plotting to appropriate the labor of others, and, in sum, the harmony that pervades the entire city as it would a piece of music.

This passage is too brief to merit a long discussion. But in its brevity it contains the seeds of two longer accounts, the first an *ekphrasis* of its physical aspects and the second an argument for the superiority of its social and political arrangements. One can infer much longer treatments based on the outline that Kydones gives here, and we can imagine him delivering them, at least in oral discussions. Kydones is the first Byzantine to praise an existing republic, though we have to remember that he spoke for a minority of Byzantines. Nevertheless, as with all texts we have examined so far, Kydones' prime concern was possibly not to speak about Venice as such but again about Byzantium, only indirectly. Instead of using the disorders of Genoa to condemn by proxy his own political enemies, as Metochites and Kantakouzenos had done, Kydones highlights the virtues of the Venetian social order clearly in order to condemn the abuses and disorders of his own native country, abuses that were being discussed in almost all the literature of the period. We can just about read the passage quoted above as saying that the Byzantine Senate was foolish, that the laws were not being enforced, criminals not being punished, good men not being rewarded, that there was no consensus among the populace, and, above all, that "lazy drones" were exploiting the labor of others, a complaint that ran through Byzantine society. Kydones' Venice is nothing but the anti-image of Byzantium viewed critically. In the many ways that we have examined, that was often the role that the Latins played in Byzantine literature. They colonized first the Byzantines' physical world, and then their minds.

Epilogue: Looking to a New World

Until the 1360s, the Palaiologan empire produced a diverse range of sources that pertain to our theme, written by intelligent men who recast traditional forms and images to fashion new perspectives and arguments. Byzantium was now a much smaller fish in a more dangerous ocean, but it nevertheless produced some of the most innovative thinkers in its history. This production peters out after 1360s, as the Ottoman Turks were solidifying their hold on Anatolia and beginning their conquest of the Balkans. It was not until after the fall of Constantinople that post-Byzantine writers produced another set of highly innovative texts about both the Latin West, now in its Renaissance phase, and the Ottoman empire of Mehmet II, already a major world power. This forces us to cope with a century-long gap and a dearth of texts for precisely the period of Ottoman expansion. The later writers, especially Laonikos, the New Herodotos and student of Plethon (the most radical philosopher in Byzantine intellectual history), belong to a different world to which we cannot do justice here. But I would like, in looking forward to that world, to outline some of the ways in which familiar tensions continued to play out in its literary production, especially regarding the Ottoman Turks. In fact, opposing trends diverged ever further into increasingly extreme formulations.

We have repeatedly seen how Byzantine sources invested in Roman and Christian ideologies tended to denigrate foreign peoples, at least when they failed to assimilate to Roman Orthodox norms. The court had an interest in projecting the image of the "Skythian" as the antithesis of Roman civilization in order to highlight the emperor's protective role and civilizing impact. We have, for example, an early image in an imperial oration by Metochites of the Ottomans as human-shaped beasts that were overrunning Asia Minor.

The function of this image in the overall argument of the oration remains to be studied, but it is worth pointing out that this was the same Metochites who, years later and in a different literary context, produced a strangely positive image of the Mongols, the archetypal Skythians of the age.[1] The historian of the Fall who reflected this negative view was Doukas, who was pro-Union. The Ottomans in Doukas have no legitimacy. He routinely calls their sultan a "tyrant" and never a *basileus*. In his eyes, the Turks not only are vile infidels but represent a new form of moral degradation, which he conveys by emphasizing their voracious and indiscriminate sexual appetites. There is no real ethnography in Doukas, only polemic. He was judging the Turks by the standards of the old Roman Orthodox empire that no longer existed.

We have seen also that Orthodox literature of the Palaiologan period did not let up at all in its polemic against Islam, even as Christian communities and the Palamite establishment were coming to terms with their Muslim masters. The rhetoric of theodicy continued unabated, viewing the barbarian enemy as a scourge sent by God to punish the Romans and not as a living culture in its own right. For Doukas, the Turks were basically indirect beneficiaries of God's desire to punish Romans (in his eyes the sins of the latter included the rejection of Union with Rome, though most Orthodox took the opposite view, namely that God was punishing them for the steps that they had taken toward communion with the heretic Latins).[2] In the Palaiologan period, as the empire seemed unable to stop the Turkish advance, the logic of theodicy was taken to its logical extreme by those who preferred an accommodation with the Turks to one with the Latins: they argued that to fight against the Turks was tantamount to opposing God's will.[3] The defeatist logic of punitive theology ultimately prevailed among some circles.

On the other hand, the fading of the Roman empire and the emergence of philosophical paganism at the school of Plethon in Mistra enabled an alternative approach to the problem of cultural and religious difference. Greek philosophical perspectives had never been completely banished from the Byzantine intellectual world, though they tended to play subordinate roles. In the Athenian historian Laonikos, who self-consciously sought to become a new Herodotos for his age, these moved to the center and shaped the expression of a new outlook. Laonikos shelved the Roman idea, following his master in advocating the radical theory that the Byzantines had really been Greeks all along. He also did not allow the Christian religion to color any aspect of his presentation of cultures and events. Plethon had revived a late antique, Platonic, and pluralist way of representing cultures, each of which was understood to have its own lawgivers and norms, both cultural and religious. In his *Histories*, Laonikos adhered to this neutrality strictly, reserving his strongest criticism for the incompetence of the Palaiologoi, whom he called "kings of the Greeks." His work actually focuses on the Turks, their institutions, and their conquests. He used Turkish sources, presented some events from their point of view, including the conquest of Constantinople, and cast some of their sultans as glorious. He was the first Greek writer to present Islam in detail *as a culture*, not a theological error, and did so moreover without overt criticism. It is impossible to do justice to Laonikos Chalkokondyles here; I have devoted a separate study to him. All I can say here is that he realizes the full potential of Greek thought in Byzantium, which had remained mostly latent or covert in previous centuries. But he would have no imitators and start no traditions: Laonikos was enabled by the unique circumstances that appeared in the interstices between the death of an old world and the rise of a new one.

ABBREVIATIONS

BA	*Byzantina Australiensia*
BF	*Byzantinische Forschungen*
BHG	*Bibliotheca Hagiographica Graeca*
BMGS	*Byzantine and Modern Greek Studies*
BZ	*Byzantinische Zeitschrift*
CFHB	*Corpus fontium historiae byzantinae*
CJ	Justinian, *Codex Iustinianus*
DAI	*De administrando imperio*
DOML	*Dumbarton Oaks Medieval Library*
DOP	*Dumbarton Oaks Papers*
GRBS	*Greek, Roman, and Byzantine Studies*
LCL	*Loeb Classical Library*
PG	J.-P. Migne, ed., *Patrologiae cursus completus, Series graeca* (Paris)
REB	*Revue des Études Byzantines*
TTH	*Translated Texts for Historians*

NOTES

PREFACE

1. Parker, *The Making of Roman India*, 82. For the classical and Hellenistic background, see Trüdinger, *Studien*; Müller, *Geschichte*; Jacob, *Géographie et ethnographie*; Dihle, "Zur hellenistischen Ethnographie"; and Dench, "Ethnography"; for the Roman contribution, Thomas, *Lands and Peoples*; Lund, *Zum Germanenbild der Römer*; and Woolf, *Tales of the Barbarians*; in Latin late antiquity, Vogt, *Kulturwelt und Barbaren*; and Merrills, *History and Geography*. Studies of individual authors will be cited below as appropriate.

2. See, for example, Ammianus: Wiedemann, "Between Men and Beasts," 193.

3. Karttunen, "The Ethnography of the Fringes," 457 calls it a subgenre but does not elaborate. For F. Jacoby and the modern debate about ethnography as a genre, see Harding, "Local History and Atthidography," 184–85; Dench, "Ethnography," 494–95.

4. Hartog, *Memories of Odysseus*; Dougherty, *The Raft of Odysseus*.

5. Previous views that Herodotos began as a geographer/ethnographer and gradually evolved into a historian were refuted by Benardete, *Herodotean Inquiries*.

6. I am not troubled by these considerations, *pace* Woolf, *Tales of the Barbarians*, 14–15, 99. By failing to mention Herodotos, he can claim the genre had no "classics" or "foundational works."

7. Tr. and discussion by Matthews, "The *Notitiae*," 86.

8. Cutler, "The Emperor's Old Clothes," 210, commenting on the silence of Byzantine sources about gifts and their "laconic treatment" of cities and buildings compared to the richness of Muslim sources; cf. Rotman, *Byzantine Slavery*, 42: "Arabs told stories of Byzantine and Arab renegades, whereas the Byzantines refrained from speaking of their own renegades."

9. E.g., it has been suspected that the Byzantines lacked curiosity: Oikonomidès, "Les marchands qui voyagent," 318. Shepard, "Imperial Information and Ignorance," 107, formulates the basic paradox, though without framing it as a problem in ethnography. Two recent volumes have no chapters on late antiquity, early Christianity, or Byzantium: Rauflaub and Talbert, *Geography and Ethnography*; and Rubiés, *Medieval Ethnographies*; a previous treatment was in Jones, "The Image of the Barbarian." One finds bizarre statements made by non-Byeantinists, e.g., Stroumsa, *The End of Sacrifice*, 39: "As far as I

know, the Byzantine millennium did not produce a single Hellenophonic Jerome, a single Christian Hebraist. In this the Byzantines were indeed the heirs of the Greeks more than those of the Romans, with a confidence in their innate cultural superiority that prevented them from being interested in other languages and cultures, all considered barbarian—a confidence that would lead them eventually to their ruin." I would not know where to begin responding to this. Then there are flat-out wrong statements: Luttwak, *The Grand Strategy*, 145: "Curiosity about foreign peoples was a Greek virtue that the Romans did not really share until they evolved into Byzantium. . . . Byzantine writings show that they were greatly interested in foreign cultures and customs, as entire nations are not even today" (repeated at 286, 288).

10. See Parani, "Byzantine Material Culture," 188. For the inclusion of foreign elements in Byzantine art—not the representation of foreign peoples as such—see now Walker, *The Emperor and the World*.

11. See the discussion by Walker, *The Emperor and the World*, 145–46.

CHAPTER I. ETHNOGRAPHY IN LATE ANTIQUE HISTORIOGRAPHY

1. There are many surveys of late antique historiography, e.g., Karpozilos, Βυζαντινοὶ ἱστορικοὶ καὶ χρονογράφοι, v. 1; Marasco, *Greek and Roman Historiography*; and Treadgold, *The Early Byzantine Historians*. There are many studies of individual authors, but no book-length study of late antique Greek ethnography. I will not be discussing here other types of late antique texts that contain ethnographic information, such as physiognomic and medical literature, Epiphanios' *De gemmis* (much work remains to be done on the transmission and restoration of this text), and Stephanos of Byzantion's *Ethnika*. I will focus on the historians.

2. Greatrex, "Lawyers and Historians."

3. For the construction of the historian's authority in antiquity, see Marincola, *Authority and Tradition*. We lack a similar study for late antiquity.

4. See below for these.

5. Prokopios, *Wars* 2.22-23; Agathias, *Histories* 2.15-17 (551 A.D.), 5.3-9 (557 A.D.), 5.10 (plague); see Kaldellis, "The Literature of Plague"; for the complex moral strategy of Agathias' earthquake accounts, see idem, "The Historical and Religious Views."

6. Agathias, *Histories* pref. 10.

7. In general, see Benedicty, "Die Milieu-Theorie bei Prokop"; Cesa, "Etnografia e geografia"; Cameron, *Procopius*; Carile, "I nomadi' (including discussion); and Maas, "Strabo and Procopius," (whose reading of Prokopios as a misogynistic Christian imperialist is doubtful).

8. Börm, *Prokop und die Perser*, on which Kaldellis, "Review of Börm."

9. Kaldellis, *Procopius of Caesarea*, 32–34.

10. Prokopios, *Wars* 4.6.5-14; cf. Merrills, ed., *Vandals, Romans and Berbers*, 18 (A. H. Merrills), 45 (W. Pohl); Pazdernik, "Xenophon's *Hellenica*," 194.

11. The two models could be used in connection with one and the same people, to sketch the terms of their decline, e.g., regarding the Persians in Xenophon, *Education of Kyros* 8.8. Curta, *The Making of the Slavs*, 44 implies that Prokopios was a climate-theorist. Cf. Boatwright, *Peoples of the Roman World*, 13: "Climatic determinism . . . was particularly ill-suited to the Romans, who moved frequently" and eventually hailed from all climates.

12. Respectively, Prokopios, *Wars* 1.3.2-7, 1.12.2-3, 4.10.13-29, 7.14.22-30, and 7.38.20-23. See Benedicty, "Prokopios' Berichte"; Curta, *The Making of the Slavs*, 36–39, 75–89; Živković, *Forging Unity*, 31–70. On the current state of scholarship regarding the early Slavs, see Barford, "Slavs." On the origin of the Moors, see Schmitz, "Procopius' Phoenician Inscriptions," with a rejoinder by A. Frendo. For Prokopios on the Moors in general, see Conant, *Staying Roman*, 252–73, and the next section of this chapter, below.

13. Respectively, Prokopios, *Wars* 1.20 and 7.34-35.

14. E.g., Prokopios, *Wars* 2.29.14-26 on Lazike and 6.4.21-30 on Vesuvius.

15. Prokopios, *Wars* 3.1.4-19, 5.12.

16. Prokopios, *Wars* 5.15, 6.14-15; Whitaker, "Late Classical and Early Mediaeval Accounts"; Alonso-Núñez, "Jordanes and Procopius."

17. Prokopios, *Wars* 6.15.8-9.

18. Respectively, Prokopios, *Wars* 8.1.7-8.6.31, 8.11.22-25, 8.17.1-8, 8.20. This list is not exhaustive. See Thompson, "Procopius on Brittia." I am skeptical that Brittia is Britain here.

19. Prokopios, *Wars* 8.6.9-10.

20. Lampe, *A Patristic Greek Lexicon*, 915–16, 917–18.

21. Prokopios, *Wars* 5.1.4.

22. Prokopios, *Wars* 5.3.5-9. For a reading of Prokopios along these lines, see Kaldellis, *Procopius of Caesarea*—though Prokopios had political ties to the last Platonists.

23. Agathias, *Histories* 1.6.3-1.7.3 and 3.17.6-9. For the Daylami in Agathias, see Mc-Geer, *Sowing the Dragon's Teeth*, 234–35.

24. Agathias, *Histories* 2.23-32, 4.24-30; Cameron, "Agathias on the Sassanians"; Questa, "Il morto e la madre"; for the Persian archives, see Lee, *Information and Frontiers*, 177.

25. Agathias, *Histories* 4.30.5.

26. Many of the fragments of Menandros deal with Central Asia. Theophylaktos Simokattes, *History* 7.7.6-7.9.12 on Central Asia (the Turks) and China; see Haussig, "Theophylakts Exkurs," 316, citing additional studies; Czeglédy, "From East to West," 107–9; Curta, "Qagan," 20; de la Vaissière, "Maurice et le qaghan"; and, for Byzantium and China, Xu-shan, *Η Κίνα και το Βυζάντιο*.

27. Theophylaktos Simokattes, *History* 1.12.8-11 and 7.16-17.

28. Libanios, *Letter* 331.1 (tr. Norman, v. 1, 467); for the embassy, see Ammianus Marcellinus, *Res gestae* 17.5.15; Eunapios, *Lives of the Philosophers* 465–66 (including observations on the tiara of the Persian king at the dinner table, echoing Libanios' list).

29. Bury, "The Treatise De administrando imperio," 539–40; Sabbah, *La méthode d'Ammien Marcellin*, on the degree to which Ammianus relied on the dispatches of Roman

generals and envoys; Lee, *Information and Frontiers*, 39. See below for the middle Byzantine period.

30. Priskos, *History* fr. 11–14. For an excellent reconstruction of the embassy to Attila, see Kelly, *Attila*, and below. For Attila's court, see Pohl, "The *regia* and the *hring*," 442–45, with some thoughts at 460–62 on the limitations of these sources and the factors that shape their accounts.

31. Nonnosos in Photios, *Bibliotheke* cod. 3; Ioannes Malalas, *Chronicle* 18.56; see also Karpozilos, Βυζαντινοὶ ἱστορικοὶ καὶ χρονογράφοι, v. 1, 449–51.

32. Menandros, *History* fr. 9–10, 19, 23. For Petros *patrikios*, see Antonopoulos, Πέτρος Πατρίκιος; for Zemarchos, see below.

33. Yuhannan of Amida (John of Ephesos), *Ecclesiastical History: Part Three* 6.23 (tr. 425). For Zemarchos' embassy, see Karpozilos, Βυζαντινοὶ ἱστορικοὶ καὶ χρονογράφοι, v. 1, 463–71; Pohl, "The *regia* and the *hring*," 447; Luttwak, *The Grand Strategy*, 97–100.

34. For the two installments of Malalas' *Chronicle* and their dates, see Croke, "Malalas," 19–21; Puech, "Malalas," 214.

35. For the geographical information presented in these accounts, see Nechaeva, "Geography and Diplomacy."

36. See Kulikowski, *Rome's Gothic Wars*, 58, for a good formulation; also Pohl, "The *regia* and the *hring*," 460–66.

37. Prokopios, *Wars* 8.5.5-6; for the term "Skythian" at this time, see Amory, *People and Identity*, 127–30.

38. Prokopios, *Wars* 6.15.23.

39. Hartog, *The Mirror of Herodotus*.

40. E.g., Said, *Orientalism*, 54–58, a great mind discussing matters almost completely unknown to it, a common problem in the book.

41. Ammianus Marcellinus, *Res gestae* 31.2; see King, "The Veracity"; Kelly, *Attila*, 17–28; in general, Wiedemann, "Between Men and Beasts."

42. Conant, *Staying Roman*, 262–263.

43. Woolf, *Tales of the Barbarians*, 112. Among many studies that read ethnography as engaged in thoughtful critiques, see, e.g., Benardete, *Herodotean Inquiries*; Thomas, *Herodotus in Context*. Tacitus' *Germania* has long been read as a critique of sorts. Gruen, *Rethinking the Other*, reviews the entire tradition and deemphasizes the rhetoric of difference (not always convincingly). Moyer, *Egypt*, ch. 1, shows how Herodotos transmitted Egyptian priestly voices.

44. Rodolfi, "Procopius and the Vandals"; also Amory, *People and Identity*, for the most part.

45. For Tacitus, see Syme, *Tacitus*; Shumate, *Nation, Empire, Decline*, 88–99; Gruen, *Rethinking the Other*, ch. 6; for Plinius, Tacitus, and others, see Romm, *The Edges of the Earth*, 48, 54–81; Kraus, "'No Second Troy'," 279; Drake, *Constantine and the Bishops*, 49–51; Parker, *The Making of Roman India*, 90–93, 106, 109 (citing additional bibliography). See also the beginning of Chapter 4, section on the "The Pechenegs in the Eleventh Century."

46. Priskos, *History* fr. 11.2.407-547; see Maas, "Fugitives and Ethnography"; Kaldellis, *Procopius of Caesarea*, 74 and 245 n. 47; and Kelly, *Attila*, 147–55, 229–30, for a subtle evaluation of Priskos' approach.

47. See, e.g., Lucian, *Anacharsis or On Gymnastics*. I owe this observation to David Sansone (University of Illinois).

48. Two exceptions are Beck, *Res Publica Romana*; Kaldellis, *Hellenism in Byzantium*, ch. 2.

49. Ando, *Law, Language, and Empire*, 114; Hankins, "Exclusivist Republicanism."

50. I am writing a book-length study of the concept of the *politeia* in late antiquity and Byzantium. The term, of course, had many concurrent meanings, and could designate the regime type, a lifestyle (e.g., of the Christians), etc. I am here tracing a specific Roman sense, which was dominant in historical texts. For Lydos on *politeia*, *tyrannis*, and *basileia*, see Kaldellis, "Republican Theory."

51. The standard discussion is Simon, "Princeps legibus solutus."

52. Cf. Lucian's *Anacharsis*.

53. Kelly, *Attila*, 147–55, 229–30: history "should challenge our assumptions. It should prompt us to look differently at the world and make us less self-assured about our own ideals and beliefs."

54. Kaldellis, *Procopius of Caesarea*, esp. 189–204 for Totila's speeches. For the speeches in the *Persian War* as vehicles of criticism, see idem, "Prokopios' *Persian War*," but Kruse, "The Speech of the Armenians," exposes the limitations of their speech that are revealed when it is compared with Prokopios' own narrative.

55. There is much scholarship on the relation between the two empires and their views of each other. See now Canepa, *The Two Eyes of the Earth*.

56. See, e.g., Ammianus Marcellinus, *Res Gestae* 17.5.1, 18.6.22, 19.1 (called Chionitae), on which Matthews, *The Roman Empire of Ammianus*, 61–62; also the metaphrastic (tenth-century) version of the *Martyrdom of Gourias, Samonas, and Abibos* refers to an attack by the Ephthalitai Huns on the eastern provinces of the Roman empire in late antiquity, especially on Edessa, and characterizes them as a "crooked and barbarous race" (151). The extant late fourth-century version, which is different in many ways, refers at this point only to "Huns" and disparages them with different adjectives: "a wicked and destructive race." In other words, it is likely that Symeon Metaphrastes was working from a different earlier version. He had no reason to add the name "Ephthalitai."

57. Kaldellis, *Procopius of Caesarea*, 69–75, for an analysis and Herodotean parallels. For the ritual sacrifice of retainers in the Central Asian context, see Beckwith, *Empires of the Silk Road*, 13, 19–20, discussing the testimony of Prokopios.

58. Blood: Prokopios, *Secret History* 11.13, 18.27, 18.30; barbarian: 14.2. For the political thought that informs the *Secret History*, see Kaldellis, *Prokopios: The Secret History*, xl–xlviii.

59. Kaldellis, *Procopius of Caesarea*, 54–55, 74, 119–28, 141–42; cf. idem, "Prokopios' *Persian War*."

60. Latin *serica*, silk from China (Seres).

61. Pazdernik, "Xenophon's *Hellenica*."

62. Kaldellis, *Procopius of Caesarea*, ch. 4 on the ideology of freedom and slavery.

63. Prokopios, *Secret History* 15.16.

64. Pazdernik, "Xenophon's *Hellenica*," 175–206, 194–95.

65. Themistios, *Oration* 10.131b–c (*On the Peace*) (tr. p. 38).

66. Connor, *Thucydides*.

67. Cameron, "Agathias on the Early Merovingians"; but cf. Kaldellis, "The Historical and Religious Views" for a different reading of the religious dimension, and "Things Are Not What They Are" for the literary aspect.

68. E.g., Agathias, *Histories* 2.25.3.

69. Prokopios, *Wars* 6.25.1-9.

70. For the moral agenda, see Kaldellis, "The Historical and Religious Views."

71. For a similar attempt by Riccoldo (ca. 1300) to use a fiction about Saracen brotherly love in order "to shame his Christian reader," see Tolan, *Saracens*, 248. Some scholars attribute Agathias' positive view of the Franks to the strategic situation of the 570s, when he was writing, and to a putative Orthodox alliance against the Arian Lombards: Cameron, *Agathias*, 50–51, 54, 120–21, 129; "Agathias on the Early Merovingians," 116, 136–39; Gottlieb, "Die Nachrichten des Agathias," esp. 151–54; and, from a different direction, Lounghis, Ιουστινιανός Πέτρος Σαββάτιος, 35–37 (and in many other publications). This interpretation, without saying so explicitly, casts Agathias as a partisan propagandist for the regime in Constantinople. The interpretation is difficult to sustain, given that he does not propagandize on its behalf in any other matter and is critical of both imperial policy and Roman society, in accordance with his moral aims as a writer. Nor can this interpretation explain the distinctive shape and thrust of his praise of the Franks, which pertains to their internal affairs (not their religion, as some wrongly maintain) and is, moreover, a fiction. However, the alliance with the Franks in the 570s would have made them a more suitable vehicle for a covert message of moral reform, so the strategic situation reinforced the moral objectives of the text, not the reverse.

72. Agathias, *Histories* 1.7.3. For the Alamanni, see Drinkwater, *The Alamanni*.

73. Agathias, *Histories* 1.7.1.

74. Agathias, *Histories* 2.23.8-9.

75. Herodotos, *Histories* 3.38; Thomas, *Herodotus in Context*, 125–27, and passim.

76. Romm, *The Edges of the Earth*, 95, and the passage of Strabo quoted and discussed there.

77. Harrison, *Writing Ancient Persia*, 85. For a similar reading of medieval literature on Muslims, see Frakes, *Vernacular and Latin Literary Discourses*.

CHAPTER 2. BYZANTINE INFORMATION-GATHERING
BEHIND THE VEIL OF SILENCE

1. Prokopios, *Secret History* 30.12; cf. *Wars* 1.21.11-13, 2.16.1. For ancient Rome, see Austin and Rankov, *Exploratio*; Sheldon, *Intelligence Activities*. For spies in late antiquity,

see Lee, *Information and Frontiers*, esp. 170–82; for Byzantium in general, see Dvornik, *Origins of Intelligence Services*; Koutrakou, "Diplomacy and Espionage," 127–29; and eadem, "Spies of Towns"; Shepard, "Imperial Information and Ignorance," 112–14. For merchants as spies, see also *CJ* 4.63.4 (of 408 or 409 A.D.).

2. Lee, "Procopius." Nechaeva, "Double Agents," argues that Justinian switched to the use of double agents.

3. Syrianos, *On Strategy* 42 (122–25). For the later date, see Baldwin, "On the Date"; Lee and Shepard, "A Double Life"; and on the attribution to Syrianos, Zuckermann, "The Compendium"; Cosentino, "The Syrianos's 'Strategikon'"; and Rance, "The Date of the Military Compendium."

4. Leon VI, *Taktika* 17.77 (*PG* 17.97).

5. Leon VI, *Taktika*, epilogue 19.

6. [*Anonymous Book on Tactics*] 18 (292–93). For spies who "possess excellent first-hand knowledge of the roads and Syrian countryside," see also Nikephoros II Phokas, *On Skirmishing* 2 (152–53).

7. Theophylaktos Simokattes, *History* 3.7.4; cf. *Life of the Emperor Basileios I* 68. For the perfect spies of the Sultan of Egypt, who travel as merchants and speak perfect French, see the fictitious account in *The Book of John Mandeville* ch. 15 (87).

8. Theophanes, *Chronographia* s.a. 6256 (436) and s.a. 6265 (447).

9. Leon the Deacon, *History* 6.11 (tr. 158). A possible source for this claim is Plutarch, *Sertorius* 3.

10. Jacoby, "Byzantine Trade," 33. See also Konstantinos VII, *Book of Ceremonies* 2.44 (v. 1, 657): in the lead-up to the invasion of Crete in 911, spies were sent to Syria to find out what the Saracens there were up to.

11. Theophanes Continuatus: *Konstantinos VII* 3 (383–84); cf. Magdalino, *L'Orthodoxie des astrologues*, 81–82. For interpreters at the middle Byzantine court, see the studies cited by Dagron, "Communication," 88 n. 29; Malamut, "La lettre diplomatique," 101 n. 21; Gastgeber, "Die lateinische Übersetzungsabteilung," 105–22; Frankopan, *The First Crusade*, 87 n. 2.

12. See Koutrakou, "Diplomacy and Espionage"; for diplomacy in general, Shepard and Franklin, eds., *Byzantine Diplomacy*. For lists of embassies and analysis, see Loughis, *Les ambassades byzantines*, with the methodological reflections of Chrysos, "Η βυζαντινή διπλωματία"; Beihammer, *Nachrichten*; and Nerlich, *Diplomatische Gesandtschaften*; for the early medieval context, see McCormick, *Origins of the European Economy*, 852–972.

13. Beard, *The Roman Triumph*, 75–76; Östenberg, *Staging the World*, 34; Kelly, *Ruling the Later Roman Empire*, 205.

14. A key text is Theophanes Continuatus: *Konstantinos VII* 17 (p. 448): τῶν ἁπανταχοῦ γὰρ στρατηγῶν καὶ βασιλικῶν πρωτονοταρίων καὶ τῶν ἐν κώμαις ἐπαρχίαις τε καὶ πόλεσιν, ἔτι μὴν καὶ εἰς ἀρχηγοὺς ἐθνῶν ἀποστελλομένων γραμμάτων, καὶ τούτων παρ' αὐτοῦ ἀναγινωσκομένων. . . .

15. Shepard, "Imperial Information and Ignorance," 114–15.

16. The date of Photios' embassy is much disputed: Treadgold, "Photius."

17. For the latter, see Beihammer, "Der harte Sturz." For western envoys, see Christou, Ἔργα καὶ ἡμέρες.

18. Nikephoros, *Short History* 49; Theophanes, *Chronographia* s.a. 6206 (384).

19. Menandros, *History* fr. 10.1.68-95. For state interpreters in late antiquity, see Clauss, *Der magister officiorum*, 19.

20. Agathias, *Histories* 4.30.3.

21. Gillett, *Envoys*.

22. Lemerle, "Thomas le Slave"; Lounghis, "Byzantine Diplomacy," 35. Alexios I holds forth on the Turks in a letter to Robert of Flanders, but this is probably spurious: de Waha, "La lettre d'Alexis I Comnène"; Schreiner, "Der Brief des Alexios I. Komnenos"; and Gastgeber, "Das Schreiben Alexios I. Komnenos"; its authenticity is defended by Frankopan, *The First Crusade*, 60–61. In general, see Shepard, "The Uses of 'History.'"

23. For the context and the content of the letter, see Lounghis, "Byzantine Diplomacy," 32–33.

24. Gerald of Wales, *The Description of Wales* 1.8 (tr. 234–35).

25. Liudprand, *Embassy to Constantinople* 37 (tr. 260–61).

26. Patoura, Οἱ αἰχμάλωτοι, 99–100, 107; Simeonova, "In the Depths of Tenth-Century Byzantine Ceremonial." Diplomatic protocol regarding forms of address is glimpsed in the *Book of Ceremonies* 2.46-28, for which see the papers in *Travaux et Mémoires* 13 (2000).

27. Eustathios, *Oration for the Emperor Manuel Komnenos* 263–64.

28. See especially the *Roman Poems* (*Rūmiyyāt*) of Abū Firās; the account of the captivity of Quābath bin Razīn in al-Tanūkhī, translated in Canard, "Les aventures d'un prisonnier"; and the account of the captivity of Hārūn bin Yaḥyā (ca. 900), translated in Vasiliev, ed., *Byzance et les Arabes*, v. 2, 379–94; see Patoura, Οἱ αἰχμάλωτοι, 93–110; Simeonova, "Foreigners"; in general, Shboul, "Byzantium and the Arabs"; El Cheikh, *Byzantium*. For prisoner-exchanges between Byzantium and the Arabs, see Toynbee, *Constantine Porphyrogenitus*, 390–93, and the studies cited by Rotman, *Byzantine Slavery*, 36–37.

29. The authenticity of the text has been debated for decades. Treadgold, *Middle Byzantine Historians*, ch. 3, is about to argue anew for its being a forgery. For its limited ethnographic information, see Patoura, Οἱ αἰχμάλωτοι, 92. For a study of Byzantine captivity accounts, which reveals how few they were and how typecast their images of the barbarian, see Messis, "La mémoire du 'je' souffrant."

30. Vasiliev, ed., *Byzance et les Arabes*, v. 1, 321; for Byzantine interpreters, see above.

31. Canard, "Les aventures d'un prisonnier."

32. *[Anonymous Book on Tactics]* 18 (292–93). See also the tale from the *One Thousand and One Nights* of an Arab accused of having agreed to work for the Christians while he was their prisoner: Rotman, *Byzantine Slavery*, 49.

33. Theophanes, *Chronographia* s.a. 6265 (447).

34. Choniates, *History* 201.

35. Theophanes, *Chronographia* s.a. 6248 (430). In late antiquity: Garsoïan, "Byzantium," 573, 585; Synelli, Οἱ διπλωματικὲς σχέσεις, 50.

36. Konstantinos VII, *Three Treatises*, 86.

37. One often encounters the theory that "intelligence as to the neighboring peoples collected by embassies, missionaries, merchants, and other means, seems to have been assembled and deposited in an office created for the purpose called *scrinium barbarorum*— Office for Barbarian Affairs. . . . It apparently functioned at least until the eleventh century." So Dvornik, *Origins of Intelligence Services*, 174, following Bury and Guilland. We know little about the late antique *scrinium barbarorum*; it handled the reception of foreign embassies, according to a sixth-century document embedded in Konstantinos VII Porphyrogennetos' *Book of Ceremonies* 1.89-90 (tr. in Greatrex and Lieu, *The Roman Eastern Frontier*, 124–28). The theory is that its functions passed to the Byzantine *epi ton barbaron* (under the *logothetes tou dromou*). But it is not clear that the *epi ton barbaron* was an office of state in the middle period: Oikonomides, "Some Byzantine State Annuitants," 23; Stavrakos, "The Elephant," 283–86.

38. Kelly, *Ruling the Later Roman Empire*, 117–20; Treadgold, *The Early Byzantine Historians*, 365; Shepard, "Imperial Information and Ignorance," 113.

39. Dvornik, *Origins of Intelligence Services*, 177–84; Shepard, "Information, Disinformation and Delay," 270–76; see also below.

40. For the mosques of Constantinople, see Reinert, "The Muslim Presence." For an anecdote from Arabic sources which shows that one could hear Arabic spoken on the streets of Constantinople, see Rotman, *Byzantine Slavery*, 42.

41. Tzetzes, *Epilogue to the Theogony*. See the sanitized translation in Kazhdan and Epstein, *Change in Byzantine Culture*, 259–60; the text itself is bowdlerized in Moravcsik, "Barbarishe Sprachreste," 286. For Constantinople as a cosmopolitan (and snobbish) city, see Simeonova, "Constantinopolitan Attitudes"; Rapp, "A Medieval Cosmopolis." For Fzetzes' distant Georgian (not Alan) amcestry, see kaldellis, *Hellonism in Byeantium*, 301.

42. Zonaras, *Commentary on the Canons of the Council in Troullo*: Canon 51 (v. 2, 425); see Webb, *Demons*, 123–24 and passim.

43. See, e.g., *The Life of Andreas the Fool* 19 (88–91).

44. For this in a later period, see Parani, "Byzantine Material Culture," 188. Associations were also made with ancient monuments of Constantinople, though it is unclear on what basis. Choniates, *History* 151, reports that "of the two bronze statues of female figures which long ago had been placed above the arch erected on the west side of the forum of Constantine, the one [was] called the Roman Woman and the other the Hungarian Woman." Cf. also Shepard, "Some Problems of Russo-Byzantine Relations," 13.

45. Oikonomidès, "Les marchands qui voyagent."

46. For the West, see Zacher, *Curiosity and Pilgrimage*; Graboïs, *Le pèlerin occidental*, 42, 117–33; in Byzantium, Kislinger, "Sightseeing."

47. Michael Choniates, *When He Traveled to the Euboian Euripos* 1 (v. 1, 180).

48. Moravcsik, "Klassizismus," and Hunger, "On the Imitation (ΜΙΜΗΣΙΣ)."

49. Ćirković, "Between Kingdom and Empire," 368 (twelfth century). For the Serbs as barbarians in Byzantine eyes, see Blangez-Malamut and Cacouros, "L'image des serbes," and Chapter 4, section on "The Representation of Orthodox Barbarians." By comparison, Arab narrative sources often give just the name of the enemy commander but dwell

on the names of the individual Arab fighters: Kennedy, *The Great Arab Conquests*, 18, 277. In part this was because of the purpose of these texts, to record heroic aspects of the conquest for later remembrance and use (cf. 30).

50. See Chapter 4, section on "The Classicism of Byzantine Ethnography."

51. Cf. Nicolet, *Space, Geography, and Politics*, with Shepard, "Emperors and Expansionism," 67.

52. Hunger, *Die hochsprachliche profane Literatur*, 507; Koder, "Sopravvivenza e trasformazione"; Oikonomidès, "Les marchands qui voyagent." The exceptions are mostly in Konstantinos VII's *De administrando imperio*, esp. 9 and 42.

53. E.g., Attaleiates, *History* 221 (impossible to make sense of); Anna Komnene, *Alexiad* 14.8.6 (Mt. Haimos continues past the Adriatic).

54. Choirosphaktes, *Letters* 76–97; eunuch: 120–23 (Kolias ed.) = 42–59, 86–93; eunuch: 78–85, with the commentary at 131–32 (Strano ed.). For the paucity of evidence in these authors, see Karpozilos, "Ταξιδιωτικές περιγραφές," 511–12.

55. Theophanes Continuatus: *Theophilos* 10 (95–99). See Ricci, "The Road from Baghdad," 132. For these embassies in general, see Magdalino, "The Road to Baghdad'" (195: "meager evidence"). For diplomatic gifts, see Cutler, "Gifts and Gift Exchange"; idem, "Significant Gifts"; and Schreiner, "Diplomatische Geschenke."

56. *Life of Demetrianos* 13 (306–7). See Grégoire, "Saint Démétrianos"; Jenkins, "The mission of St. Demetrianus of Cyprus"; Canard, "Deux épisodes des relations diplomatiques"; for the context, Metcalf, *Byzantine Cyprus*, 440–41.

57. See Chapter 5, section on "The Politics of Palaiologan Travel Literature."

58. Fledelius, "Royal Scandinavian Travellers," 215; see also Ciggarr, *Western Travellers*, ch. 4 (and passim); and Raffensperger, *Reimagining Europe*, 25.

59. Christides, "The Image of the Sudanese," 17 (quatation modified); also Hendrickx, "Le roi africain"; O'bweng-Okwess, "Τό ἱστορικό ἐνδιαφέρον." The source is Robert de Clari, *The Conquest of Constantinople* 54 (130–31; tr. 79–80). For Nubia and the early Byzantine Commonwealth, see Fowden, *Empire to Commonwealth*, 116–19, 135–37; Patoura-Spanou, *Χριστιανισμός*, 323–72 (to be used with caution); Godlewski, "Nubia, Egypt, and Byzantium" (also to be used with caution).

60. "An inscription in Greek characters, discovered at Philae, mentions the visit in 360 of an Aksumite viceroy, a Christian named Abratoeis, to the Roman emperor, who received him with all the honours due to his rank": Mekouria, "Christian Aksum," 406. He appears to be unknown to modern historians of the later Roman empire.

61. Lamma, "Venezia"; and Dagron, "Le 'Mythe de Venise'"; for the background, Nicol, *Byzantium and Venice*; Martin, "The Venetians"; for recent bibliography, Angold, "The Venetian Chronicles."

62. A notice on the origins and topography of Venice and Pippin's attack is in Konstantinos VII, *De administrando imperio* 27.71-96; on which Dagron, "Le 'Mythe de Venise'," 66. Later sources will be discussed in separate chapters below.

63. Kinnamos, *History* 6.10; in general, see Ljubarskij, "John Kinnamos."

64. Choniates, *History* 86.

65. Eustathios, *Commentary on Ioannes Damaskenos' Pentecostal Hymn* 210 (col. 717) (a new edition is expected from P. Cesaretti and S. Ronchey; I thank the former for sending me an advance copy of this passage and his argument concerning the date). See Cesaretti, "Su Eustazio," 221 for the text; also Magdalino, "Aspects of Twelfth-Century Byzantine *Kaiserkritik*," 335; Browning, "Eustathios," 89. For the notion of the mixed constitution, see von Fritz, *The Theory of the Mixed Constitution*; Aalders, *Die Theorie der gemischten Verfassung*; Lintott, "The Theory of the Mixed Constitution"; Hahm, "The Mixed Constitution"; for its medieval reception, Blythe, *Ideal Government*.

66. Lemerle, *Le premier humanisme*, 280–88; for a closer study, see Németh, *Imperial Systematization*.

67. Theophanes' collaborator Georgios Synkellos excerpted the list of Sasanian Persian kings and reign lengths from Agathias, but none of his ethnographical information: *Ecloga chronographica* 440–42 (tr. 518–21). I bypass the issue of the authorship of Theophanes' *Chronographia*.

68. Photios, *Bibliotheke* codd. 3 (Nonnosos), 60 (Herodotos), 63 (Prokopios), 65 (Theophylaktos Simokattes), 72 (Ktesias), 80 (Olympiodoros). In general, see Schamp, "La réception de l'histoire"; Efthymiades, *Φώτιος*; Croke, "Tradition and Originality."

69. Benardete, *Herodotean Inquiries*. Herodotos was not an ethnographer / geographer who later turned to history. His *Histories* had a Persian orientation from the start.

70. Mendels, "Greek and Roman History," 204.

71. Nicolle, "Byzantine and Islamic Arms"; Ducellier, *Chrétiens d'Orient*, 203–16; Dagron, "Apprivoiser la guerre"; Mavroudi, *A Byzantine Book*; Sezgin, *Wissenschaft*, 84–167; Magdalino, *L'Orthodoxie des astrologues*; Mavroudi, "Occult Science."

72. See the texts discussed in Kaldellis, *Hellenism in Byzantium*, 220–21 (Ioannes Italos on the Arab appropriation of Greek philosophy), 375 (Theodoros II Laskaris on the rise of philosophy in the West). For the theme in antiquity of personified Philosophy's rejection by the Greeks and her acceptance by the barbarians, see Johnson, *Ethnicity and Argument*, 132–34; Parker, *The Making of Roman India*, 269–70. The closest to an admission of borrowing that has been postulated is Leon VI's conception of Holy War and his proposals regarding military recruitment: Dagron, "Byzance," and even here the debt (if it is that) is not acknowledged. In neither case is it clear that Leon was inspired by Islamic practice, which he distorts and condemns.

73. Leon VI, *Taktika* 18.95 (*PG* 18.101).

74. Herrin, "Aspects of the Process of Hellenization"; and Dunn, "Evangelization." For the problem of Hellenism in this instance, see Kaldellis, *Hellenism in Byzantium*, 116. For Leon's account of the Slavs in the empire, see Chapter 4, section on "The *Taktika* and *De administrando imperio*."

75. Ševčenko, "Religious Missions," 13, 20 (extensive bibliography on the Byzantine missions is cited at 7–8 n. 1). For the silence of Konstantinos VII on Cyril and Methodios, see Wolfram, "The Image of Central Europe"; Eggers, "Das De Administrando Imperio," 67–73. In general, Ivanov, "Casting Pearls," 299.

76. Treadgold, "Three Byzantine Provinces," 132.

77. *Life of the Emperor Basileios I* 97; tr. Ševčenko, "Religious Missions," 23–25; see the discussion by Peri, "La brama e lo zelo," 127–29; in general, Franklin, "Constantine Porphyrogenitus."

78. Shepard, "Imperial Outliers," 373.

79. Ivanov, "Mission Impossible." See Chapter 4, section on "The Representation of Orthodox Barbarians."

80. Theophylaktos of Ochrid, *Life of St Kliment of Ochrid*; likewise, his account of *The Martyrdom of the Fifteen Holy Martyrs of Tiberioupolis* 35 (coll. 186–201), presents the pre-conversion Bulgarians as generic (Hellenic) pagans; there is almost no distinctive information. In general, see Mullett, *Theophylact of Ochrid*, 235–39; Ivanov, "Mission Impossible," 259. Other lives of Slavic saints written in Greek (in the middle period) survive only in Slavonic translation. For Kliment, see Obolensky, *Six Byzantine Portraits*, ch. 1.

81. Obolensky, *The Byzantine Commonwealth*, 5, 353–56; cf. Kaldellis, *Hellenism in Byzantium*, ch. 2.

CHAPTER 3 EXPLAINING THE RELATIVE DECLINE
OF ETHNOGRAPHY IN THE MIDDLE PERIOD

1. Moravcsik, "Klassizismus"; Hunger, "On the Imitation (ΜΙΜΗΣΙΣ)"; Aerts, "Imitatio and Aemulatio." For surveys of middle Byzantine historiography, see Karpozilos, *Βυζαντινοὶ ἱστορικοὶ καὶ χρονογράφοι*, v. 2–3; Treadgold, *Middle Byzantine Historians*; in brief, Kaldellis, "The Corpus of Byzantine Historiography."

2. For Theophanes' sources, see Mango and Scott, *The Chronicle of Theophanes Confessor*, lxxv–xcv; Karpozilos, *Βυζαντινοὶ ἱστορικοὶ καὶ χρονογράφοι*, v. 2, 124–35; Treadgold, "Trajan the Patrician."

3. Theophanes, *Chronicle* s.a. 6171 (pp. 356–59); from the same source in Nikephoros, *Short History* 36.

4. See Chapter 4, section on "Ethnographic Moments in the Byzantine Historians."

5. Mango, "The Tradition of Byzantine Chronography," 370–72.

6. See Chapter 4, section on "The Representation of Orthodox Barbarians."

7. For their diversity, see Afinogenov, "Some Observations on Genres"; Kaldellis, "The Corpus of Byzantine Historiography."

8. For hagiography, see Chapter 3, section on "Ethnography and Christianity."

9. Mango, "The Tradition of Byzantine Chronography," 370.

10. Kazhdan, *A History of Byzantine Literature*, v. 2, 43–52; Magdalino, "Orthodoxy and History," 158.

11. Jenkins, "Constantine VII's Portrait"; idem, "The Classical Background"; for hagiography as the model, Alexander, "Secular Biography."

12. Theophanes Continuatus: *Romanos I* 40–41 (426–27); for his career, Whittow, *The Making of Byzantium*, 344–45.

13. Morris, "The Two Faces of Nikephoros"; Roueché, "Byzantine Writers," 127–29; Ljubarskij, "Nikephoros Phokas"; Karpozilos, Βυζαντινοὶ ἱστορικοὶ καὶ χρονογράφοι, v. 2, 477–83; Holmes, *Basil II*, ch. 4–5; and Kiapidou, Ἡ Σύνοψη Ἱστοριῶν.

14. Angold, ed., *The Byzantine Aristocracy*; Cheynet, *Pouvoir et contestations*; Vlysidou, Αριστοκρατικές οικογένειες.

15. Lieberich, *Studien zu den Proömien*, 22; Talbot and Sullivan, *The History of Leo the Deacon*, 11 (the notes document his use of ancient sources, as does the Index, 262–64); Hoffmann, "Geschichtsschreibung oder Rhetorik?" 106 n. 6, cites previous bibliography.

16. Leon the Deacon, *History* 2.6, 3.11.

17. Holmes, *Basil II*, 134–35.

18. Book 14 of Zonaras' *Chronicle* discusses the internal politics of the Persians, but only to explain their wars with the Romans; 15.1 gives a brief statement of Abasgian customs, especially relating to the production of eunuchs, lifted from Prokopios, *Wars* 8.3.12-21. Zonaras displaced it from the reign of Justinian I to that of Leon III, and added a contemporary reference. For a proposal about his motives in doing this, see Messis, "Public hautement affiché."

19. Kazhdan, *A History of Byzantine Literature*, v. 1.

20. Anna Komnene, *Alexiad* 6.9 ff. For Byzantine views of the Turks, see Messina, "Tipologia." For Anna as an author, see the papers in Gouma-Peterson, ed., *Anna Komnene*.

21. Robert and the Normans: Anna Komnene, *Alexiad* 1.10-14. Byzantine views of the Latins have been studied by many in an often repetitve body of scholarship: Lamma, "Venezia"; Asdracha, "L'image de l'homme occidental"; Impellizzeri, "Romani, Latini e barbari"; Hunger, *Graeculus perfidus*; Shepard, "Aspects of Byzantine Attitudes"; Origone, "Genova vista da Bizanzio"; Hörandner, "Das Bild des Anderen"; Lilie, "Anna Komnene"; Gounaridis, "Η εικόνα των Λατίνων"; Reinsch, "Ausländer und Byzantiner"; Prinzing, "Vom Umgang der Byzantiner"; Laiou, "L'interprétation byzantine"; Kolbaba, *The Byzantine Lists*; Jeffreys, "The 'Wild Beast from the West' "; Koder, "Latinoi"; Tounta, "The Perception of Difference."

22. For Anna's possible sources, see Loud, "Anna Komnena"; Savvides and Nikoloudis, Ο ύστερος μεσαιωνικός κόσμος, 46–47.

23. For the increasing complexity in the historians' representations of individuals, see Ljubarskij, "Man in Byzantine Historiography." This affected the representation of foreigners too.

24. Howard-Johnston, "Anna Komnene," 296–300, surveys previous explanations and offers his own, which is countered by Macrides, "The Pen of the Aunt." But the absence of ethnography does not set Anna apart from other Byzantine historians, a point that obviates part of the discussion.

25. Kinnamos, *History* 1.4, 2.14 and 2.18, 2.20, 3.1-2 and 4.1-2, 5.12, and 6.10, respectively. For his account of Venice in particular, see p. 36 above; in general, Ljubarskij, "John Kinnamos."

26. Only the second installment of Psellos' *Chronographia* is panegyrical, though probably sarcastic even then: Kaldellis, *The Argument*, 11. The panegyrical account of

Nikephoros III Botaneiates in the *History* of Attaleiates is superimposed on the work and is undermined by the critical outlook of the remainder: see Krallis, *Michael Attaleiates*. Finally, the *History* of Choniates may have been more conventionally panegyrical in early versions, but after 1204 its outlook became consistently more critical: Simpson, "Before and After 1204"; "Niketas Choniates"; and *Niketas Choniates*. For his break with the ideals of the panegyrics, see ibid., ch. 1; Magdalino, *The Empire of Manuel I*, 477–83.

27. Psellos, *Chronographia* 7.67-69; see Chapter 4, section on "The Pechenegs in the Eleventh Century."

28. Kaldellis, *The Argument*. A conventional treatment in Pietsch, *Die Chronographia*. For the lack of information about foreign peoples in Psellos, see Koutrakou, "Psellus, Romanus III and an Arab Victory."

29. Esp. Psellos, *Chronographia* 7.49-59.

30. Attaleiates, *History* 5.

31. Beck, *Das byzantinische Jahrtausend*, 304–5.

32. It is no accident that Prokopios, Psellos, and Choniates feature prominently in Tinnefeld's *Kategorien der Kaiserkritik* (I am not suggesting that Psellos and Choniates knew the *Secret History*). For the language and style of the *Secret History*, see Kaldellis, *Prokopios: The Secret History*, xxxv–xl.

33. Simpson, *Niketas Choniates*, ch. 1.2.

34. Choniates, *History* 365.

35. Choniates, *History* 477 ; see Kaldellis, "Niketas Choniates," 90.

36. Choniates, *History* 594.

37. Attaleiates, *History* 90.

38. Attaleiates, *History* 164–65.

39. Attaleiates, *History* 197 ; see Kaldellis, "A Byzantine Argument."

40. Attaleiates, *History* 109–10.

41. Attaleiates, *History* 158–59.

42. Attaleiates, *History* 30–31; see Chapter 4, section on "The Pechenegs in the Eleventh Century."

43. Krallis, *Michael Attaleiates*, discusses previous studies, which are mainly socioeconomically deterministic in approach.

44. Attaleiates, *History* 193–94, 220.

45. Prokopios, *Secret History* 1.3.

46. Kaldellis, *Hellenism in Byzantium*, ch. 5.

47. Jouanno, "Les barbares."

48. Howard-Johnston, "Anna Komnene," 296–300.

49. Momigliano, *The Classical Foundations*, ch. 1; cf. Strauss, *An Introduction*, 272–82.

50. On this matter, the field of classical studies is divided between those who (following Said) believe that classical texts project and refine cultural stereotypes and those who believe that many of them try to challenge such assumptions from a more philosophical perspective. I side with the second camp, which tends to attract literary scholars who read the texts carefully, while the first camp tends to consist of cultural historians

who do not practice close readings but fold texts into their social background in order to approximate the results of modern social science. Thus, false impressions of "the culture" are created by stringing together passages from a variety of works that, when examined individually, appear to be subversive, not complicit. An example of such a study, albeit a sophisticated and insightful one, is Sassi, *The Science of Man*, which distills a homogeneous mentality. A case-by-case, text-by-text approach yields different results.

51. Among a large bibliography, see Smith, *The Early History of God*. For the dominant narrative of exclusivity, see Gruen, *Rethinking the Other*, 277–86, followed by an exposition of "the other side" that is based largely on noncanonical texts and often strained.

52. Stroumsa, *The End of Sacrifice*, 40: "In late antiquity, one may sometimes discern among some Christian authors a certain ethnological curiosity. This curiosity, though, does not go so far as to develop any sympathy for the various religions of humanity." Cf. idem, "Philosophy of the Barbarians," 64–65 ("did not encourage ethnological curiosity"), 69 ("no interest in barbarians, repeating the prejudices about them common in ancient literature"), and 83; Schott, *Christianity, Empire*, 152–53.

53. E.g., Pseudo-Clement, *Recognitions* 9.17-28; copied in the sixth century into Pseudo-Kaisarios, *Erotapokriseis* 108–9 (83–86). Against Julian: Gregory of Nazianzos, *Or.* 4.107-9; Georgios the Monk, *Chronicle*, v. 1, 73–81.

54. Olster, "Classical Ethnography"; Buell, *Why This New Race*; Martin, *Inventing Superstition*, 213–17; Johnson, *Ethnicity and Argument*. Following this line of reasoning, Boatwright, *Peoples of the Roman World*, 160, 186–87 purposely treats Christians as an ethnic group in the empire.

55. This polemical religious taxonomy was created by the early Apologists and codified in the fourth century by the great bishops, e.g., Eusebios, *Evangelical Preparation*; Athanasios, *Against the Gentiles*, etc.

56. Eusebios, *Ecclesiastical History* 1.2.19; cf. Wood, *"We have no king but Christ"*, 23.

57. Eusebios, *Life of Constantine* 3.7–8; he was a master of such appropriation.

58. Stroumsa, "Philosophy of the Barbarians," 65.

59. Wood, *"We have no king but Christ"*, 67.

60. Cf. Wood, *"We have no king but Christ"*, 36–37.

61. Sarris, *Empires of Faith*, 200, 204–8, 226. Scholars are now rewriting the history of the early medieval West as premised on a substratum of Roman norms, whether real or imagined: Smith, *Europe After Rome*; Wickham, *The Inheritance of Rome*.

62. Olster, "From Periphery to Center," 96; also Fauvarque, "Les visions providentialistes"; Chauvot, *Opinions romaines*, ch. 8–11; Fletcher, *The Barbarian Conversion*, 25; Ivanov, "Casting Pearls," 298, citing additional studies that have come to this conclusion.

63. Jones, "The Image of the Barbarian," 380–81, who discusses western authors at 381–86.

64. Johnson, *Ethnicity and Argument*, 215 and 232.

65. Smith, *Chosen Peoples*; Garrison, "Divine Election," 277–78 and passim.

66. For a translation and discussion of the relevant sources, see Heather and Matthews, *The Goths*, 103–31; for the representation of Gothic Christianity in Byzantine

texts, Messis and Papaioannou, "Histoires 'gothiques'." I omit from the following discussion texts that were not written in Greek or never translated into it, for they could have played little or no role in the formation of later Byzantine ethnography. Some are interesting from an ethnographic standpoint, especially Bardaisan, *The Book of the Laws of Countries*; cf. Teixidor, *Bardesane*; Ramelli, *Bardaisan*.

67. Most of the geography is in *Martyrdom of Arethas* 1–2; see the extensive introduction of the Detoraki edition.

68. *Martyrdom of Sire*; see the introduction of the editor, Devos; also idem, "La jeune martyre Perse"; for the context, Walker, *The Legend of Mar Qardagh*, 230–32.

69. Romm, *The Edges of the Earth*, 82; Mayerson, "A Confusion of Indias"; Koutrakou, "The Image of Egypt," 227 n. 65; and see now Lenski, "Captivity and Slavery," 249.

70. For editions and bibliography, including a translation, see Elliott, *The Apocryphal New Testament*, 439–511; more recent studies in Bremmer, ed., *The Apocryphal Acts*; Parker, *The Making of Roman India*, 297–301; Seland, "Trade and Christianity," 78–79. Likewise the traditions associated with Bartholomew and Frumentius.

71. Symeon Logothetes, *Chronicle* 88.13 (110).

72. Philostorgios, *Ecclesiastical History* 2.6, 3.4-6 (tr. pp. 40–44); see Fiaccadori, "Teofilo Indiano"; Dihle, "Die Sendung"; idem, "L'embassade de Théophile." For the Persian Gulf connection, see Potts, *The Arabian Gulf*, 330–32. For the eastern Churches, see Finneran, "Beyond Byzantium." For Philostorgios, see now Meyer, ed., *Philostorge*.

73. Philostorgios, *Ecclesiastical History* 3.4 (tr. 40). For the rise of Himyar, see Breton, *Arabia Felix*, 159–63.

74. For the antecedents of that argument (in Eudoxos), see Romm, *The Edges of the Earth*, 150.

75. Kaldellis, *Hellenism in Byzantium*, 174–76.

76. Berg, "The Letter of Palladius"; Stoneman, "Who Are the Brahmans?"; Parker, *The Making of Roman India*, 284–85, citing previous bibliography; also Seland, "Trade and Christianity," 82.

77. Palladios, *On the Peoples of India and the Brahmans* 1.1 (p. 3).

78. Palladios, *On the Peoples of India and the Brahmans* 1.8 (p. 6).

79. Palladios, *On the Peoples of India and the Brahmans* 1.10 (p. 8).

80. Respectively, Palladios, *On the Peoples of India and the Brahmans* 1.4 (p. 4), 1.5 (p. 4), 1.7 (p. 6), 1.14 (p. 10).

81. Palladios, *On the Peoples of India and the Brahmans* 1.11-12 (p. 8).

82. Palladios, *On the Peoples of India and the Brahmans* 1.13 (p. 10).

83. Palladios, *On the Peoples of India and the Brahmans* 1.11 (p. 8).

84. Parker, *The Making of Roman India*, 285.

85. Pseudo-Kaisarios, *Erotapokriseis* 108 (p. 84), based on the pseudo-Clementine *Recognitions*.

86. For the function of ancient utopias, see Clay and Purvis, *Four Island Utopias*, esp. 46–48, 107–14 on Iamboulos.

87. Pseudo-Neilos of Ankyra, *Narrations* 3 (94–103 in Caner's translation); and Messis, "La mémoire du 'je' souffrant'," 115–20, 130–32. For the concept of the hagiographical romance, see Elliot, *Roads to Paradise*, ch. 3.

88. I owe this reading to Messis (pers. comm.).

89. For his own travels, see, e.g., Kosmas Indikopleustes, *Christian Topography* 2.29-30, 2.65. For a discussion of the illustrated manuscript, see Brubaker, "The *Christian Topography*."

90. Kosmas Indikopleustes, *Christian Topography* 2.49-53, 2.54-64, and 3.65-66 respectively.

91. Kosmas Indikopleustes, *Christian Topography*, book 11. See Parker, *The Making of Roman India*, 135–40, 236–40. For Christian geography in late antiquity, see Kordosis, Ιστορικογεωγραφικά; Inglebert, *Interpretatio Christiana*, 25–108; Humphries, "A New Created World"; also Philostorgios above.

92. Inglebert, *Interpretatio Christiana*, 109–92; and Caire, "Le Diamérismos." The key text was Hippolytos' early third-century *Diamerismos*. For the modern impact of this Biblical ethnology, see Trautmann, *Aryans*, 42–61. For the classical analogues, see Curty, *Les parentés légendaires*.

93. See pp. 39–43 above.

94. See p. 35 above.

95. *Life of Elias the Younger* 16, 18–22 (24–33); see Koutrakou, "The Image of Egypt," 220–22.

96. E.g., *Life of Ioannes of Gotthia*; Ignatios the Deacon, *Life of Gregorios Dekapolites*; *Life of Blasios of Amorion*.

97. Ignatios the Deacon, *Life of Georgios of Amastris* 64–68; tr. and discussion in Treadgold, "Three Byzantine Provinces," 136–39.

98. See p. 129 above.

99. For the problem of fictionality, see Kaldellis, "The Emergence of Literary Fiction."

100. Berger, *Life and Works*, 45; 33 for Rome. Elsewhere there is an awareness of the difference between Latin and Greek, and Armenian.

101. Relying on a Greek translation of an Arabic work that preserved sixth-century traditions such as are found in the *Martyrdom of Arethas*, a text written originally in Syriac but of which there was a Greek version: Fiaccadori, "Gregentios." The bibliography on the events in question is large. If the *Life* of Gregentios was not written in Constantinople, as Berger proposes, but, say, in Rome or Alexandria, as others have suggested, then these texts may not belong to the Byzantine milieu to begin with.

102. For a thorough introduction, see the new edition by Volk.

103. *Life of Makarios of Rome* 139.

104. Ktesias, *Indika*, summarized in Photios, *Bibliotheke* cod. 72. The *Alexander Romance* survives in many versions; for the Byzantine ones, see now Jouanno, *Histoire merveilleuse*, especially the bibliography at 325–28. For the origins of the text, see Fraser, *Cities of Alexander*, 205–26. For Makarios and the *Alexander Romance*, see Gero, "The Alexander Legend." For the monstrous races in western thought, see Friedman, *The*

Monstrous Races; for the *kynokephaloi* in east and west, Bartlett, *The Natural and the Supernatural*, 95.

105. For the ancient material, see Karttunen, "The Ethnography of the Fringes"; Romm, *The Edges of the Earth*, 77–81 on Ktesias' *kynokephaloi*. For the *vita* of Makarios, see Elliot, *Roads to Paradise*, esp. ch. 5 on journeys through exotic places .

106. Cheynet, "Les limites du pouvoir," 17. For ancient explorers, see Roller, *Through the Pillars of Herakles*.

107. Mango, "A Journey," 255.

108. Galatariotou, "Travel and Perception"; Malamut, "Des voyages"; Külzer, *Peregrinatio graeca*; idem, "Reisende und Reisenliteratur"; and the papers in Macrides, ed., *Travel*.

109. Epiphanios the Monk, *Life and Deeds of the Apostle Andreas* 221.

110. Epiphanios the Monk, *Life and Deeds of the Apostle Andreas* 241. For a commentary, see Mango, "A Journey."

111. See pp. 101–2 below. The same is true of Epiphanios of Jerusalem's *Proskynetarion* (of the eighth or ninth century), which describes his journey to the Holy Land via Cyprus; see the discussion by Schneider, "Das Itinerarium." He may have been identical with the Epiphanios who traveled around the Black Sea.

112. Galatariotou, "Travel and Perception"; Külzer, "Konstantinos Manasses."

113. Petros of Sicily, *History of the Paulicians* 37 (p. 21) indignantly notes that the Paulicians were calling themselves Christians and other Byzantines "Romans," indicating a process of ethnic differentiation. Ludwig, "The Paulicians," 23 claims that "the Paulicians saw themselves as Byzantines: segregation of the group as a distinct heretical sect is a Constantinopolitan construct."

114. Kolbaba, *The Byzantine Lists*.

115. Quoted and discussed in Ivanov, "Mission Impossible," 260.

116. See esp. Chapter 4, section on "The Representation of Orthodox Barbarians."

117. For sixth-century texts on this theme, see Maas, "'Delivered from Their Ancient Customs." For taming barbarians through conversion in the middle period, see Ivanov, "Mission Impossible."

118. Leon VI, *Taktika* 18.59 (*PG* 18.61). I have a file with dozens of references to texts saying the same thing ("convert them, tame them, make them more like us").

119. Nicolaus I, *Responsa ad consulta Bulgarorum*; for the context, and a study of the letters of Nicolaus and Photios (below), see Sullivan, "Khan Boris"; Simeonova, *Diplomacy*; and Curta, *Southeastern Europe*, 169–72. The bibliography on these events and texts is vast.

120. Photios, *Letter to Khan Boris*; see Simeonova, *Diplomacy*, 112–52 and 156; Odorico, "La Lettre de Photius" and "Les miroirs des princes," 233–40, citing previous bibliography.

121. Gautier, "Moeurs populaires."

122. For a detailed case study, see Kaldellis, "The Kalends."

123. Pope Nicolaus I, quoted and discussed by Fögen, "Reanimation of Roman Law," 19.

124. See Chapter 4, section on "The Representation of Orthodox Barbarians."

125. See Athanassiadi, *Vers la pensée unique*, with the subtitle *La montée de l'intolérance dans l'antiquité tardive*.

126. Prokopios, *Wars* 8.6.9-10; see p. 5 above.

127. Haldon, *Byzantium in the Seventh Century*, 348–55; Hatlie, *The Monks and Monasteries*, 246.

128. Chiefly Cameron, "Images of Authority," citing previous studies; also eadem, "The Theotokos." For the reign of Herakleios, see Reinink and Stolte, eds., *The Reign of Heraclius*.

129. See pp. 24–25 above. Of course, "even as they pursued transcendence, philosophers were not insulated from the political and social realities of Roman imperialism": Schott, *Christianity, Empire*, 48–50.

130. *Questions to doux Antiochos* 42 (col. 624); for this text, see Brubaker and Haldon, *Byzantium*, 269; cf. Olster, *Roman Defeat*, 133.

131. Cf. Dagron, "L'ombre"; Kaldellis, "The Hagiography."

132. Haldon and Brubaker, *Byzantium in the Iconoclastic Era*, 17 n. 27.

133. I know two exceptions. Ioannes Mauropous expresses an attitude of forgiveness toward the heretic Theodoretos in his *Epigram* 49 (p. 27): "He was a man, so, man, don't judge him badly." Theophylaktos of Ochrid conceded that some of the errors of the Latins in theology "come not so much from wickedness of judgment as from ignorance of the truth," in this case partially due to the "poverty of Latin vocabulary"; quoted and discussed by Obolensky, *Six Byzantine Portraits*, 43. But he may have been commissioned by the emperor to effect a rapprochement with the pope: Frankopan, *The First Crusade*, 20. In general, see Kolbaba, *The Byzantine Lists*, 91–92, 176.

134. Kaldellis, *A New Herodotos*, and see the Epilogue of the present book.

135. Cassiodorus, *Variae* 1.1; tr. and discussion in Heather, *Empires and Barbarians*, 359–60. The ideological supremacy of Constantinople over the barbarian West is emphasized by Sarris, *Empires of Faith*; Raffensperger, *Reimagining Europe*, 11–15 (into the eleventh century). Meserve, *Empires of Islam*, 151 has characterized the difference between the ethnographers of antiquity and those of the Renaissance by invoking the "detached and neutral curiosity which ultimately [the former] derived from a sense of cultural confidence, bolstered by the political and military security that empire affords."

136. Cf. Kaegi, *Byzantium and the Decline*.

137. Güterbock, *Byzanz und Persien*; Fowden, *Empire to Commonwealth*; see now Dignas and Winter, *Rome and Persia*; and Canepa, *The Two Eyes of the Earth*. For the "Iranian Commonwealth," see Rapp, "Chronology."

138. Chrysos, "The Title ΒΑΣΙΛΕΥΣ."

139. Maas, "'Delivered from Their Ancient Customs'"; cf. also Sizgorich, "Reasoned Violence."

140. Heather, "The Barbarian," 250. For the shock delivered to the Roman system by the Arab conquests, see esp. Whittow, *The Making of Orthodox Byzantium*, ch. 6.

141. Ducellier, *Chrétiens d'Orient*, 174.

142. For the gap between what they knew and what they wrote about Islam, see Ducellier, *Chrétiens d'Orient*, 137–45.

143. For a survey, see Kazhdan, *A History of Byzantine Literature*, v. 1.

144. Ljubarskij, "Man in Byzantine Historiography," for one aspect of this development.

145. For Christian triumphalism, see Brown, *Power and Persuasion*, ch. 4; for imperial victory, see McCormick, *Eternal Victory*.

146. Heather, *The Fall*, 293 and 300.

147. Whitby, "Greek Historical Writing," 73; Olster, *Roman Defeat*, esp. 2, 44, 180–82; Croke, "Late Antique Historiography," 572. For the inability of western writers to come to terms with the success of Islam, see Tolan, *Saracens*, 19.

148. Efthymiades, "Chrétiens et sarrasins," 618.

149. Karapli, "Speeches of Arab Leaders."

150. Kaldellis, *Procopius of Caesarea*, ch. 5; for enemy speeches in Roman historiography, see Adler, *Valorizing the Barbarians*.

151. For general studies, see Meyendorff, "Byzantine Views of Islam"; Sahas, *John of Damascus*; Khoury, *Polémique byzantine*; Ducellier, *Chrétiens d'Orient*, esp. 146–66 for polemics; Hoyland, *Seeing Islam*. The main sources for the middle period are Glei and Khoury, *Johannes Damaskenos*; Förstel, *Niketas von Byzanz*; and Förstel, *Schriften zum Islam*; and, for a neglected philosophical source (Eustratios of Nikaia), Trizio, "A Neoplatonic Refutation." For Byzantine translations and polemics against the Koran, see now Simelides, "The Byzantine Understanding," esp. 892–93. For Byzantine views of the Arabs in general, see Jeffreys, "The Image of the Arabs"; Koutrakou, "The Image of the Arabs," and "The Arabs Through Byzantine Eyes."

152. Cf. Shboul, "Byzantium and the Arabs"; El Cheikh, *Byzantium*.

153. For this passage, see Cosentino, "The Syrianos's 'Strategikon'," 266; in general, Rance, "The Date of the Military Compendium."

154. For Leon, Psellos, and Mauropous, see pp. 102–5 and 118–24 below.

155. Howard-Johnston, "The *De administrando imperio*," 310. For this text, see Chapter 4, section on "The *Taktika* and *De administrando imperio*."

156. Howard-Johnston, *Witnesses*, ch. 7; Hoyland, *Theophilus of Edessa* (starting at 86).

157. Kaegi, "Initial Byzantine Reactions"; Constantelos, *Christian Hellenism*, 125–43; Haldon, *Byzantium in the Seventh Century*, 353–54, 364; Kaegi, *Byzantium and the Early Islamic Conquests*, 206, 210–18; Olster, *Roman Defeat*, 36–43; Hoyland, *Seeing Islam*, ch. 12; Haldon and Brubaker, *Byzantium in the Iconoclastic Era*, 18–22. I cite additional and later sources and studies in Kaldellis, "A Byzantine Argument," 5–6 n. 10. For the same schema in western sources, see Tolan, *Saracens*, 41–44.

158. Euodios, *The Martyrdom of the Forty-Two* 4–11 (62–65).

159. Ducellier, *Chrétiens d'Orient*, 180–81.

160. Olster, *Roman Defeat*, 81; cf. Johnson, *Ethnicity and Argument*, 181.

161. For Saracens as beasts, see the sources quoted by Jeffreys, "The Image of the Arabs," 313–15; Constantelos, *Christian Hellenism*, 126–29, 135. For lions to rabbits, see Koutrakou, "The Image of the Arabs," 216, citing Theodosios the Grammarian on the

siege of 717–718. For similar language used of the Turks in liturgical texts of the four-teenth century, see Slavin, "From Constantinople to Moscow," 206.

162. Ducellier, *Chrétiens d'Orient*, 169–72.

163. Anastasios of Sinai, *Quaestio* 101 (161–63) (seventh century); in general, Haldon, "The Works of Anastasius."

164. Photios, *Homily* 4 (tr. 95–110).

165. Many such passages are cited at Kaldellis, "A Byzantine Argument," 14 n. 24.

166. Photios, *Homily* 6.4 (tr. 129, slightly modified).

167. For Attaleiates, see also Chapter 3, section on "The Genres of Historiography."

168. Krallis, *Michael Attaleiates*.

169. Attaleiates, *History* 96–97.

170. Attaleiates, *History* 164–65.

171. Attaleiates, *History* 193–97, esp. 193–94; cf. 220.

172. Attaleiates, *History* 197.

CHAPTER 4. THE GENRES AND POLITICS OF MIDDLE
BYZANTINE ETHNOGRAPHY

1. For the *ethnika* in the military manuals, see especially Wiita, *The Ethnika*, who showed how the *Taktika* depends on the *Strategikon* for all nations but the Saracens, and provided a commentary on the information in the *Strategikon*; also Dagron, "'Ceux d'en face'"; briefly, Dvornik, *Origins of Intelligence Services*, 158–62; Luttwak, *The Grand Strategy*, 287–99. Leon VI had worked over the material in the *Strategikon* in his own *Problemata*, considered a precursor to the *Taktika*. Here he recasts much of the material of the *Strategikon* in the form of questions and answers.

2. Leon VI, *Taktika*, epilogue 19. See p. 27 above. (I will cite the *PG* numeration of the *Taktika* only where it is different.)

3. Noted, albeit in passing, by Dagron, "'Ceux d'en face'," 212 n. 14, 218.

4. Leon VI, *Taktika* 18.17 and Maurikios, *Strategikon* 11.1.4-5.

5. Leon VI, *Taktika* 18.18 and Maurikios, *Strategikon* 11.1.6-7.

6. Leon VI, *Taktika* 18.19 and Maurikios, *Strategikon* 11.1.8-10.

7. Leon VI, *Taktika* 18.21 and Maurikios, *Strategikon* 11.1.12-14.

8. Leon VI, *Taktika* 18.25, 18.27, 18.29-39.

9. We know, however, that he had, because of the *Problemata*.

10. Leon VI, *Taktika* 18.41-73 (*PG* 18.42-76) and Maurikios, *Strategikon* 11.2. For Leon on the Turks, see Moravcsik, "La Tactique de Léon le Sage," mostly on his dependence on the *Strategikon*. For such classicizing transfers of ethnonyms, see the section on "The Classicism of Byzantine Ethnography" below.

11. Leon VI, *Taktika* 18.42-43, 18.59 (*PG* 18.43, 18.45, 18.61); cf. Moravcsik, "La Tactique de Léon le Sage," 232–33; Tougher, "The Imperial Thought-World," 53–54.

12. Shepard, "Manners Maketh Romans?" 141–45.

13. Leon VI, *Taktika* 18.40 (*PG* 18.42).

14. Konstantinos VII, *De administrando imperio* 40; cf. 51.110-28; cf. Malamut, "L'image byzantine," 105–7; Antonopoulos, *Ο Αυτοκράτορας Κωνσταντίνος Z'*, 136–43 for sources and discussion.

15. Leon VI, *Taktika* 18.59 (*PG* 18.61).

16. Leon VI, *Taktika* 18.74-92 (*PG* 18.78-98) and Maurikios, *Strategikon* 11.3.

17. Leon VI, *Taktika* 18.76 (*PG* 18.80) and Maurikios, *Strategikon* 11.3.3.

18. Leon VI, *Taktika* 18.84 (*PG* 18.89) and Maurikios, *Strategikon* 11.3.23-24.

19. Leon VI, *Taktika* 18.74 (*PG* 18.78).

20. Leon VI, *Taktika* 18.93-102 (*PG* 18.99-108) and Maurikios, *Strategikon* 11.4. Note that Leon does not mention the Antai, who are in the *Strategikon*: Moravcsik, "La Tactique de Léon le Sage," 229.

21. Leon VI, *Taktika* 18.93-95 (*PG* 18.99-101); cf. 18.75 (*PG* 18.79); see the discussion at p. 39 above.

22. Leon VI, *Taktika* 18.96 (*PG* 18.102). For the best case that can be made for the *Strategikon's* discussion of Slavic hospitality and openness, see Heather, *Empire and Barbarians*, 434–35.

23. Leon VI, *Taktika* 18.103-34 (*PG* 18.109-42). See Dagron, "Byzance," with more thoughts in idem, "Apprivoiser la guerre"; a summary of some aspects of this section in Kolias, "The *Taktika*."

24. Leon VI, *Taktika* 18.117 (*PG* 18.123).

25. Leon VI, *Taktika* 18.104 (*PG* 18.110).

26. Leon VI, *Taktika* 18.105 (*PG* 18.111). The question of the existence of a concept of Holy War in Byzantium has been much debated recently.

27. Leon VI, *Taktika* 18.118 (*PG* 18.124); cf. 18.108, 18.120 (*PG* 18.114, 18.126).

28. Leon VI, *Taktika* 18.135 (*PG* 18.142).

29. Leon VI, *Taktika* 18.24 (οὐ γὰρ δουλείᾳ καὶ στρατείᾳ ἐκστρατεύουσι Σαρακηνοί, ἀλλὰ φιλοκερδίᾳ μᾶλλον καὶ ἐλευθερίᾳ, ἢ τὸ πλέον εἰπεῖν λῃστείᾳ καὶ τῆς ἑαυτῶν πίστεως, μᾶλλον δὲ εἰπεῖν ἀπιστίας τῇ δεισιδαιμονίᾳ, ὡς ἐνταῦθα τάχα πάσχοντες παρ' ἡμῶν, καὶ Θεὸν ἡγοῦνται πολέμιον ἔχειν, καὶ τὴν ζημίαν μὴ ὑποφέρειν).

30. Leon VI, *Taktika* 18.122-27 (*PG* 18.128-33); see Ducellier, *Chrétiens d'Orient*, 133–34; Dagron, "Byzance," 221 n. 14 and 237–39, whose suggestion requires further discussion.

31. Dagron, " 'Ceux d'en face'," 216. For heresiology and ethnography, see p. 102 below.

32. McGeer, *Sowing the Dragon's Teeth*, provides an excellent analysis of late tenth-century warfare based on both the historical sources and the military manuals.

33. For general studies, see Jenkins, ed., *Commentary*; Toynbee, *Constantine Porphyrogenitus*; Markopoulos, ed., *Κωνσταντίνος Z'*; Eggers, "Das De Administrando Imperio" (who does not, however, discuss the theories regarding the composition of the text).

34. Howard-Johnston, "The *De administrando imperio*," 319, has mounted a defense of the text's utility, but it is hard to believe that imperial planners did not already know how to do all that.

35. The theory was championed in Jenkins, ed., *Commentary*, but see Sode, "Untersuchungen"; Moysidou, *To Βυζάντιο*, 190.

36. Shepard, "Information, Disinformation and Delay," 270–76.

37. Živković, "Sources de Constantin VII."

38. Frankopan, "Some Notes," 2.

39. Živković, "Constantine Porphyrogenitus' Kastra Oikumena," 14, 19, which is not to say that the suggestion is not correct. For an overview, see Curta, *Southeastern Europe*, 137–46.

40. Shepard, "Imperial Information and Ignorance"; "Information, Disinformation and Delay," 270–72; and Beaud, "Le savoir et le monarque" (an article with a misleading title).

41. Howard-Johnston, "The *De administrando imperio*," 320–30.

42. Cf. Jenkins, ed., *Commentary*, 1, 2, 12, 18 (and passim) with Shepard, "Information, Disinformation and Delay," 270–72; and Lounghis, *Κωνσταντίνου Ζ'*, 106–12, on which see below. Howard-Johnston seems to be of two minds about this chapter: cf. "The *De administrando imperio*," 302 and 308 with 313. For Konstantinos VII and the Pechenegs, see Malamut, "L'image byzantine," 109–15.

43. Lounghis, *Κωνσταντίνου Ζ'*. Howard-Johnston, "The *De administrando imperio*," 303 n. 5, notes the existence of Lounghis' book but does not discuss it. Magdalino, "A History of Byzantine Literature," 177–81, offers some tentative support to Lounghis.

44. Cf. Yannopoulos, "Histoire et légende."

45. A convincing argument for misunderstanding in one instance has been made by Živković, "Constantine Porphyrogenitus' Kastra Oikoumena."

46. Howard-Johnston, "The *De administrando imperio*," 304.

47. *DAI* proem 19–21, 13.197-200; cf. Jenkins, ed., *Commentary*, 3.

48. *DAI* 9.71-78.

49. Jenkins, ed., *Commentary*, 55–56; on the linguistic aspect, see the discussion of the etymology of the geographical names in that chapter by Melin, "The Names of the Dnieper Rapids."

50. For the Rus' in Leon the Deacon, see pp. 102–5 below.

51. See also the discussion at *DAI* 31.31-42 of the (fictitious) papal "oracle and injunction" that allegedly prevents the Croats from waging offensive war.

52. *DAI* 15.

53. Cf. Bickermann, "Origines Gentium."

54. See esp. *DAI* 27.30-58 on the Lombards; less so 28 on the Venetians; 30.61-90 on the Croats; 32 Serbs; 37 Pechenegs; 38 Magyars (Turks); 41 Moravians; and 45 Iberians.

55. Cf. *DAI* 29 with *Life of the Emperor Basileios I* 52–58 (288–92).

56. Ševčenko, "Re-reading Constantine Porphyrogenitus," esp. 191; Howard-Johnston, "The *De administrando imperio*," 328; Németh, *Imperial Systematization*, 57–58.

57. Theophanes, *Chronicle* s.a. 6171 (356–59); from the same source in Nikephoros, *Short History* 35–36.

58. Skylitzes, *Synopsis Historion: Konstantinos IX* 9–10 (442–47) and 16–18 (455–61) respectively.

59. Anna Komnene, *Alexiad* 6.9.

60. E.g., the sources of *The Miracles of St. Demetrios* 2.5. Howard-Johnston, "Byzance avant l'an mil," 55, proposes that the second book of the *Miracles* generally has its origin in materials similar to that which later made up the *De administrando imperio.*

61. See Curta, "Qagan," 4–10; Fielder, "Bulgars." For the geography, see Curta, *Southeastern Europe*, 78–80, citing previous scholarship. Such passages have only begun to be studied as literary artifacts: Todorov, "Byzantine Myths," 66–67.

62. Treadgold, "Trajan the Patrician," argues that this may have been Traianos *patrikios* (early to mid-eighth century).

63. Skylitzes, *Synopsis Historion: Konstantinos* IX 9–10 (442–47). For the events, see Golden, *An Introduction*, 216–22; Peacock, *Early Seljuq History*; for a commentary on the passage, Meserve, *Empires of Islam*, 131–34, who finds it garbled, but this is a relative verdict (she also discusses its reception among Renaissance historians); for Byzantine views of the Turks, Messina, "Tipologia"; Savvides, "Η γνώση."

64. Holmes, *Basil II*, ch. 2; Flusin and Cheynet, *Jean Skylitzès*, xii–xvi.

65. Attaleiates, *History* 43–44; see the notes in Pérez Martín's edition, *Miguel Ataliates*, 251–52.

66. There are no solid indicators for the date of Skylitzes' *Synopsis*. Kiapidou, *Ἡ Σύνοψη Ἱστοριῶν*, 125–36, has argued for an earlier date, in the 1060s or 1070s, which would invalidate my argument, though her position is based, like those it aims to replace, on vague conjectures. It is just as likely that the present argument invalidates her proposed dating.

67. Bryennios, *Materials for a History* 1.7-10; cf. Zonaras, *Chronicle* 17.25. I follow Neville, *Heroes and Romans*, ch. 5. For Bryennios' changes to Skylitzes, see also Carile, "La *Hyle Historias*," 57–59.

68. Bickermann, "Origines Gentium." Todorov, "Byzantine Myths," uses the classical term but does not make any comparisons.

69. Parker, *The Making of Roman India*, 82.

70. Skylitzes, *Synopsis Historion: Konstantinos* IX 17 (459); cf. Moravcsik, *Byzantinoturcica*, v. 2, 11–13.

71. Bryennios, *Materials for a History* 4.10.

72. Attaleiates, *History* 48–49; see Ševčenko, "Wild Animals"; Drocourt, "Les animaux." For elephant images in middle Byzantine art, see Stavrakos, "The Elephant," 287–93. For an ethnographic analysis of a similar passage in a later historian, see Petrides, "Georgios Pachymeres." For exotic animals as markers of ethnographic discourse, Dieterich, *Byzantinische Quellen*, 28–34; Parker, *The Making of Roman India*, 127 and passim; in triumphs, Östenberg, *Staging the World*, 168–84, 275.

73. Kaminiates, *Capture of Thessalonike* 49, 52. For the debate over the authenticity of this text and its ethnographic deficiencies, see pp. 30–31 above. For these ethnic traits, see O'bweng-Okwess, "Le portrait du soldat noir."

74. Choniates, *Orations* 8.57.

75. Choniates, *History* 94.

76. The contemporary digression on the Cumans by Robert de Clari also focuses on their horses, albeit without the salacious detail: *Conquest of Constantinople* 65 (142–45; tr. 87–88).

77. Ammianus Marcellinus, *Res Gestae* 31.2; see Magoulias' translation of Choniates, *O City of Byzantium*, 378 n. 270; and Stephenson, "Byzantine Conceptions," 252. For Ammianus' account of the Huns, see p. 10 above.

78. Treadgold, *The Early Byzantine Historians*, 314, 317; idem, "The Byzantine World Histories." The indirect influence of Ammianus in the Greek tradition is traceable through Zonaras: Banchich and Lane, *The History of Zonaras*, 222–23.

79. Choniates, *History* 395–96. They are mentioned also by Anna Komnene, *Alexiad* 6.12.5.

80. Ioannes Phokas, *Ekphrasis* 3 (col. 932; Troickij ed. 4). See Külzer, *Peregrinatio graeca*, 20–21; and Galatariotou, "Travel and Perception," esp. 224–25. For a reading of the text and the correction of the name, see Messis, "Littérature, voyage et politique."

81. Genesios, *On the Reigns of the Emperors* 3.3-4 and Theophanes Continuatus: *Theophilos* 19–21 (109–12) is not an ethnography of the Persians, but a set of romantic and unhistorical stories that circulated about the leaders of Persian units who took up service under the empire after their revolt against the Caliphate had failed; see, in general, Venetis, "Korramis." Future research may indicate whether these stories owe anything to Persian tradition; at first sight they appear to be constructed around ancient Greek stereotypes about Persian culture. For a Zoroastrian view of their activities in the Byzantine empire, see Daryaee, "A Historical Episode."

82. Kaldellis, "The Original Source"; for the campaign itself, Stephenson, *Byzantium's Balkan Frontier*, 51–55.

83. Leon the Deacon, *History* 9.6 (tr. 193–94).

84. Herodotos, *Histories* 4.62, 4.76-78.

85. For the debate, see Kaldellis, *Procopius of Caesarea*, ch. 1.

86. Prokopios, *Wars* 6.25.9-10.

87. Terras, "Leo Diaconus."

88. Leon the Deacon, *History* 9.8 (tr. 195).

89. Moravcsik, "Zum Bericht des Leon Diakonos"; Terras, "Leo Diaconus," 401.

90. See p. 47 above.

91. For these, see p. 50 above.

92. Leon the Deacon, *History* 9.11.

93. Leon the Deacon, *History* 6.3.

94. Östenberg, *Staging the World*, 130–35, on the interplay between the victor and the vanquished. For the limits of the connection between ethnography and the triumph, see Woolf, *Tales of the Barbarians*, 84–85.

95. Leon the Deacon, *History* 9.12; cf. Plutarch, *Camillus* 7.1; see Kaldellis, "The Original Source."

96. Östenberg, *Staging the World*, 94–97, 283.

97. Rance, "The Date of the Military Compendium," 708.

98. For outdated notions of "classicizing imitation," see Moravcsik, "Klassizismus," and Hunger, "On the Imitation (MIMHΣIΣ)"; for "atavism," Dieterich, *Byzantinische Quellen*, xvii–xviii; for "distortion," Mango, *Byzantine Literature*, and Cameron, *Procopius*. For the use of ancient ethnonyms and classical ethnography as a template, Amantos, "Τὰ ἐθνολογικὰ ὀνόματα"; Moravcsik, "Die archaisierenden Namen", and *Byzantinoturcica*, v. 2, 13–17 on names for Turks; Savvides, "Η γνώση," 717–20 on "Skythians" and Turks, 721 on "Persians" and Turks; Tapkova-Zaimova, "L'emploi des ethnica"; Ditten, "'Germanen' und 'Alamannen'"; Bibikov, "Das 'Ausland'," 66–67; Spadaro, "I barbari"; Vratimos, "The Identification of the Scythians"; as well as in many studies of the Byzantine "image" of various peoples; see also below.

99. For the belief that modern names (for rivers and the like) are more "accurate" than medieval names, see Luttwak, *The Grand Strategy*, 34, 42.

100. For an example of how modern racial and linguistic terms emerged from an engagement with the Byzantine sources in the nineteenth century, see Stamatopoulos, *Το Βυζάντιο*, 163–209.

101. Rapp, "Hellenic Identity," 129 on the Greek bias.

102. Mango, *Byzantine Literature*, 5–6 for his experience of Greek comp courses, 8 for flavor.

103. Brown, *Society and the Holy*, 93.

104. See Kaldellis, *Procopius of Caesarea*, 38–45.

105. E.g., MacMullen, *Voting About God*, 13: "rappers."

106. From Williams, *Style*, 5. The Latin bias of modern English and its extremes were ridiculed by George Orwell in his essay "Politics and the English Language," reprinted often and available online.

107. Browning, *Medieval and Modern Greek*, 16–17 n. 35. The texts are Konstantinos VII, *De administrando imperio* 42.24 and Theophanes Continuatus: *Theophilos* 28 (122).

108. For the early Roman empire, see Swain, *Hellenism and Empire*, ch. 1–2; Brown, *An Atticist Lexicon*.

109. Diller, "Byzantine Lists"; Fraser, *Greek Ethnic Terminology*, 154–55.

110. Quoted by Theophanes, *Chronographia* s.a. 5870 (66); see Treadgold, "Trajan the Patrician."

111. Attaleiates, *History* 30, 66.

112. Attaleiates, *History* 66, 97.

113. Choniates, *Orations* 9. For the parallel use of classicizing and non-classicizing ethnonyms, see Durak, "Defining the 'Turk'."

114. Anna Komnene, *Alexiad* 10.10.4.

115. Anna Komnene, *Alexiad* 10.8.1.

116. Konstantinos VII, *De administrando imperio* 1.10-15; see Moravcsik, "Τὰ συγγράματα."

117. For an argument that it was the Frankish, "Latin," core of western Europe that absorbed peripheral peoples (thereby indirectly vindicating Byzantine terminology), see Bartlett, *The Making of Europe*.

118. Cf. Heather, *The Fall*, 523 n. 44, for a more positive reaction. Durak, "Defining the 'Turk'," discusses some of the ways by which the Byzantines themselves decoded classical ethnonyms.

119. The obscure reference in Attaleiates, *History* 87, can perhaps be explained through Leon the Deacon, *History* 9.6.

120. Stephenson, "Byzantine Conceptions," 253–56. I would not, however, follow him in calling this a Byzantine form of "Orientalism," because Orientalism is (or was) a modern scholarly discipline professing objectivity." Generic labels (e.g., Skythian) served imperial propaganda, but in a different way. For the term "Mysian," see Papadopoulou, "Οι όροι ʻΜυσίαʼκαι ʻΜυσόςʼ," which offers only an inventory, not an interpretation.

121. The general Priskos in Theophylaktos Simokattes, *History* 7.7.5 ("this is Roman land"); and Daphnopates, *Letter* 5.116 ff. (64–65); in general, Chrysos, "Die Nordgrenze." For the justice of restoring lost lands to the empire, see Laiou, "Economic Thought," 1126.

122. Leon the Deacon, *History* 8.2, 8.8.

123. Moravcsik, *Byzantinoturcica*, v. 2, 279–83 for a partial list. "Skythian" as a *topos*: see Zástěrová, "Zur Problematik"; Bibikov, "Das ʻAuslandʼ," 67–68; Carile, "I nomadi," esp. 69–71; Amory, *People and Identity*, 127–30; Spadaro, "I barbari"; Stephenson, *Byzantium's Balkan Frontier*, 108–10.

124. Anna Komnene, *Alexiad* 8.5.6.

125. Vásáry, *Cumans and Tartars*, 4–12; cf. Savvides, "Οι Κομάνοι."

126. Cf. Lindner, "Nomadism"; Bartha, "The Typology" (including discussion); Shaw, "ʻEaters of Fleshʼ"; Ahrweiler, "Byzantine Concepts" (which lacks a clear point); and Donner, "The Role of Nomads."

127. Bibikov, "Das ʻAuslandʼ," 67–72; Dagron, "ʻCeux d'en faceʼ," 215.

128. Prokopios, *Wars* 8.5.6; cf. Herodotos, *Histories* 4.6-7 and 4.17-18: despite their particular tribal names, the generic "Skythian" suffices. Liebeschuetz, "Making a Gothic History," 201: "Writers of the later empire were well aware that Getae and Scythians were collective designations, covering a large number of different peoples, settled at different times in the eastern Balkans and southeastern Ukraine."

129. Bibikov, "Die alte Rusʼ," 199–205; Patlagean, "Nommer les Russes."

130. Attaleiates, *History* 43–44.

131. Attaleiates, *History* 78, 104–5. For Prokopios on the Ephthalitai, see pp. 17–20 above.

132. Chalkokondyles, *Histories* 1.10.

133. Freeman, *The Philosopher and the Druids*; Östenberg, *Staging the World*, 155 cites many sources; Woolf, *Tales of the Barbarians*.

134. Anna Komnene, *Alexiad* 15.3.2; also 5.5.5, 13.4.2-3; cf. Aristotle, *Nicomachean Ethics* 3.6-9. For Byzantine views of the Latins, see pp. 201 n 21 above.

135. Barber and Jenkins, eds., *Medieval Greek Commentaries*.

136. Aristotle, *Nicomachean Ethics* 3.7 (1115b27-28).

137. Anna Komnene, *Alexiad* 1.15.1, 4.6.5; Boatwright, *Peoples of the Roman World*, 36.

138. It has been proposed that this was what the Magyars called themselves, at least initially: Jenkins, ed., *Commentary*, 13–14. Luttwak, *The Grand Strategy*, 156, proposes that the Byzantines called them "Turks" because they lived "an entirely Turkic way of life as nomadic herdsmen and mounted archers." But in that case they would have called them "Huns" or "Skythians." Meserve, *Empires of Islam*, 140, says that "because of their [the Hungarians'] perceived kinship with the Khazar 'Turks' (a relationship much debated in modern scholarship), they were often called Tourkoi in Greek sources." But this kinship is not highlighted in Byzantine sources. For Byzantine Tourkia as Hungary, see Tóth, "The Territories."

139. Rance, "The Date of the Military Compendium," 713–14, citing previous bibliography.

140. Venetis, "Korramis."

141. See p. 213 n 81 above.

142. Durak, "Defining the 'Turk'," 72.

143. Kaldellis, *Hellenism in Byzantium*, 285 (and ch. 5 generally); for the increasing use of Persian figures in the twelfth century, Cresci, "*Exempla* storici greci," 124–28, 133, 141–42.

144. Vidal-Naquet, *The Black Hunter*, 208: "it is the Greek polis that is being defined by historians and its 'ethnographers' in terms of its opposite"; Hartog, *The Mirror of Herodotus*; Dauge, *Le barbare*, esp. pt. 2; Heather, "The Barbarian," 235–36, 238, 242; Kaldellis, *Procopius of Caesarea*, ch. 2, esp. 75, 87; and Messis, "La mémoire du 'je' souffrant," 112–13, 129–40; in the Roman triumph, Östenberg, *Staging the World*, 262; generally, Webb, *Demons and Dancers*, 198–202, 208 (attacks on the theater by preachers served to define the Church); Wilken, *John Chrysostom* (attacks on the Jews served to define Christian identity), etc.

145. Psellos, *Chronographia* 7.67-69; see Malamut, "L'image byzantine," 122. Pietsch, *Die Chronographia*, does not discuss this passage.

146. Psellos, *Chronographia* 7B.16; see Moore, *Iter Psellianum*, 416, for editions and discussions.

147. Kaldellis, *The Argument*.

148. See pp. 10 and 100 above.

149. Mauropous, *Oration on the Feast-Day of the Victorious Standard-Bearer [St Georgios] and the Recent Miracle Involving the Barbarians* 9–14 (144–45 Lagarde). For the context of this speech, see below. For Mauropous, see Karpozilos, *Συμβολή*.

150. Psellos, *Chronographia* 7.69.

151. See Chapter 1, section on "The Politics of Ethnography."

152. Maas, "'Delivered from their Ancient Customs'."

153. Cf. MacMullen, *Christianizing the Roman Empire*, esp. ch. 1.

154. For this saying, see Massing, "Greek Proverbs"; cf. Jeremiah 13.23.

155. Attaleiates, *History* 30–31 (Ausones is an archaic term for Romans); in general, Cresci, "Michele Attaliata," 198; and the notes to Pérez Martín's edition, *Miguel Ataliates*, 248–49.

156. So Ivanov, "Mission Impossible," 256. Mauropous as the only one: Malamut, "L'image byzantine," 123 (but cf. 144 nothing changed in the representation of the Pechenegs between the tenth and the twelfth centuries).

157. Mauropous, *Poem* 96 (50 Lagarde).

158. MacCormack, *Art and Ceremony*, masterfully reveals how panegyric encoded shared values but takes the genre at face value, dismissing cynics even when they were contemporaries (esp. Augustine, *Confessions* 6.6.9). Much evidence, both lying on the surface and between the lines, suggests that contemporaries were less gullible than scholars think and that they knew well the difference between panegyric and reality. For Psellos in particular, see Kaldellis, *The Argument*, esp. ch. 20; for Choniates, Magdalino, *The Empire of Manuel I*, 477–82; Simpson, *Niketas Choniates*. Sometimes even emperors found the praise to be over-the-top: Dennis, "Imperial Panegyric," 134.

159. Lefort, "Rhétorique et politique"; Karpozilos, Συμβολή, 141–42. For the context, see Malamut, "L'image byzantine," 118–23; Stephenson, *Byzantium's Balkan Frontier*, 89–98, but at 111 he does not note that Mauropous' speech was nixed due to controversy, nor does Kolia-Dermitzaki, "Τὸ ἐμπόλεμο Βυζάντιο," 230–31, though they cite Lefort's study. For another speech we can tell was revised at the last minute to suit the propaganda needs of the regime, see Heather, "Liar in Winter," 201–3.

160. Psellos, *Chronographia* 6.109; cf. Attaleiates, *History* 24; Skylitzes, *Synopsis Historion: Konstantinos IX* 8 (440).

161. Psellos, *Letter* 207 (239); cf. Stephenson, *Byzantium's Balkan Frontier*, 111–12; for Psellos' militarism, see Kaldellis, *The Argument*. Skylitzes also seems to have favored a policy of exterminating the Pechenegs: *Synopsis Historion: Konstantinos IX* 17 (459).

162. See the devastating analysis of the panegyrics of Themistios by Heather, "Themistius"; Heather and Moncour, *Politics*. For the middle period, one may substitute "Christianity" in Heather's analysis for "philosophy." Little of substance is affected.

163. Stephenson, *Byzantium's Balkan Frontier*, 107–14.

164. Odorico, ed., *La face cachée*.

165. Attaleiates, *History* 158–59; see pp. 54–55 above.

166. *pace* Lefort, "Rhétorique et politique," 287.

167. Skylitzes, *Synopsis Historion: Konstantinos IX* 16 (456–57).

168. Nikephoros Ouranos, *Letter* 35 (234–35).

169. E.g., Theophanes Continuatus: *Michael III* 27 (185–91) ; Psellos, *Praise of Italos*, discussed in Kaldellis, *Hellenism in Byzantium*, 220–21.

170. Angold, *Byzantium*, 2.

171. The relevant bibliography is vast. I am preparing a separate study of this question that is not linked to the issues of ethnography and the perception of foreign peoples. Notable exceptions include J. B. Bury, S. Runciman, and H.-G. Beck. For a preliminary statement, see Kaldellis, *Hellenism in Byzantium*, ch. 2; cf. Ando, "Decline, Fall," 32–33 on the exclusion of Byzantium from the Roman legacy.

172. I plan to discuss the Byzantine meaning of *oikoumene* in a separate study.

173. Daphnopates, *Oration on the Peace* 264. The author's identity is immaterial here.

174. Angelov, "The Bulgarians," 22 (slightly modified).

175. Nikolaos Mystikos, *Letter* 12 (82). More passages are cited by Kolia-Dermitzaki, Ὁ βυζαντινός "ἱερός πόλεμος," 308–9.

176. Nikolaos Mystikos, *Letter* 17 (118). Stouraitis, "Byzantine War," 95 realizes that Nikolaos was exaggerating but does not grasp that the Byzantines deployed this rhetoric only when they were in a position of weakness.

177. Theophanes Continuatus: *Romanos I* 15 (408–9).

178. Daphnopates, *Oration on the Peace* 274. For the occasion, see Shepard, "A Marriage Too Far?' 127–31.

179. Daphnopates, *Letter* 5.47-48 (58–59).

180. Kaldellis, "Review of Page."

181. Leon the Deacon, *History* 4.5 (tr. 110).

182. Psellos, *Enkomion for Ioannes [Mauropous] the Metropolitan of Euchaita* 69–73 (146). This was Bishop Leon.

183. *Life of the Emperor Basileios I* 12.

184. Ivanov, "Casting Pearls," starting from Theophanes Continuatus: *Leon V* 20 (31).

185. Page, *Being Byzantine*, 54. Ivanov, "Mission Impossible," 257 cites condescending texts but runs religious and ethnic differences together, e.g., when he translates *ethnē* as "pagans."

186. E.g., *Life of Athanasios of Athos* A 55, B20 (27, 145); *Life of Loukas of Steiris* 32, 50 (52–55, 80–83); *Life of Nikon* 40 (140–41).

187. Shepard, "A Marriage Too Far?' 125.

188. Psellos, *Chronographia* 4.39-40. This idea occurs in many sources and is studied in the papers in Nikolaou and Tsiknakis, eds., Βυζάντιο.

189. Attaleiates, *History* 297.

190. Choniates, *History* 369–74; but see Stephenson, *Byzantium's Balkan Frontier*, 288–94.

191. Akropolites, *History* 11, 34, 54; for thirteenth-century attitudes, Kaldellis, *Hellenism in Byzantium*, 360–68.

192. Mesarites, *Funeral Oration for His Brother Ioannes* 49 (I, 62); for Benedictus, see Hoeck and Loenertz, *Nikolaos-Nektarios*, 30–54.

193. Kanaboutzes, *Commentary on Dionysios of Halikarnassos* 35. There used to be confusion as to whether this author was of Latin background writing in Greek or of "Greek" Orthodox origin addressing Latin masters. The quoted passage, along with the reference to "our Justinian" (at 12), proves that he was Orthodox. See Efthymiades and Mazarakis, "La chronique familiale."

194. Koutrakou, "The Image of the Arabs," 217. From the later period, and from an official document no less, see Pitsakis, "A propos de la citoyenneté romaine," 98–99.

195. Koutrakou, ""Animal Farm" in Byzantium?' 332–34.

196. See pp. 83–85 above.

197. Leon the Deacon, *History* 5.3.

198. For "Mysian" applied to the Bulgarians, see Kolia-Dermitzaki, "Η εικόνα," 64.

199. Moysidou, *Το Βυζάντιο*, 117–18, 125–28.

200. Treadgold, "Byzantium," 212.

201. Cf. Koutrakou, *La propagande impériale*, 377. Stouraitis, "Byzantine War," does not realize that Byzantines (sometimes) called themselves Christians rather than Romans almost exclusively during those centuries when they were surrounded by non-Christians. But he correctly demonstrates that the Roman-barbarian distinction was primary at all other times.

202. Mîrşanu, "The Imperial Policy," 497; cf. Thompson, *The Goths*, 28 (the policies of the Gothic kingdom show the same nonconfessional pattern: "Heresy did not make another nation an enemy, just as orthodoxy did not make it a friend").

203. Nikolaos Mystikos, *Letter* 23 (156–59).

204. Cf. Ševčenko, "Three Paradoxes," 229 n. 32, with Obolensky, *Six Byzantine Portraits*, 34–82; Mullett, *Theophylact of Ochrid*, 261, 266–77 (with a useful survey of past discussions); Stephenson, "Byzantine Conceptions," 249–52; idem, *Byzantium's Balkan Frontier*, 152–54; Curta, *Southeastern Europe*, 286–88; Kolia-Dermitzaki, "Η εικόνα," 60–62.

205. Theophylaktos of Ochrid, *Letter* 4 (141). Full references in Mullett, *Theophylact of Ochrid*, 269–70, 274; the animal comparisons are highlighted by Obolensky, *Six Byzantine Portraits*, 31, 58, 66.

206. Theophylaktos of Ochrid, *The Martyrdom of the Fifteen Holy Martyrs of Tiberioupolis* 35 (col. 200); see Obolensky, *Six Byzantine Portraits*, 71–77; Stephenson, "Byzantine Conceptions," 250–51; idem, *Byzantium's Balkan Frontier*, 152–54. For the *Life of Kliment of Ochrid*, see p. 200 n 80 above.

207. Quotation and summary from Kazhdan, *Studies on Byzantine Literature*, 220.

208. Galatariotou, "Travel and Perception," 229.

209. Magdalino, "Byzantine Snobbery"; idem, "Constantinople"; Mullett, "Originality"; eadem, *Theophylact of Ochrid*, 247–60. For Eustathios at Thessalonike, see Angold, *Church and Society*, ch. 8; for Choniates at Athens, Kaldellis, *The Christian Parthenon*, ch. 6. For provincial stereotypes, see Magdalino, "Paphlagonians."

210. See pp. 32–33 above.

211. Tzetzes, *Letter* 67 (96–97).

212. Tzetzes, *Histories (Chiliades)* 10.316.

213. Tzetzes, *Histories (Chiliades)* 10.317; Herodotos, *Histories* 5.12.

214. Hesiod, *Works and Days* 373.

215. Tzetzes, *Histories (Chiliades)* 10.318.

216. Blangez-Malamut and Cacouros, "L'image des Serbes," 97; for the context, Stephenson, *Byzantium's Balkan Frontier*, ch. 8.

217. Eustathios. *Oration for Isaakios Angelos in Philippoupolis* 10 (43–44), followed by an account of their Cuman, "Skythian," allies.

218. Choniates, *History* 90–92; cf. Akropolites, *History* 70.

219. Cf. Choniates, *Oration* 4 (to emperor Isaakios II Angelos) (26–34) for extended comments on the Serbs in the same vein.

220. Bibikov, "Die alte Rus'," 205–6.

221. Cited by Blangez-Malamut and Cacouros, "L'image des Serbes," 99.

222. Theodoros II Laskaris, *Letter* 44 (58).

223. Frankopan, "Some Notes," 1.

224. Efthymiades, "Νοεροί και πραγματικοί"; Magdalino, "Ο οφθαλμός," 121–23; in general, Malamut, *Sur la route.*

225. E.g., Gregorios Dekapolites (arrested); Neilos of Rossano (mocked as a Bulgarian); and the four cases of arrested saints discussed by Dvornik, *Origins of Intelligence Services*, 152–53 ("it appears that they arrested everyone unable to produce a written permit to account for his presence near the border").

226. See the Greek monks at the monastery of Mar Saba in Dalrymple, *From the Holy Mountain.*

227. Pakourianos, *Typikon* 24 (105); for Pakourianos, see Lemerle, *Cinq études*, 115–91. Ethnic monasteries (e.g., Iviron and Chilandar on Mt. Athos, or "of the Romans," i.e., from Rome, in Constantinople) are an understudied phenomenon (individually they have received much attention from their respective national scholars). For ethnicity and monasticism, see Obolensky, *Six Byzantine Portraits*, 125, 128–30; Shahîd, *Byzantium and the Arabs*, 167 n. 103; Hatlie, *The Monks and Monasteries*, 246. For the Armenian monastery at Philippopolis, see Bartikian, Αρμενοβυζαντινά, 186; at 191 identified with the monastery founded by Pakourianos.

228. Fowden, *Empire to Commonwealth*; Shepard, "Byzantium's Overlapping Circles"; Raffensperger, "Revisiting the Idea," 160–64 and *Reimagining Europe*, passim; Kaldellis, *Hellenism in Byzantium*, 110; Rapp, "Chronology," 183; idem, "The Iranian Heritage," 648 n. 7 ("so narrowly to Greek and Slavic elements"); Wood, *"We have no king but Christ"*, 255 (Nestorianism and Monophysitism in the East were rivals to Constantinopolitan Orthodoxy); and Arnason, "Byzantium," 502–3.

229. Huntington, *The Clash of Civilizations.* The map is fascinating. For the modern ideological roots of Obolensky's schema, see Stamatopoulos, *Το Βυζάντιο*, 20.

230. Shepard, "The Byzantine Commonwealth."

231. Obolensky, *The Byzantine Commonwealth*, 14–15.

232. See Moysidou, *Το Βυζάντιο*, 128–29, 243. Franklin, "The Empire of the Rhomaioi," complements this conclusion on the Rus' side, as does Raffensperger, "Revisiting the Idea," who adds that the Commonwealth theory has harmed scholarship on the Rus'.

233. Obolensky, *The Byzantine Commonwealth*, 353–56; idem, *Six Byzantine Portraits*, 2; also Ivanov, "Mission Impossible," 254 ("innate cultural snobbery"), 260 ("Greek arrogance"), 264 ("Greek snobbery") (257 is a crucial page because there Ivanov translates *ethnē* alternately as "pagans" and "barbarians," revealing fundamental confusions); also, in a limited form, Angelov, "The Bulgarians," 28. The Hellenist interpretation predates Obolensky's *magnum opus*: Ševčenko, "Three Paradoxes," 226, 229. A fantastic formulation of the Byzantines' ecumenical ideology and their view of others can be found in Obolensky, *Byzantium and the Slavs*, 11–13, which verges on fiction. Among other claims, he asserts that there was no distinction between Roman and barbarian in the Byzantine view, and then has to rationalize away its appearance in the sources.

234. For the Rus', see Raffensperger, *Reimagining Europe*, 168.

235. Geertz, *The Interpretation of Culture*, 18.

236. Cf. Heather, *Empires and Barbarians*, 519: "the fact that they adopted Christianity did mean that they could not be viewed as barbarian 'outsiders' in the same unrelenting fashion that classical authors had adopted toward all non-Romans."

CHAPTER 5. ETHNOGRAPHY IN PALAIOLOGAN LITERATURE

1. The emperors in question were Ioannes V and his many sons, especially Manuel II. He tries to cope with this development in letters that he wrote on campaign in Asia Minor in the retinue of Bayezid: see Barker, *Manuel II*, ch. 2.

2. Kaldellis, *A New Herodotos* (forthcoming).

3. Pachymeres, *History* 1.3 (v. 1, 27).

4. Siniossoglou, *Radical Platonism in Byzantium*.

5. Mullett, "In Peril on the Sea"; for travel information in epistolography, Karpozilos, "Ταξιδιωτικές περιγραφές."

6. For the ambassadors of this period, see Mergiali-Sahas, "A Byzantine Ambassador"; Barker, "Emperors, Embassies, and Scholars."

7. Barker, *Manuel II*, 192, who gathers the information in Manuel's letters about his travels; Karpozilos, "Ταξιδιωτικές περιγραφές," 512.

8. Homeyer, "Zur Synkrysis des Manuel Chrysoloras"; Saradi-Mendelovici, "Christian Attitudes Toward Pagan Monuments," 59; for the addressee, Thorn, "Das Briefcorpus des Manuel Chrysoloras," 21.

9. See Chapter 2, section on "Byzantine Sources of Information."

10. Lippard, *The Mongols and Byzantium*, 213; in general, Oikonomidès, "Byzantine Diplomacy"; Malamut, "De 1299 à 1451"; for a snapshot of this complex culture, Obolensky, "A Byzantine Grand Embassy." See below for individual cases.

11. Gregoras, *Roman History* 6.8 (v. 1, 193–95), who comments on the moral qualities appropriate to ambassadors. For the mission, see also Pachymeres, *History* 9.5 (v. 3, 230–33). For all passages in Gregoras, one should consult the commentary in van Dieten, *Nikephoros Gregoras*.

12. Metochites, *Presbeutikos* 91–92; in general, Laiou, *Constantinople and the Latins*, 96–98; de Vries-van der Velden, *Théodore Métochite*, 66–76 (who proves, at 73–74 n. 86, the falsity of the traditional notion that Metochites went on five embassies to the Serbs: in reality he presented himself five times before the kral on this one).

13. Metochites, *Presbeutikos* 93–95. That winter is also described by Pachymeres, *History* 9.33 (v. 3, 304–5); for the route, Belke, "Roads and Travel," 83, citing previous bibliography.

14. Metochites, *Presbeutikos* 98–99.

15. Metochites, *Presbeutikos* 90. For hostile perceptions by the Byzantines of other Balkan peoples in the fourteenth century, see Barker, "The Question of Ethnic Antagonisms"; Malamut, "Les discours de Démétrius Cydonès." For the middle period, see Chapter 4, section on "The Representation of Orthodox Barbarians."

16. Metochites, *Presbeutikos* 103–6.

17. See p. 133 above.

18. Gregoras, *Letter* 32; *Roman History* 8.14 (v. 1, 373–83); see Karpozilos, "Ταξιδιω-τικές περιγραφές," 529–31; Belke, "Roads and Travel," 83–84; Vlachakos, Νικηφόρος Γρηγοράς, 226–32.

19. Gregoras, *Roman History* 8.14 (v. 1, 383).

20. Libadenos, *A Narrative of Travel and Anabasis*; see the discussion by the editor Lampsides, 136–38; for the date, see 138–42; for autobiographical modes in later literature, Angold, "Autobiography and Identity"; Hinterberger, *Autobiographische Traditionen*, esp. 290–94 for Libadenos; Dimitroukas, "Andreas Libadenos," extracts historical information.

21. Libadenos, *A Narrative of Travel and Anabasis* 45–49.

22. For Doukas ("Phokas"), see p. 67 above. The *Ekphrasis of the Sights of Jerusalem* by Perdikas of Ephesos (fourteenth century) contains one reference to the polluted Saracens and their vile religion (vv. 91–93, 168) and some allusions to the presence of the "impious." These texts do, however, contain valuable indirect information regarding local guide culture in Jerusalem. In general, see Külzer, *Peregrinatio graeca*.

23. Gregoras, *Roman History* 24.4 (v. 3, 7); for Odysseus, van Dieten, *Nikephoros Gregoras*, v. 5, 11. I follow van Dieten in numbering this book as 24 (in the Bonn edition it is 22—followed by 25). This is a complicated problem.

24. Gregoras, *Roman History* 24.5 (v. 3, 9–10).

25. See the review in van Dieten, *Nikephoros Gregoras*, v. 1, 26–30; v. 5, 10–31; Vlachakos, Νικηφόρος Γρηγοράς, 230–31.

26. Gregoras, *Roman History* 24.5 (v. 3, 10).

27. Gregoras, *Roman History* 24.10 (16–17) and 25.1 (19).

28. Gregoras, *Roman History* 24.8 (14) and 24.9 (15–16).

29. Kaldellis, *The Christian Parthenon*.

30. Gregoras, *Roman History* 25.1 (18–19).

31. Rhodes: Gregoras, *Roman History* 24.6 (11–13).

32. Alexandria: Gregoras, *Roman History* 24.7 (13–14).

33. Damascus: Gregoras, *Roman History* 24.8 (14–15).

34. van Dieten, *Nikephoros Gregoras*, v. 5, 207 n. 29 suggests that this was a way of saying that the "capital" (i.e., Constantinople) was less free in religious matters than other places. But Alexandria was not the capital of the Mamluk realm, and why would Gregoras need to be indirect about it? He says more damning things about the Palamite establishment openly.

35. Antioch: Gregoras, *Roman History* 24.9 (15–16).

36. Issos: Gregoras, *Roman History* 24.10 (16–17). I cannot explain why he goes on at such length about it.

37. For Gregoras' own account of Mongol expansion, at the beginning of the *Roman History*, see the section on "The Mongols" below.

38. Hierapolis and Tarsos: Gregoras, *Roman History* 25.1 (18–20).

39. Gregoras, *Roman History* 25.2 (20–21).

40. Gregoras, *Roman History* 25.7 (27).

41. Cyprus and Lapithos: Gregoras, *Roman History* 25.8–10 (27–32).

42. Gregoras, *Roman History* 25.12 (34–35).

43. Gregoras, *Roman History* 25.12-13 (34–37).

44. Crete: Gregoras, *Roman History* 25.15-16 (38–40).

45. The prefatory letter of Lucius Septimius to the Latin version of Dictys of Crete's *Journal of the Trojan War* (of the Severan period) says that the text was found when an earthquake caused Dictys' tomb at Knossos to open, and some shepherds found a box containing the tablets, written in Phoenician letters. All this is a fiction, of course, but people knew there were antiquities there, and tombs. For "Septimius," see Champlin, "Serenus Sammonicus."

46. Surveys begin in the Renaissance: Karadimas, "The Unknown Past."

47. Gregoras, *Roman History* 25.17 (41–42).

48. Troy: Gregoras, *Roman History* 25.26 (51).

49. Siniossoglou, *Radical Platonism*, 89–113.

50. For an edition, translation, and commentary on the texts, see Philippidis-Braat, "La captivité de Palamas," with the texts at 137–90; also Arnakis, "Gregory Palamas"; Karpozilos, "Ταξιδιωτικές περιγραφές," 537–39; Messis, "La mémoire du 'je' souffrant."

51. For later polemics, see Ducellier, *Chrétiens d'Orient*, 277–84, 289–310 (296 for *sklerosis*); also Karpozilos, "Byzantine Apologetic"; Vryonis, "Byzantine Attitudes"; for more texts and studies, Necipoğlu, *Byzantium Between the Ottomans and the Latins*, 200 n. 63.

52. Bryer, "Greek Historians," 488.

53. Barker, *Manuel II*, 136.

54. Palamite (especially monastic) accommodation with the Turks is discussed by Siniossoglou, *Radical Platonism*.

55. Philotheos Kokkinos, *Life of Sabas the Fool* 24, 41, 50 (206–7, 237, 257–58). I thank Charis Messis for this reference; in general, Congourdeau, "La Terre Sainte au XIVe siècle."

56. Gregoras, *Roman History* 29.7-9 (v. 3, 227–29). The first text I know to mention Turks sodomizing bishops is Alexios' possibly spurious letter to Robert of Flanders: Frankopan, *The First Crusade*, 61.

57. See p. 114 above.

58. See Chapter 4, section on "The Pechenegs in the Eleventh Century."

59. Morgan, "The Mongols"; Lippard, *The Mongols and Byzantium*; Langdon, "Byzantium's Initial Encounter."

60. Runciman, "The Ladies of the Mongols"; Morgan, "The Mongols," 206; Langdon, "Byzantium's Initial Encounter," 100, 127, 137–38; for Maria, Lippard, *The Mongols and Byzantium*, 159–60.

61. Connell, "Western Views"; Meserve, *Empires of Islam*.

62. A variant of "Tocharians" (used later by Pachymeres; see below), the name of a Central Asian tribe mentioned in classical sources: Zachariadou, "The Oğuz Tribes," 286.

63. Pachymeres, *History* 2.24 (v. 1, 180–87); for the author and his critical stance, Lambakis, Γεώργιος Παχυμέρης; for his Mongol geography, Laiou, "On Political Geography."

64. Pachymeres, *History* 2.25 (v. 1, 186–87).

65. Pachymeres, *History* 3.3 (v. 1, 234–39).

66. Pachymeres, *History* 3.4 (v. 1, 238–39).

67. Pachymeres, *History* 3.5 (v. 1, 240–43). The same events in Gregoras, *Roman History* 4.7-8 (v. 1, 101–7), with an excursus on the Crusader origin of those cities. Michael seems to have been aware of the slave trade: Lippard, *The Mongols and Byzantium*, 93.

68. Petrides, "George Pachymeres"; also Laiou, "On Political Geography," 109–12.

69. In general, see Laiou, "On Political Geography," 112–14, though a "political" reading can be pushed further.

70. Pachymeres, *History* 5.4 (v. 2, 444–47).

71. See Chapter 1, section on "The Politics of Ethnography."

72. Pachymeres, *History* 5.4 (v. 2, 446–49).

73. Laiou, "On Political Geography," 119–20 on Pachymeres, *History* 12.1 (v. 4, 502–7); it is not that he "mistook" him for a Christian (Lippard, *The Mongols and Byzantium*, 160–62, 170). The virtuous Muslim, as a foil for Christian failings, appears prominently in Attaleiates' *History*, in the figure of Alp Arslan; see p. 80 above.

74. Pachymeres, *History* 9.26-27 (v. 3, 288–95), 12.1 (v. 4, 502–9).

75. In general, see Bydén, "The Nature and Purpose of the *Semeioseis*"; Featherstone, "Theodore Metochites."

76. A similar paradox in Choniates, who promises in the preface of his *History* to write such simple prose that common day-laborers will be able to read him, and then delivers one of the most challenging works of Greek prose: Kaldellis, "Niketas Choniates." We are clearly dealing with deliberate contrasts in both cases, though it is still not clear what we are to make of them.

77. Metochites, *Moral Essays* 37–40.

78. The four Roman essays: Metochites, *Moral Essays* 106–9; for the argument for Christian monarchy and its background, see Shawcross, " 'Do Thou Nothing," 110–11.

79. Metochites, *Moral Essays* 109 (722).

80. Metochites, *Moral Essays* 110 (723–34).

81. Metochites, *Moral Essays* 110 (729).

82. Metochites buttresses this with an exposition of Homer, *Iliad* 13.4-6, where Zeus looks past the Thracians to the peoples of the north, "drinkers of milk . . . most just of all men." On this passage see Strabo, *Geography* 7.3.4-9; and Romm, *The Edges of the Earth*, 53.

83. Metochites, *Moral Essays* 110 (732: τὸ πᾶν ἀποδιδόασιν ὄφλημα τῇ φύσει).

84. Strabo, *Geography* 7.3.7; cf. Shumate, *Nation, Empire, Decline*, 81.

85. Metochites, *Moral Essays* 110 (734), quoting, and slightly altering, Thucydides, *History* 2.97.

86. Garzya, "Byzantium," 33–35, 50 n. 22; and esp. de Vries-van der Velden, *Théodore Métochite*. In *Moral Essay* 6 he argues that all men like what they are accustomed to, but

this can be trained and redirected; at 6.2.6 he seems to quote Agathias in saying that everyone thinks his own to be the best.

87. Gregoras, *Roman History* 9.13 (v. 1, 459).

88. Gregoras, *Letter* 23; discussion in Bydén, "The Nature and Purpose of the *Semeioseis*," 269–73. Gregoras praises Metochites' learning and writings also in the *Roman History* 7.11 (v. 1, 272). For Gregoras' geography, see Laiou, "Italy and the Italians," 88–90; Vlachakos, Νικηφόρος Γρηγοράς (consisting of lists).

89. Gregoras, *Roman History* 2.4 (v. 1, 30). Langdon, "Byzantium's Initial Encounter," 104–5 compares Gregoras' account with that of Ammianus on the Huns, but seems unaware of his textual debts to Pachymeres and Metochites; as is Vlachakos, Νικηφόρος Γρηγοράς, 198, 226.

90. Gregoras, *Roman History* 2.4 (v. 1, 32–33).

91. For this subgenre, see Chapter 4, section on "Ethnographic Moments."

92. Gregoras, *Roman History* 2.5 (v. 1, 35–40).

93. Gregoras, *Roman History* 2.5 (v. 1, 38).

94. Gregoras, *Roman History* 2.5 (v. 1, 40).

95. Gregoras viewed the effect of Mongol expansion at the expense of the Turks as detrimental to the interests of the Byzantine frontier, while Pachymeres seems to have viewed it as positive: Lippard, *The Mongols and Byzantium*, 35. This may have contributed to his demythologization of their image. Note that Gregoras similarly undermines his account of the First Crusade, which begins panegyrically and heroically—but notice its last sentence: 4.7 (v. 1, 106).

96. Bartlett, *The Making of Europe*, esp. 20. The term "Latins" could be used self-ascriptively by western medieval writers, e.g., Roger Bacon: Bartlett, *The Natural and the Supernatural*, 134.

97. Konstantinos VII, *De administrando imperio* 13.116-22; see Shepard, "A Marriage Too Far?' 122 n. 4.

98. Laiou, "Italy and the Italians," 80, for this sense of familiar otherness in Pachymeres.

99. Numerous studies of these images are cited at p. 201 n 21 above; for the Palaiologan period, Laiou, "Italy and the Italians"; Messis, "Venise." For the gender dynamic, see Messis, "Lectures sexuées d l'altérité." For ancient Roman views of northerners and Greeks, see Woolf, *Tales of the Barbarians*; Boatwright, *Peoples*, ch. 2–3; Gruen, *Rethinking the Other*, ch. 5–6. For the Trojan War background of the Fourth Crusade, see Shawcross, "Re-Inventing the Homeland."

100. For Chalkokondyles on the "Romans" (western Europeans or Catholics), see Kaldellis, *A New Herodotos*, ch. 5.

101. For the circumstances and social dynamics of this choice at the end, see Necipoğlu, *Byzantium Between the Ottomans and the Latins*.

102. See Manuel II, *Funeral Oration for his Brother Theodoros* 194–95 (cf. 128-31) defending the plan by his brother, Theodoros I, to sell the Peloponnese to the Hospitallers, a plan scotched by his own subjects ("there were two options left open—either to accept the rule of the Turks or that of the Christians").

103. See p. 50 above.

104. E.g., Choniates, *History* 301, 365, 402, 410, 414–15, 453, 594, 477.

105. Choniates, *History* 199, 204–5; see Magdalino, *The Empire of Manuel I*, e.g., 221–24.

106. See Chapter 3, section on "Ethnography and Christianity."

107. Konstantinos Stilbes, *Errors of the Latin Church*; for the eleventh- and twelfth-century origin of this charge, see Kolbaba, *The Byzantine Lists*, 95, 135, 178; Kaldellis, *Hellenism in Byzantium*, 358–59.

108. Akropolites, *Against the Latins* 1.1 (30–31).

109. Akropolites, *Against the Latins* 2.27 (64); discussion in Hunger, *Graeculus perfidus*, 44–45; Kaldellis, *Hellenism in Byzantium*, 381–83.

110. Theodoros II Laskaris, *Letter* 5 (8); discussion in Kaldellis, *Hellenism in Byzantium*, 375; for the theme in general, see Tinnefeld, "Das Niveau." Yet at the same time westerners could complain about "the poverty of the Latins" in philosophy: Bartlett, *The Natural and the Supernatural*, 136.

111. Kydones, *Apologia* 364.

112. Kydones, *Apologia* 365–66 (tr. 28); see Hunger, *Graeculus perfidus*, 21–22.

113. Kydones, *Speech of Advice to the Romans* 977d; see Ryder, *The Career and Writings*, 71–72, 80, 103.

114. Kydones, *Apologia* 401.

115. Kydones, *Apologia* 372.

116. Kydones, *Apologia* 400.

117. Koder, "Latinoi," 37: Kydones refers to the Italians as barbarians only ironically, to critique his imagined opponent's usage. The adversaries that he constructs, who might have been calling the westerners barbarians, are called straw men by Ševčenko, "The Decline of Byzantium," 172, but I'm not so sure.

118. Necipoğlu, *Byzantium Between the Ottomans and the Latins*.

119. Kaldellis, *A New Herodotos*.

120. Gregoras, *Roman History* 6.1 (v. 1, 165); see Kaldellis, *Hellenism in Byzantium*, 384–85.

121. Pachymeres, *History* 7.34 (v. 3, 101).

122. Gregoras, *Roman History* 37.48 (v. 3, 555–56); also 11.11 (v. 1, 567–68). For the import of foreign luxury goods in the later period, see Laiou and Morrisson, *The Byzantine Economy*, 191–92.

123. Gregoras, *Roman History* 9.1 (v. 1, 396); for these markers see Page, *Being Byzantine*, ch. 5; for Theodoros, Laiou, "A Byzantine Prince Latinized"; Shawcross, " 'Do Thou Nothing'."

124. Gregoras, *Roman History* 4.5 (v. 1, 98).

125. For these clichés, see Laiou, "Italy and the Italians," 73–74.

126. Gregoras, *Roman History* 5.6 (v. 1, 147).

127. Dennis, "The Byzantines in Battle," 165; Luttwak, *The Grand Strategy*.

128. Maurikios, *Strategikon* 2.16 (tr. 32).

129. Maurikios, *Strategikon* 3.5 (tr. 37).

130. See Dennis, "The Byzantines in Battle," 176 for examples.

131. *Praecepta militaria* 4.19 (50–51).

132. Psellos, *Chronographia* 1.32-33. For the role of Basileios in this text, see Kaldellis, *The Argument*.

133. Kinnamos, *History* 4.13 (tr. 129–30); cf. 2.14 (for Aristotle: 6.13).

134. E.g., Shawcross, *The Chronicle of Morea*, 196–97.

135. Kazhdan, "The Aristocracy."

136. E.g., Anna Komnene, *Alexiad* 11.6.3.

137. See pp. 114–15 above.

138. Chalkokondyles, *Histories* 2.20.

139. Gregoras, *Roman History* 10.3 (v. 1, 482–83).

140. Choniates, *History* 108–10; and Jones and Maguire, "A Description of the Jousts." Ioannes Kantakouzenos, *History* 1.42 (v. 1, 205) claims that these customs were only just then introduced among the Romans and that emperor Andronikos III bested his western teachers in the art. The former claim should be investigated.

141. See pp. 36–37 above.

142. See Chapter 3 above; for the monarchical bias, see Angelov, *Imperial Ideology*, 200–202.

143. Laiou, "Italy and the Italians"; Syros, "Between Chimera and Charybdis"; Messis, "Venise." For Genoa in particular, which I will be focusing on, see Origone, "Genova vista da Bizanzio," and *Bisanzio e Genova*, esp. 251–61.

144. Angelov, *Imperial Ideology*, 68–69.

145. Holobolos, *Oration 1 in Praise of Michael Palaiologos* 45; for the oration, the Genoese, and the date, see Macrides, "The New Constantine," 33–35; and esp. Hilsdale, "The Imperial Image"; for the name of Genoa, Chalkokondyles, *Histories* 5.58; and Ditten, "Die Namen für Venedig."

146. Holobolos, *Oration 1 in Praise of Michael Palaiologos* 46. The event referred to was the treaty of Nymphaion (1261); its oaths could, by a stretch, be interpreted this way: Angelov, *Imperial Ideology*, 341 n. 113; for the change in context between 1261 and 1265, Hilsdale, "The Imperial Image."

147. Metochites, *Moral Essays* 96 (esp. 616–18).

148. Shawcross, " 'Do Thou Nothing' "; Syros, "Between Chimera and Charybdis," 463–67.

149. Gregoras, *Roman History* 7.5 (v. 1, 233–37). The differences in political orders were real. For a contrast, see Jacoby, "The Encounter of Two Societies." For the debate over Theodoros, see Laiou, "A Byzantine Prince Latinized."

150. Metochites, *On Character or on High Culture* 22–24 (126–37).

151. Syros, "Between Chimera and Charybdis," 464 claims the point is "to establish the cultural superiority of the ancient Athenians." But if "culture" here means literature, who would deny it?

152. Syros, "Between Chimera and Charybdis," 469–70, building on Laiou, "Italy and the Italians," 86–88; for Gregoras' different use of the same upheavals, see ibid. 90; a review of the facts in Origone, "Genova vista da Bizanzio," 488–92.

153. Kydones, *Letter* 24 (v. 1, 53–54); see Syros, "Between Chimera and Charybdis," 484–86; Messis, "Venise." For Kydones and Venice, see Dennis, "Demetrios Kydones," esp. 499 for this letter; and Kianka, "Demetrios Kydones."

EPILOGUE

1. Metochites, *Second Imperial Oration* 14 (376–87); cf. Ševčenko, "The Decline of Byzantium," 172–73, 178.

2. Doukas, *History* 5.1, and passim.

3. Texts cited and contextualized by Ducellier, *Chrétiens d'Orient*, 180–81, 317–20; Moustakas, "Byzantine 'Visions' of the Ottoman Empire," 215–16; Necipoğlu, *Byzantium Between the Ottomans and the Latins*, 46. Luther argued much the same: Heath, "Renaissance Scholars," 462.

BIBLIOGRAPHY

PRIMARY SOURCES

The following does not include standard texts from classical antiquity. I cite English translations, where available, for the convenience of the interested reader even when I have not quoted from them directly. I use "v." to designate specific volumes within a multi-volume publication, and "vols." to designate the total number of volumes. "Ed." means only that the publication contains the original text, not necessarily the most recent critical edition (though often that is the case). Byzantine authors are listed by their family or second names, unless they are conventionally known by their first names or are emperors.

Agathias. *Histories*; ed. R. Keydell, *Agathiae Myrinaei Historiarum Libri Quinque* (Berlin 1967 = *CFHB* v. 2); tr. J. D. Frendo, *Agathias: The Histories* (Berlin and New York 1976 = *CFHB* v. 2A).

Akropolites, Georgios. *Against the Latins*; ed. A. Heisenberg, rev. P. Wirth, *Georgii Acropolitae opera*. v. 2 (Stuttgart 1978).

———. *History*; ed. A. Heisenberg, rev. P. Wirth, *Georgii Acropolitae opera*. v. 1 (Stuttgart 1978); tr. R. Macrides, *George Akropolites: The History* (Oxford 2007).

Alexander Romance; ed. W. Kroll, *Historia Alexandri Magni* (Berlin 1926); tr. R. Stoneman, *The Greek Alexander-Romance* (London 1991).

Ammianus Marcellinus. *Res Gestae*; ed. and tr. J. C. Rolfe, *Ammianus Marcellinus* (Cambridge, Mass. and London 1935–1939 = *LCL*).

Anastasios of Sinai. *Quaestiones*; ed. M. Richard and J. A. Munitiz, *Anastasii Sinaitae qvaestiones et responsiones* (Turnhout 2006).

Anna Komnene. *Alexiad*; ed. D. R. Reinsch and A. Kambylis, *Annae Comnenae Alexias* (Berlin 2001 = *CFHB* v. 40); tr. E. R. A. Sewter, rev. P. Frankopan, *Anna Komnene: Alexiad* (London 2009).

[*Anonymous Book on Tactics*]; ed. and tr. in G. Dennis, *Three Byzantine Military Treatises* (Washington, D.C. 1985 = *CFHB* v. 25) 246–327.

Antiochos, Gregorios. *Letters*; ed. J. Darrouzès, "Deux lettres de Grégoire Antiochos écrites de Bulgarie vers 1173," *Byzantinoslavica* 23 (1962): 276–84.

Attaleiates, Michael. *History*; ed. and tr. I. Pérez Martín, *Miguel Ataliates: Historia* (Madrid 2002); ed. and tr. A. Kaldellis and D. Krallis, *Michael Attaleiates: History* (Washington, D.C. 2012 = *DOML*).

Bardaisan. *The Book of the Laws of Countries: Dialogue on Fate of Bardaisan of Edessa*; ed. and tr. H. J. W. Drijvers (Assen 1964).

Barlaam and Ioasaph; ed. R. Volk, *Die Schriften des Johannes von Damascus*, v. 6.1-2: *Historia animae utilis de Barlaam et Ioasaph (spuria)* (Berlin 2006–2009); tr. G. R. Woodward and H. Mattingly, *John Damascene: Barlaam and Ioasaph* (Cambridge, Mass. and London 1967 = LCL).

The Book of John Mandeville with Related Texts; tr. I. M. Higgins (Indianapolis 2011).

Bryennios, Nikephoros. *Materials for a History*; ed. and tr. P. Gautier, *Nicephori Bryennii Historiarum libri quattuor (Nicéphore Bryennios: Histoire)* (Brussels 1975 = CFHB v. 9).

Cassiodorus. *Variae*; tr. S. J. B. Barnish (Liverpool 1992 = TTH v. 12).

Chalkokondyles, Laonikos. *Histories*; ed. and tr. A. Kaldellis (Washington, D.C. 2014 = DOML).

Choirosphaktes, Leon. *Letters*; ed. and tr. G. Kolias, *Léon Choerosphactès: Magistre, proconsul et patrice* (Athens 1939); and G. Strano, *Leone Choirosphaktes: Corrispondenza* (Catania 2008).

Choniates, Michael.; ed. S. Lambros, Μιχαὴλ Ἀκομινάτου τοῦ Χωνιάτου τὰ σωζόμενα, 2 vols. (Athens 1879–1880).

Choniates, Niketas. *History*; ed. J.-L. van Dieten, *Nicetae Choniatae Historia* (Berlin 1975 = CFHB v. 11); tr. H. J. Magoulias, *O City of Byzantium, Annals of Niketas Choniates* (Detroit 1984).

———. *Orations*; ed. J.-L. van Dieten, *Nicetae Choniatae orationes et epistulae* (Berlin 1972 = CFHB v. 3).

CJ = Codex Iustinianus; ed. P. Krueger in *Corpus Iuris Civilis*: v. 2 (Berlin 1895).

Daphnopates, Theodoros. *Letters*; ed. and tr. J. Darrouzès and L. G. Westerink, *Théodore Daphnopatès: Correspondance* (Paris 1978).

———. *Oration on the Peace*; ed. and tr. I. Dujčev, "On the Treaty of 927 with the Bulgarians," *DOP* 32 (1978): 219–95.

Doukas. *History*; ed. and tr. V. Grecu, *Istoria Turco-Bizantina* (Bucharest 1958); tr. H. Magoulias, *Decline and Fall of Byzantium to the Ottoman Turks, by Doukas* (Detroit 1975).

Epiphanios of Jerusalem. *Proskynetarion*; ed. H. Donner, "Palästina-Beschreibung des Epiphanios Hagiopolita," *Zeitschrift des deutschen Palästina-Vereins* 87 (1971): 42–91.

Epiphanios the Monk. *Life and Deeds of the Apostle Andreas*; ed. PG 120: 215–60.

Eunapios. *Lives of the Philosophers*; ed. and tr. W. C. Wright, *Philostratus and Eunapius: Lives of the Philosophers* (Cambridge, Mass. and London 1921 = LCL).

Euodios. *The Martyrdom of the Forty-Two*; ed. V. Vasil'evskij and P. Nikitin, *Skazanija o 42 amorijskich mučenikach* (St. Petersburg 1905).

Eusebios. *Ecclesiastical History*; ed. and tr. K. Lake and J. E. L. Oulton, 2 vols. (Cambridge, Mass. 1926–1932).

———. *Life of Constantine*; tr. A. Cameron and S. G. Hall, *Eusebius: Life of Constantine* (Oxford 1999).

Eustathios of Thessalonike. *Commentary on Ioannes Damaskenos' Pentecostal Hymn*; ed. PG 136: 503–754.

————. *Oration for Isaakios Angelos in Philippoupolis*; ed. T. L. F. Tafel, *Eustathii metropolitae Thessalonicensis opuscula* (Frankfurt 1832) 41–45.

————. *Oration for the Emperor Manuel Komnenos*; ed. Wirth, *Eustathii Thessalonicensis opera minora* (Berlin and New York 2000 = *CFHB* v. 32) 261–88.

Genesios, Ioseph. *On the Reigns of the Emperors*; ed. A. Lesmüller-Werner and I. Thurn, *Josephi Genesii regum libri quattuor* (Berlin 1978 = *CFHB* v. 14); tr. A. Kaldellis, *Genesios: On the Reigns of the Emperors* (Canberra 1998 = *BA* v. 11).

Georgios Synkellos. ed. A. Mosshammer, *Ecloga chronographica* (Leipzig 1984); tr. W. Adler and P. Tuffin, *The Chronography of George Synkellos: A Byzantine Chronicle of Universal History from the Creation* (Oxford 2002).

Gerald of Wales. *The Description of Wales*; tr. L. Thorpe, *Gerald of Wales: The Journey through Wales / The Description of Wales* (London 1978).

Gregoras, Nikephoros. *Letters*; ed. P. A. M. Leone, *Nicephori Gregorae Epistulae*, 2 vols. (Milan 1982–1983).

————. *Roman History*; ed. L. Schopen and I. Bekker, *Byzantina Historia*, 3 vols. (Bonn 1829–1855); German tr. and commentary in van Dieten, *Nikephoros Gregoras* (q.v.).

Holobolos, Manuel. *Orations*; ed. M. Treu, *Programm des könlichen Victoria-Gymnasiums zu Potsdam* (Potsdam 1906).

Ignatios the Deacon. *Life of Georgios of Amastris*; ed. V. G. Vasil'evskij, *Trudy*, v. 3 (St. Petersburg 1915) 1–71.

————. *Life of Gregorios Dekapolites*; ed. G. Makris, *Ignatios Diakonos und die vita des hl. Gregorios Dekapolites* (Stuttgart and Leipzig 1997).

Kaminiates, Ioannes. *Capture of Thessalonike*; ed. G. Böhlig, *Ioannis Caminiatae De expugnatione Thessalonicae* (Berlin and New York 1973 = *CFHB* v. 4); ed. and tr. D. Frendo and A. Fotiou, *John Kameniates: The Capture of Thessaloniki* (Canberra and Perth 2000 = *BA* v. 12).

Kanaboutzes, Ioannes. *Commentary on Dionysios of Halikarnassos*; ed. M. Lehnerdt, *Ioannis Canabutzae magistri ad principem Aeni et Samothraces in Dionysium Halicarnasensem Commentarius* (Leipzig 1890).

Kantakouzenos, Ioannes. *History*; ed. L. Schopen, *Ioannis Cantacuzeni eximperatoris Historiarum Libri IV*, 3 vols. (Bonn 1828–1832).

Kinnamos, Ioannes. *History*; ed. *PG* 133: *Historiarum libri VII*; tr. C. Brand, *Deeds of John and Manuel Comnenus* (New York 1976).

Konstantinos VII Porphyrogennetos. *Book of Ceremonies*; ed. J. J. Reiske, *Constantini Porphyrogeniti imperatoris de cerimoniis aulae byzantinae*, 2 vols. (Bonn 1829–1830).

————. *De administrando imperio*; ed. G. Moravcsik and tr. R. J. H. Jenkins, *Constantine Porphyrogenitus: De administrando imperio* (Washington, D.C. 1967 = *CFHB* v. 1); annotated tr. K. Belke and P. Soustal, *Die Byzantiner und ihre Nachbarn: Die* De administrando imperio *genannte Lehrschrift des Kaisers Konstantinos Porphyrogennetos für seinen Sohn Romanos* (Vienna 1995).

————. *On Embassies*; ed. C. de Boor, *Excerpta de legationibus* (Berlin 1903) = U. Ph. Boissevain et al., eds., *Excerpta historica iussu imp. Constantini Porphyrogeniti confecta*, v. 1.

————. *Three Treatises*; ed. and tr. J. Haldon, *Constantine Porphyrogenitus: Three Treatises on Imperial Military Expeditions* (Vienna 1990 = *CFHB* v. 28).

Kosmas Indikopleustes. *Christian Topography*; ed. and tr. W. Wolska-Conus, *Cosmas Indicopleustès: Topográphie chrétienne*, 3 vols. (Paris 1968–1973); tr. J. W. McCrindle, *The Christian Topography of Cosmas, An Egyptian Monk* (London 1897).

Ktesias. *Indika*; ed. and tr. D. Lenfant, *Ctésias de Cnide: la Perse, l'Inde, autre fragments* (Paris 2004); tr. A. Nichols, *Ctesias: On India* (Bristol 2011).

Kydones, Demetrios. *Apologia for his Faith*: ed. G. Mercati, *Notizie di Procoro e Demetrio Cidone, Manuele Caleca e Teodoro Meliteniota* (Vatican City 1931) 359–437; tr. (based on a German tr.) in J. Likoudis, *Ending the Byzantine Greek Schism* (New Rochelle, N.Y. 1992) 22–70.

————. *Letters*; ed. R.-J. Loenertz, *Démétrius Cydonès: Correspondance*, 2 vols. (Rome 1956–1960).

————. *Speech of Advice to the Romans*; ed. *PG* 154: 961–1007.

Leon VI. *Problemata*; ed. A. Dain, *Leonis VI Sapientis Problemata* (Paris 1935).

————. *Taktika*; ed. and tr. G. T. Dennis, *The Taktika of Leo VI* (Washington, D.C. 2010 = *CFHB* v. 49); prior edition in *PG* 107: 669–1120 (references to the *PG* enumeration of chapters are given in parentheses as Dennis does not provide cross-references).

Leon the Deacon. *History*; ed. C. B. Hase, *Leonis diaconi Historae libri X* (Bonn 1828); tr. A.-M. Talbot and D. F. Sullivan, *The History of Leo the Deacon: Byzantine Military Expansion in the Tenth Century* (Washington, D.C. 2005).

Libadenos, Andreas. *A Narrative of Travel and Anabasis*; ed. O. Lampsides, Ἀνδρέου Λιβαδηνοῦ βίος καὶ ἔργα (Athens 1975) 39–87.

Libanios. *Letters*; ed. R. Foerster, *Libanii opera*, 12 vols. (Leipzig 1903–1927) v. 10–11: *Epistulae*; partial tr. A. F. Norman, *Libanius: Autobiography and Selected Letters*, 2 vols. (Cambridge, Mass. and London 1992 = *LCL*); partial tr. S. Bradbury, *Selected Letters of Libanius from the Age of Constantius and Julian* (Liverpool 2004 = *TTH* v. 41).

Life of Andreas the Fool; ed. and tr. L. Rydén, *The Life of St. Andrew the Fool*, 2 vols. (Uppsala 1995).

Life of Athanasios of Athos; ed. J. Noret, *Vitae dvae antiqvae sancti Athanasii Athonitae* (Turnhout 1982).

Life of Blasios of Amorion; ed. *Acta Sanctorum Nov.* 4, 657c–669d.

Life of Demetrianos; ed. H. Delehaye, *Acta Sanctorum Novembris*, v. 3 (Brussels 1910) 300–308; ed. H. Grégoire, "Saint Démétrianos, évêque de Chytri (île de Chypre)," *BZ* 16 (1907): 204–40, here 217–40.

Life of Elias the Younger; ed. G. R. Taibbi, *La vita di Sant'Elia il Giovane* (Palermo 1962).

Life of Gregentios of Zaphar; ed. and tr. in Berger, *Life and Works of Saint Gregentios* (q.v.).

Life of Ioannes of Gotthia; ed. M.-F. Auzépy, "La vie de Jean de Gothie (*BHG* 891)," in C. Zuckermann, ed., *La Crimée entre Byzance et le khaganat khazar* (Paris 2006) 69–85.

Life of Loukas of Steiris; ed. and tr. C. L. and W. R. Connor, *The Life and Miracles of Saint Luke of Steiris* (Brookline, Mass. 1994).

Life of Makarios of Rome; ed. A. Vassiliev, *Anecdota graeco-byzantina* (Moscow 1893) 135–65.

Life of Nikon; ed. and tr. D. F. Sullivan, *The Life of Saint Nikon* (Brookline, Mass. 1987).

Life of the Emperor Basileios I; ed. and tr. I. Ševčenko, *Chronographiae quae Theophanis Continuati nomine fertur liber quo Vita Basilii imperatoris amplectitur* (Berlin 2011 = *CFHB* v. 42).

Liudprand of Cremona. *Embassy to Constantinople*; tr. P. Squatriti, *The Complete Works of Liudprand of Cremona* (Washington, D.C. 2007) 238–82.

Malalas, Ioannes. *Chronicle*; ed. I. Thurn, *Ioannis Malalae Chronographia* (Berlin 2000 = *CFHB* v. 35); tr. E. Jeffreys et al., *The Chronicle of John Malalas* (Melbourne 1986 = *BA* v. 4).

Manasses, Konstantinos. *Hodoiporikon*; ed. K. Horna, "Das *Hodoiporikon* des Konstantin Manasses," *BZ* 13 (1904): 313–55.

———. *Short Chronicle*; ed. O. Lampsides, *Constantini Manassis Breviarium Chronicum*, 2 vols. (Athens 1996 = *CFHB* v. 36).

Manuel II Palaiologos. *Funeral Oration for his Brother Theodoros*; ed. and tr. J. Chrysostomides, *Manuel II Palaeologus: Funeral Oration on his Brother Theodore* (Thessalonike 1985).

Martyrdom of Arethas; ed. M. Detoraki and tr. J. Beaucamp, *Le Martyre de saint Aréthas et de ses compagnons (BHG 166)* (Paris 2007).

Martyrdom of Gourias, Samonas, and Abibos; ed. O. von Gebhardt, *Die Akten der edessenischen Bekenner Gurjas, Samonas und Abibos* (Leipzig 1911).

Martyrdom of Sire; ed. P. Devos, "Sainte Sirin, martyre sous Khosrau Ier Anosarvan," *Analecta Bollandiana* 64 (1946): 87–131.

Maurikios. *Strategikon*; ed. G. T. Dennis and tr. E. Gamillscheg, *Das Strategikon des Maurikios* (Vienna 1981 = *CFHB* v. 17); tr. G. T. Dennis, *Maurice's Strategikon: Handbook of Byzantine Military Strategy* (Philadelphia 1984).

Mauropous, Ioannes. ed. P. de Lagarde, *Iohannis Euchaitorum Metropolitae quae in codice Vaticano Graeco 676 supersunt* (Göttingen 1882).

Menandros. *History*; ed. and tr. R. C. Blockley, *The History of Menander the Guardsman* (Liverpool 1985).

Mesarites, Nikolaos. *Funeral Oration for his Brother Ioannes*; ed. A. Heisenberg, *Neue Quellen zur Geschichte des lateinische Kaisertums und der Kirchenunion, I–III* (Munich 1922).

Metochites, Theodoros. *On Character or on High Culture*; ed. and tr. I. Polemis, Θεόδωρος Μετοχίτης: Ἠθικὸς ἢ περὶ παιδείας (Athens 1995).

———. *Second Imperial Oration*; ed. and tr. I. Polemis, Θεόδωρος Μετοχίτης: Οἱ δύο βασιλικοί λόγοι (Athens 2007) 285–421.

———. *Moral Essays*; ed. M. C. G. Müller and M. T. Kiessling, *Theodori Metochitae Miscellanea philosophica et historica* (Leipzig 1821); partial ed. and tr. K. Hult, *Theodore*

*Metochites On Ancient Authors and Philosophy (*Semeioseis gnomikai *1–26 & 71)* (Göteborg 2002).

———. *Presbeutikos*; ed. in L. Mavromatis, *La fondation de l'empire Serbe: Le Kralj Milutin* (Thessalonike 1978) 89–119.

The Miracles of St. Demetrios; ed. and tr. P. Lemerle, *Les plus anciens recueils des miracles de Saint Démétrius et la pénétration des Slaves dans le Balkans*, 2 vols. (Paris 1979–1981).

Nicolaus I, pope. *Responsa ad consulta Bulgarorum*; ed. L. Heiser, *Die Responsa ad consulta Bulgarorum des Papstes Nikolaus I. (858–867): Ein Zeugnis päpstlicher Hirtensorge und ein Dokument unterschiedlicher Entwicklungen in den Kirchen von Rom und Konstantinopel* (Trier 1979); tr. W. L. North on the *Medieval Sourcebook* website of Fordham University; tr. S. N. Scott, "The Collapse of the Moravian Mission of Saints Cyril and Methodius, the Fate of Their Disciples, and the Christianization of the Southern Slavs" (PhD dissertation, University of California, 1989) 222–99.

Nikephoros II Phokas. *On Skirmishing*; ed. and tr. in G. Dennis, *Three Byzantine Military Treatises* (Washington, D.C. 1985 = *CFHB* v. 25) 143–239.

Nikephoros, patriarch of Constantinople. *Short History*; ed. and tr. C. Mango (Washington , D.C. 1990 = *CFHB* v. 13).

Nikolaos Mystikos, patriarch of Constantinople. *Letters*; ed. and tr. R. J. H. Jenkins and L. G. Westerink, *Nicholas I Patriarch of Constantinople: Letters* (Washington, D.C. 1973 = *CFHB* v. 6).

Pachymeres, Georgios. *History*; ed. A. Failler, tr. Failler and V. Laurent, *Georges Pachymérès: Relations historiques*, 5 vols. (Paris 1984–2000 = *CFHB* 24.1-4).

Pakourianos, Gregorios. *Typikon*; ed. and tr. P. Gautier, "Le typikon du sébaste Grégoire Pakourianos," *REB* 42 (1984): 5–145; tr. R. Jordan in J. Thomas and A. Constantinides Hero, eds., *Byzantine Monastic Foundation Documents*, 5 vols. (Washington, D.C. 2000) 507–63.

Palladios. *On the Peoples of India and the Brahmans*; ed. W. Berghoff, *Palladius de gentibus Indiae et Bragmanibus* (Meisenheim am Glan 1967).

Perdikas of Ephesos. *Ekphrasis of the Sights of Jerusalem*; ed. T. Baseu-Barabas, "Perdikas von Ephesos und seine Beschreibung Jerusalems: Die heiligen Stätten gesehen von einem Byzantiner des 14. Jh.s," Σύμμεικτα 11 (1997): 151–88.

Petros of Sicily. *History of the Paulicians*; ed. and tr. Ch. Astruc et al., "Les sources grecques pour l'histoire des Pauliciens d'Asie mineure," *Travaux et Mémoires* 4 (1970): 2–226, here 6–67; partial tr. J. and B. Hamilton, *Christian Dualist Heresies in the Byzantine World, c. 650–1405* (Manchester and New York 1998) 65–92.

Philotheos Kokkinos. *Life of Sabas the Fool*; ed. D. G. Tsames, Φιλοθέου Κωνσταντινουπόλεως τοῦ Κοκκίνου ἁγιολογικὰ ἔργα, A: Θεσσαλονικεῖς ἅγιοι (Thessalonike 1985) 161–325.

Phokas (*recte* Doukas), Ioannes. *Condensed Ekphrasis of the Holy Lands from Antioch to Palestine*; ed. *PG* 133: 928–61; ed. J. Troickij, *Pravoslavnyj Palestinsij Sbornik* 23 (St. Petersburg 1889) 1–28.

Photios. *Homilies*; tr. C. Mango, *The Homilies of Photius Patriarch of Constantinople* (Cambridge, Mass. 1958).

———. *Bibliotheke*; ed. and tr. R. Henry, *Photius: Bibliothèque*, 8 vols. (Paris 1959–1977); partial tr. N. G. Wilson, *Photius: The Bibliotheca* (London 1993).

———. *Letter to Khan Boris*; ed. B. Laourdas and L. G. Westerink, *Photii patriarchae Constantinopolitani Epistulae et Amphilochia*, v. 1 (Leipzig 1983) 1–39; tr. D. Stratoudaki White and J. R. Berrigan, *The Patriarch and the Prince: The Letter of Patriarch Photios of Constantinople to Khan Boris of Bulgaria* (Brookline, Mass. 1982).

Philostorgios. *Ecclesiastical History*; ed. J. Bidez, *Philostorgius: Kirchengeschichte*, 3rd ed. rev. F. Winkelmann (Berlin 1981); tr. P. R. Amidon, *Philostorgius: Church History* (Atlanta 2007).

Piacenza Pilgrim; ed. P. Geyer, *Itineraria et alia geographica* (Turnhout 1965) 129–74 (two versions); tr. J. Wilkinson, *Jerusalem Pilgrims Before the Crusades*, 2nd ed. (Warminster 2002) 129–51; annotated tr. of the Sinai section in D. F. Caner, *History and Hagiography from the Late Antique Sinai* (Liverpool 2010 = *TTH* v. 53) 252–62.

Praecepta militaria; ed. and tr. E. McGeer, *Sowing the Dragon's Teeth: Byzantine Warfare in the Tenth Century* (Washington, D.C. 1995) 12–59.

Priskos. *History* (frag.); ed. and tr. R. C. Blockley, *The Fragmentary Classicising Historians of the Later Roman Empire: Eunapius, Olympiodorus, Priscus and Malchus*, 2 vols. (Liverpool 1981–1983).

Prokopios. *Wars* and *Secret History*; ed. J. Haury, rev. G. Wirth, *Procopii Caesariensis opera omnia*, 4 vols. (Leipzig 1962–1964); tr. H. B. Dewing, *Procopius*, 6 vols. (Cambridge, Mass. and London 1914–1935 = *LCL*); tr. A. Kaldellis, *Prokopios: The Secret History with Related Texts* (Indianapolis 2010).

Psellos, Michael. *Chronographia*; ed. S. Impellizeri and tr. S. Ronchey, *Michele Psello: Imperatori di Bisanzio (Cronografia)*, 2 vols. (Milan 1984); tr. E. R. A. Sewter, *Michael Psellus: Fourteen Byzantine Rulers* (London 1966).

———. *Enkomion for Ioannes [Mauropous] the Metropolitan of Euchaita*; ed. G. T. Dennis, *Michaelis Pselli orationes panegyricae* (Stuttgart and Leipzig 1994) 143–74.

———. *Letters*; ed. E. Kurtz and F. Drexl, *Michaelis Pselli scripta minora*, v. 2 (Milan 1941).

———. *Praise of Italos*; ed. A. Littlewood, *Michaelis Psellis oratoria minora* (Leipzig 1985) 69–72.

Pseudo-Clement. *Recognitions*; ed. F. Paschke and B. Rehm, *Die Pseudoklementinen II. Rekognitionen* (Berlin 1965).

Pseudo-Kaisarios. *Erotapokriseis*; ed. R. Riedinger (Berlin 1989).

Pseudo-Neilos of Ankyra, *Narrations*; ed. and tr. M. Link, *Die Erzählung des Pseudo-Neilos: Ein spätantiker Märtyrerroman* (Leipzig 2005); tr. D. F. Caner, *History and Hagiography from the Late Antique Sinai* (Liverpool 2010 = *TTH* v. 53) 73–135.

Ouranos, Nikephoros. *Letters*; ed. J. Darrouzès, *Épistoliers byzantins du Xe siècle* (Paris 1960).

Robert de Clari. *The Conquest of Constantinople*; ed. and tr. J. Dufournet, *Robert de Clari: La conquête de Constantinople* (Paris 2004); tr. E. H. McNeal, *Robert de Clari: Conquest of Constantinople* (New York 1936).

Questions to doux Antiochos (pseudo-Athanasian *Erotapokriseis*); ed. *PG* 28: 556–708.

Skylitzes, Ioannes. *Synopsis of Histories*; ed. J. Thurn, *Ioannis Scylitzae Synopsis Historiarum* (Berlin and New York 1973 = *CFHB* v. 5); tr. J. Wortley, *John Skylitzes: A Synopsis of Byzantine History, 811–1057* (Cambridge 2010).

Stilbes, Konstantinos. *Errors of the Latin Church*; ed. and tr. J. Darrouzès, "Le mémoire de Constantin Stilbès contre les Latins," *REB* 21 (1963): 50–100.

Symeon Logothetes. *Chronicle*; ed. Wahlgren, *Symeonis Magistri et Logothetae Chronicon* (Berlin 2006 = *CFHB* v. 44).

Syrianos. *On Strategy*; ed. and tr. in G. Dennis, *Three Byzantine Military Treatises* (Washington, D.C. 1985 = *CFHB* v. 25) 9–135.

Themistios. *Oration 10 (On the Peace)*; ed. G. Downey and A. F. Norman, *Themistii Orationes quae supersunt*, 2 vols. (Leipzig 1965–1971) v. 1, 195–214; tr. P. Heather and J. Matthews, *The Goths in the Fourth Century* (Liverpool 1991 = *TTH* v. 11) 36–50.

Theodoros II Laskaris. *Letters*; ed. N. Festa, *Theodori Ducae Lascaris epistulae CCXVII* (Florence 1898).

Theophanes. *Chronographia*; ed. C. de Boor, *Theophanis Chronographia*, 2 vols. (Leipzig 1883–1885); tr. C. Mango and R. Scott, *The Chronicle of Theophanes Confessor: Byzantine and Near Eastern History A.D. 284–813* (Oxford 1997).

Theophanes Continuatus. ed. I. Bekker (Bonn 1838). See also *Life of the Emperor Basileios I*.

Theophylaktos of Ochrid. *Letters*; ed. and tr. P. Gautier, *Théophylacte d'Achrida: Lettres* (Thessalonike 1986 = *CFHB* v. 16.2).

———. *Life of Kliment of Ochrid*; ed. *PG* 126: 1194–1240; also in N. L. Tunickij, *Monumenta ad SS Cyrilli et Methodii successorum vitas resque gestas pertinentia* (London, 1972) 66–141; tr. I. Duichev, *Kiril and Methodius: Founders of Slavonic Writing*, tr. S. Nikolov (Boulder, Colo. 1985) 93–126; tr. S. N. Scott, *The Collapse of the Moravian Mission of Saints Cyril and Methodius, the Fate of their Disciples, and the Christianization of the Southern Slavs* (Ph.D. dissertation, University of California 1989) 76–181.

———. *The Martyrdom of the Fifteen Holy Martyrs of Tiberioupolis*; ed. *PG* 126: 152–221.

Theophylaktos Simokattes. *History*; ed. C. de Boor, rev. P. Wirth, *Theophylacti Simocattae Historiae* (Stuttgart 1972); tr. M. and M. Whitby, *The History of Theophylact Simocatta* (Oxford 1986).

Tzetzes, Ioannes. *Epilogue to the Theogony*; ed. H. Hunger, "Zum Epilog der Theogonie des Johannes Tzetzes," in Tzetzes, *Byzantinische Grundlagensforschung* (London 1973) XVIII, 302–7.

———. *Histories (Chiliades)*; ed. P. A. Leone, *Ioannis Tzetzae Historiae* (Naples 1968).

———. *Letters*; ed. P. A. M. Leone, *Ioannis Tzetzes epistulae* (Leipzig 1972).

Yuhannan of Amida (John of Ephesos). *Ecclesiastical History: Part Three*; tr. R. P. Smith, *The Third Part of the Ecclesiastical History of John, Bishop of Ephesus* (Oxford 1860).

Zonaras, Ioannes. *Chronicle*; ed. *PG* 134–35; ed. M. Pinder and T. Büttner-Wobst, *Ioannis Zonarae Epitomae historiarum*, 3 vols. (Berlin 1841–1897).

————. *Commentary on the Canons of the Council in Troullo*; ed. G. A. Rhalles and M. Potlis, Σύνταγμα τῶν θείων καὶ ἱερῶν κανόνων, v. 2 (Athens 1852).

MODERN SCHOLARSHIP

Aalders, G. J. D. *Die Theorie der gemischten Verfassung im Altertum* (Amsterdam 1968).

Adler, E. *Valorizing the Barbarians: Enemy Speeches in Roman Historiography* (Austin, Tex. 2011).

Aerts, W. J. "Imitatio and Aemulatio in Byzantium with Classical Literature, Especially in Historical Writing," in H. Hokwerda, ed., *Constructions of Greek Past: Identity and Historical Consciousness from Antiquity to the Present* (Groningen 2003) 89–99.

Afinogenov, D. E. "Some Observations on Genres of Byzantine Historiography," *Byzantion* 62 (1992): 13–33.

Ahrweiler, H. "Byzantine Concepts of the Foreigner: The Case of the Nomads," in Ahrweiler and A. E. Laiou, eds., *Studies on the Internal Diaspora of the Byzantine Empire* (Washington, D.C. 1988) 1–15.

Alexander, P. "Secular Biography at Byzantium," *Speculum* 15 (1940): 194–209.

Alonso-Núñez, J. M. "Jordanes and Procopius on Northern Europe," *Nottingham Mediaeval Studies* 31 (1987): 1–16.

Amantos, K. "Τὰ ἐθνολογικὰ ὀνόματα εἰς τοὺς Βυζαντινοὺς συγγραφεῖς," Ἑλληνικά 2 (1929): 97–104.

Amory, P. *People and Identity in Ostrogothic Italy, 489–554* (Cambridge 1997).

Ando, C. "Decline, Fall, and Transformation," *Journal of Late Antiquity* 1 (2008): 30–60.

————. *Law, Language, and Empire in the Roman Tradition* (Philadelphia 2011).

Angelov, P. D. "The Bulgarians Through the Eyes of the Byzantines," *Bulgarian Historical Review* 22 (1994): 18–32.

Angold, M., ed. "Autobiography and Identity: The Case of the Later Byzantine Empire," *Byzantinoslavica* 60 (1999): 36–59.

————. *The Byzantine Aristocracy: IX to XIII Centuries* (Oxford 1984).

————. *Byzantium: The Bridge from Antiquity to the Middle Ages* (London 2001).

————. *Church and Society in Byzantium Under the Comneni, 1081–1261* (Cambridge 1995).

————. "The Venetian Chronicles and Archives as Sources for the History of Byzantium and the Crusades (992–1204)," in M. Whitby, ed., *Byzantines and Crusaders in Non-Greek Sources, 1025–1204* (Oxford 2007), 59–94.

Antonopoulos, P. Πέτρος Πατρίκιος: Ὁ Βυζαντινός διπλωμάτης, ἀξιωματοῦχος καί συγγραφέας (Athens 1990).

————. Ο Αυτοκράτορας Κωνσταντίνος Ζ' Πορφυρογέννητος και οι Ούγγροι (Athens 1996).

Arnakis, G. G. "Gregory Palamas Among the Turks and Documents of his Captivity as Historical Sources," *Speculum* 26 (1951): 104–18.

Arnason, J. P. "Byzantium and Historical Sociology," in P. Stephenson, ed., *The Byzantine World* (London 2010) 491–504.

Asdracha, C. "L'image de l'homme occidental à Byzance: Le témoignage de Kinnamos et de Choniates," *Byzantinoslavica* 44 (1983): 31–40.

Athanassiadi, P. *Vers la pensée unique: La montée de l'intolérance dans l'antiquité tardive* (Paris 2010).

Austin, N. J. E. and N. B. Rankov. *Exploratio: Military and Political Intelligence in the Roman World from the Second Punic War to the Battle of Adrianople* (London 1995).

Baldwin, B. "On the Date of the Anonymous περὶ στρατηγικῆς," *BZ* 81 (1988): 290–93.

Banchich, T. M., and E. N. Lane. *The History of Zonaras from Alexander Severus to the Death of Theodosius the Great* (London 2008).

Barber, C., and D. Jenkins, eds. *Medieval Greek Commentaries on the* Nicomachean Ethics (Leiden 2009).

Barford, P. M. "Slavs beyond Justinian's Frontiers," *Studia Slavica et Balcanica Petropolitana* 2 (2008): 21–32.

Barker, J. W. *Manuel II Palaeologus (1391–1425): A Study in Late Byzantine Statesmanship* (New Brunswick, N.J. 1969).

———. "Emperors, Embassies, and Scholars: Diplomacy and the Transmission of Byzantine Humanism to Renaissance Italy," in D. G. Angelov, ed. *Church and Society in Late Byzantium* (Kalamazoo, Mich. 2009) 158–79.

———. "The Question of Ethnic Antagonisms Among Balkan States of the Fourteenth Century," in T. S. Miller and J. Nesbitt, eds., *Peace and War in Byzantium: Essays in Honor of George T. Dennis, S.J.* (Washington, D.C. 1995) 165–77.

Bartha, A. "The Typology of Nomadic Empires," in *Popoli delle steppe: Unni, Avari, Ungari*, v. 1 (Spoleto 1988) 151–79.

Bartikian, H. *Αρμενοβυζαντινά: Σχέσεις του αρμενικού έθνους με το μεσαιωνικό Ελληνισμό* (Thessalonike 2007).

Bartlett, R. *The Making of Europe: Conquest, Colonization and Cultural Change, 950–1350* (Princeton, N.J. 1993).

———. *The Natural and the Supernatural in the Middle Ages* (Cambridge 2008).

Beard, M. *The Roman Triumph* (Cambridge, Mass. 2007).

Beaud, B. "Le savoir et le monarque: le *Traité sur les nations* de l'empereur byzantin Constantin VII Porphyrogénète," *Annales* 45 (1990): 551–64.

Beck, H.-G. *Das byzantinische Jahrtausend* (Munich 1982).

———, *Res Publica Romana: Vom Staatsdenken der Byzantiner* (Munich 1970).

Beckwith, C. I. *Empires of the Silk Road: A History of Central Aurasia from the Bronze Age to the Present* (Princeton, N.J., and Oxford 2009).

Beihammer, A. "Der harte Sturz des Bardas Skleros: Eine Fallstudie zu zwischenstaatliche Kommunikation und Konfliktführung in der byzantinisch-arabischen Diplomatie des 10. Jahrhunderts," *Römische historische Mitteilungen* 45 (2003): 21–57.

———. *Nachrichten zum byzantinischen Urkundenwesen in arabischen Quellen (565–811)* (Bonn 2000).

Belke, K. "Roads and Travel in Macedonia and Thrace in the Middle and Late Byzantine Period," in R. Macrides, ed., *Travel in the Byzantine World* (Aldershot 2002) 73–90.

Belke, K., and P. Soustal, *Die Byzantiner und ihre Nachbarn: Die* De administrando imperio *genannte Lehrschrift des Kaisers Konstantinos Porphyrogennetos für seinen Sohn Romanos* (Vienna 1995).

Benardete, S. *Herodotean Inquiries* (The Hague 1969).

Benedicty, R. "Die Milieu-Theorie bei Prokop von Kaisareia," *BZ* 55 (1962): 1–10.

———. "Prokopios' Berichte über die slavische Vorzeit: Beiträge zur historiographischen Methode des Prokopios von Kaisareia," *Jahrbuch der österreichischen Byzantinistik* 14 (1965): 51–78.

Berg, B. "The Letter of Palladius on India," *Byzantion* 44 (1974): 5–16.

Berger, A. *Life and Works of Saint Gregentios, Archbishop of Taphar* (Berlin 2006).

Bibikov, M. V. "Das 'Ausland' in der byzantinischen Literatur des 12. und der ersten Hälfte des 13. Jahrhunderts," in J. Herrmann et al., eds., *Griechenland—Byzanz—Europa: Ein Studienband* (Berlin 1985) 61–72.

———. "Die alte Rus' und die russisch-byzantinischen Beziehungen im Spiegel der byzantinischen Quellen (Ende 11.-13. Jh)," *Jahrbuch der österreichischen Byzantinistik* 35 (1985): 197–222.

Bickermann, E. J. "Origines Gentium," *Classical Philology* 47 (1952): 65–81.

Blangez-Malamut, E., and M. Cacouros. "L'image des Serbes dans la rhétorique byzantine de la second moitie du XIIe siècle," in K. Fledelius, ed., *Byzantium: Identity, Image, Influence* (Copenhagen 1996) 97–122.

Blythe, J. M. *Ideal Government and the Mixed Constitution in the Middle Ages* (Princeton, N.J. 1992).

Boatwright, M. T. *Peoples of the Roman World* (Cambridge 2012).

Börm, H. *Prokop und die Perser: Untersuchungen zu den römisch-sasanidischen Kontakten in der ausgehenden Spätantike* (Stuttgart 2007).

Bremmer, J. N., ed. *The Apocryphal Acts of Thomas* (Leuven 2001).

Breton, J.-F. *Arabia Felix from the Time of the Queen of Sheba: Eighth Century B.C. to First Century A.D.*, tr. A. LaFarge (Notre Dame, Ind. 1999).

Brown, C. G. "An Atticist Lexicon of the Second Sophistic: Philemon and the Atticist Movement" (Ohio State University, Ph.D. dissertation 2008).

Brown, P. *Power and Persuasion in Late Antiquity: Towards a Christian Empire* (Madison, Wis. 1992).

———. *Society and the Holy in Late Antiquity* (Berkeley, Calif. 1982).

Browning, R. "Eustathios of Thessalonike Revisited," *Bulletin of the Institute of Classical Studies* 40 (1995): 83–90.

———. *Medieval and Modern Greek* (Cambridge 1983).

Brubaker, L., and J. Haldon. *Byzantium in the Iconoclastic Era (ca 680–850): The Sources* (Aldershot 2001).

———. "The *Christian Topography* (Vat. gr. 699) Revisited: Image, Text, and Conflict in Ninth-Century Byzantium," in E. Jeffreys, ed., *Byzantine Style, Religion and Civilization: In Honour of Sir Steven Runciman* (Cambridge 2006) 3–24.

Bryer, A. "Greek Historians on the Turks: The Case of the First Byzantine-Ottoman Marriage," in R. Davis and J. Wallace-Hadrill, eds., *The Writing of History in the Middle Ages* (Oxford 1981): 471–93.

Buell, D. K. *Why This New Race: Ethnic Reasoning in Early Christianity* (New York 2005).

Bury, J. B. "The Treatise De administrando imperio," *BZ* 15 (1906): 517–77.

Bydén, B. "The Nature and Purpose of the *Semeioseis gnomikai*: The Antithesis of Philosophy and Rhetoric," in K. Hult, *Theodore Metochites On Ancient Authors and Philosophy (Semeioseis gnomikai 1–26 & 71)* (Göteborg 2002) 245–88.

Caire, E. "Le Diamérismos selon Jean Malalas," in J. Beaucamp, ed., *Recherches sur la Chronique de Jean Malalas*, v. 1 (Paris 2004) 19–36.

Cameron, A. *Agathias* (Oxford 1970).

———. "Agathias on the Early Merovingians," *Annali della Scuola Normale Superiore di Pisa. Classe di lettere e filosofia* ser. 2, 37 (1968): 95–140.

———. "Agathias on the Sassanians," *DOP* 23–24 (1969–70): 67–183.

———. "Images of Authority: Élites and Icons in Late Sixth-Century Byzantium," in M. Mullett and R. Scott, eds., *Byzantium and the Classical Tradition* (Birmingham 1981) 204–34.

———. *Procopius and the Sixth Century* (London 1985).

———. "The Theotokos in Sixth-Century Constantinople," *Journal of Theological Studies* 29 (1978): 79–108.

Canard, M. "Les aventures d'un prisonnier arabe et d'un patrice byzantine à l'époque des guerres bulgaro-byzantines," *DOP* 11 (1956): 51–72.

———. "Deux épisodes des relations diplomatiques arabo-byzantines au Xe siècle," *Bulletin d'Études Orientales* 13 (1949–50): 51–69.

———. Canepa, M. *The Two Eyes of the Earth: Art and Ritual of Kingship Between Rome and Sasanian Iran* (Berkeley, Calif. 2009).

Carile, A. "La *Hyle Historias* del cesare Niceforo Briennio," *Aevum* 43 (1969): 56–87.

———. "I nomadi nelle fonti bizantine," in *Popoli delle steppe: Unni, Avari, Ungari*, v. 1 (Spoleto 1988) 55–99.

Cesa, M. "Etnografia e geografia nella visione storica di Procopio di Cesarea," *Studi classici e orientali* 32 (1982): 189–215.

Cesaretti, P. "Su Eustazio e Venezia," *Aevum* 62 (1988): 218–27.

Champlin, E. "Serenus Sammonicus," *Harvard Studies in Classical Philology* 85 (1981): 189–212.

Chauvot, A. *Opinions romaines face aux barbares au IVe siècle ap. J.-C.* (Paris 1998).

Cheynet, J.-C. "Les limites du pouvoir à Byzance: une forme de tolérance?' in A. Nikolaou, ed., Ανοχή και καταστολή στους μέσους χρόνους: Μνήμη Λένου Μαυρομάτη (Athens 2002) 15–28.

———. *Pouvoir et contestations à Byzance (963–1210)* (Paris 1996).

Christides, V. "The Image of the Sudanese in Byzantine Sources," *Byzantinoslavica* 43 (1982): 8–17.

Christou, E. Έργα και ημέρες δυτικών απεσταλμένων στην Κωνσταντινούπολη (Athens 2000).

Chrysos, E. "Die Nordgrenze des byzantinischen Reiches im 6. bis 8. Jahrhundert," in B. Hänsel, ed. *Die Völker Südosteuropas im 6. bis 8. Jahrhundert* (Berlin 1987) 27–40.

———. "Ἡ βυζαντινή διπλωματία ὡς μέσο επικοινωνίας," in N. G. Moschonas, ed., *Ἡ ἐπικοινωνία στὸ Βυζάντιο* (Athens 1993) 399–407.

———. "The Title ΒΑΣΙΛΕΥΣ in Early Byzantine International Relations," *DOP* 32 (1978): 31–75.

Ciggaar, K. N. *Western Travellers to Constantinople: The West and Byzantium, 962–1204* (Leiden 1996).

Ćirković, S. M. "Between Kingdom and Empire: Dušan's State 1346–1355 Reconsidered," in E. Papadopoulou and D. Dialeti, eds., *Βυζάντιο και Σερβία κατά τον ΙΔ΄ αιώνα* (Athens 1996) 110–20.

Clauss, M. *Der magister officiorum in des Spätantike (4.–6. Jahrhundert): Das Amt und sein Einfluss auf die kaiserliche Politik* (Munich 1980).

Clay, D., and A. Purvis. *Four Island Utopias* (Newburyport, Mass. 1999).

Conant, J. *Staying Roman: Conquest and Identity in Africa and the Mediterranean, 439–700* (Cambridge 2012).

Congourdeau, M.-H. "La Terre sainte au XIVe siècle: La Vie de Sabas de Vatopédi par Philothée Kokkinos," in B. Caseau et al., eds. *Pèlerinages et lieux saints dans l'Antiquité et le Moyen Age: Mélanges offerts à Pierre Maraval* (Paris 2006) 121–33.

Connell, C. W. "Western Views of the Origin of the 'Tartars': An Example of the Influence of Myth in the Second Half of the Thirteenth Century," *Journal of Medieval and Renaissance Studies* 3 (1973): 115–37.

Connor, W. R. *Thucydides* (Princeton, N.J. 1984).

Constantelos, D. J. *Christian Hellenism: Essays and Studies in Continuity and Change* (New Rochelle, N.Y. 1998).

Cosentino, S. "The Syrianos's 'Strategikon': A 9th Century Source?' *Byzantinistica: Rivista di studi bizantini e slavi* 2 (2000): 243–80.

Cresci, L. R. "*Exempla* storici greci negli encomi e nella storiografia bizantini del XII secolo," *Rhetorica* 22 (2004): 115–45.

———. "Michele Attaliata e gli ἔθνη scitici," *Νέα Ῥώμη: Rivista di richerche bizantinistiche* 1 (2004): 185–207.

Croke, B. "Late Antique Historiography, 250–650 C.E.," in J. Marincola, ed., *A Companion to Greek and Roman Historiography* (Malden, Mass. 2011) 567–81.

———. "Malalas, the Man and His Work," in E. Jeffreys, ed., *Studies in John Malalas* (Sydney 1990) 1–25.

———. "Tradition and Originality in Photius' Historical Reading," in J. Burke et al., eds., *Byzantine Narrative: Papers in Honour of Roger Scott* (Melbourne 2006) 59–70.

Curta, F. *The Making of the Slavs: History and Archaeology of the Lower Danube Region, c. 500–700* (Cambridge 2001).

———. "Qagan, Khan, or King? Power in Early Medieval Bulgaria (Seventh to Ninth Century)," *Viator* 37 (2006): 1–31.

———. *Southeastern Europe in the Middle Ages, 500–1250* (Cambridge 2006).

Curty, O. *Les parentés légendaires entre cités grecques: catalogue raisonnée des inscriptions contenant le terme ΣΥΓΓΕΝΕΙΑ et analyse critique* (Geneva 1995).

Cutler, A. "The Emperor's Old Clothes: Actual and Virtual Vesting and the Transmission of Power in Byzantium and Islam," in M. Balard et al., eds., *Byzance et le monde extérieur: Contacts, relations, échanges* (Paris 2005) 195–210.

———."Gifts and Gift Exchange as Aspects of the Byzantine, Arab, and Related Economies," *DOP* 55 (2001): 247–78.

———. "Significant Gifts: Patterns of Exchange in Late Antique, Byzantine, and Early Islamic Diplomacy," *Journal of Medieval and Early Modern Studies* 38 (2008): 79–101.

Czeglédy, K. "From East to West: The Age of Nomadic Migrations in Eurasia (tr. P. B. Golden)," *Archivum Eurasiae medii Aevi* 3 (1983): 25–125.

Dagron, G. "Apprivoiser la guerre: Byzantins et Arabes ennemis intimes," in K. Tsiknakis, ed., *Το εμπόλεμο Βυζάντιο (9ος–12ος αι.)* (Athens 1997) 36–49.

———. "Byzance et le modèle islamique au Xe siècle à propos des *Constitutions Tactiques* de l'empereur Léon VI," *Comptes-rendus des séances de l'Académie des inscriptions et belles-lettres* 127 (1983).

———. " 'Ceux d'en face': Les peuples dans les traités byzantins," *Travaux et mémoires* 10 (1987): 207–32.

———. "Communication et stratégies linguistiques," in N. G. Moschonas, ed., *Ἡ ἐπικοινωνία στὸ Βυζάντιο* (Athens 1993) 81–92.

———. "Le 'Mythe de Venise' vu de Byzance," in P. Schreiner, ed., *Il mito di Venezia: una città tra realta e rappresentazione* (Rome 2006) 61–80.

———. "L'ombre d'un doubte: L'hagiographie en question, VIe–XIe siècle," *DOP* 46 (1992): 59–69.

Dalrymple, W. *From the Holy Mountain: A Journey in the Shadow of Byzantium* (London 1998).

Darrouzès J. "Deux lettres de Grégoire Antiochos écrites de Bulgarie vers 1173," *Byzantinoslavica* 23 (1962): 276–84.

———, ed. *Épistoliers byzantins du Xe siècle* (Paris 1960).

Daryaee, T. "A Historical Episode in the Zoroastrian Apocalyptic Tradition: The Romans, the Abbasids, and the Khorramdins," in T. Daryaee and M. Omidsalar, eds., *The Spirit of Wisdom: Essays in Memory of Ahmad Tafazzoli* (Costa Mesa, Calif. 2004) 64–76.

Dauge, Y. A. *Le barbare: Recherches sur la conception romaine de la barbarie et de la civilisation* (Brussels 1981).

Dench, E. "Ethnography and History," in J. Marincola, ed., *A Companion to Greek and Roman Historiography* (Malden, Mass. 2011) 493–503.

Dennis, G. T. "The Byzantines in Battle," in K. Tsiknakis, ed., *Το εμπόλεμο Βυζάντιο (9ος–12ος αι.)* (Athens 1997) 165–78.

———. "Demetrios Kydones and Venice," in C. Maltezou and P. Schreiner, eds., *Bisanzio, Venezia e il mondo franco-greco (XIII–XV secolo)* (Venice 2002) 495–502.

———. "Imperial Panegyric: Rhetoric and Reality," in H. Maguire, ed., *Byzantine Court Culture from 829 to 1204* (Washington, D.C. 1997) 132–40.

Devos, P. "La jeune martyre Perse Sainte Sirin (+ 559) [*BHG* 1637]," *Analecta Bollandiana* 112 (1994): 5–31.

van Dieten, J.-L. *Nikephoros Gregoras: Rhomäische Geschichte*, 5 vols. (Stuttgart 1973–2003).

Dieterich, K. *Byzantinische Quellen zur Länder- und Völkerkunde*, v. 1 (Leipzig 1912).

Dignas, B., and E. Winter. *Rome and Persia in Late Antiquity: Neighbors and Rivals* (Cambridge 2007).

Dihle, A. "L'embassade de Théophile l'Indien ré-examinée," in T. Fahd, ed., *L'Arabie préislamique et son environnement historique et culturel* (Leiden 1989) 461–68.

———. "Die Sendung des Inders Theophilos," in P. Steinmetz, ed., *Politeia und Res Publica: Beiträge zum Verständnis von Politik, Recht und Staat in der Antike* (Wiesbaden 1969) 330–36.

———. "Zur hellenistischen Ethnographie," *Entretiens sur l'antiquité classique* 8 (1962): 205–39.

Diller, A. "Byzantine Lists of Old and New Geographical Names," *BZ* 63 (1970): 27–42.

Dimitroukas, J. "Andreas Libadenos' Travel to Egypt and Palestine and its Description (1325 or 1326)," in J. P. Monferrer-Sala et al., eds., *East and West: Essays on Byzantine and Arab Worlds in the Middle Ages* (Piscataway, N.J. 2009) 277–84.

Ditten, H. "'Germanen' und 'Alamannen' in antiken und byzantinischen Quellen," in J. Herrmann et al., eds., *Griechenland—Byzanz—Europa: Ein Studienband* (Berlin 1985) 20–31.

———. "Die Namen für Venedig und Genua bei den letzten byzantinische Geschichtsschreiber (15. Jahrhundert)," *Helikon: rivista di tradizione e cultura classica* 6 (1966): 51–70.

Donner, F. M. "The Role of Nomads in the Near East in Late Antiquity (400–800)," in F. M. Clover and R. S. Humphreys, eds., *Tradition and Innovation in Late Antiquity* (Madiso, Wis. 1989) 73–85.

Dougherty, C. *The Raft of Odysseus: The Ethnographic Imagination of Homer's* Odyssey (Oxford 2001).

Drake, H. A. *Constantine and the Bishops: The Politics of Intolerance* (Baltimore 2000).

Drinkwater, J. F. *The Alamanni and Rome 213–496 (Caracalla to Clovis)* (Oxford 2007).

Drocourt, N. "Les animaux comme cadeaux d'ambassade entre Byzance et ses voisins (VIIe–XIIe siècle)," in B. Doumerc and C. Picard, eds., *Byzance et ses périphéries: hommage à Alain Ducellier* (Toulouse 2004): 67–93.

Ducellier, A. *Chrétiens d'Orient et Islam au Moyen Age, VIIe–XVe siècle* (Paris 1996).

Dujčev, I. "On the Treaty of 927 with the Bulgarians," *DOP* 32 (1978): 219–95.

Dunn, M. "Evangelization or Repentance? The Re-Christianization of the Peloponnese in the Ninth and Tenth Centuries," *Studies in Church History* 14 (*Renaissance and Renewal in Christian History*) (1977): 71–86.

Durak, K. "Defining the 'Turk': Mechanism of Establishing Contemporary Meaning in the Archaizing Language of the Byzantines," *Jahrbuch der Österreichischen Byzantinistik* 59 (2009): 65–78.

Dvornik, F. *Origins of Intelligence Services* (New Brunswick, N.J. 1974).

Efthymiades, S. *Φώτιος Πατριάρχης Κωνσταντινουπόλεως, Βιβλιοθήκη ὅσα τῆς ἱστορίας: Ἀνθολογία* (Athens 2000).

———. "Chrétiens et sarrasins en Italie mériodionale et en Asie Mineure (IXe–XIe siècle)," in A. Jacob et al., eds., *Histoire et culture dans l'Italie byzantine* (Rome 2006) 589–618.

———. "Νοεροί και πραγματικοί ταξιδιώτες στο Βυζάντιο του 8ου, 9ου και 10ου αιώνα," *Βυζαντινά* 20 (1999): 155–65.

Efthymiades, S., and A. Mazarakis. "La chronique familiale du Parisinus gr. 1601 et l'identité de son rédacteur," *BZ* 102 (2009): 615–25.

Eggers, M. "Das De Administrando Imperio des Kaisers Konstantin VII. Porphyrogennetos und die historisch-politische Situation Südosteuropas im 9. und 10. Jahrhundert," *Ostkirchliche Studien* 56 (2007): 15–100.

El Cheikh, N. M. *Byzantium Viewed by the Arabs* (Cambridge, Mass. 2004).

Elliot, A. G. *Roads to Paradise: Reading the Lives of the Early Saints* (Providence, R.I. 1987).

Elliott, J. K. *The Apocryphal New Testament: A Collection of Apocryphal Christian Literature in an English Translation* (Oxford 1993).

Fauvarque, B. "Les visions providentialistes du barbare chez les Romains des IVe–Ve siècles ap. J.-C.," in J. Boulogne et J. Sys, eds., *Le Barbare, le primitif et le sauvage = Études Inter-ethniques* 10 (1995): 75–88.

Featherstone, M. "Theodore Metochites's *Semeioseis Gnomikai*: Personal Encyclopedism," in P. van Deun and C. Macé, eds., *Encyclopedic Trends in Byzantium?* (Leuven 2011) 333–44.

Fiaccadori, G. "Teofilo Indiano," *Studi classici e orientali* 33 (1983): 295–331; 34 (1984): 271–308.

———. "Gregentios in the Land of the Homerites," in Berger, *Life and Works of Saint Gregentios* (q.v.) 48–81.

Fielder, U. "Bulgars in the Lower Danube Region: A Survey of the Archaeological Evidence and the State of Current Research," in F. Curta, ed., *The Other Europe in the Middle Ages: Avars, Bulgars, Kazhars, and Cumans* (Leiden 2008) 151–236.

Finneran, N. "Beyond Byzantium: The Non-Chalcedonian Churches," in L. James, ed., *A Companion to Byzantium* (Oxford and Malden, Mass. 2010) 199–223.

Fledelius, K. "Royal Scandinavian Travellers to Byzantium," in idem, ed., *Byzantium: Identiy, Image, Influence* (Copenhagen 1996) 212–18.

Fletcher, R. *The Barbarian Conversion from Paganism to Christianity* (Berkeley, Calif. 1997).

Flusin, B., and J.-C. Cheynet. *Jean Skylitzès: Empereurs de Constantinople* (Paris 2003).

Fögen, T. M. "Reanimation of Roman Law in the Ninth Century: Remarks on Reasons and Results," in L. Brubaker, ed., *Byzantium in the Ninth Century: Dead or Alive?* (Aldershot 1998) 11–22.

Förstel, K. *Niketas von Byzanz: Schriften zum Islam* (Würzburg 2000).

———. *Schriften zum Islam von Arethas und Euthymios Zigabenos und Fragmente der griechischen Koranübersetzung* (Wiesbaden 2009).

Fowden, G. *Empire to Commonwealth: Consequences of Monotheism in Late Antiquity* (Princeton, N.J. 1993).

Frakes, J. C. *Vernacular and Latin Literary Discourses of the Muslim Other in Medieval Germany* (New York 2011).

Franklin, S. "The Empire of the Rhomaioi as Viewed from Kievan Russia: Aspects of Byzantino-Russian Cultural Relations," *Byzantion* 53 (1983): 507–37.

———. "Constantine Porphyrogenitus and Russia," in A. Markopoulos, ed., *Κωνσταντίνος Ζ' ὁ Πορφυρογέννητος καὶ ἡ ἐποχὴ του* (Athens 1989) 57–68.

Frankopan, P. "Some Notes on Byzantine Foreign Policy in the 9th–11th Centuries: Was there really such a thing as steppe diplomacy?" *Journal of Medieval and Islamic History* 2 (2003): 1–11.

———. *The First Crusade: The Call from the East* (Cambridge, Mass. 2012).

Fraser, P. M. *Cities of Alexander the Great* (Oxford 1996).

———. *Greek Ethnic Terminology* (Oxford 2009).

Freeman, P. *The Philosopher and the Druids: A Journey Among the Ancient Celts* (New York 2006).

Friedman, J. B. *The Monstrous Races in Medieval Art and Thought* (Cambridge, Mass. 1981).

von Fritz, K. *The Theory of the Mixed Constitution in Antiquity: A Critical Analysis of Polybius' Political Ideas* (New York 1954).

Galatariotou, C. "Travel and Perception in Byzantium," *DOP* 47 (1993): 221–41.

Garrison, M. "Divine Election for Nations—A Difficult Rhetoric for Medieval Scholars?" in L. B. Mortensen, ed., *The Making of Christian Myths in the Periphery of Latin Christendom (c. 1000–1300)* (Copenhagen 2006) 275–314.

Garsoïan, N. "Byzantium and the Sasanians," in E. Yarshater, ed., *The Cambridge History of Iran*, v. 3.1 (Cambridge 1983) 568–92.

Garzya, A. "Byzantium," in K. J. Dover, ed., *Perceptions of the Ancient Greeks* (Cambridge, Mass. 1992) 29–53.

Gastgeber, C. "Das Schreiben Alexios' I. Komnenos an Robert I. von Flandern: Sprachliche Untersuchung," in G. de Gregorio and O. Kresten, eds., *Documenti medievali greci e latini: Studi comparativi* (Spoleto 1998) 141–85.

———. "Die lateinische Übersetzungsabteilung der byzantinischen Kaiserkanzlei unter den Komnenen und Angeloi," in M. Balard et al., eds., *Byzance et le monde extérieur: Contacts, relations, échanges* (Paris 2005) 105–22.

Gautier, P. "Moeurs populaires bulgares au tournant des 12e/13e siècles," in *Byzance et les Slaves: Etudes de civilisation (Mélanges Ivan Dujčev)* (Paris 1979) 181–89.

———. "Le typikon du sébaste Grégoire Pakourianos," *REB* 42 (1984): 5–145.

———, tr. and ed., *Théophylacte d'Achrida: Lettres*, v. 2 (Thessalonike 1986).

Geertz, C. *The Interpretation of Culture: Selected Essays* (New York 1973).

Gero, S. "The Alexander Legend in Byzantium: Some Literary Gleanings," *DOP* 46 (1992): 83–87.

Geyer, P., ed. *Itineraria et alia geographica* (Turnhout 1965).

Gillett, A. *Envoys and Political Communication in the Late Antique West, 411–533* (Cambridge 2003).

Glei, R., and A. D. Khoury. *Johannes Damaskenos und Theodor Abū Qurra: Schriften zum Islam* (Würzburg 1995).

Godlewski, W. "Nubia, Egypt, and Byzantium," in O. Pevny, *Perceptions of Byzantium and Its Neighbors: 843–1261* (New York 2000) 168–80.

Golden, P. B. An *Introduction to the History of the Turkic Peoples: Ethnogenesis and State-Formation in Medieval and Early Modern Eurasia and the Middle East* (Wiesbaden 1992).

Gottlieb, G. "Die Nachrichten des Agathias aus Myrina über des Christentum der Franken und Alamannen," *Jahrbuch des Römisch-Germanischen Zentralmuseums Mainz* 16 (1969): 149–58.

Gouma-Peterson, T., ed. *Anna Komnene and her Times* (New York 2000).

Gounaridis, P. "Η εικόνα των Λατίνων την εποχή των Κομνηνών," *Βυζαντινά Σύμμεικτα* 9 (1994): 157–71.

Graboïs, A. *Le pèlerin occidental en Terre sainte au Moyen Âge* (Brussels 1998).

Greatrex, G. "Lawyers and Historians in Late Antiquity," in R. W. Mathisen, ed., *Law, Society, and Authority in Late Antiquity* (Oxford 2001) 148–61.

Greatrex, G., and S. N. C. Lieu. *The Roman Eastern Frontier and the Persian Wars, part II (A.D. 363–630): A Narrative Sourcebook* (London 2002).

Grégoire, H. "Saint Démétrianos, évêque de Chytri (île de Chypre)," *BZ* 16 (1907): 204–40.

Gruen, E. *Rethinking the Other in Antiquity* (Princeton, N.J. 2011).

Güterbock, K. *Byzanz und Persien in ihren diplomatisch-völkerrechtlichen Beziehungen im Zeitalter Justinians: Ein Beitrag zur Geschichte des Völkerrechts* (Berlin 1906).

Hahm, D. "The Mixed Constitution in Greek Thought," in R. Balot, ed., *A Companion to Greek and Roman Political Thought* (Oxford 2009) 178–98.

Haldon, J. *Byzantium in the Seventh Century: The Transformation of a Culture* (Cambridge 1990).

———. "The Works of Anastasius of Sinai: A Key Source for the History of the Seventh-Century East Mediterranean Society and Belief," in A. Cameron and L. Conrad, eds., *The Byzantine and Early Islamic Near East*, v. 1: *Problems in the Literary Source Material* (Princeton, N.J. 1992) 107–48.

Haldon, J., and L. Brubaker. *Byzantium in the Iconoclast Era (ca. 680–850): A History* (Cambridge 2011).

Hankins, J. "Exclusivist Republicanism and Non-Monarchical Republic," *Political Theory* 38 (2010): 452–82.

Harding, P. "Local History and Atthidography," in J. Marincola, ed. *A Companion to Greek and Roman Historiography* (Oxford 2011): 180–88.

Harrison, T. *Writing Ancient Persia* (Bristol 2011).

Hartog, F. *The Mirror of Herodotus: The Representation of the Other in the Writing of History*, tr. J. Lloyd (Berkeley, Calif. 1988).

———. *Memories of Odysseus: Frontier Tales from Ancient Greece*, tr. J. Lloyd (Chicago 2001).

Hatlie, P. *The Monks and Monasteries of Constantinople, ca. 350–850* (Cambridge 2007).

Haussig, H. W. "Theophylakts Exkurs über die skythischen Völker," *Byzantion* 23 (1953): 275–462.

Heath, M. J. "Renaissance Scholars and the Origins of the Turks," *Bibliotheque d'humanisme et Renaissance* 41 (1979): 453–71.

Heather, P. "The Barbarian in Late Antiquity: Image, Reality, and Transformation," in R. Miles, ed., *Constructing Identities in Late Antiquity* (London 1999).

———. *Empire and Barbarians: Migration, Development and the Birth of Europe* (London 2009).

———. *The Fall of the Roman Empire: A New History* (London 2005).

———. "Liar in Winter: Themistius and Theodosius," in S. McGill et al., eds., *From the Tetrarchs to the Theodosians: Later Roman History and Culture, 284–450 C.E.* (Cambridge 2010 = *Yale Classical Studies* v. 34) 185–213.

———. "Themistius: A Political Philosopher," in M. Whitby, ed., *The Propaganda of Power: The Role of Panegyric in Late Antiquity* (Leiden 1998) 125–50.

Heather, P., and J. Matthews. *The Goths in the Fourth Century* (Liverpool 1991 = *TTH* v. 11).

Heather, P. and D. Moncour. *Politics, Philosophy, and Empire in the Fourth Century: Select Orations of Themistius* (Liverpool 2001).

Hendrickx, B. "Le roi africain à Constantinople en 1203," Βυζαντινά 13 (1985): 893–98.

Herrin, J. "Aspects of the Process of Hellenization in the Early Middle Ages," *Annual of the British School at Athens* 68 (1973): 113–26.

Hilsdale, C. "The Imperial Image at the End of Exile: The Byzantine Embroidered Silk in Genoa and the Treaty of Nymphaion (1261)," *DOP* 64 (2010): 151–99.

Hinterberger, M. *Autobiographische Traditionen in Byzanz* (Vienna 1999).

Hoeck, J. M., and R. J. Loenertz. *Nikolaos-Nektarios von Otranto, Abt von Casole: Beiträge zur Geschichte der ost-westlichen Beziehungen unter Innozenz III. und Friedrich II* (Ettal 1965).

Hoffmann, L. "Geschichtsschreibung oder Rhetorik? Zum *logos parkleitikos* bei Leon Diakonos," in M. Grünbart, ed., *Theatron: Rhetorische Kultur in Spätantike und Mittelalter* (New York 2007) 105–39.

Holmes, C. *Basil II and the Governance of Empire (976–1025)* (Oxford 2005).

Homeyer, H. "Zur Synkrysis des Manuel Chrysoloras, einem Vergleich zwischen Rom und Konstantinopel: Ein Beitrag zum italienischen Frühhumanismus," *Klio* 62 (1980): 525–34.

Hörandner, W. "Das Bild des Anderen: Lateiner und Barbaren in der Sicht der byzantinischen Hofpoesie," *Byzantinoslavica* 54 (1993): 162–68.

Howard-Johnston, J. "Anna Komnene and the *Alexiad*," in M. Mullett and D. Smythe, eds., *Alexios I Komnenos*, v. 1, *Papers* (Belfast 1996) 260–302.

———. "Byzance avant l'an mil: L'étranger européen aux marges de l'Europe," in *Byzance et l'Europe: Colloque à la Maison de l'Europe* (Paris 2001) 51–62.

———. "The *De administrando imperio*: a Re-Examination of the Text and a Re-Evaluation of its Evidence about the Rus'," in M. Kazanski et al., eds., *Les centres proto-urbain russes entre Scandinavie, Byzance et Orient* (Paris 2000) 301–36.

———. *Witnesses to a World Crisis: Historians and Histories of the Middle East in the Seventh Century* (Oxford 2010).

Hoyland, R. G. *Seeing Islam as Others Saw It: A Survey and Evaluation of Christian, Jewish and Zoroastrian Writings on Early Islam* (Princeton, N.J. 1997).

―――. *Theophilus of Edessa's Chronicle and the Circulation of Historical Knowledge in Late Antiquity and Early Islam* (Liverpool 2011 = *TTH* v. 57).

Humphries, M. "A New Created World: Classical Geographical Texts and Christian Contexts in Late Antiquity," in J. H. D. Scourfield, ed., *Texts and Culture in Late Antiquity: Inheritance, Authority, and Change* (Swansea 2007) 33–67.

Hunger, H. "On the Imitation (ΜΙΜΗΣΙΣ) of Antiquity in Byzantine Literature," *DOP* 23–24 (1969–1970): 17–38.

―――. *Die hochsprachliche profane Literatur der Byzantiner*, v. 1 (Munich 1978).

―――. *Graeculus perfidus, Ἰταλὸς ἰταμός: Il senso dell'alterità nei rapporti Greco-Romani ed Italo-Bizantini* (Rome 1987).

Huntington, S. *The Clash of Civilizations and the Remaking of World Order* (New York 1996).

Impellizzeri, S. "Romani, Latini e barbari nell' 'Alessiade' di Anna Comnena," in *Da Roma alla terza Roma*. Studi II: *La nozione di "Romano" tra cittadinanza e universalità* (Naples 1984) 377–83.

Inglebert, H. *Interpretatio Christiana: Les mutations des savoirs (cosmographie, géographie, ethnographie, histoire) dans l'Antiquité chrétienne, 30–630 après J.-C.* (Paris 2001).

Ivanov, S. A. "Casting Pearls Before Circe's Swine: The Byzantine View of Mission," *Travaux et mémoires* 14 (2002): 295–301.

―――. "Mission Impossible: Ups and Downs in Byzantine Missionary Activity from the Eleventh to the Fifteenth Century," in J. Shepard, ed., *The Expansion of Orthodox Europe: Byzantium, the Balkans and Russia* (Aldershot 2007) 251–65.

Jacob, C. *Géographie et ethnographie en Grèce ancienne* (Paris 1991).

Jacoby, D. "The Encounter of Two Societies: Western Conquerors and Byzantines in the Peloponnesus After the Fourth Crusade," *American Historical Review* 78 (1973): 873–906.

―――. "Byzantine Trade with Egypt from the Mid-Tenth Century to the Fourth Crusade," *Thesaurismata* 30 (2000): 25–77.

Jeffreys, E. "The Image of the Arabs in Byzantine Literature," in *The 17th International Byzantine Congress: Major Papers* (New Rochelle, N.Y. 1986) 305–23.

Jeffreys, M. and E. "The 'Wild Beast from the West': Immediate Literary Reactions in Byzantium to the Second Crusade," in A. Laiou and R. P. Mottahedeh, eds., *The Crusades from the Perspective of Byzantium and the Muslim World* (Washington, D.C. 2001) 101–16.

Jenkins, R. J. H. "Constantine VII's Portrait of Michael III," *Bulletin de la classe des lettres et des sciences morales et politiques: Académie Royale de Belgique* ser. 5, 34 (1948): 71–77.

―――. "The mission of St. Demetrianus of Cyprus to Baghdad," *Annuaire de l'Institut de Philologie et d'Histoire Orientales et Slaves* (= *Mélanges Henri Grégoire* v. 1) 9 (1949): 267–75.

―――. "The Classical Background of the Scriptores post Theophanem," *DOP* 8 (1954): 11–30.

————, ed. *Constantine Porphyrogenitus: De administrando Imperio*, v. 2, *Commentary* (London 1962).

Johnson, A. P. *Ethnicity and Argument in Eusebios' Praeparatio Evangelica* (Oxford 2006).

Jones, L., and H. Maguire, "A Description of the Jousts of Manuel I Komnenos," *BMGS* 26 (2002): 104–48.

Jones, W. R. "The Image of the Barbarian in Medieval Europe," *Comparative Studies in Society and History* 13 (1971): 376–407.

Jouanno, C. "Les barbares dans le roman byzantin du XIIe siècle: fonction d'un topos," *Byzantion* 62 (1992): 264–300.

————. *Histoire merveilleuse du roi Alexandre maître du monde* (Toulouse 2009).

Ludwig, C. "The Paulicians and Ninth-Century Byzantine Thought," in L. Brubaker, ed., *Byzantium in the Ninth Century: Dead or Alive?* (Aldershot 1998) 23–35.

Kaegi, W. *Byzantium and the Decline of Rome* (Princeton, N.J. 1968).

————. "Initial Byzantine Reactions to the Arab Conquest," *Church History* 38 (1969): 139–49.

————. *Byzantium and the Early Islamic Conquests* (Cambridge 1992).

Kaldellis, A. "The Historical and Religious Views of Agathias: A Reinterpretation," *Byzantion* 69 (1999): 206–52.

————. *The Argument of Psellos' Chronographia* (Leiden 1999).

————. "Things Are Not What They Are: Agathias *Mythistoricus* and the Last Laugh of Classical Culture," *Classical Quarterly* 53 (2003): 295–300.

————. *Procopius of Caesarea: Tyranny, History, and Philosophy at the End of Antiquity* (Philadelphia 2004).

————. "Republican Theory and Political Dissidence in Ioannes Lydos," *BMGS* 29 (2005): 1–16.

————. "A Byzantine Argument for the Equivalence of All Religions: Michael Attaleiates on Ancient and Modern Romans," *International Journal of the Classical Tradition* 14 (2007): 1–22.

————. "The Literature of Plague and the Anxieties of Piety in Sixth-Century Byzantium," in F. Mormando and T. Worcester, eds., *Piety and Plague: From Byzantium to the Baroque* (Kirksville, Mo. 2007) 1–22.

————. *Hellenism in Byzantium: The Transformations of Greek Identity and the Reception of the Classical Tradition* (Cambridge 2007).

————. Review of Börm, *Prokop und die Perser* (see above) *BZ* 101 (2008): 806–11.

————. "Niketas Choniates: Paradox, Reversal, and the Meaning of History," in A. Simpson and S. Efthymiades, eds., *Niketas Choniates: A Historian and a Writer* (Geneva 2009) 75–99.

————. *The Christian Parthenon: Classicism and Pilgrimage in Byzantine Athens* (Cambridge 2009).

————. "The Corpus of Byzantine Historiography: An Interpretive Essay," in P. Stephenson, ed., *The Byzantine World* (London 2010) 211–22.

————. *Prokopios: The Secret History with Related Texts* (Indianapolis 2010).

————. Review of Page, *Being Byzantine* (q.v.) in *Medieval Review* 09.04.10 (online).

————. "Prokopios' *Persian War*: A Thematic and Literary Analysis," in R. Macrides, ed., *Byzantine History as Literature* (Aldershot 2010) 253–73.

————. "The Kalends in Byzantium, 400–1200 AD: A New Interpretation," *Archiv für Religionsgeschichte* 13(2012): 187–203.

————. "The Original Source for Ioannes Tzimiskes' Balkan Campaign (971)," *BMGS* 13 37 (2013): 1–18.

————. "The Emergence of Literary Fiction in Byzantium and the Paradox of Plausibility," in P. Roilos, ed., *Byzantine and Early Modern Greek Fictional Writing* (forthcoming).

————. "The Hagiography of Doubt and Skepticism," in S. Efthymiades, ed., *A Companion to Byzantine Hagiography*, v. 2 (forthcoming).

————. *A New Herodotos: Laonikos Chalkokondyles on the Ottoman Empire, the Fall of Byzantium, and the Emergence of the West* (forthcoming).

Karadimas, N. "The Unknown Past of Minoan Archaeology from the Renaissance Until the Arrival of Sir Arthur Evans in Crete," in D. Panagiotopoulos et al., eds., *Minoan Archaeology: Challenges and Perspectives for the 21st Century* (Heidelberg forthcoming).

Karapli, K. "Speeches of Arab Leaders to Their Warriors According to Byzantine Texts," *Graeco-Arabica* 5 (1993): 233–42.

Karpozilos, A. "Byzantine Apologetic and Polemic Writings of the Palaeologian Epoch Against Islam," *Greek Orthodox Theological Review* 15 (1970): 213–48.

————. Συμβολὴ στὴ μελέτη τοῦ βίου καὶ τοῦ ἔργου τοῦ Ἰωάννη Μαυρόποδος (Ioannina 1982).

————. "Ταξιδιωτικές περιγραφές και εντυπώσεις σε επιστολογραφικά κείμενα," in N. G. Moschonas, ed., Ἡ Ἐπικοινωνία στὸ Βυζάντιο (Athens 1993) 511–41.

————. Βυζαντινοὶ ἱστορικοὶ καὶ χρονογράφοι, 3 vols. (Athens 1997–2009).

Karttunen, K. "The Ethnography of the Fringes," in E. J. Bakker et al., eds., *Brill's Companion to Herodotus* (Leiden 2002) 457–74.

Kazhdan, A. P. (in collaboration with S. Franklin). *Studies on Byzantine Literature of the Eleventh and Twelfth Centuries* (Cambridge and Paris 1984).

————. "The Aristocracy and the Imperial Idea," in M. Angold, ed., *The Byzantine Aristocracy IX to XII Centuries* (Oxford 1984) 43–57.

————. (in collaboration with L. F. Sherry and C. Angelidi). *A History of Byzantine Literature*, v. 1: *650–850* (Athens 1999).

————. (ed. C. Angelidi). *A History of Byzantine Literature*, v. 2: *850–1000* (Athens 2006).

Kazhdan, A. P., and A. W. Epstein. *Change in Byzantine Culture in the Eleventh and Twelfth Centuries* (Berkeley, Calif. 1985).

Kelly, C. *Ruling the Later Roman Empire* (London 2004).

————. *Attila the Hun: Barbarian Terror and the Fall of the Roman Empire* (London 2009).

Kennedy, H. *The Great Arab Conquests: How the Spread of Islam Changed the World We Live in* (Cambridge, Mass. 2007).

Khoury, A. T. *Polémique byzantine contre l'Islam: VIIIe–XIIIe s.* (Leiden 1972).

Kianka, F. "Demetrios Kydones and Italy," *DOP* 49 (1995): 99–110.

Kiapidou, E.-S. *Ἡ Σύνοψη Ἱστοριῶν τοῦ Ἰωάννη Σκυλίτζη καὶ οἱ πηγές της (811–1057)* (Athens 2010).

King, C. "The Veracity of Ammianus Marcellinus' Description of the Huns," *American Journal of Ancient History* 12 (1987): 77–95.

Kislinger, E. "Sightseeing in the Byzantine Empire," in N. G. Moschonas, ed., *Ἡ Ἐπικοινωνία στὸ Βυζάντιο* (Athens 1993) 457–68.

Koder, J. "Sopravvivenza e trasformazione delle concezioni geografiche antiche in età bizantina," in F. Prontera, ed., *Geografia storica della Grecia antica: Tradizioni e problemi* (Rome 1991) 46–66.

———. "Latinoi-The Image of the Other According to Greek Sources," in C. Maltezou and P. Schreiner, eds., *Bisanzio, Venezia e il mondo franco-greco (XIII–XV secolo)* (Venice 2002) 25–39.

Kolbaba, T. *The Byzantine Lists: Errors of the Latins* (Urbana 2000).

Kolia-Dermitzaki, A. *Ὁ βυζαντινός «ἱερός πόλεμος»: Ἡ ἔννοια καί ἡ προβολή τοῦ θρησκευτικοῦ πολέμου στό Βυζάντιο* (Athens 1991).

———. "Τὸ ἐμπόλεμο Βυζάντιο στὶς ὁμιλίες καὶ τὶς ἐπιστολὲς του 10ου καὶ 11ου αἰ.: Μία μεθοδολογικὴ προσέγγιση," in K. Tsiknakis, ed., *Τὸ ἐμπόλεμο Βυζάντιο (9ος–12ος αι.)* (Athens 1997) 213–38.

———. "Ἡ εἰκόνα των Βουλγάρων και της χώρας τους στις βυζαντινές πηγές του 11ου και 12ου αιώνα," in K. Nikolaou and K. Tsiknakis, eds., *Βυζάντιο και Βούλγαροι (1018–1185)* (Athens 2008) 59–89.

Kolias, T. G. "The *Taktika* of Leo VI the Wise and the Arabs," *Graeco-Arabica* 3 (1984): 129–35.

Kordosis, M. S. *Ιστορικογεωγραφικά πρωτοβυζαντινών και εν γένει παλαιοχριστιανικών χρόνων* (Athens 1996).

Koutrakou, N. "The Image of the Arabs in Middle-Byzantine Politics: A Study in the Enemy Principle (8th-10th Centuries)," *Graeco-Arabica* 5 (1993): 213–24.

———. *La propagande impériale byzantine: Persuasion et réaction (VIIIe–Xe siècles)* (Athens 1994).

———. "Diplomacy and Espionage: Their Role in Byzantine Foreign Relations, 8th–10th Centuries," *Graeco-Arabica* 6 (1995): 125–44.

———. "'Spies of Towns': Some Remarks on Espionage in the Context of Arab-Byzantine Relations," *Graeco-Arabica* 7–8 (2000): 243–66.

———. "The Image of Egypt in the Byzantine Thought-World: Reminiscence and Reality (7th–12th Centuries)," *Graeco-Arabica* 9–10 (2004): 211–33.

———. "The Arabs Through Byzantine Eyes (11th–12th Centuries); A Change in Perception?" in J. P. Monferrer-Sala et al., eds., *East and West: Essay on Byzantine and Arab Worlds in the Middle Ages* (Piscataway, N.J. 2009) 27–54.

———. "'Animal Farm' in Byzantium? The Terminology of Animal Imagery in Middle Byzantine Politics and the Eight 'Deadly Sins'," in I. Anagnostakis, T. G. Kolias, and E. Papadopoulou, eds., *Ζώα και περιβάλλον στο Βυζάντιο (7ος–12ος αι.)* (Athens 2011) 319–77.

――――. "Psellus, Romanus III and an Arab Victory 'Beyond any Reasonable Expectation': Some Remarks on Psellus' Perception of Foreign Relations," *Graeco-Arabica* 11 (2011): 319–45.

Krallis, D. *Michael Attaleiates and the Politics of Imperial Decline in Eleventh-Century Byzantium* (Tempe, Ariz. 2012).

Kraus, C. " 'No Second Troy': Topoi and Refoundation in Livy, Book V," *Transactions of the American Philological Association* 124 (1994): 267–89.

Kruse, M. "The Speech of the Armenians in Procopius: Justinian's Foreign Policy and the Transition Between Books 1 and 2 of the *Wars*," *Classical Quarterly* 63 (2013) forthcoming.

Kulikowski, M. *Rome's Gothic Wars from the Third Century to Alaric* (Cambridge 2007).

Külzer, A. *Peregrinatio graeca in Terram Sanctam: Studien zu Pilgerführern und Reisebeschreibungen über Syrien, Palästina und den Sinai aus byzantinischer und metabyzantinischer Zeit* (Frankfurt am Main 1994).

――――. "Reisende und Reisenliteratur im Byzantinischen Reich," *Βυζαντινά Σύμμεικτα* 14 (2001): 77–93.

――――. "Konstantinos Manasses und Johannes Phokas: Zwei byzantinische Orientreisende des 12. Jahrhunderts," in X. von Ertzdorff and G. Giesemann, eds., *Erkundung und Beschreibung der Welt: Zur Poetik der Reise- und Länderberichte* (Amsterdam 2003) 185–209.

Laiou, A. E. "A Byzantine Prince Latinized: Theodore Palaeologus, Marquis of Montferrat," *Byzantion* 38 (1968): 386–410.

――――. *Constantinople and the Latins: The Foreign Policy of Andronicus II 1282–1328* (Cambridge, Mass. 1972).

――――. "On Political Geography: The Black Sea of Pachymeres," in R. Beaton and C. Roueché, eds., *The Making of Byzantine History: Studies Dedicated to Donald M. Nicol* (Aldershot 1993) 94–121.

――――. "Italy and the Italians in the Political Geography of the Byzantines (14th Century)," *DOP* 49 (1995): 73–98.

――――. "L'interprétation byzantine de l'expansion occidentale (XIe–XIIe siècles)," in M. Ballard and A. Ducellier, eds., *Le partage du monde: Echanges et colonisation dans la Méditerranée médiévale* (Paris 1998) 163–79.

――――. "Economic Thought and Ideology," in Laiou, ed., *The Economic History of Byzantium from the Seventh Through the Fifteenth Century* (Washington, D.C. 2002) v. 3, 1123–44.

Laiou, A. E., and C. Morrisson, *The Byzantine Economy* (Cambridge 2007).

Lambakis, S. *Γεώργιος Παχυμέρης, πρωτέκδικος καὶ δικαιοφύλαξ: Εἰσαγωγικὸ δοκίμιο* (Athens 2004).

Lamma, P. "Venezia ne giudizio delle fonti bizantine dal X al XII secolo," *Rivista storica italiana* 74 (1962): 457–79.

Lampe, G. W. H. *A Patristic Greek Lexicon* (Oxford 1961).

Langdon, J. S. "Byzantium's Initial Encounter with the Chinggidids: An Introduction to the Byzantino-Mongolica," *Viator* 29 (1998): 95–140.

Lee, A. D. "Procopius, Justinian and the *kataskopoi*," *Classical Quarterly* 39 (1989): 569–72.

———. and J. Shepard, "A Double Life: Placing the Peri Presbeon," *Byzantinoslavica* 52 (1991): 14–39.

———. *Information and Frontiers: Roman Foreign Relations in Late Antiquity* (Cambridge 1993).

Lefort, J. "Rhétorique et politique: Trois discours de Jean Mauropous en 1047," *Travaux et Mémoires* 6 (1976): 265–303.

Lemerle, P. "Thomas le Slave," *Travaux et Mémoires* 1 (1965): 255–97.

———. *Cinq études sur le XIe siècle Byzantin* (Paris 1977).

———. *Les plus anciens recueils des miracles de Saint Démétrius et la pénétration des slaves dans le Balkans* (Paris 1979–1981).

———. *Le premier humanisme byzantin: notes et remarques sur enseignement et culture à Byzance des origines au Xe siècle* (Paris 1971); tr. H. Lindsay and A. Moffatt, *Byzantine Humanism, The First Phase: Notes and Remarks on Education and Culture in Byzantium from Its Origins to the 10th Century* (Canberra 1986).

Lenski, N. "Captivity and Slavery Among the Saracens in Late Antiquity (ca. 250–630 CE)," *Antiquité tardive* 19 (2011): 237–266.

Lieberich, H. *Studien zu den Proömien in der griechischen und byzantinischen Geschichtsschreibung*, 2 vols. (Munich 1898–1900).

Liebeschuetz, J. H. W. G. "Making a Gothic History: Does the *Getica* of Jordanes Preserve Genuinely Gothic Traditions?" *Journal of Late Antiquity* 4 (2011): 185–216.

Lilie, R.-J. "Anna Komnene und die Lateiner," *Byzantinoslavica* 54 (1993): 169–82.

Lindner, R. P. "Nomadism, Horses, and Huns," *Past and Present* 92 (1981): 3–19.

Lintott, A. "The Theory of the Mixed Constitution at Rome," in J. Barnes and M. Griffin, eds., *Philosophia Togata II: Plato and Aristotle at Rome* (Oxford 1997) 70–85.

Lippard, B. G. *The Mongols and Byzantium, 1243–1341* (Ph.D. dissertation, Indiana University 1983).

Ljubarskij, J. N. "Man in Byzantine Historiography from John Malalas to Michael Psellos," *DOP* 46 (1992): 177–86.

———. "Nikephoros Phokas in Byzantine Historical Writings," *Byzantinoslavica* 54 (1993): 245–53.

———. "John Kinnamos as a Writer," in C. Scholz and G. Makris, eds., *Polypleuros Nous: Miscellanea für Peter Schreiner zu seinem 60. Geburtstag* (Munich 2000) 164–73.

Loud, G. A. "Anna Komnena and Her Sources for the Normans of Southern Italy," in I. Wood and G. A. Loud, eds., *Church and Chronicle in the Middle Ages: Essays Presented to John Taylor* (London 1991) 41–57.

Lounghis, T. *Les ambassades byzantines en Occident: Depuis la fondation des états barbares jusqu' aux Croisades (407–1096)* (Athens 1980).

————. *Κωνσταντίνου Ζ′ Πορφυρογέννετου De administrando imperio (Πρὸς τὸν ἴδιον υἱὸν ʿΡωμανόν): Μία μέθοδος ανάγνωσης* (Thessalonike 1990).

————. *Ιουστινιανός Πέτρος Σαββάτιος: Κοινωνία, Πολιτική και Ιδεολογία τον 6ο μ.Χ. Αιώνα* (Thessalonike 2005).

————. "Byzantine Diplomacy," in S. Lampakis et al., eds., *Byzantine Diplomacy: A Seminar* (Athens 2007) 15–82.

Lund, A. *Zum Germanenbild der Römer: Eine Einführung in der antike Ethnographie* (Heidelberg 1990).

Luttwak, E. *The Grand Strategy of the Byzantine Empire* (Cambridge, Mass. 2009).

Maas, M. "Fugitives and Ethnography in Priscus of Panium," *BMGS* 19 (1995): 146–60.

————. " 'Delivered from Their Ancient Customs': Christianity and the Question of Cultural Change in Early Byzantine Ethnography," in K. Mills and A. Grafton, eds., *Conversion in Late Antiquity and the Early Middle Ages: Seeing and Believing* (Rochester, N.Y. 2003) 152–88.

————. "Strabo and Procopius: Classical Geography for a Christian Empire," in H. Amirar and B. T. H. Romeny, eds., *From Rome to Constantinople: Studies in Honour of Averil Cameron* (Leuven 2007) 67–83.

MacCormack, S. *Art and Ceremony in Late Antiquity* (Berkeley, Calif. 1981).

MacMullen, R. *Christianizing the Roman Empire, A.D. 100–400* (New Haven, Conn. 1984).

————. *Voting About God in Early Church Councils* (New Haven, Conn. 2006).

Macrides, R. "The New Constantine and the New Constantinople—1261?' *BMGS* 6 (1980): 13–41.

————. "The Pen of the Aunt: Echoes of the Mid-Twelfth Century in the *Alexiad*," in T. Gouma-Peterson, ed., *Anna Komnene and Her Times* (New York 2000) 15–43.

————. ed. *Travel in the Byzantine World* (Aldershot 2002).

Magdalino, P. "Aspects of Twelfth-Century Byzantine *Kaiserkritik*," *Speculum* 58 (1983): 326–46.

————. "Byzantine Snobbery," in M. Angold, ed., *The Byzantine Aristocracy: IX to XIII Centuries* (Oxford 1984) 58–78.

————. *The Empire of Manuel I Komnenos, 1143–1180* (Cambridge 1993).

————. "Paphlagonians in Byzantine High Society," in S. Lambakis, ed., *Η Βυζαντινή Μικρά Ασία (6ος—12ος αι.)* (Athens 1998) 141–50.

————. "The Road to Baghdad in the Thought-World of Ninth-Century Byzantium," in L. Brubaker, ed., *Byzantium in the Ninth Century: Dead or Alive?* (Aldershot 1998) 195–213.

————. "Constantinople and the Outside World," in D. Smythe, ed., *Strangers to Themselves: The Byzantine Outsider* (Aldershot 2000) 149–62.

————. "A History of Byzantine Literature for Historians," in P. Odorico and P. A. Agapitos, eds., *Pour une "nouvelle" histoire de la littérature byzantine: Problèmes, méthodes, approches, propositions* (Paris 2002) 167–84.

————. "Ο οφθαλμός της οικουμένης και ο ομφαλός της γης," in E. Chrysos, ed., *Το Βυζάντιο ως Οικουμένη* (Athens 2005) 107–23.

————. *L'Orthodoxie des astrologues: La science entre le dogme et la divination à Byzance (VIIe-XIVe siècle)* (Paris 2006).

————. "Orthodoxy and History in Tenth-Century Byzantine 'Encyclopedism,'" in P. Van Deun and C. Macé, eds., *Encyclopedic Trends in Byzantium?* (Leuven 2011) 143–59.

Magoulias, H. J. *O City of Byzantium, Annals of Niketas Choniates* (Detroit 1984).

Malamut, É. *Sur la route des saints byzantines* (Paris 1993).

————. "L'image byzantine des Petchénègues," *BZ* 88 (1995): 105–47.

————. "Des voyages et de la littérature voyageuse à Byzance: Un autre espace, une autre société (IVe–XIIe siècles)," in A. Dierkens and J.-M. Sansterre, eds., *Voyages et voyageurs à Byzance et en Occident du VIe au XIe siècle* (Geneva 2000) 189–213.

————. "Les discours de Démétrius Cydonès comme témoignage de l'idéologie byzantine vis-à-vis des peuples de l'Europe orientale dans les années 1360–1372," in G. Prinzing and M. Salamon, eds., *Byzantium and East Central Europe* (Cracow 2001) 203–19.

————. "De 1299 à 1451 au coeur des ambassades byzantines," in C. Maltezou and P. Schreiner, eds., *Bisanzio, Venezia e il mondo franco-greco (XIII–XV secolo)* (Venice 2002) 79–124.

————. "La lettre diplomatique: Introduction," in M. Balard et al., eds., *Byzance et le monde extérieur: Contacts, relations, échanges* (Paris 2005) 99–104.

Mango, C. *Byzantine Literature as a Distorting Mirror* (Oxford 1975).

————. *Byzantium: The Empire of New Rome* (New York 1980).

————. "A Journey Round the Coast of the Black Sea in the Ninth Century," in P. Schreiner and O. Strakhov, eds. *Chrysai Pylai = Palaeoslavica* 10 (2002): 255–64.

————. "The Tradition of Byzantine Chronography," *Harvard Ukrainian Studies* 12–13 (1988–1989): 360–72.

Mango, C., and R. Scott, *The Chronicle of Theophanes Confessor: Byzantine and Near Eastern History, A.D. 284–813* (Oxford 1997).

Marasco, G., ed. *Greek and Roman Historiography in Late Antiquity: Fourth to Sixth Century A.D.* (Leiden 2003).

Marincola, J. *Authority and Tradition in Ancient Historiography* (Cambridge 1997).

Markopoulos, A., ed. *Κωνσταντίνος Ζ' ὁ Πορφυρογέννητος καὶ ἡ ἐποχὴ του* (Athens 1989).

Martin, D. *Inventing Superstition from the Hippocratics to the Christians* (Cambridge, Mass. 2004).

Martin, M. E. "The Venetians in the Byzantine Empire Before 1204," *BF* 13 (1988): 201–14.

Massing, J. M. "Greek Proverbs to Soap Advert: Washing the Ethiopian," *Journal of the Warburg and Courtauld Institutes* 58 (1995): 108–201.

Matthews, J. *The Roman Empire of Ammianus* (London 1989).

————. "The *Notitia Urbis Constantinopolitanae*," in L. Grig and G. Kelly, eds., *Two Romes: Rome and Constantinople in Late Antiquity* (Oxford 2012) 81–115.

Mavroudi, M. *A Byzantine Book on Dream Interpretation: The* Oneirocriticon *of Achmet and its Arabic Sources* (Leiden 2002).

———. "Occult Science and Society in Byzantium: Considerations for Future Research," in Mavroudi and P. Magdalino, eds., *The Occult Sciences in Byzantium* (Geneva 2006) 39–95.

Mayerson, P. "A Confusion of Indias: Asian India and African India in the Byzantine Source," *Journal of the Americal Oriental Society* 113 (1993): 169–74.

McCormick, M. *Eternal Victory: Triumphal Rulership in Late Antiquity, Byzantium and the Early Medieval West* (Cambridge 1990).

———. *Origins of the European Economy: Communications and Commerce, A.D. 300–900* (Cambridge 2001).

McGeer, E. *Sowing the Dragon's Teeth: Byzantine Warfare in the Tenth Century* (Washington, D.C. 1995).

Mekouria, T. T. "Christian Aksum," in G. Mokhtar, ed., *General History of Africa*, v. 2, *Ancient Civilizations of Africa* (Berkeley, Calif. 1981) 401–22.

Melin, E. "The Names of the Dnieper Rapids in Chapter 9 of Constantine Porphyrogenitus' De administrando imperio," *Scando-Slavica* 49 (2003): 35–62.

Mendels, D. "Greek and Roman History in the Bibliotheca of Photius—A Note," *Byzantion* 56 (1986): 196–206.

Mergiali-Sahas, S. "A Byzantine Ambassador to the West and his Office During the Fourteenth and Fifteenth Cenuries," *BZ* 94 (2001): 588–604.

Merrills, A. H., ed. *Vandals, Romans and Berbers: New Perspectives on Late Antique North Africa* (Aldershot 2004).

———. *History and Geography in Late Antiquity* (Cambridge 2005).

Meserve, M. *Empires of Islam in Renaissance Historical Thought* (Cambridge, Mass. 2008).

Messina, R. G. "Tipologia della rappresentazione dei Turchi in fonti bizantine dei secc. XI–XII," *BF* 25 (1999): 305–21.

Messis, C. "La mémoire du 'je' souffrant: Construire et écrire la mémoire personnelle dans les récits de captivité," in P. Odorico et al., eds., *L'écriture de la mémoire: La littérarité de l'historiographie* (Paris 2006) 107–46.

———. "Littérature, voyage et politique au XIIe siècle: L'*Ekphrasis des lieux saints* de Jean 'Phokas,'" *Byzantinoslavica* 69 (2011): 146–66.

———. "Lectures sexuées d l'altérité: Les latins et identité romaine menacée les derniers siècles de Byzance," *Jahrbuch der österreichischen Byzantinistik* 61 (2011): 151–70.

———. "Public hautement affiché et public réellement visé dans certaines créations littéraires byzantines: Le cas de l'Apologie de l'eunuchisme de Théophylacte d'Achrida," in P. Odorico, ed., *La face cachée de la litterature byzantine: Le texte en tant que message immediat* (Paris 2012) 41–85.

———. "De l'invisible au visible: Venise dans la littérature byzantine des derniers siècles", in idem and P. Odorico, eds., *Villes de toute beauté: L'ekphrasis des cités dans les littératures byzantine et byzantino-slaves* (Paris 2012) 149–79.

Messis, C., and E. Papaioannou, "Histoires 'gothiques': Le *Miracle* de l'Euphemie et du Goth (*BHG* 739) et le voyage transversal des sujets littéraires dans la production écrite à Byzance," *DOP* (forthcoming).

Metcalf, D. M. *Byzantine Cyprus, 491–1191* (Nicosia 2009).

Meyendorff, J. "Byzantine Views of Islam," *DOP* 18 (1964): 113–32.

Meyer, D., ed. *Philostorge et l'historiographie de l'antiquité tardive / Philostorg im Kontext der spätantiken Geschichtsschreibung* (Stuttgart 2011).

Mîrşanu, D. "The Imperial Policy of Otherness: Justinian and the Arianism of Barbarians as a Motive for the Recovery of the West," *Ephemerides Theologicae Lovanienses* 84 (2008): 477–98.

Momigliano, A. *The Classical Foundations of Modern Historiography* (Berkeley, Calif. 1990).

Moore, P. *Iter Psellianum* (Toronto 2005).

Moravcsik, G. "Zum Bericht des Leon Diakonos über den Glauben an die Dienstleistung im Jenseits," *Studia Antiqua Antonio Salač septuagenario oblata* (Prague 1955) 74–76.

———. *Byzantinoturcica*, v. 2: *Sprachreste der Türkvölker in den byzantinischen Quellen* (Berlin 1958).

———. "Klassizismus in der byzantinischen Geschichtsschreibung," in P. Wirth, ed., *Polychronion: Festschrift Franz Dölger zum 75. Geburtstag*, v. 1 (Heidelberg 1966) 366–77.

———. "Barbarishe Sprachreste in der Theogonie des Johannes Tzetzes," in Moravcsik, *Studia Byzantina* (Amsterdam 1967) 283–92.

———. "Die archaisierenden Namen der Ungarn in Byzanz," in Moravcsik, *Studia Byzantina* (Amsterdam 1967) 320–25.

———. "Τὰ συγγράμματα Κωνσταντίνου τοῦ Πορφυρογεννήτου ἀπὸ γλωσσικῆς ἀπόψεως," in Moravcsik, *Studia Byzantina* (Amsterdam 1967) 260–66.

———. "La Tactique de Léon le Sage comme source historique hongroise," in Moravcsik, *Studia Byzantina* (Amsterdam 1967) 221–39.

Morgan, D. O. "The Mongols and the Eastern Mediterranean," in B. Arbel et al., eds., *Latins and Greeks in the Eastern Mediterranean After 1204* (London 1989) 198–211.

Morris, R. "The Two Faces of Nikephoros Phokas," *BMGS* 12 (1988): 83–115.

Moustakas, K. "Byzantine 'Visions' of the Ottoman Empire: Theories of Ottoman Legitimacy by Byzantine Scholars After the Fall of Constantinople," in A. Lymberopoulou, ed., *Images of the Byzantine World: Visions, Messages and Meanings. Studies Presented to Leslie Brubaker* (Aldershot 2011) 215–29.

Moyer, I. *Egypt and the Limits of Hellenism* (Cambridge 2011).

Moysidou, J. *Το Βυζάντιο και οι βόρειοι γείτονές του τον 10ο αιώνα* (Athens 1995).

Müller, K. E. *Geschichte der antiken Ethnographie und ethnologischen Theoriebildung von den Anfängen bis auf die byzantinischen Historiographen* (Wiesbaden 1972–1980).

Mullett, M. "Originality in the Byzantine Letter: The Case of Exile," in A. Littlewood, ed., *Originality in Byzantine Literature, Art, and Music: A Collection of Essays* (Oxford 1995) 39–58.

———. *Theophylact of Ochrid: Reading the Letters of a Byzantine Archbishop* (Aldershot 1997).

———. "In Peril on the Sea: Travel Genres and the Unexpected," in R. Macrides, ed., *Travel in the Byzantine World* (Aldershot 2002) 259–84.

Nechaeva, E. "Double Agents in the Intelligence Service Under Justinian: Evidences of Procopius of Caesaria," *Živa Antika* 54 (2004): 137–47.

———. "Geography and Diplomacy: Journeys and Adventures of Late Antique Envoys," in S. Conti et al., eds., *Geografia e viaggi nell'antichità* (Ancona 2007) 149–61.

Necipoğlu, N. *Byzantium Between the Ottomans and the Latins: Politics and Society in the Late Empire* (Cambridge 2009).

Németh, A. *Imperial Systematization of the Past: Emperor Constantine VII and his Historical Excerpts* (Ph.D. dissertation, Central European University, 2010).

Nerlich, D. *Diplomatische Gesandtschaften zwischen Ost- und Westkaisern, 756–1002* (Bern 1999).

Neville, L. *Heroes and Romans in Twelfth-Century Byzantium: The "Material for History" of Nikephoros Bryennios* (Cambridge 2012).

Nicol, D. M. *Byzantium and Venice: A Study in Diplomatic and Cultural Relations* (Cambridge 1988).

Nicolle, D. "Byzantine and Islamic Arms and Armour: Evidence for Mutual Influence," *Graeco-Arabica* 4 (1991): 299–326.

Nicolet, C. *Space, Geography, and Politics in the Early Roman Empire* (Ann Arbor, Mich. 1991).

Nikolaou, K., and K. Tsiknakis, eds. *Βυζάντιο και Βούλγαροι (1018–1185)* (Athens 2008).

Obolensky, D. *The Byzantine Commonwealth: Eastern Europe, 500–1453* (London 1971).

———. "A Byzantine Grand Embassy to Russia in 1400," *BMGS* 4 (1978): 123–32.

———. *Six Byzantine Portraits* (Oxford 1988).

———. *Byzantium and the Slavs* (Crestwood, N.Y. 1994).

O'bweng-Okwess, K. "Τὸ ἱστορικὸ ἐνδιαφέρον τοῦ ταξιδιοῦ ἑνὸς νεγρο-αφρικανοῦ βασιλιᾶ στὴν Κωνσταντινούπολη στὶς ἀρχὲς τοῦ 13ου αἰώνα," *Βυζαντινὸς Δόμος* 2 (1988): 35–39.

———. "Le portrait du soldat noir chez les Arabes et les Byzantines d'après l'anonyme 'Foutouh al-Bahnasâ' et 'De expurgatione Thessalonicae' de Jean Caminiatès," *Βυζαντινὸς Δόμος* 2 (1988): 41–47.

Odorico, P. "La lettre de Photius à Boris de Bulgarie," *Byzantinoslavica* 54 (1993): 83–88.

———. "Les miroirs des princes à Byzance: une lecture horizontale," in Odorico, ed., *"L'éducation au gouvernement et à la vie": La tradition des "Régles de vie" de l'antiquité au Moyen-Âge* (Paris 2009) 223–46.

———, ed. *La face cachée de la litterature byzantine: Le texte en tant que message immediat* (Paris 2012).

Oikonomidès, N. "Byzantine Diplomacy, A.D. 1204–1453," in J. Shepard and S. Franklin, eds., *Byzantine Diplomacy* (Aldershot 1992) 73–88.

———. "Les marchands qui voyagent, ceux qui ne voyagent pas et la pénurie des textes géographiques byzantins," in A. Dierkens and J.-M. Sansterre, eds., *Voyages et voyageurs à Byzance et en Occident du VIe au XIe siècle* (Geneva 2000) 307–19.

———. "Some Byzantine State Annuitants: *Epi tes [Megales] Hetaireias* and *Epi ton Barbaron*," *Βυζαντινά Σύμμεικτα* 14 (2001): 9–28.

Olster, D. M. *Roman Defeat, Christian Response, and the Literary Construction of the Jew* (Philadelphia 1994).

———. "Classical Ethnography and Early Christianity," in K. B. Free, ed., *The Formulation of Christianity by Conflict Through the Ages* (Lewiston, N.Y. 1995) 9–31.

———. "From Periphery to Center: The Transformation of Late Roman Self-Definition in the Seventh Century," in R. Mathisen and H. S. Sivan, eds., *Shifting Frontiers in Late Antiquity* (Aldershot 1996) 93–101.

Origone, S. "Genova vista da Bizanzio," in *La Storia dei Genovesi (Atti del Convegno internazionale di studi sui ceti dirigenti nelle istituzioni della Repubblica di Genova, Genova, 7–10 Giugno 1988)* v. 9 (Genoa 1989) 485–505.

———. *Bisanzio e Genova* (Genoa 1992).

Östenberg, I. *Staging the World: Spoils, Captives, and Representations in the Roman Triumphal Procession* (Oxford 2009).

Page, G. *Being Byzantine: Greek Identity Before the Ottomans* (Cambridge 2008).

Papadopoulou, T. "Οι όροι 'Μυσία' και 'Μυσός' στις Βυζαντινές πηγές της μέσης και ύστερης περιόδου," in C. Stavrakos et al., eds., *Hypermachos: Studien zu Byzantinistik, Armenologie und Georgistik. Festschrift für Werner Seibt zum 65. Geburtstag* (Wiesbaden 2008) 257–81.

Parani, M. G. "Byzantine Material Culture and Religious Iconography," in M. Grünbart et al., eds., *Material Culture and Well-Being in Byzantium (400–1453)* (Vienna 2007) 181–92.

Parker, G. *The Making of Roman India* (Cambridge 2008).

Patlagean, E. "Nommer les Russes en grec, 1081–1294," in S. W. Swierkosz-Lenart, ed., *Le origini e lo sviluppo della christianità slavo-bizantina* (Rome 1992) 123–41.

Patoura, S. *Οἱ αἰχμάλωτοι ὡς παράγοντες ἐπικοινωνίας καὶ πληροφόρησης (4ος–10ος αἰ.)* (Athens 1994).

Patoura-Spanou, S. *Χριστιανισμός και παγκοσμιότητα στο πρώιμο Βυζάντιο: Από τη θεωρία στην πράξη* (Athens 2008).

Pazdernik, C. "Xenophon's *Hellenica* in Procopius' *Wars*: Pharnabazus and Belisarius," *GRBS* 46 (2006): 175–206.

Peacock, A. *Early Seljuq History: A New Interpretation* (London 2010).

Pérez Martín, I. *Miguel Ataliates: Historia* (Madrid 2002).

Peri, V. "La brama e lo zelo della fede del popolo chiamato 'Rhos'," in *Harvard Ukrainian Studies* 12–13 (1988–1989 = *Proceedings of the International Congress Commemorating the Millennium of Christianity in Rus'-Ukraine*): 114–31.

Petrides, A. "Georgios Pachymeres Between Ethnography and Narrative: Συγγραφικαὶ Ἱστορίαι 3.3-5," *GRBS* 49 (2009): 295–318.

Philippidis-Braat, A. "La captivité de Palamas chez les Turcs: Dossier et commentaire," *Travaux et mémoires* 7 (1979): 109–21.

Pietsch, E. *Die Chronographia des Michael Psellos: Kaisergeschichte, Autobiographie und Apologie* (Wiesbaden 2005).

Pitsakis, G. "A propos de la citoyenneté romaine dans l'Empire d'Orient: Un survol à travers les textes grecs," *Méditarranées* 12 (1997): 73–100.

Pohl, W. "The *regia* and the *hring*—Barbarian Places of Power," in M. de Jong and
    F. Theuws, eds., *Topographies of Power in the Early Middle Ages* (Leiden 2001) 439–66.
Potts, D. T. *The Arabian Gulf in Antiquity*, v. 2: *From Alexander the Great to the Coming
    of Islam* (Oxford 1990).
Prinzing, G. "Vom Umgang der Byzantiner mit den Fremden," in C. Lüth et al., eds.,
    *Der Umgang mit den Fremden in der Vormoderne: Studien zur Akkulturation in bil-
    dungshistorischer Sicht* (Cologne et al. 1997) 117–43.
Puech, V. "Malalas et la prosopographie di VIe siècle: Un éclairage sur le régime de Jus-
    tinien," in S. Agusta-Boularot et al., eds., *Recherches sur la Chronique de Jean Mala-
    las*, v. 2 (Paris 2006) 213–26.
Questa, C. "Il morto e la madre: Romei e Persiani nelle 'Storie' de Agatia," *Lares* 55
    (1989): 375–405.
Raffensperger, C. "Revisiting the Idea of the Byzantine Commonwealth," *BF* 28 (2004):
    159–74.
———. *Reimagining Europe: Kievan Rus' in the Medieval World* (London 2012).
Ramelli, I. *Bardaisan of Edessa: A Reassessment of the Evidence and a New Interpretation*
    (Piscataway, N.J. 2009).
Rance, P. "The Date of the Military Compendium of Syrianus Magister (formerly the
    Sixth-Century Anonymus Byzantinus)," *BZ* 100 (2007): 701–37.
Rapp, C. "A Medieval Cosmopolis: Constantinople and its Foreign Inhabitants," in J. M.
    Asgeirsson and N. van Deusen, eds., *Alexander's Revenge: Hellenistic Culture Through
    the Centuries* (Reykjavík 2002) 153–71.
———. "Hellenic Identity, *Romanitas*, and Christianity in Byzantium," in K. Zacharia,
    ed., *Hellenisms: Culture, Identity and Ethnicity from Antiquity to Modernity* (Alder-
    shot 2008) 127–47.
Rapp, S. "Chronology, Crossroads, and Commonwealths: World-Regional Schemes and
    the Lessons of Caucasia," in J. H. Bentley et al., eds., *Interactions: Transregional
    Perspectives on World History* (Honolulu 2005) 167–201.
———. "The Iranian Heritage of Georgia: Breathing New Life into the Pre-Bagratid
    Historiographical Tradition," *Iranica Antiqua* 44 (2009): 645–92.
Rauflaub, K., and R. J. A. Talbert, eds. *Geography and Ethnography: Perceptions of the
    World in Pre-Modern Societies* (Malden, Mass. 2010).
Reinert, W. "The Muslim Presence in Constantinople, 9th-15th Centuries: Some Pre-
    liminary Observations," in H. Ahrweiler and A. E. Laiou, eds., *Studies on the Internal
    Disapora of the Byzantine Empire* (Washington, D.C. 1998) 125–50.
Reinink, G. J., and B. H. Stolte, eds. *The Reign of Heraclius (610–641): Crisis and Confronta-
    tion* (Leuven et al. 2002).
Reinsch, D. R. "Ausländer und Byzantiner im Werk der Anna Komnene," *Rechtshisto-
    risches Journal* 8 (1996): 257–74.
Ricci, A. "The Road from Baghdad to Byzantium and the Case of the Bryas Palace in
    Istanbul," in L. Brubaker, ed., *Byzantium in the Ninth Century: Dead or Alive?* (Al-
    dershot 1998) 131–49.

Rodolfi, A. "Procopius and the Vandals: How the Byzantine Propaganda Constructs and Changes African Identity," in M. G. Berndt and R. Steinacher, eds., *Das Reich der Vandalen und seine (Vor)Geschichte* (Vienna 2008) 233–42.

Roller, D. *Through the Pillars of Herakles: Greco-Roman Exploration of the Atlantic* (London 2006).

Romm, J. S. *The Edges of the Earth in Ancient Thought: Geography, Exploration, and Fiction* (Princeton, N.J. 1992).

Rotman, Y. *Byzantine Slavery and the Mediterranean World* (Cambridge, Mass. 2009).

Roueché, C. "Byzantine Writers and Readers: Story Telling in the Eleventh Century," in R. Beaton, ed., *The Greek Novel* (London 1988) 123–32.

Rubiés, J.-P., ed. *Medieval Ethnographies: European Perceptions of the World Beyond (The Expansion of Latin Europe, 1000–1500)* (Aldershot 2009).

Runciman, S. "The Ladies of the Mongols," in Εἰς μνήμην Κ. Ἄμαντου, *1874–1960* (Athens 1960) 46–53.

Ryder, J. R. *The Career and Writings of Demetrius Kydones: A Study of Fourteenth-Century Byzantine Politics, Religion and Society* (Leiden 2010).

Sabbah, G. *La méthode d'Ammien Marcellin: Recherches sur la construction du discours historique dans les* Res Gestae (Paris 1978).

Sahas, D. *John of Damascus on Islam: The "Heresy of the Ishmaelites"* (Leiden 1972).

Said, E. W. *Orientalism* (New York 2003; originally 1978).

Saradi-Mendelovici, H. "Christian Attitudes Toward Pagan Monuments in Late Antiquity and their Legacy in Later Byzantine Centuries," *DOP* 44 (1990): 47–61.

Sarris, P. *Empires of Faith: The Fall of Rome to the Rise of Islam, 500–700* (Oxford 2011).

Sassi, M. M. *The Science of Man in Ancient Greece*, tr. P. Tucker (Chicago 2001).

Savvides, A. G. K. "Οἱ Κομάνοι (Κουμάνοι) καὶ τὸ Βυζάντιο, 11ος–13ος αἰ. μ.Χ.," *Βυζαντινά* 13.2 (1985): 937–55.

———. "Ἡ γνώση τῶν Βυζαντινῶν γιά τον τουρκόφωνο κόσμο της Ασίας, τῶν Βαλκανίων και της κεντρικής Ευρώπης μέσα από την ονοματοδοσία," in N. G. Moschonas, ed., *Ἡ ἐπικοινωνία στὸ Βυζάντιο* (Athens 1993) 711–27.

Savvides, A. G. K., and N. G. Nikoloudis. *Ο ύστερος μεσαιωνικός κόσμος (11ος–16ος αιώνες): Βυζάντιο, Μεσαιωνική Δύση, Ανατολή και Ισλάμ, Βαλκάνια και Σλάβοι* (Athens 2007).

Schamp, J. "La réception de l'histoire chez Photios sous bénéfice d'inventaire," in I. Lewandowski and L. Mrozewics, eds., *L'image de l'Antiquité chez les auteurs postérieurs* (Poznán 1996) 9–26.

Schmitz, P. C. "Procopius' Phoenician Inscriptions: Never Lost, Not Found," *Palestine Excavation Quarterly* 139 (2007): 99–104.

Schneider, A. M. "Das Itinerarium des Epiphanios Hagiopolita," *Zeitschrift des deutschen Palästina-Vereins* 63 (1940): 143–54.

Schott, J. *Christianity, Empire, and the Making of Religion in Late Antiquity* (Philadelphia 2008).

Schreiner, P. "Byzanz und der Westen: Die gegenseitige Betrachtungsweise in der Literatur des 12. Jahrhunderts," in A. Haverkamp, ed., *Friedrich Barbarossa: Handlungsspielräume und Wirkungsweisen des staufischen Kaisers* (Sigmaringen 1992) 551–80.

———. "Der Brief des Alexios I. Komnenos an den Grafen Robert von Flandern und das Problem gefälschter byzantinischer Kaiserschreiben in den westlischen Quellen," in G. de Gregorio and O. Kresten, eds., *Documenti medievali greci e latini: Studi comparativi* (Spoleto 1998) 111–40.

———. "Diplomatische Geschenke zwischen Byzanz und dem Westen ca. 800–1200: Eine Analyse der Texte mit Quellenanhang," *DOP* 58 (2004): 251–82.

Seland, E. H. "Trade and Christianity in the Indian Ocean during Late Antiquity," *Journal of Late Antiquity* 5 (2012): 72–86.

Ševčenko, I. "The Decline of Byzantium Seen Through the Eyes of Its Intellectuals," *DOP* 15 (1961): 167–86.

———. "Three Paradoxes of the Cyrillo-Methodian Mission," *Slavic Review* 23 (1964): 220–36.

———. "Religious Missions Seen from Byzantium," *Harvard Ukrainian Studies* 12–13 (1988–1989): 7–27.

———. "Re-reading Constantine Porphyrogenitus," in J. Shepard and S. Franklin, eds., *Byzantine Diplomacy* (Aldershot 1992) 167–89.

Ševčenko, N. P. "Wild Animals in the Byzantine Park," in A. Littlewood et al., eds., *Byzantine Garden Culture* (Washington, D.C. 2002) 69–86.

Sezgin, F. *Wissenschaft und Technik im Islam*, v. 1: *Einführung in die Geschichte der arabischislamischen Wissenschaften* (Frankfurt 2003).

Shahîd, I. *Byzantium and the Arabs in the Sixth Century*, v. 2, pt. 1 (Washington, D.C. 2002).

Shaw, B. " 'Eaters of Flesh, Drinkers of Milk': The Ancient Mediterranean Ideology of the Pastoral Nomad," *Ancient Society* 13–14 (1982–1983): 5–31.

Shawcross, T. "Re-Inventing the Homeland in the Historiography of Frankish Greece: The Fourth Crusade and the Legend of the Trojan War," *BMGS* 27 (2003): 120–52.

———. " 'Do Thou Nothing Without Counsel': Political Assemblies and the Ideal of Good Government in the Thought of Theodore Palaeologus and Theodore Metochites," *Al-Masaq* 20 (2008): 89–118.

———. *The Chronicle of Morea: Historiography in Crusader Greece* (Oxford 2009).

Shboul, A. M. H. "Byzantium and the Arabs: The Image of the Byzantines as Mirrored in Arabic Literature," in E. Jeffreys et al., eds., *Byzantine Papers* (Canberra 1981) 43–68.

Sheldon, R. M. *Intelligence Activities in Ancient Rome: Trust in the Gods, but Verify* (London 2005).

Shepard, J. "Some Problems of Russo-Byzantine Relations c. 860–c. 1050," *Slavonic and East European Review* 52 (1974): 10–33.

———. "Information, Disinformation and Delay in Byzantine Diplomacy," *BF* 10 (1985): 233–93.

———. "Aspects of Byzantine Attitudes and Policy Towards the West in the Tenth and Eleventh Centuries," *BF* 13 (1988): 67–118.

———. "A Marriage Too Far? Maria Lekapena and Peter of Bulgaria," in A. Davids, ed., *The Empress Theophano: Byzantium and the West at the Turn of the First Millennium* (Cambridge 1995) 121–49.

———. "Imperial Information and Ignorance: A Discrepancy," *Byzantinoslavica* 56 (1995): 107–16.

———. "Emperors and Expansionism: From Rome to Middle Byzantium," in D. Abulafia and N. Berend, eds., *Medieval Frontiers: Concepts and Practices* (Aldershot 2002) 55–82.

———. "The Uses of 'History' in Byzantine Diplomacy: Observations and Comparisons," in C. Dendrinos et al., eds., *Porphyrogenita: Essays on the History and Literature of Byzantium and the Latin East in Honour of Julian Chrysostomides* (Aldershot 2003) 91–115.

———. "Byzantium's Overlapping Circles," in E. Jeffreys, ed., *Proceedings of the 21st International Congress of Byzantine Studies,* v. 1 (Aldershot 2006) 15–55.

———. "The Byzantine Commonwealth 1000–1500," in M. Angold, ed., *The Cambridge History of Christianity,* v. 5: *Eastern Christianity* (Cambridge 2006) 1–52.

———. "Manners maketh Romans? Young Barbarians at the Emperor's Court," in E. Jeffreys, ed., *Byzantine Style, Religion and Civilization: In Honour of Sir Steven Runciman* (Cambridge 2006) 135–58.

———, ed. *The Expansion of Orthodox Europe: Byzantium, the Balkans and Russia* (Aldershot 2007).

———. "Imperial Outliers: Building and Decorating Works in the Borderlands and Beyond," in P. Stephenson, ed., *The Byzantine World* (London 2010) 372–85.

Shepard, J., and S. Franklin, eds. *Byzantine Diplomacy* (Aldershot 1992).

Shumate, N. *Nation, Empire, Decline: Studies in Rhetorical Continuity from the Romans to the Modern Era* (London 2006).

Simelides, C. "The Byzantine Understanding of the Qur'anic Term *al-Samad* and the Greek Translation of the Qur'an," *Speculum* 86 (2011): 887–913.

Simeonova, L. *Diplomacy of the Letter and the Cross: Photios, Bulgaria and the Papacy, 860s–880s* (Amsterdam 1998).

———. "In the Depths of Tenth-Century Byzantine Ceremonial: The Treatment of Arab Prisoners of War at Imperial Banquets," *BMGS* 22 (1998): 74–103.

———. "Foreigners in Tenth-Century Byzantium: A Contribution to the History of Cultural Encounter," in D. C. Smythe, ed., *Strangers to Themselves: The Byzantine Outsider* (Aldershot 2000) 229–44.

———. "Constantinopolitan Attitudes Toward Aliens and Minorities, 860s–1020s," *Études balkaniques* (2000): 91–112; (2001): 83–98.

Simon, D. "Princeps legibus solutus: Die Stellung des byzantinischen Kaisers zum Gesetz," in Simon and D. Nörr, eds., *Gedächtnisschrift für W. Kunkel* (Frankfurt a.M. 1984) 449–92.

Simpson, A. "Before and After 1204: The Versions of Niketas Choniates' *Historia*," *DOP* 60 (2006): 189–221.

————. "Niketas Choniates: The Historian," in Simpson and S. Efthymiadis, eds., *Niketas Choniates: A Historian and a Writer* (Geneva 2009) 13–34.

————. *Niketas Choniates: A Historiographical Study* (Oxford) forthcoming.

Simpson, A. and S. Efthymiadis, eds., *Niketas Choniates: A Historian and a Writer* (Geneva 2009).

Siniossoglou, N. *Radical Platonism in Byzantium: Illumination and Utopia in Gemistos Plethon* (Cambridge 2011).

Sizgorich, T. "Reasoned Violence and Shifty Frontiers: Shared Victory in the Late Roman East," in H. A. Drake, ed., *Violence in Late Antiquity: Perceptions and Practices* (Aldershot 2006) 167–76.

Slavin, P. "From Constantinople to Moscow: The Fourteenth-Century Liturgical Response to the Muslim Incursions in Byzantium and Russia," in D. Angelov, ed., *Church and Society in Late Byzantium* (Kalamazoo, Mich. 2009) 201–29.

Smith, A. D. *Chosen Peoples: Sacred Sources of National Identity* (Oxford 2003).

Smith, J. M. H. *Europe After Rome: A New Cultural History 500–1000* (Oxford 2005).

Smith, M. S. *The Early History of God: Yahweh and the Other Deities in Ancient Israel*, 2nd ed. (Grand Rapids, Mich. 2002).

Sode, C. "Untersuchungen zum de Administrando Imperio," *Poikila Byzantina* 13 (1994): 149–260.

Spadaro, M. D. "I barbari: luoghi comuni di etnografia bizantina presso gli storici," in U. Criscuolo and R. Maisano, eds., *Categorie linguistiche e concettuali della storiografia bizantina* (Napoli 2000) 233–47.

Squatriti, P. *The Complete Works of Liudprand of Cremona* (Washington, D.C. 2007).

Stamatopoulos, D. A. *Το Βυζάντιο μετά το έθνος: Το πρόβλημα της συνέχειας στις βαλκανικές ιστοριογραφίες* (Athens 2009).

Stavrakos, Ch. "The Elephant: A Rare Motif on the Byzantine Lead Seal ἐπὶ τῶν βαρβάρων," in Stavrakos, ed., *Proceedings of the 1st International Congress for Sino-Greek Studies, Ioannina, 2–4 October 2004* (Ioannina 2008) 281–99.

Stephenson, P. "Byzantine Conceptions of Otherness After the Annexation of Bulgaria (1018)," in D. Smythe, ed., *Strangers to Themselves: The Byzantine Outsider* (Aldershot 2000) 245–57.

————. *Byzantium's Balkan Frontier: A Political Study of the Northern Balkans, 900–1204* (Cambridge 2000).

Stoneman, R. "Who are the Brahmans? Indian Lore and Cynic Doctrine in Palladius' *De Bragmanibus* and Its Models," *Classical Quarterly* 44 (1994): 500–510.

Stouraitis, I. "Byzantine War Against Christians—An *Emphylios Polemos*?" *Βυζαντινά Σύμμεικτα* 20 (2010): 85–110.

Strauss, L. *An Introduction to Political Philosophy: Ten Essays by Leo Strauss*, ed. H. Gildin (Detroit 1989).

Stroumsa, G. "Philosophy of the Barbarians: On Early Christian Ethnological Representations," in Stroumsa, *Barbarian Philosophy: The Religious Revolution of Early Christianity* (Tübingen 1999) 57–84.

———. *The End of Sacrifice: Religious Transformations in Late Antiquity* (Cambridge, Mass. 2009).

Sullivan, R. "Khan Boris and the Conversion of Bulgaria: A Case Study of the Impact of Christianity on a Barbarian Society," *Studies in Medieval and Renaissance History* 3 (1966): 55–139.

Swain, S. *Hellenism and Empire: Language, Classicism, and Power in the Greek World A.D. 50–250* (Oxford 1996).

Syme, R. *Tacitus* (Oxford 1963).

Synelli, K. *Οἱ διπλωματικὲς σχέσεις Βυζαντίου καὶ Περσίας ἕως τὸν ΣΤ΄ αἰώνα* (Athens 1986).

Syros, V. "Between Chimera and Charybdis: Byzantine and Post-Byzantine Views on the Political Organization of the Italian City-States," *Journal of Early Modern History* 14 (2010): 451–504.

Talbot, A.-M., and D. F. Sullivan. *The* History *of Leo the Deacon: Byzantine Military Expansion in the Tenth Century* (Washington, D.C. 2005).

Tapkova-Zaimova, V. "L'emploi des ethnica et les problèmes de la communication à Byzance," in N. G. Moschonas, ed., *Ἡ ἐπικοινωνία στὸ Βυζάντιο* (Athens 1993) 701–9.

Teixidor, J. *Bardesane d'Édesse: La première philosophie syriaque* (Paris 1992).

Terras, V. "Leo Diaconus and the Ethnology of the Kievan *Rus*'," *Slavic Review* 24 (1965): 395–406.

Thomas, R. *Lands and Peoples in Roman Poetry: The Ethnographic Tradition* (Cambridge 1982).

———. *Herodotus in Context: Ethnography, Science and the Art of Persuasion* (Cambridge 2000).

Thompson, E. A. *The Goths in Spain* (Oxford 1969).

———. "Procopius on Brittia and Britannia," *Classical Quarterly* 30 (1980): 498–507.

Thorn, L. "Das Briefcorpus des Manuel Chrysoloras: eine Blütenlese," in E. Konstantinou, ed., *Der Beitrag der byzantinischen Gelehrten zur abendländischen Renaissance des 14. und 15. Jahrhunderts* (Frankfurt am Main 2006) 17–28.

Tinnefeld, F. *Kategorien der Kaiserkritik in der byzantinischen Historiographie von Prokop bis Niketas Choniates* (Munich 1971).

———. "Das Niveau der abendländischen Wissenschaft aus der Sicht gebildeter Byzantiner im 13. und 14. Jh.," *BF* 6 (1979): 241–80.

Todorov, B. A. "Byzantine Myths of Origins and Their Functions," *Studia Slavica et Balcanica Petropolitana* 2 (2008): 64–72.

Tolan, J. V. *Saracens: Islam in the Medieval European Imagination* (New York 2002).

Tóth, L. S. "The Territories of the Hungarian Tribal Federation Around 950 (Some Observations on Constantine VII's 'Tourkia')," in G. Prinzing and M. Salamon, eds., *Byzanz und Ostmitteleuropa, 950–1453* (Wiesbaden 1999) 23–33.

Tougher, S. "The Imperial Thought-World of Leo VI: The Non-Campaigning Emperor of the Ninth Century," in L. Brubaker, ed., *Byzantium in the Ninth Century: Dead or Alive?* (Aldershot 1998) 51–62.

Tounta, E. "The Perception of Difference and the Differences of Perception: The Image of the Norman Invaders of Southern Italy in Contemporary Western Medieval and Byzantine Sources," *Βυζαντινά Σύμμεικτα* 20 (2010): 111–42.

Toynbee, A. *Constantine Porphyrogenitus and His World* (Oxford 1973).

Trautmann, T. *Aryans and British India* (Berkeley, Calif. 1997).

Treadgold, W. "Three Byzantine Provinces and the First Byzantine Contacts with the Rus,' " *Harvard Ukrainian Studies* 12–13 (1988–1989 = *Proceedings of the International Congress Commemorating the Millennium of Christianity in Rus'-Ukraine*): 132–44.

———. "Photius Before His Patriarchate," *Journal of Ecclesiastical History* 53 (2002): 1–17.

———. "Byzantium, the Reluctant Warrior," in N. Christie and M. Yazigi, eds., *Noble Ideals and Bloody Realities: Warfare in the Middle Ages* (Leiden 2006) 209–33.

———. *The Early Byzantine Historians* (New York 2007).

———. "The Byzantine World Histories of John Malalas and Eustathius of Epiphania," *International History Review* 29 (2007): 709–45.

———. "Trajan the Patrician, Nicephorus, and Theophanes," in D. Bumazhnov et al., eds., *Bibel, Byzanz und christlicher Orient: Festschrift für Stephen Gero zum 65. Geburtstag* (Louvain 2011) 589–623.

———. *Middle Byzantine Historians* (forthcoming).

Trizio, M. "A Neoplatonic Refutation of Islam from the Time of the Komneni," in A. Speer and D. Wirmer, eds., *Knotenpunkt Byzanz: Wissensformen und kulturelle Wechselbeziehungen* (Berlin 2012) 145–66.

Trüdinger, K. *Studien zur Geschichte des griechisch-römischen Ethnographie* (Basel 1918).

de la Vaissière, É. "Maurice et le qaghan: à propos de la digression de Théophylacte Simocatta sur les Turcs," *REB* 68 (2010): 219–24.

Vásáry, I. *Cumans and Tartars: Oriental Military in the Pre-Ottoman Balkans, 1185–1365* (Cambridge 2005).

Vasiliev, A. A. ed. *Byzance et les Arabes*, v. 1 (Brussels 1935).

———. *Byzance et les Arabes*, v. 2 (Brussels 1950).

Venetis, E. "Korramis in Byzantium," *Encyclopedia Iranica*. http://www.iranica.com/articles/korramis-in-byzantium.

Vidal-Naquet, P. *The Black Hunter: Forms of Thought and Forms of Society in the Greek World*, tr. A. Szegedy-Masazk (Baltimore 1986).

Vlachakos, P. K. *Νικηφόρος Γρηγοράς: Φυσική γεωγραφία και ανθρωπογεωγραφία στο έργο του* (Thessalonike 2003).

Vlysidou, V. *Αριστοκρατικές οικογένειες και εξουσία (9ος–10ος αι.): Έρευνες πάνω στα διαδοχικά στάδια αντιμετώπισης της αρμενο-παφλαγονικής και της καππαδοκικής αριστοκρατίας* (Thessalonike 2001).

Vogt, J. *Kulturwelt und Barbaren zum Menschheitsbild der spätantiken Gesellschaft* (Wiesbaden 1967).

Vratimos, A. "The Identification of the Scythians in the Service of Romanos IV's First Expedition to Anatolia," *Byzantinoslavica* 67 (2009): 191–98.

de Vries-van der Velden, E. *Théodore Métochite: un réévaluation* (Amsterdam 1987).

Vryonis, S. "Byzantine Attitudes Toward Islam During the Late Middle Ages," *GRBS* 12 (1971): 263–86.

de Waha, M. "La lettre d'Alexis I Comnène à Robert I le Frisson: une révision," *Byzantion* 47 (1977): 113–25.

Walker, A. *The Emperor and the World: Exotic Elements and the Imaging of Middle Byzantine Imperial Power, Ninth to Thirteenth Centuries C.E.* (Cambridge 2012).

Walker, J. *The Legend of Mar Qardagh: Narrative and Christian Heroism in Late Antique Iraq* (Berkeley, Calif. 2006).

Webb, R. *Demons and Dancers: Performance in Late Antiquity* (Cambridge, Mass. 2008).

Whitaker, I. "Late Classical and Early Mediaeval Accounts of the Lapps (Sami)," *Classica et Mediaevalia* 34 (1983): 283–303.

Whitby, M. *The Emperor Maurice and his Historian: Theophylact Simocatta on Persian and Balkan Warfare* (Oxford 1988).

———. "Greek Historical Writing After Procopius: Variety and Vitality," in A. Cameron and L. I. Conrad, eds., *The Byzantine and Early Islamic Near East*. v. 1, *Problems in the Literary Source Material* (Princeton, N.J. 1992) 25–80.

Whittow, M. *The Making of Orthodox Byzantium, 600–1025* (Berkeley, Calif. 1996).

Wickham, C. *The Inheritance of Rome: Illuminating the Dark Age, 400–1000* (London 2009).

Wiedemann, T. E. J. "Between Men and Beasts: Barbarians in Ammianus Marcellinus," in I. S. Moxon et al., eds., *Past Perspectives: Studies in Greek and Roman Historical Writing* (Cambridge 1986) 189–201.

Wiita, J. E. *The Ethnika in Byzantine Military Treatises* (Ph.D. dissertation, University of Minnesota, 1977).

Wilken, R. *John Chrysostom and the Jews: Rhetoric and Reality in the Late Fourth Century* (Berkeley, Calif. 1983).

Williams, J. M. *Style: Toward Clarity and Grace* (Chicago 1990).

Wolfram, H. "The Image of Central Europe in Constantine VII Porphyrogenitus," in A. Markopoulos, ed., *Κωνσταντίνος Ζ' ὁ Πορφυρογέννητος καὶ ἡ ἐποχὴ του* (Athens 1989) 5–14.

Wood, P. *"We have no king but Christ": Christian Political Thought in Greater Syria on the Eve of the Arab Conquest (c. 400–585)* (Oxford 2010).

Woolf, G. *Tales of the Barbarians: Ethnography and Empire in the Roman West* (London 2011).

Xu-shan, Zhang. *Η Κίνα και το Βυζάντιο: Σχέσεις, εμπόριο, αμοιβαίες γνώσεις απο τις αρχές του 6ου ως τα μέσα του 7ου αι.* (Ioannina 1998).

Yannopoulos, P. "Histoire et légende chez Constantin VII," *Byzantion* 57 (1987): 158–66.

Zachariadou, E. A. "The Oğuz Tribes: The Silence of the Byzantine Sources," in R. Curiel and R. Gyselen, eds., *Itinéraires d'Orient: Hommages à Claude Cahen* (Bures-sur-Yvette 1994) 285–89.

Zacher, C. K. *Curiosity and Pilgrimage: The Literature of Discovery in Fourteenth-Century England* (Baltimore and London 1976).

Zástěrová, B. "Zur Problematik der ethnographischen Topoi," in J. Herrmann et al., eds., *Griechenland—Byzanz—Europa: Ein Studienband* (Berlin 1985) 16–19.

Živković, T. *Forging Unity: The South Slavs Between East and West: 550–1150* (Belgrade 2008).

———. "Constantine Porphyrogenitus' Kastra Oikoumena in the Southern Slav Principalities," *Istorijski casopis* 57 (2008): 9–28.

———. "Sources de Constantin VII Porphyrogénète concernant le passé le plus ancien des Serbes et des Croates," *Βυζαντινά Σύμμεικτα* 20 (2010): 11–37.

Zuckermann, C. "The Compendium of Syrianus Magister," *Jahrbuch der Österreichischen Byzantinistik* 40 (1990): 209–24.

INDEX

ACKNOWLEDGMENTS

As with much that I have written, this book owes its inception to a question casually posed to me by Stephanos Efthymiades in 2001: Why does it seem that the Byzantines abandoned the classical genre of ethnography after the seventh century? The question nagged at me for years, but I did not take it up in earnest until later, when Paolo Odorico generously invited me to teach a seminar in May 2010 at the École des Hautes Études en Sciences Sociales (Paris). Paolo's own work and the orientation of the Byzantine seminar he conducts, which focuses on the analysis of literature against its historical background, were ideal for the study of this question. I wish to express my heartfelt thanks to him for this opportunity, as well as to Charis Messis, with whom I had many stimulating discussions during my stay. Both are articulate and persuasive advocates of distinctively French approaches to Byzantine literature. I also thank others who provided me with texts and ideas: Cliff Ando, Jean-Claude Cheynet, Scott Kennedy, Dimitris Krallis, David Olster, Vasilis Syros, and the readers for the Press.

A practical French version of the book, stemming from those Paris lectures, is being published by Belles Lettres as *Le discours ethnographique à Byzance: continuités et ruptures*, in the series Séminaires Byzantins that is under Paolo's direction. This English version differs from that one in that the chapters have been arranged differently to reorient the argument; much new material and bibliography have been added here throughout; and, most important, I have added the Palaiologan material, extending the discussion to the fifteenth century.